THE RISE AND DECLINE OF THE PROGRAM OF EDUCATION FOR BLACK PRESBYTERIANS OF THE UNITED PRESBYTERIAN CHURCH U.S.A., 1865–1970

THE RISE AND DECLINE OF THE PROGRAM OF EDUCATION FOR BLACK PRESBYTERIANS OF THE UNITED PRESBYTERIAN CHURCH U.S.A., 1865–1970

by Inez Moore Parker

Trinity University Press • San Antonio

"God has brought them out of Egypt and though they are yet in the wilderness, they have their faces toward the Promised Land."
General Assembly,
PCUSA, 1870

To my daughter, Amelia L'Angela Parker
and
that host of founders, builders, and supporters
who devoted their talents, services, and substance
to the continuing emancipation
of
Black Americans

Presbyterian Historical Society Publication Series

1. *The Presbyterian Enterprise* by M. W. Armstrong, L. A. Loetscher and C. A. Anderson (Westminster Press, 1956; Paperback reprinted for P.H.S., 1963 & 1976)
2. *Presbyterian Ministry in American Culture* by E. A. Smith (Westminster Press, 1962)
3. *Journals of Charles Beatty, 1762–1769*, edited by Guy S. Klett (Pennsylvania State University Press, 1962)
4. *Hoosier Zion, The Presbyterians in Early Indiana* by L. C. Rudolph (Yale University Press, 1963)
5. *Presbyterianism in New York State* by Robert Hastings Nichols, edited and completed by James Hastings Nichols (Westminster Press, 1963)
6. *Scots Breed and Susquehanna* by Hubertis M. Cummings (University of Pittsburgh Press, 1964)
7. *Presbyterians and the Negro — A History* by Andrew E. Murray (Presbyterian Historical Society, 1966)
8. *A Bibliography of American Presbyterianism During the Colonial Period* by Leonard J. Trinterud (Presbyterian Historical Society, 1968)
9. *George Bourne and "The Book and Slavery Irreconcilable"* by John W. Christie and Dwight L. Dumond (Historical Society of Delaware and Presbyterian Historical Society, 1969)
10. *The Skyline Synod: Presbyterianism in Colorado and Utah* by Andrew E. Murray (Golden Bell Press, 1971)
11. *The Life and Writings of Francis Makemie*, edited by Boyd S. Schlenther (Presbyterian Historical Society, 1971)
12. *A Younger Church in Search of Maturity: Presbyterianism in Brazil from 1910 to 1959* by Paul Pierson (Trinity University Press, 1974)
13. *Presbyterians in the South*, Vols. II and III, by Ernest Trice Thompson (John Knox Press, 1973)
14. *Ecumenical Testimony* by John T. McNeill and James H. Nichols (Westminster Press, 1974)
15. *Iglesia Presbiteriana: A History of Presbyterians and Mexican Americans in the Southwest* by R. Douglas Brackenridge and Francisco O. Garcia-Treto (Trinity University Press, 1974)
16. *The Rise and Decline of the Program of Education for Black Presbyterians of the United Presbyterian Church U.S.A., 1865–1970* by Inez M. Parker (Trinity University Press, 1977)
17. *Minutes of the Presbyterian Church in America, 1706–1788*, edited by Guy S. Klett (Presbyterian Historical Society, 1977)

FOREWORD

The Presbyterian Historical Society is pleased to bring to publication *The Rise and Decline of the Program of Education for Black Presbyterians* by Inez M. Parker, professor emeritus at Johnson C. Smith University. The study presents a historical survey of a very important phase of education among Black people in America, the educational and cultural development of the freedmen and their descendants in Presbyterian schools and colleges. Professor Parker not only has devoted more than forty years of research to this study, but has also studied and taught at some of the institutions about which she writes. She has procured information, both oral and written, that few living Americans could obtain. Her sources include conversations with persons no longer living, personal letters from teachers and students at schools that no longer exist, nineteenth and early twentieth century photographs of people who attended or taught at schools for the freedmen, letters from persons who supported educational work among the freedmen, speeches made at freedmen's schools, school catalogs and other school publications, and her personal involvement in some of these schools. These sources supplement Professor Parker's extensive investigation and study of official church records and reports, especially Minutes of the General Assembly and annual reports of the Board of Missions for Freedmen and the Board of National Missions of the Presbyterian Church in the U.S.A., and helped her to produce a study of unique value.

Since Professor Parker's research covered such a long period of time, the exact source for a few facts is no longer known, as footnotes indicate.

For this same reason, a small number of quotations are imprecise in exact wording, although they are accurate in meaning. Similarly, some items are missing from the bibliography. The present location of the files on Negro schools compiled by staff members of the Unit of Work with Colored People of the Board of National Missions is not known; this made it impossible to check a few passages. However, the Publications and Editorial Committee of the Presbyterian Historical Society is satisfied with the reliability of meaning and fact presented in Professor Parker's very thorough study.

The members of the committee, together with the full membership of the Board of Directors, have had an abiding interest in Professor Parker's study since she was first asked to prepare her history of Presbyterian-sponsored education among the Freedmen and their descendants as a volume in the Society's Publication Series. The members of the committee and the board would also like to thank Catherine Gunsalus Gonzalez and Clara Beth Van de Water for their assistance in preparing the manuscript for publication. The officials of the Society take pleasure in adding Professor Parker's historical study to this series.

Charles J. Speel II
For the Publications and Editorial Committee

PREFACE

The old order is passing rapidly, and the new generation, both black and white, has less than a cursory knowledge of the sacrificial efforts and tremendous funds which went into the founding and development of schools for black Americans following the Civil conflict. So that these early strides toward the progressive emancipation of the transplanted African may never be forgotten, this study is offered as a constant reminder and from a deep sense of gratitude of the black constituency of the United Presbyterian Church, U.S.A.

Authentic records of the educational program are scarce and scattered and, in many instances, extinct. Those which are still extant have been listed and evaluated in the bibliography. Far more significant, however, were the author's more than four decades of involvement in the program as pupil and teacher. Personal experiences instilled insights, engendered understanding, and provided knowledgeable contacts which were unavailable in print.

Of necessity, greater coverage is made of those schools which operated over an extended period of time and kept records of their programs. In many instances, available records of parochial schools that made outstanding contributions to the community and inspired individuals toward achievements of high recognition are to be found in scant church minutes, obituaries, and reports to presbyteries and synods.

In this endeavor the writer has accumulated many debts of gratitude to persons who contributed enrichment to this study. Mrs. Virginia Ray Randall suggested the project during the time she was Assistant Secretary of the Unit of Work with Colored People, and her concern and encouragement supported me along the way. Dr. Eugene Carson Blake, while serving as Stated Clerk of the General Assembly, introduced the manuscript to the Presbyterian Historical Society. Dr. Leland Stanford Cozart, President Emeritus of Barber-Scotia College, made significant contributions toward the completion of the study. Mrs. Hardy Liston, widow of the late President Hardy Liston of Johnson C. Smith University, enriched the study through her lifetime connection with the program. Dr. Walter P. Moser, Chairman of the Board of Trustees of Johnson C. Smith University, made valiant efforts toward the publication of the study. Dr. H. N. Morse, who served as Secretary of the Board of National Missions (retired), checked the authenticity of the content. His secretary, Mrs. Wester, made available important records from the Pittsburgh office. Dr. Catherine Gunsalus Gonzalez edited the manuscript and made valuable revisions. Miss Catherine Gladfelter, who was Secretary of Medical and Educational Work, made available historical cards of various schools. Dr. A. H. George, Dean Emeritus of the Johnson C. Smith University Theological Seminary, provided rare materials and shared his thorough knowledge of the black experience in the Presbyterian Church, U.S.A. To each of these, I wish to express my deepest appreciation.

In addition, I wish to record my indebtedness to a number of people whose personal records and memories provided me with information: Dr. Harold Stinson, Principal of Boggs Academy; and his mother, Mrs. H. M. Stinson (on schools west of the Mississippi); the Reverend Robert Meachem, late President of the Alice Lee Elliott School, and Mrs. Meachem, their son and daughter-in-law Mr. and Mrs. Robert Meachem, Jr. (on schools in Oklahoma); Mr. Henry Blue and his grandmother (on schools in North Carolina); Mrs. Myrtle McCreary (on the Mount Herman School); Dr. Richard Allen Carroll, Chairman of the English Department, Spelman College (on the Monticello School, where his father was principal); and Miss Una Houston (on Ingleside Academy and Knoxville College). To these and to numerous others it is my privilege to express genuine thanks and appreciation.

This endeavor has been long and grueling, and yet rewarding—requiring something of sacrifice, something of patience and perseverance. There were many unbelievable and traumatic experiences through which to pass. Yet, if any ill-feeling or bitterness of spirit emits from these pages, it is completely without intent, but is rather the inevitable result of dealing with issues that touch upon the deepest of human passions.

I. M. P.

CONTENTS

THE RISE AND DECLINE OF THE PROGRAM OF EDUCATION FOR BLACK PRESBYTERIANS OF THE UNITED PRESBYTERIAN CHURCH U.S.A., 1865–1970

INTRODUCTION: THE CONDITION OF BLACKS AT EMANCIPATION

Let us go back over the route of the Rebel into the Wilderness[1] where a strange and powerful aristocracy emerged and a new nation was born. The route leads through a curtain of weeping willows, before a background of cypress, oak, and pine trees. Leaping out from all around is a jumbled array of contrasts: bluebirds and buzzards; colonnaded manor houses and smoke-painted shanties; frock coats and calico sackcloth; verdant fertile swamplands and wide stretches of gullied wasteland; saintly humanitarians with Book in hand and hooded nightriders with flaming crosses.

Many incidents of the pageant staged in this setting were experienced by one who was born "before the surrender" and who reiterated the stories to her posterity. This self-made historian, an offspring of a wealthy white planter and his quadroon housekeeper, was a dynamic storyteller, and the present writer was a devoted listener. Over and over this chronicler recreated the incidents which cut the pattern of the life which her listener inherited. Her mind and memory were filled with vivid details, which she narrated as though she had never told them before, without malice or discernible emotion, except occasionally when she came to some martyr or some valorous defeat in the Wilderness. Then her copious body quivered as if with some chill, and she would stop

---

[1] See p. 7 for geographical extent of what is here called "the Wilderness."

and stare back into the times that had been. A search of her gray eyes for a twinkle of jest revealed only loneliness. And yet, she never seemed to tire of recreating the scenes of that tragedy in the Wilderness which now unfold in these pages.

This verdant forest had been discovered and rediscovered by Europeans. Spain, France, and England, as well as other seekers in their turn, had claimed it by little more than squatters' rights. As time passed, however, England gained supremacy. Oppressed but ambitious bands of "freedom lovers" renounced their English bonds and, gambling with a turbulent ocean, staked their lives on a bid for freedom in a distant land. Those who won the contest with nature were amazed at the potential of the new land with its green rolling hills, tumbling streams, towering mountains, long sandy beaches, black loam, red clay, tropical forests alive night and day with birds.

For these settlers the possibilities of a new nation began to form, but they lacked enough physical stamina to lay its foundation. Although force was applied to the redskinned natives, they moved stubbornly and fought back, leaving the settlers with their dreams unfulfilled. Some of the newcomers perished while others languished, even longing for their previous low status in England. Help from the king was slow and meager. Yet the migrants eked out a scanty existence until the year of 1619. In that year, a Portuguese pirate cruising in a Dutch freighter loaded with strange cargo steered into the James River harbor. For the weary settlers, the cargo consisted of manna from the Congo, for the Dutch ship "sold us twenty Negars."[2] The importance of the black gold did not readily excite the settlers; it was not until they learned of the "Negars" ability to labor under adverse circumstances and survive the menaces of the Wilderness that they saw that labor force was now available to make their dreams come true.

In the beginning, the supply of blacks had come primarily by way of the West Indies, but by the 1700s ships plied the Atlantic directly between Africa and the Wilderness. A large majority of the transplanted Africans came from Guinea, Gambia, the Gold Coast, and Senegal. The natives of Senegal, who were often skilled artisans, brought the highest prices. On the other hand, the Elies from Calabar were rated as undesir-

---

[2] Master John Rolfe, "A Relation from Master John Rolfe," in Captain John Smith, *The General Historie of Virginia* (1624), Book IV of *Works, 1608–1631,* ed. Edward Arbor (Birmingham, England: 1884, and New York: AMS Press, Inc., 1967), p. 543.

ables since they frequently chose suicide rather than bondage. Those from the Gaboans were considered weaklings.[3] Each tribe had its own language, which made communication among the members of a slave gang next to impossible, and, the settlers' seeing the advantages of this, made up the slave gangs of blacks from different tribes. The slave-vendors knew the market value of various tribes and persuaded their accomplices in Africa to herd natives accordingly into corrals near the coast to wait for the slave ships.[4] Selectivity and separation, therefore, became a sound business practice of the pirates.

In the Wilderness, the blacks were pushed viciously into action. Timber began to fall, swamps ran dry, gullies were leveled; venomous creatures struck back and crawled off to a remoter hideaway. Plowshares began to pulverize the moist black loam, and out of this sod came indigo, sugarcane, cotton, rice, goobers, and tobacco, each of which by turn established a lucrative market which formed the foundation for the kingdom.

The mother country's demand for more and more rum, rice, indigo, cotton, and molasses increased. Tobacco production in the Piedmont section of Virginia and the Carolinas was overworked. Hard labor was the needed ingredient; hence, the market-in-men grew into a big business: transporting, breeding, buying, and selling. To obtain such a commodity, the ancient continent of Africa was raped by pirates.

Local retail business establishments of this piracy set up lucrative trading posts at Philadelphia, Richmond, Charleston, and New Orleans. These dispensaries hung out their "For Sale" signs, printed personal business cards, ran advertisements in the daily newspapers, and employed professional auctioneers. In this manner the market was securely established. Many historians, however, have stated that this local business was frowned on by planters, as the dealers often stole slaves from one plantation and sold them to another in a different locality.[5]

Many slave ships were outfitted in New York harbor until 1860. Since more slaves meant greater profits, the normal capacity of a ship was seldom observed. Some slaves were shackled together and stapled to the decks. Others were packed in the dungeonlike holds of the ships, while

[3] Carter G. Woodson, *The Negro In Our History* (Washington, D.C.: Associated Publishers, 1927), pp. 60–70.

[4] John Hope Franklin, *From Slavery to Freedom; a history of American Negroes* (New York: Alfred A. Knopf, 1956), pp. 54–55.

[5] Langston Hughes and Milton Meltzer, *A Pictorial History of Negroes in America* (New York: Crown Publishers, Inc., 1963), pp. 69–70.

still others were stacked and stapled in layers, berth upon berth to the top. Many of these open-air dwellers died while crossing and were tossed overboard.[6] Because of this system of packing and overloading, a slave ship became a filthy, unsanitary structure and could often be smelled for miles at sea and before docking. Frequently the slave ship had to be junked after unloading.

Because of the expense involved in crossing the "Middle Passage" and the loss of life, the practice of local breeding developed and breeding stations were established in the Wilderness. Particularly in great demand were the ones in Maryland and Virginia. For this new phase of the market-in-men, hardy, virile males, black and white, were mated with well-kept black females conditioned for propagation.

Slave trading constituted the big business by virtue of which the Wilderness grew into an aristocracy. The entire land was involved in transporting, breeding, bartering, or exploiting the human commodity. By economic supremacy, land control, and monopoly of every facet of the government, the slaveowners created a power structure which determined the destinies of poor whites as well as the enslaved.

By 1803 the soul-vendors had landed more than twenty thousand Africans in Georgia and South Carolina.[7] The chains of bondage were riveted tighter by law and greed. Slaveocracy created a thriving aristocracy with the market-in-men at the hub of its economic, political, social, and governmental machinery. The wealthy planters who owned many slaves were masters of the church, the courts, the schools, the legislative halls, and the polls. They directed all in their own interests and to their own advantage. Those who owned few or no slaves were forced, in many instances, to compete with skilled slaves who had been taught trades and crafts. Carpenters, brick masons, wagoners, blacksmiths, shoe cobblers, spinners, weavers, boat workers, seamstresses, sawmill attendants, barbers, steamboat pilots, midwives, millwrights, and saddlers were hired out by their wealthy masters for much less than the smaller farmer or businessman could afford to charge.

By 1860, although historians differ slightly in citing the results of the 1860 census, of a white population of 8,000,000, there were 384,000 slaveowners. Of this number, 2,000 owned one hundred or more slaves; 338,000 owned fewer than twenty; the remaining slaveholders owned five

---

[6] Franklin, *From Slavery*, p. 56.
[7] Hughes and Meltzer, *A Pictorial History*, p. 26.

or fewer.[8] This latter group operated on the perimeter of slaveocracy as did those who were unable financially to buy slaves.

The effects of slavery on the bonded black varied in degree according to the area of labor to which he or she was confined. The two major categories were the house slave and the field slave. The house slave, placed in contact with the luxury and culture of the wealthy aristocrat and afforded a degree of confidence, absorbed behavioral patterns and speech similar to that of his immediate environment. In unique instances, some member of the wealthy planter's family introduced the house slave secretly to the rudiments of education. The house slave was sometimes permitted to have a family, with certain rights reserved by the master. In addition, for turning informer, he or she would be granted freedom. Black history records that more than three hundred fifty planned revolts by the field slaves were quelled by the house slave turning informer. The house slave was often indoctrinated into feeling superior to the field slave. This division favored strongly the master's cause.[9]

Closely related to the house slave was the slave trained as a mechanic or craftsman. This slave benefitted from an occupation which stimulated intellectual faculty and produced a marketable skill. One slave craftsman, Phillip Reed, cast in bronze the plaster model of the Statue of Freedom which was lifted to the Capitol dome in Washington, December 2, 1863. The *Charlotte Observer*, July 3, 1960, tells the story under the title "The Lady on The Capitol Dome?":

> Thomas Crawford, outstanding sculptor in his day, got $3,000 for the job. He executed it in his studios in Rome, supposedly using his daughter as the model of freedom. A plaster model of the statue was shipped to America in April, 1858, but didn't arrive until a year later. The bark on which it was traveling, the Emily Taylor, sprung a leak and was sold for kindling wood in Bermuda, where the statue languished for eight months. After its arrival in the U.S. the statue was cast in bronze, thanks to the know-how of the only man around with the skill to do the job—a Negro slave, named Phillip Reed.

The field slave's wretched lot contrasted sharply with that of the house slave. The field slave was forced to labor from sunup to sundown, from

[8] John P. Davis, Jr., *A Brief History of the Negro In the United States* (Englewood, New Jersey: Prentice-Hall, 1966), p. 27.

[9] Janet Harris and Julius Hobson, *Black Pride* (New York: McGraw-Hill Book Co., 1969), p. 26.

six to seven days weekly. There was no hope of remuneration, but forty-nine lashes were certain for failure to perform up to peak. The field slaves were confined to debasing influences until their consciences were crushed, their self-respect ineffective, their sensibilities blunted, and cowardice became a way of life.

From this slave system evolved a rift among the blacks. Hatred and jealousy were a natural result. The field slave was suspicious of the serious concern of the house slave for the master's welfare. The house slave was viewed as a snooper, squealer, and informer. Hence there developed the division between the "black aristocracy" and the "black commoner."

In general, the slaves were taught in this rigid school that their master's will was supreme and that they had no alternative but to obey. The female was indoctrinated into believing that her body was the absolute property of her master and that she had no personal rights which he was obligated to respect. The black male's paternal feeling was submerged, and he was taught to look upon his own offspring merely as his master's chattel and responsibility.

Through this system of apprenticeship, the transplanted African was taught the principles of a new religion—to be obedient to the master, that meekness and dutiful industry were conducive to longevity and well-being on earth and promised rest, peace, and happiness in the hereafter. The slaves were, therefore, to give all of themselves to another just to exist in this world with a promise of better days in the world to come. This new faith taught the slaves to sing: "Swing low, sweet chariot, coming for to carry me home"; "You kin take all this world but give me Jesus"; "Soon I will be donna with the troubles of this world."

The "Christian" master was an ever-present example that precept and practice need not agree in the faith. The masters rose to a high position of respectability by exploiting the defenseless. The words which came over white pulpits to black ears in the balconies about the meek, the merciful, and the compassionate bore little resemblance to the daily life of the black. The slaves learned to lie to avoid the lash and to steal to appease the pangs of hunger.

The dignity of honest, hard labor was also taught in a distorted fashion. To work "like a nigger" was degrading. Conversely, to bask supinely in leisure and luxury was the life of the blessed. This the sweating blacks and the sulking poor whites observed from their separate but ignoble places while their "betters" enjoyed the fruits of the earth.

The concept of sanitation and beauty was likewise learned in a dual system. Crowded in the squalor of their cramped cabins, the slaves learned to associate cleanliness with the "Big House." At the end of a day's work, they plodded to their filthy quarters, which they altered only in anticipation of a visitor from the "Big House."

The new land's reputation as a wealthy and powerful nation filled with churchgoing people spread. It sent missionaries abroad to abate the heathenish practices of those who did not know that Christ had come. It sent some of its profits from slavery to redeem benighted lands, even to the continent of Africa, that the pagans might learn "to do justice, to love kindness, and to walk humbly with your God."[10] But, at the same time, the Fugitive Slave Law of 1850, the Kansas-Nebraska Act of 1854, the Dred Scott Decision of 1857, the rise of the new Republican party, the Lincoln-Douglas debates of 1858, John Brown's Raid at Harper's Ferry in 1859-60, and the election of Abraham Lincoln as president were incidents portending civil strife.

The utterances of the new president were a threat to the slaveowners and caused uneasiness behind a curtain that gradually descended across the Wilderness: "A house divided against itself cannot stand"; "My oft expressed personal wish, that all men everywhere could be free"; "Where one man governs himself, that is self government, when he governs himself and another with the consent of the other, that is representative government; but when a man governs himself and another without the consent of the other, that is not democracy, that is despotism."

Christian sentiment or humanitarianism began to breathe stronger in sections where slavery was less profitable. A new system of transportation was devised whereby blacks moved secretly to non-southern regions. Station managers, conductors, and crewmen were strategically concealed along the route. The Fugitive Slave Law of 1850 was ineffective and the Underground Railroad system continued to operate.

By this time the kingdom had reached its peak in luxury and misery and extended from Virginia and the Carolinas through the Georgia swamps and across the Alabama lowlands. It had topped the fertile loam of the Mississippi Delta and looked westward toward the Golden Gate. With this westward movement emerged the query: Shall this new land be slave or free? The Homestead Act accelerated this movement and the Dred Scott decision intensified the rush. Signs of the approaching conflict were evident. The blacks in the lofts of the barns, shucking corn or shelling goobers, sensed the temper of the times and made the rafters ring with their "sorrow songs": "Over my head I see trouble in the air and

[10] Mic. 6:8.

there must be a God somewhere." Or those picking cotton under the noonday sun would hear the lilting notes of a songmaker rise above their bending backs: "My Lord's gonna move this wicked race; Gonna rise up a nation that shall obey."

The nation did rise against the injustices inflicted on the slaves. The defenders of "the cause that was just" mobilized, and at 4:30 a.m. April 12, 1861, muskets were fired on Fort Sumter. Seven cotton-growing states—South Carolina, Mississippi, Florida, Alabama, Louisiana, Texas, and Georgia—formed a coalition and were joined later by the tobacco-growing states—Virginia, Arkansas, Tennessee, and North Carolina. This coalition marked the geographical route of the Rebel.

The entire region was enveloped in strife and confusion. In the states forming the coalition, some poor whites who had been pushed to the out-skirts of the economy began to realize that "the cause that was just" was in reality the cause of the wealthy planter. The ranks of the Rebel began to thin. Typical of this reaction was the situation in Winston County, Alabama. In the rough uplands of red clay and sparse timberland, these deprived whites had groveled and grumbled. They refused to fight with the Rebels and sent five infantry companies into the Union army. Tom Dygard recalled the incident in 1960 in the *Charlotte Observer*:

> In 1860, there were only 122 slaves and 14 slaveholders in Winston County. When the State of Alabama voted to secede from the Union, Winston County residents gathered at a tavern in a mass meeting and voted to secede from the State of Alabama. Their reso-lution said, if it is legal for a state to secede from the Union, then it follows that it is legal for a county to secede from a state, by the same process of reasoning.[11]

The Rebels suffered serious setbacks at Vicksburg, Gettysburg, and later at Richmond. On January 1, 1863, the Emancipation Proclamation was issued as a necessary war measure. The lifeline of the Rebel was cut. When the firing finally ceased, and the mist of battle lifted, a piteous array of wasteland was revealed. In the wreckage of their land, the de-feated groped in misery, but the tragic figure in this group was the liber-ated slave, gripped by fear. At first the former slaves remained near their dispossessed masters, but finding little or no relief they turned with mis-

[11] Tom Dygard, "G. O. P. Outpost in Democratic Camp," *Charlotte Ob-server,* 9 October 1960, pp. 1A and 4D.

givings to the stranger in blue. During this period of shock and consternation, the president was murdered and, to the liberated, their Moses was dead and he had no brother Aaron.

The church learned soon after 1865 how the transplanted African had been introduced to western civilization and both the army and the church were startled and amazed at what they found. The Union army was first to make the discovery of the conditions. Even before the final stages of the Civil conflict, the Union soldiers' quarters were beseiged by contrabands from abandoned plantations. They were hungry, ill-clad, and fearful. Emaciated men, women, and children formed a continuous stream which emerged out of the surrounding thickets. Gen. Oliver O. Howard dispatched urgent pleas for relief to the federal government and the churches. This was a plight for which their military training had not prepared them, and they were baffled and shocked at what they found.

Congress responded through the Freedmen's Bureau, which was organized on March 3, 1865, with General Howard as commissioner. It was established as a temporary measure. On February 6, 1866, Congress voted to extend its powers and functions, but President Andrew Johnson vetoed it. On July 16, 1866, another act was passed over the president's veto extending the bureau's tenure to July 1868. It was later further extended. The Freedmen's Bureau established the right to marriage for freedmen and the right to choose employers; it issued supplies and funds and acted as a court of law where there was none or where Negroes were not recognized as free. The bureau ended its main work in 1869, but its aid to education continued until 1872. It had about nine hundred agents in 1868 and expended in all some $20 million. General Howard published a report of the work of the Freedmen's Bureau in the House Executive Documents, Forty-first Congress, Second Session.

The pioneer teachers were a second group to enter the Wilderness immediately after the close of the war. Their reports were replete with such words as "incredible," "amazed," "shocked," and "unbelievable" in describing the dehumanized masses that assembled for instruction. The pupils ranged in age from the very young to the very old, in knowledge from illiterate to those who had a cursory acquaintance with the rudiments of education. In complexion they varied from pure ebony to nut-brown, to creamy olive, to near-white with blue or gray eyes and fleecy locks. They were anxious and glad to learn, and in oral communication they spoke a dialect of English (a foreign language to them) learned by rote and accented by their native tongue.

The pioneer teachers who labored in the Wilderness were dedicated to the work of the church. For the most part, they had been trained in the New England Latin academies and higher branches of education. Sincerity of purpose characterized their effort. While the "carpetbaggers"—the political and economic opportunists from the North who invaded the South after the war—were detested, these "other carpetbaggers" were different. They brought with them their passion for religion, order, cleanliness and their Puritan yen for honesty and regard for knowledge. They were a dedicated, praying band of industrious people insistent upon frugality and the value of time. Whether under an old oak tree, in a blacksmith shop, or in the basement of a church, they created an atmosphere conducive to learning and devised casual techniques which began the desired transformation in their pupils.

They were in the classroom six hours, five days weekly, taught night school from seven to nine o'clock, three nights weekly, and usually spent one day in each week visiting the homes and teaching the people how to manage their households. They also held prayer meetings, taught Sabbath school, and assisted catechists in the conduct of Sunday morning services in the absence of the minister. The work of these "other carpetbaggers" was truly an adventure in pure faith. They helped to dispel fear and to develop a sense of true Christian values; motivated a sense of pride and personal dignity; aided in the acquisition of academic skills and habits of cleanliness; gave back the power to dream and create. Among the teachers were found occasionally some Southern whites. For their dedication, they were scoffed at by former friends and labelled "nigger-lover," robbed of all social prestige, frequently disinherited by family, and often socially ostracized.

These teachers were working in an emerging climate of terror for the ex-slaves. Those who wished to uproot and unseat the freedmen who had been given a step into freedom under the supervision of "carpetbaggers" exploded with pent-up animosity and the inevitable happened: terror stalked the defunct kingdom. Reason was snuffed out, human decency was dead, conscience was slain, and passion ruled. Night riders, practicing the medieval code of ethics in reverse and hooded in cowardice, lit the symbol of the crucifixion to assure the resurrection of the fallen kingdom. In the darkness of the night, the flaming cross illumined the path for hot tar and feathers; hempen cord and rusty muskets left charred bodies or mutilated carcasses. Lynching, hanging, and other brutalities permeated the Wilderness.

The insecure ex-slaves were given every cause to create a defiant cynicism or counter-hate defense, but reciprocity was stayed either by intense fear, or the steadying and sobering effects of their inherent gentleness of spirit, or by the lack of unity among the freedslaves.

This was the situation discovered by the church when its redemptive mission program was launched in the Wilderness.

STRUCTURING THE RESPONSE
OF THE CHURCH

The Presbyterian Church, U.S.A. was tardy in responding to the urgent plea for immediate missionary activity in the Wilderness. There had been a division within the church in 1837–1838, caused by a combination of theological and social issues, including abolition, and differing attitudes on polity questions. The two branches were referred to as the Old School branch, which was the more conservative, and the New School branch.[1] Feelings were still deep and tense in 1864, and the division remained, although the Old School branch had lost its heavy Southern constituency in 1861 when the Presbyterian Church, U.S. had been founded in the South. In view of this and other facts, efforts to activate a concerted movement toward the mission field had to be cautious and astute. The church was reluctant to attack vigorously due to potentially explosive emotions, particularly in the South, combined with complacency and apathy among many in the North.

During the Presbyterian delay, however, other denominations, many with strong emotional appeal, entered the mission field and, as a result, these denominations had a head start. However, Presbyterianism was being fostered in the Wilderness by the voluntary services of individuals who were pioneering in the region even before the church officially

---

[1] George M. Marsden, *The Evangelical Mind and the New School Experience* (New Haven: Yale University Press, 1970), pp. 64–67, 96.

began its work. Some of this voluntary work had begun well before the Civil War.

Among the earliest Presbyterian pioneers was John Chavis, the first black man to be ordained by the Presbyterian church. He was commissioned in 1801 as a missionary to his own people. He preached to both black and white audiences in Virginia and the Carolinas until a law forbidding Negroes to preach was passed following the Nat Turner rebellion. Chavis then turned his talents to teaching. He taught at various times in Chatham, Wake, Orange, and Granville counties in North Carolina, from 1808 to 1830, when he retired. Among his pupils were free Negroes and children of prominent white families, many of whom became physicians, preachers, lawyers, teachers, and politicians of distinction.[2]

Another of the early pioneers was Mrs. Samantha J. Neil, a Civil War widow from Pennsylvania, who went to Amelia County, Virginia in search of the bodies of her husband and three brothers. She searched for them in vain but what she discovered became her life's work. She returned home, sold her possessions, and went back to Amelia County to do what she could to relieve the plight of the destitute freedmen in that area. She began teaching under a large oak but later moved into a deserted, dilapidated blacksmith shop. Seven churches, an orphanage, and three schools, one of which evolved into Ingleside Seminary, resulted from her years of voluntary missionary services.[3]

In the North, both the Old School and New School branches of the church began planning their approach to the mission problem in 1864. The General Assembly (Old School) had delayed every denouncement of slavery until 1864, but in that year it appointed two committees "to investigate the possibility of missions for Negroes." One of the committees, with headquarters in Philadelphia, was to operate in the eastern area, and the other, with headquarters in Indianapolis, was to function throughout the western area. Both committees were charged specifically to work chiefly in connection with military and contraband camps and hospitals, and to "call upon our people for funds to be expended in this work—by circulars, by printed or personal appeals through the pastors and sessions."[4] Accurate records were to be reported to the Assembly

[2] Janet E. Seville, *Like A Spreading Tree* (New York: Presbyterian Church in the U.S.A., Board of National Missions, 1936), p. 27.

[3] Jesse Belmont Barber, *Climbing Jacob's Ladder* (New York: Presbyterian Church in the U.S.A., National Missions, 1952), p. 36.

[4] Presbyterian Church in the U.S.A. (Old School). General Assembly,

the following year. The committee stationed at Philadelphia consisted of the Reverends W. P. Breed, S. F. Colt, and ruling elders John McArthur and W. Hall. The committee located at Indianapolis consisted of the Reverends J. Nixon, S. C. Logan and ruling elders J. Ray, Charles Todd, and Jesse L. Williams. The Old School committees worked for a year establishing schools and churches. The eastern committee said in a circular:

> In the providence of God, a new and touching cause reaches our ears for Christian sympathy, effort and contribution. Without any agency of their own, colored people, lately in servitude, to the number it is believed, of nearly half a million, have been thrown within the national lines, in a condition, in most cases, of almost utter physical and moral destitution. Their sufferings in long weary journeys—often almost without clothing, often without shelter in inclement weather, and long without bread, sinking exhausted by the way, sickening and dying in large numbers—have been such as no tongue can tell.
>
> They are now congregated in vast numbers in various localities, East and West—15,000 on the sea islands in South Carolina and Georgia; 20,000 at Newbern and in Eastern North Carolina; 20,000 at Portsmouth and Norfolk and vicinity; and 50,000 in and around Washington.
>
> Beneficient associations have done much toward relieving their physical wants. But these people are more than mere animals; they have immortal souls.
>
> They need the ministration of the gospel, in health, in sickness and in the hour of death.
>
> They need to be taught to read the word of God. Such as can read, need the ministrations of the colporteur, conveying to them the pages of religious truth.
>
> Masters now of their persons, time and families, they need instruction in the new duties that thus develop upon them.
>
> In a word, they need everything that the ignorant, destitute and the perishing can need.
>
> Other Christian denominations are at work. Shall our beloved church sit with folded hands? Our General Assembly has answered, NO! and has appointed committees for the work.[5]

Minutes (Philadelphia: Presbyterian Board of Education, 1864), pp. 322–323.

[5] Presbyterian Church in the U.S.A., Board of National Missions, Unit of Work with Colored People, Card File on Negro Schools. The current location of the file is not known.

This and other circulars were sent out according to the General Assembly's directions but enthusiasm was not easily aroused. In addition, the committees ran into difficulties stemming from loosely defined functional areas. After one year of operation, they sent an overture to the General Assembly recommending the appointment of one central committee with two secretaries, one to operate in the East and the other in the West. The General Assembly approved the recommendation, and the central committee was to be known as "the General Assembly's Committee on Freedmen." [6] The Committee was organized on June 21, 1865.[7] Immediately it went to work, sending out a circular which merits quoting at length, because it shows the rationale behind much of the church's mission:

To the Pastors and People of the Presbyterian Church:
The last General Assembly established its "Committee on Freedmen" in the city of Pittsburgh and directed it to take charge of the effort of our church for the elevation of this long degraded people.
The Committee was organized on the 21st day of June, and has entered upon its work.
There are now more than 40 missionaries and teachers in the field, and the expense of the Committee in sustaining the work, at present, is a little more than $2,000 per month. There is in the treasury now about $4,000—sufficient to carry on the work for about two months, though only $300 and a little over came into the treasury during the month of June.
The missions and schools are in successful operation but thousands of poor people must be turned away for the lack of sufficient help. Many more missionaries are ready to go and others only wait for the advance of the season to make it safe.
Four million of perishing people, long degraded and abused are calling to the Christian heart and hand of our Church for education and gospel privileges. Fields "White to the harvest" and of unlimited promise, bid the Church in the name of the Lord, "Thrust in the sickle and reap."
What can the Committee do without the speedy, earnest, and persevering cooperation of God's people?
Brethren, we ought to be sure today of one hundred thousand dollars, to be expended the present year for the elevation of the Freedmen. Is not the cry of this people the voice of the Master saying, "Withhold not good from them to whom it is due, when it is in

[6] *Minutes* (Old School), 1865, p. 544.
[7] *Minutes* (Old School), 1865, p. 545.

the power of thine hand to do it." They plead the wrongs and sorrows of 200 years. While we hesitate, one generation perishes and another passes beyond our reach. The demand is made upon our GRATITUDE. They fought for our country; they fed our prisoners; they guided our hunted wanderers and they buried and wept over our dead.

The demand is made upon our PATRIOTISM. If we fail to elevate and educate this people, they will justly be the enemies of the nation and country; and woe to us if God "require" the wrongs of this race of our generation.

The demand is made upon our RELIGION. Under the shadow of the "Judgment of the Great Day," for Jesus will say, "In as much as ye have done it unto the least of these, my brethren, ye have done it unto me."[8]

This Committee worked with great haste for a year, meeting bimonthly and upon call by the secretary, exercising direct control over the entire program for freedmen. In July, 1866, it elected the following officers: the Reverend Elijah E. Swift, chairman, and the Reverend S. F. Scoval, recording secretary. The tone and dismay of the Committee came through in its second annual report to the General Assembly:

The Committee has been especially embarrassed by the uncertain posture in which the last Assembly left the whole subject of the mission among the Freedmen. It was supposed that no plans ought to be laid reaching farther than the meeting of the Assembly as the Committee was unwilling to even seem to forestall the action of the Church upon the pending resolution to dissolve the Committee. But considering the whole case and concluding that an actual abandonment of this mission was not thought of the Committee entered upon their labor with zeal and carried it on with energy, working by such plans as looked toward an enlarged and permanent mission.[9]

Following this discouraging introduction, the committee on Freedmen made a detailed report of activities and the progression made during the past year:

II of Labourers
1. The experiences of last year and more definite and reliable information of the field led the Committee in the beginning of the year to the conclusion that it would be better to attempt to sustain schools only in such localities as afforded a reasonable prospect for

[8] Card File on Negro Schools.
[9] *Minutes* (Old School), 1867, p. 441.

the organization of a church to have a minister as superintendent of each station occupied. With the conviction that the whole work must ultimately fall into the hands of ministers and teachers of their own race, special efforts were made to secure all such qualified men and women as could be sustained. The Committee would report gratifying results as following this plan.

2. The special difficulty in enlisting qualified ministers of our Church, in the work, has arisen chiefly from two causes.

The First is the KIND of WORK which has been required. The Committee were not able to sustain a sufficient number of teachers in central points to meet the necessities of the case. Hence last year, almost every minister was required to go into the school, and to teach daily the simplest rudiments of education, spending only Saturday and Sunday in the direct duties of his office. It was necessary to do this because it was useless to attempt to build a church without teaching the people, at least, to read the Bible.

The Second difficulty arose from the PECULIAR TRIALS of the work. The complete social ostracism of any minister who enters the field, if he does his duty, is hard to bear. To be despised by a wicked world, through graces, leads the servants of Jesus to be strong but to be disgraced in the eyes of those who profess to follow the common Lord, saps the strength and wounds the soul. To preach the gospel in Africa makes a hero in the Church, and gives one a place in the prayers of all Christian households; but to preach the same gospel to the Africans in our own land secures neither honor nor sympathy from the large body of Christian people. And the fear of a supposed difficulty of obtaining a pastorate, even in northern churches, after having engaged in the work, has deterred many, while others were led to decline by the persuasion that the Church would not sustain a permanent mission among Freedmen.

Many were willing to enter the field as an experiment or spend a year under its discomforts. The same is true of teachers but to a far less extent. Some have gone without counting the cost and have been soon discouraged. This, with the plan of sustaining schools only in connection with churches will account for the fact that, while 104 missionaries have held commissions since the last report only 21 are in commission at the present time.[10]

With this revised plan as a guideline, the Committee redoubled its efforts toward preparing trained leaders among the freedmen. To this end, normal and theological courses were added to the upper level schools for freedmen with a view of ultimately turning the execution of the program

[10] *Minutes* (Old School), 1867, pp. 442–443.

over to them. Under the new plan also it became mandatory for each
minister to operate a parochial school without additional expense to the
Committee. A nominal fee was permitted to cover operational expenses
and a small stipend for the minister. The parochial school thereafter became an adjunct to the work of the church.

The catechists, who were chiefly black candidates for the ministry,
were closely associated with the minister in his extended responsibilities.
As a necessity of the work, the office of catechist had been revived by the
Catawba Presbytery in December, 1866. In this association with the
minister the catechist gained practical experience in gathering congregations, maintaining public worship, and superintending Sabbath schools.
In addition, a part of each week was spent in study under the guidance of
the teacher or minister. During the early years of intense hostility, the
white minister accompanied by a black catechist on his pastoral visits was
less likely to stir up animosity within the white community than a white
minister alone visiting black parishioners.

The more liberal New School branch of the church also began structuring an approach to the mission field in the Wilderness, and in 1864 its
committee of Home Missions appointed a Freedmen's Committee. In
1868, this became the Freedman's Department of Missions, with an
associate secretary and headquarters in New York City. By 1868, the
New School branch was operating sixty-one schools in nine states and
the District of Columbia, most of them at the elementary level, although
a few were more advanced. The strongest concentration of schools was in
Tennessee and South Carolina. The Reverend Willard Richardson and
his family established the Fairfield Institute at Winnsboro, South Carolina, and the Reverend Samuel Loomis was making great progress with
the Brainerd Institute at Chester and nearby vicinity in the same state.[11]

Both branches met in their separate assemblies in 1869, made their
final reports and voted to reunite. When the historic reunion of the Old
and New School branches was effected in 1870, the separate programs
for freedmen of the two branches were consolidated by the General
Assembly, June 10, 1870.[12] The General Assembly also ruled that the
united committee should be known as "The Presbyterian Committee of
Missions for Freedmen" and should maintain headquarters in Pittsburgh.
The two former agencies were directed to turn over all their holdings to

[11] Barber, *Climbing,* pp. 38–39.
[12] Presbyterian Church in the U.S.A., General Assembly, *Minutes* (New
York: Presbyterian Board of Publication, 1870), p. 105. Hereafter cited as
Minutes.

the new Committee. During the first meeting, June 16, 1870, the Reverend E. E. Swift, the chairman of the Old School's Committee on Freedmen, became the chairman of the new Committee, and the Reverend A. C. McClelland was elected secretary.

The new Committee prosecuted its responsibilities without further major changes in plan or organization for twelve years. In 1882, however, it became evident that the Committee would have to be incorporated to settle matters of ownership and legally handle bequests. The General Assembly, therefore, while convening at Saratoga Springs, New York in 1883, sanctioned the incorporation under the title, "The Presbyterian Board of Missions for Freedmen of the Presbyterian Church in the U.S. of A."[13] This was a great help. The former organization had operated from 1865 to 1882 under the disadvantage of being an organization which was appointed from year to year without a sense of permanence. Yet all was not well with the new Board. It had inherited a large number of schools from the two branches and a staggering debt with which to start its new career. This was no small obstacle in view of the fact that the church still had to be educated to appreciate the finances necessary to operate an effective program for the freedmen. The Board felt constrained to highlight this factor in each annual report.

The general structure of the Board continued for more than forty years without major changes. In the 1923 reorganization of the church's boards and agencies, four boards emerged: the Board of National Missions, the Board of Foreign Missions, the Board of Christian Education, and the Board of Pensions. The Board of Missions for Freedmen was placed under the Board of National Missions as the Division of Work for Colored People. Dr. John M. Gaston, who had been appointed director of the Board of Missions for Freedmen in 1910, retained his headquarters in Pittsburgh until he retired in 1938, whereupon Dr. Albert B. McCoy became secretary of the unit. He was succeeded in 1950 by Dr. Jesse Belmont Barber.

Despite the fact that women had been among the early pioneers to the mission field in the Wilderness, it was not until 1884 that the General Assembly recognized and authorized them as an adjunct of the Board of Missions for Freedmen. Thereupon the Women's Executive Committee of Home Missions, which had been established in 1878, created its Department of Freedmen, also called the "Women's Committee," with Mrs. Caroline E. Coulter as its first general secretary. With its headquarters in Pittsburgh, the women had easy access to the Board's plans, policies, and

[13] *Minutes,* 1883, p. 592.

problems. At that early date the Board of Missions for Freedmen did not envision what a tremendous asset this new department would be to the program.

In 1885, the General Assembly adopted a resolution which strengthened and encouraged the organized women. It affectionately urged all the women's Home Mission societies of the church to give the work a place in their sympathies, their prayers, and their benefactions. The women were gratified by this commendation and increased their activities as they grew stronger and more effective. The women's interest was centered primarily in the schools. An attempt in 1888 and 1889 to merge the Women's Department with the rest of the church's mission to the freedmen failed after a long deliberation.

With the entrance of the women into the organized machinery of operation, a new dimension was added to the program. The missionary outreach was greatly extended and a creative force vitalized the activities. In 1892, in its eighth annual report, the Women's Committee of the Department of Freedmen made the following explanation of its method of gaining support:

> Our plan of work is very simple. We have local Home Mission Societies in which the actual work is done—Presbyterial Societies, where work is planned, methods discussed and information disseminated; Synodical Societies where Presbyterial reports are read, addresses made by workers from the field, or others specially interested, enthusiasm aroused, suggestions made and much done to unify the work. It is a part of our plan to have a Secretary for Freedmen in every Synodical and Presbyterial Society. We have now, as far as reported to us, seventy Presbyterial Secretaries for work among the Freedmen, whose duty it is to see that the claims of the Freedmen are brought before every auxiliary society in the Presbytery during the year. Where we have no Freedmen Secretary, the Presbyterial Secretary kindly takes charge of the work in addition to her other duties.[14]

Through this methodical approach the women boosted the Board's expansion dreams.

The Women's Executive Committee considered 1888 its most successful year since its organization. By this time the women's "simple plan of

[14] Presbyterian Church in the U.S.A., Women's Executive Committee of Home Missions, Freedmen's Department, *Annual Report,* Pittsburgh Office of the Board, 1892, p. 95. Hereafter cited as Women's Committee, *Annual Report.*

operation" had crystallized, and the Board had learned the value of their influence, industry, and devotion to the program. In 1911 the Board of Missions for Freedmen made the following estimate of the women's value to the program:

> One of the most efficient aids to the Board in the prosecution of its work is our Women's Department. It is not only a present help in time of need, but it is indispensible to the growing success of the work. Through this Department the Board receives nearly all of the scholarship money that goes to the support of the needy students in our many institutions. Many of the salaries of the teachers are obtained in this way, and nearly all of the money used for buildings is raised through this department and usually raised before the buildings are begun.
>
> If a new teacher is called for in some one of our growing schools, the Board approves of this addition . . . provided a salary can be found through the Woman's Department. If a poor and needy student wants to enter one of our schools but cannot be taken in unless the prescribed scholarship money is secured, the case is turned over to the Woman's Department with favorable recommendation.[15]

It is obvious that after 1884 the women relieved the Board of a tremendous portion of its responsibility. Whether in the classroom or in the promotional phase of the program they were the support that energized the work. Their innovativeness and their ability to win friends and financial aid for the program constituted a life-giving factor without which it is difficult to envision how the Board might have fared during the lean years.

From 1884 until the reorganization of the boards in 1923, this Women's Committee rendered an invaluable service to the program of the Board of Missions for Freedmen. The new structure created in 1923 no longer included a separate women's board, much to the annoyance of many of the women who had not been properly consulted about the change in structure.[16] Between 1923 and 1932, the organized women's work functioned within the framework of the Unit of Schools and Hospitals, dealing primarily with boarding schools for the blacks. The day schools were operated primarily within the framework of the Division of

[15] Presbyterian Church in the U.S.A., Board of Missions for Freedmen, *Annual Report* (Pittsburgh: Office for the Board, 1911), p. 13–14. Hereafter cited as BMF, *Annual Report.*

[16] Margaret Gibson Hummel, *The Amazing Heritage* (Philadelphia: The Geneva Press, 1970), p. 52.

Work for Colored People. In 1938 the title was changed from the Division of Work for Colored People to the Unit of Work with Colored People. Between 1923 and 1932, the schools for blacks were shifted from one of these units to the other causing a great deal of confusion and concern within the black community. The dynamic impact of the women's work, however, was greatly changed. The Board of Missions for Freedmen and its supporting agencies lost their identity. The black community felt that the spirit of missions had become submerged and all but lost in the mechanized, consolidated machinery. The concern was great, and apprehension and skepticism began to mount.

The discussion thus far has concerned the organization in the North necessary to establish the missions. But the missionary field in the South had to be structured also in order to operate within the church's organized machinery. To this end churches, presbyteries, and synods had to be organized. These were structures of the Presbyterian Church, U.S.A. in an area that was outside of that northern church's previous boundary.

On October 6, 1866, the Catawba Presbytery was organized by three white ministers, the Reverends Samuel C. Alexander, Willis L. Miller, and Sidney S. Murkland, at Freedom Church, Dunlap, North Carolina. The establishment of this presbytery was so intimately related to the founding of Biddle (now Johnson C. Smith) University that further history will be given in connection with the history of that institution.[17] Catawba Presbytery was at first attached to the Synod of Baltimore, Old School. The same year, 1866, the Presbytery of Hopewell of the Presbyterian Church, U.S. ordained three Negroes: David Laney,[18] Joseph Williams, and Robert Casters. These three ministers, all residents of Georgia, withdrew from their presbytery in 1867 and organized Knox Presbytery. This presbytery, the first in the United States to be composed entirely of Negroes, was received into the Northern Assembly, Old School, in 1868. A third presbytery, Atlantic, was organized on January 1, 1868, with both white and black ministers who lived in the vicinity of Charleston, South Carolina.

The Synod of Atlantic was authorized by the Old School Assembly of 1868, composed of the presbyteries of Catawba, Atlantic, and Knox. The initial meeting was set for October 11 at Charlotte, North Carolina. This was the first black synod to be organized. Fairfield Presbytery of the New School branch of the church was formed in 1869 and was added to this

[17] See Chapter V, "The North Carolina Schools," sec. on Biddle University.
[18] He is the father of Lucy Craft Laney, the founder of Haines Institute, Augusta, Georgia.

synod in 1870. The oldest church in this synod is reported to be Zion Church, Charleston, South Carolina, which was organized by Dr. John B. Adger in 1846.[19]

By action of the General Assembly in 1887, that part of the Synod of Atlantic north of the boundary line between the states of North and South Carolina was set apart as the Synod of Catawba. The initial meeting of this new synod was held November 2, 1887. To the three charter member presbyteries of the new synod—Cape Fear, Catawba, and Yadkin—was added the Presbytery of Southern Virginia, formed in 1887.

In Oklahoma, two churches were organized for Negroes in 1872, one called New Hope, at Frogville, and the other Hebron, at Hugo. These churches, however, do not appear on the rolls of a presbytery until 1885, when they are listed under the Presbytery of Indian Territory, Synod of Kansas.[20] The first presbytery to be organized for blacks west of the Mississippi was Allen Presbytery, which was listed in 1889 as being part of the synod of Missouri. The next year the name was changed to the Presbytery of White River.

In 1905, the General Assembly acted to permit the establishment of new presbyteries and synods within the geographical bounds of already established judicatories. This allowed the creation of black presbyteries and synods in areas where there were white structures. Canadian Synod and the Synod of East Tennessee, both Negro, were created in 1907 under this action.

The Canadian Synod was established on October 8, 1907 and consisted of the presbyteries of White River, Kiamichi, and Rendall. The first meeting was held on that date in the First Presbyterian Church in Oklahoma City, with the pioneer minister, the Reverend William L. Bethel, as the first moderator. Rendall and Kiamichi presbyteries were created out of the presbyteries in the Synod of Indian Territory.

The Synod of East Tennessee was organized on October 25, 1907. In 1935 the name was changed to the Blue Ridge Synod. It contained the presbyteries of Birmingham, LeVere, and Rogersville, with churches in Mississippi, Tennessee, and Alabama. The beginnings of the development of black churches in this area go back to the work of missionaries of the New School branch of the church. The Reverend George W. LeVere, a Negro missionary, organized in 1865 the Knoxville Shiloh Church, which remained one of the strongest black Presbyterian churches

[19] Seville, *Like A Spreading,* pp. 30–31.
[20] Barber, *Climbing,* p. 28.

in the South. He also established churches at New Market and Maryville. These churches were received into Union Presbytery, which was made up largely of white churches.[21] In 1907 they became part of the new LeVere Presbytery in Blue Ridge Synod.

In an effort to strengthen these new structures in the mission field the Workers' Conferences were begun. Under the direction of the Board of Missions for Freedmen, the annual Workers' Conference was organized in 1914 for the Atlantic, Blue Ridge, Catawba and Canadian synods. The idea of the Workers' Conference originated with Dr. John M. Gaston soon after he became assistant secretary of the Board of Missions for Freedmen in the spring of 1914. He called together the workers in the four synods for the first session of the Conference to convene and organize at the Mary Potter School at Oxford, North Carolina.

The purpose of the annual Conference was to bring together for fellowship and inspiration all workers involved in the programs for blacks. Here they discussed common problems, exchanged techniques and ideas, and received such information and instruction as would enhance the progress of the program across the field. It was also intended that the host communities would benefit through contact with the Conference personnel and program. The sessions brought together hundreds of delegates, informed speakers, and expertly trained singing groups. The Conference gradually developed into one of the most valuable and unique organizations under the Board.

With the passing of time, the Conference expanded in interest, number of participants, and value to the progress of the program. This made it necessary to abandon the original policy of shifting the annual sessions from school to school. In view of this change in policy, the Workers' Conference took advantage of Biddle University's larger facilities for several years. In 1951, the last session of the Conference was held at Biddle University, by this date renamed Johnson C. Smith University. At this time controversial issues arose over changing policies relative to the work with black Presbyterians and disintegration set in. Fewer and smaller sessions were held and the Workers' Conference eventually ceased to function.

---

[21] Clifford Drury, *Presbyterian Panorama: One Hundred and Fifty Years of National Missions History* (Philadelphia: Presbyterian Church in the U.S.A., Board of Christian Education, 1952), p. 86.

NEGRO WORK

OF THE PRESBYTERIAN CHURCH, U.S.A.

PRESBYTERIAN CHURCH, UNITED STATES OF AMERICA, BOARD OF NATIONAL MISSIONS, 156 FIFTH AVENUE, NEW YORK, NEW YORK, 1947

A PROGRAM OF EDUCATION 2

The schools established in the field were classified for practical purposes as parochial or boarding. The parochial schools were nonresidence coeducational elementary and high schools which often operated day and night in the early years. The boarding schools—academies, seminaries, colleges, institutes and a university—made up the rest of the school system of the Committee of Home Missions. The complete program is best visualized as a university system, with all of the lower level schools, with a few exceptions, geared to a common training program. From the elementary to the university, there was a gradation, uniform in character and purpose, leading to fulfillment at the highest level of the academic program. Thus the parochial and high schools became feeders for the centers of higher learning as well as terminal training centers for many.

In some of the larger schools, superintendents, principals, secretaries, treasurers and, sometimes, deans were employed. But for the vast majority of the schools at the parochial level, only one or two teachers were commissioned, who, in the early years, were a white minister or his wife, or both. As the formative years crystallized, the white teachers were replaced by the freedmen.

In the early stages of development of the program, the parochial schools were considered by the Freedmen's Committee to be the most immediate necessity. Unable to read, the masses of the liberated could make only superficial shows of advancement toward meaningful worship.

The Committee also reasoned that intelligent worship involved knowledge and use of certain range of information. Because particular principles had to be understood and applied; specific attitudes and loyalties cultivated; correct choice in habits, tastes, and actions encouraged and directed into channels of Christian conduct and character, the parochial schools were established to meet these basic needs.

These new parochials, like new frontiers, experienced rustic beginnings, accompanied by haste and limited funds. But for old and young, inspired and understanding teachers worked miracles. They were the doors to a new way of life, and through them much intellectual power, creativity, and innate leadership ability were discovered. The higher level schools took pride in the parochials and encouraged the parochials' promising pupils to accept the larger advantages which the higher level provided.

Many of the boarding schools began as parochials. However, in the parochials at the end of the school day, the pupils went back to the same drab huts, the same ill-prepared and deficient diet, and the same demoralizing temptations which infested their communities.

The Committee realized early the grave need for the pupils to have worthy contacts, sane guidance, and sound instruction. These students were not considered to be "outpatients" with minor irregularities, to be treated and released. They were, on the contrary, socially, educationally, religiously, and in some cases morally ill, neglected over a long period of time, and in need of sympathetic understanding, counseling, and love at work and at play. The boarding schools were designed to meet these needs. In the boarding schools, the pupils were placed in a wholesome environment, around the clock, under the precept and influences of Christian instructors, in an atmosphere where just to live was an educational experience. Skills, tastes, and choices were formed in daily routine, and habits of getting things done promptly and correctly were formed. The Committee, therefore, established such schools at widely separated but strategic points from Virginia to Texas.

There were other varied and numerous advantages to the boarding schools: the students gained strength, poise, pride, and dignity through the study of other peoples, ancient and modern, who had passed through and overcome experiences similar to theirs; they learned to contrast the clean life with the sordid; and the philosophy of the family as a primary social and Christian unit was taught. In this atmosphere of singing, working, playing, sharing, praying, and sacrificing for worthy objectives, a sense of personal dignity and respectability emerged. The pupils learned to view Africa through new eyes as they learned about its ancient cultures and contributions to history and civilization, its glamorous queens and kings of intelligence and power, as well as its natural and abundant resources. As they studied and played with students from "the dark continent," a sense of belonging in the society of mankind was awakened. The intrinsic value of black people to civilization was illumined.

Respect for the rights, opinions, and property of others was a by-product of living democratically in a Christian environment. Comradeships approached the depth of blood relations, and frequently lifetime mates and friendships developed. In many ways, they were finishing schools for black students.

It was not uncommon for some pupils to remain in the boarding schools for six, eight, or more years, absorbing the principles of the "better life." With few exceptions, they left the schools reluctantly but capable of wielding strong influences without damaging effects to themselves. The Committee expressed its estimate of these boarding schools in the following words:

> In mission schools where the aim is to touch every phase of life, raise the standard of living, instill the ideals of sanitation, improve the conditions of health, and express the love of Christ, as well as spread general knowledge, perhaps the dormitory is a more important factor in the work of the school than is the laboratory. Here it is that the students live. Here it is that habits of neatness and orderliness are definitely built up.[1]

The majority of the parochial schools convened in one or two rooms and frequently in the basement of a church or a rented structure. The churches were, in most instances, constructed with a view of temporarily housing a parochial school. Some of the larger schools, however, had separate buildings which grew in number and quality as the program progressed.

Likewise, there was a type of uniformity in the universal training program—rudimentary theological, classical, industrial courses. At the core of the curriculum was the Bible as a textbook and the Shorter Catechism as a type of workbook. Supplementary to these were courses in reading, writing, and arithmetic. Memorization was a common method utilized throughout the system until well into the 1930s. Especially was this true

---

[1] Presbyterian Church in the U.S.A., Board of National Missions *Annual Report* (New York: Presbyterian Building, 1932), p. 133. Hereafter cited as BNM, *Annual Report*.

in the instruction of the Catechism, arithmetic, spelling, history, poetry, and public speaking. The spelling bee, historical dates, and mathematical tables were popular contest activities.

For the most part, the pattern of the curriculum for these schools followed the general outline of the New England academies in which the majority of the early white teachers had received their training. Very few, if any, of the educational frills were stressed. Undergirding the total program was the common objective of intelligent Christian living, proper social relationships, adequate industrial skills, and basic practices of morality and cleanliness.

Music, especially singing, had played a long and important role in the black community. This continued to be the pattern in the schools. As far back as 1871, some of the larger schools had organized groups of singers —male, female, and mixed—to travel and sing in the interest of the schools. A natural urge to sing was utilized to achieve both moral and material ends. Through the throbbing sobs of the "sorrow songs" the groups sang to the heart of America. These spirituals which made up the greater portion of the groups' repertoire had their dateless and anonymous origin back in the wretched days of slavery. During that dark age, pent-up passion and sorrow were released, and a song was born. America was given a truly great folk song, and the singers were given something to live by. The universal appeal of these spirituals captured the hearts of thousands, black and white, and won the respect of music lovers who more than the singers realized how well the blacks sang. The descendants of the songmakers sang for greater deliverance as their forebears had sung to survive. The Committee made use of the singing groups for promotional purposes and sent them over the states and abroad to win friends and funds for the program. The response was gratifying.

In the beginning, these singing groups rendered the spirituals with something of the same feeling and fervor of the songmakers but, as pride was awakened and a sense of human dignity was aroused, there was a vigorous resentment by the students against anything that brought back memories of the days of slavery. This resentment was most intense during the middle 1920s, but began to wane shortly thereafter. Choirs and ensembles were still used for promotional purposes but their repertoires consisted primarily of religious and classical numbers.

The Beginnings (1865–1870)

The first five years of the divided church's missionary endeavors in the Wilderness were spent in structuring, fact-finding, and getting acquainted with the character of the mission field. When the two branches, the Old School and the New School, reunited in 1870, their work among the freedmen extended largely through North Carolina, South Carolina, Georgia, and Tennessee.

Involving the freedmen, the united church had 1 synod, 4 presbyteries, 85 churches, 138 schools, 1 normal school, 3 colleges, and 35 ministers, 14 of whom were Negroes.

An Era of Gradual Expansion (1870–1890)

Fifteen of the next twenty years were characterized by the expansion of the missionary outreach into previously untouched states and shifting the emphasis from the parochial to the higher level schools. The increasing necessity for black leadership and the gesture of the Southern states toward establishing a public system of education for Negroes, at least in the primary level, had strong bearing on this shift of focus. The states were dependent on the church schools to train teachers for their new systems.

By 1872, parochial schools in Washington, D.C. and Georgetown were merged with the public schools by the Freedmen's Bureau, and the Presbyterian teachers were withdrawn. These changes were suggestive of the trend and procedure which the Committee of Missions for Freedmen would take as it progressed into the decade ahead. Some parochial schools were transferred to other denominations when this was considered feasible.

One factor which kept the progress of the Committee at a gradual pace between 1870 and 1890 was its inherited debt which curtailed the scope and nature of all its activities. The Committee expressed this in the following report:

> It will be remembered that while the balance in hand, May 1, 1870, on the part of one of the organizations to which it became successor on the 16th of the month following, was but $3,878.12, the indebtedness upon that part of the work which had been conducted by the other organization to which it was made successor, as shown by an audited balance-sheet presented by its acting Secretary, August 31, of the same year, was, at this date $17,789.15.[2]

[2] Presbyterian Church in the U.S.A., Committee of Missions for Freedmen, *Annual Report* (Pittsburgh: Office of the Committee, 1873), p. 5. Hereafter cited as CMF, *Annual Report*.

This report also revealed the difficulties which arose from the loss of the $12,000 annual grant from the federal government, which was stopped July 1, 1870. The Freedmen's Bureau had given out large sums of money for educational purposes among the freedmen between 1865 and 1872. Some funds went to individual schools such as Hampton, Howard, and Atlanta Universities, but for the general work of the Presbyterian Church, U.S.A., the federal money for the freedmen went to the Committee of Missions for Freedmen. The report also spoke of the reduction in aid received from church boards. The debt, nevertheless, had been reduced to $5,000 in 1873. The total number of schools in 1873 was forty-six.[3] This number reflects a loss of seventy-two of the parochial schools inherited by the Committee following the 1870 merger.

The number of schools reported for the year 1874 was forty. This decrease of six additional schools was attributed to a scarcity of funds which necessitated retrenchment. Biddle, Scotia, Wallingford, and Brainerd were cited as the four schools under the Committee's care for the training of teachers of a higher order than "common."[4]

Getting a substantial footing in the state of Georgia was not easy for the Committee. First of all, migration had almost depopulated some farm areas. Also, hostility had been a stubborn barrier. Prior to the arrival of Presbyterians, other denominations with greater emotional appeal had begun work in Georgia among the freedmen after 1865. Although some intellectual alertness was desirable for meaningful worship, certain of these denominations utilized the human emotions that were readily responsive in an illiterate and oppressed people. By 1874, however, the Presbyterians, who had constantly insisted upon an educated ministry and an enlightened congregation, were successful in establishing rather permanent missions in some sections of the state.

In 1875, the Committee of Missions for Freedmen announced that its old debt had at last been lifted, yet the total number of schools had been reduced to thirty-nine. The Committee, in 1876, could again announce that it was able to close its books for the year clear of debt, with the exception of a small sum amounting to $1,354.00. The report also included a tribute to the mission teachers:

> In the missionary spirit of our teachers, as we think, lies one grand power of our work. With daily access to the minds and hearts of thousands, at a period when the memory and the heart are most

[3] CMF, *Annual Report*, 1873, pp. 6–7.
[4] *Minutes*, 1874, p. 174.

susceptible, their opportunities for doing good cannot well be over-estimated. . . .[5]

The Committee sent the Reverend Daniel Jackson Sanders to Scotland in 1876 to represent the work. He sailed for Scotland in October and by March 22 had collected $3,880.00. The total amount which came from Scotland that year up to the time of the meeting of the General Assembly was $4,359.43. The net proceeds went for missionaries' salaries. The Committee's secretary also went abroad to Ireland and received funds for the work. By 1877, Scotland had increased its contributions to the Committee by $1,508.51 and expressed a sentiment of continued sympathy for its work among the freedmen. The report of 1876 announced that the number of schools remained at thirty-nine and made mention of a new periodical:

A felt necessity in our work had been a periodical adapted to the work under our care and about two years ago *The Christian Freedmen*, a small monthly sheet was started with Professor Shedd of Biddle Memorial Institute, Charlotte, N.C. as editor and manager. About a year later this paper was enlarged to nearly double its former size under the name of *The Southern Evangelist*. It is now published by Rev. W. A. Patton, Superintendent of Wallingford Academy, Charleston, S.C. Rev. J. D. Shedd and Rev. D. J. Sanders, editors and proprietors—all missionaries in the Committee's employ. So far as we know, this is the only paper published specially for the moral and spiritual education of the Freedmen and we deem it very creditable both to them and its conductors that it proves self-sustaining, and with monthly information which it contains, "fresh from the field," it would prove very readable to any one interested in the proper elevation of this people.[6]

In a continued study of its progress the Committee stated that the cutting off of government aid and the burden of liquidating the inherited debt of 1870 had prevented it making any direct effort to enlarge its program. It also felt that though the geographical area was still limited, the size was too large for proper cultivation with the funds at its command. The Committee noted that since the last report Biddle Memorial Institute had obtained a new charter under the name "Biddle University" with enlarged powers and full collegiate grade.[7]

[5] CMF, *Annual Report*, 1876, p. 5.
[6] CMF, *Annual Report*, 1876, p. 10.
[7] *Minutes*, 1877, p. 675.

In 1878, the higher level schools were listed as follows:

Biddle University (Charlotte, North Carolina)
Wallingford Academy (Charleston, South Carolina)
Scotia Seminary (Concord, North Carolina)
Brainerd Institute (Chester, South Carolina)
Fairfield Institute (Winnsboro, South Carolina)
Blufton Institute (Blufton, Beauford County, South Carolina)

Sanders, in 1879, recognized the need for a larger medium of publicity through which the church and schools could dispense valuable information. In this interest he began the publication of a journal which he named *The Africo-American Presbyterian*. The editor hoped that this organ would be the answer to the wider publicity needs of the program. The journal grew in respect, popularity, and usefulness. The editor later bought the interest and good will of the *Southern Evangelist*.[8]

Because it had been haunted constantly by its inability to extend its outreach, the Committee had, by 1880, expansion at the core of its plans. The Committee said in 1882:

> The work of the committee is, by the limitation of its funds, confined to four of the Southern States: the two Carolinas, Virginia and Tennessee, with a few missions and schools in three others, Georgia, Kentucky, and Florida. There are the great states of Alabama, Mississippi, Texas, Louisiana and Arkansas, with a colored population of 2,360,381, not touched yet.[9]

In addition to the lack of sufficient funds there were other factors which retarded the advancement of the program. As mentioned earlier, for "social expediency" catechists and licentiates had to be trained to accompany ministers on their missionary responsibilities, thus doubling personnel unnecessarily. The menace of fire hazards, accidental and incendiary, had to be fought periodically at almost every mission center. As will be seen in the accounts of individual schools which follow, some schools went up in flames again and again; some lives were lost; valuable property and the tithings of many people were consumed almost annually by fires.

At the national level significant changes began to affect the work in the field. The Reverend A. C. McClelland, who had been a vital influence in the Committee, died April 19, 1880. He was succeeded by the Reverend

[8] *Biddle Institute Catalogue,* 1874–1875, front endpaper.
[9] *Minutes,* 1882, p. 217.

R. H. Allen, who had been pastor of the Old Pine Street Presbyterian Church in Philadelphia from 1867 to 1880.[10] Another event of major interest was the appointment of the Reverend Henry N. Payne as the first field secretary.[11] The specific function of this office was loosely defined, and its value to the program was hotly contested. Some opposed "the unnecessary expense involved," and the black community contended that his activities resembled too vividly that of the overseer of days gone by. On the other hand, the mission field was expanding and the Committee felt the need for a liaison factor.

In 1881, the Committee of Missions for Freedmen compared the work of the Presbyterian church with what other denominations were doing in the mission field:

> A great and inviting field spreads out all around us, into which we have made no entrance whatever—Alabama, with her 600,249 of colored people; Louisiana, with her 485,794; Mississippi, with her 650,337; Texas, with her 394,001; and others of the original slave states have not been touched by the Committee. There are earnest appeals coming to us from these states, and if we had the men and the money we would enter them at once. Sister protestant denominations have taken up the work among the Freedmen with earnestness and zeal, and we certainly bid them Godspeed. The Methodist Episcopal Church has 6 chartered institutions, 3 theological schools, 1 medical college, and 10 other schools, in 11 of the most populous southern states. . . . The American Missionary Association has flourishing colleges and schools in Virginia, North and South Carolina, Georgia, Alabama and Florida. . . . The Episcopal Church has missions among the Freedmen in 11 different states. . . .[12]

The work was greatly enlarged between 1881 and 1882. The Committee felt that Southern opposition to the program was on the wane, and especially was this true among Southern Presbyterians. In 1883 the Committee was incorporated with enlarged powers. At last its work was beginning to spread into the "region beyond." Swift Memorial College was established at Rogersville, Tennessee, and in the Indian Territory the Pittsburgh Mission was founded at Cold Creek. The effects of permanence, made possible by the Board's incorporation, were felt immediately. By 1884, the incorporated body under the new name, "The Board

---

[10] *A Sketch of the Life and Work of Mrs. Mary E. Allen* (Philadelphia: Press of Henry B. Ashmead, 1886), p. 13.

[11] *Minutes,* 1886, p. 11.

[12] CMF, *Annual Report,* 1881, p. 11.

of Missions for Freedmen," was operating sixty-seven schools, manned by 133 teachers, with an enrollment of 7,388 pupils. The Board's annual report for that year listed thirteen new schools and eleven new churches. Mary Allen Junior College was established at Crockett, Texas the same year. Most significant was the creation of the Women's Committee for Freedmen under the control of the Board of Missions for Freedmen. This was done at the request of Mrs. Mary E. Allen, the wife of the Reverend R. H. Allen, who had a leading role in the Board of Missions for Freedmen. Long had Mrs. Allen been interested and involved in this work, and the new Women's Committee was to have specific concern for freedwomen and children. The term "Our New Work" was often used thereafter by churchwomen to refer to projects under this committee.[13]

The expansion trend was well underway by 1885, and the Board set out to make Mary Allen [Junior College] in Texas what Scotia was in North Carolina—the "Mount Holyoke of the Southwest." This concept grew out of the similarity of the school's program to that of Scotia and the original school in the North which furnished the pattern. The schools established at Maryville, Tennessee, and Hendersonville, North Carolina, were growing rapidly, and the expansion had moved well into Oklahoma by 1886. Four additional missions were established in Oklahoma: Oak Hill, Valliant, Lukfatah, and Wheelock. During the year also the Board tried again to establish itself in the state of Louisiana, which had already been well occupied by the Roman Catholic church and various Protestant denominations. A mission was established at Pointee Coupi, Louisiana, and two women were sent to take charge of it. Two other women were sent to Gainesville, Florida to take charge of a newly established school there.[14]

The Women's Committee considered 1888 the most successful year since it entered the work in 1884. With a systematic approach and sincerity of purpose, the Committee boosted the Board's expansion dreams into the "region beyond." Financial support of the program had risen to a new high, and the program had grown in the esteem of the general church. Eighty-two schools with 203 teachers were under the Board's care that year.

In this same year, 1888, the founding of Richard Allen Institute in Pine Bluff, Arkansas was accomplished, with more than two hundred pupils enrolled.

The Reverend E. E. Swift, the first chairman of the Committee on

[13] *A Sketch of Mary E. Allen,* p. 17.
[14] BMF, *Annual Report,* 1886, pp. 9–11 and pp. 15–16.

Freedmen, died in 1888, and he was succeeded by the Reverend E. P. Cowan, as president of the Board of Missions.

Transition, Recession, and Curtailment (1890–1900)

The momentum of the expansion thrust of the two previous decades moved the program progressively into the 1890s before its progress was curtailed. The decade, 1890–1900, was characterized by recession—the national economy dropped; benevolence was curtailed; several parochial schools were closed; debts rose, and a near-calamitous situation developed for the Board's program. However, the decade began propitiously. In 1890, the Immanuel School at Aiken, South Carolina, was brought entirely under the Board's control, and the property, valued at more than $4,000, was transferred by deed to the Board.

Under Swift's long administration, only a moderate emphasis had been placed on the industrial phase of the Board's program and the major stress had been academic. Cowan's point of view was different, however:

> Industrial training is now a special feature in all our Seminaries and Academies. It has been introduced at Biddle during the year with marked success. In Scotia and Mary Allen, it has been carried on most prosperously. At Brainerd Institute, nearly every new building needed for the Institution, for the past three or four years, has been put up by the students.[15]

This report glossed over a serious controversy, however, and it is not clear whether the Board was aware of the depth of the feeling on this point. Within the black community militant voices were expressing disdain for the more conciliating philosophy of the post-Reconstruction period.

One of the major points at issue was industrial education rather than academic education. Many within the black community viewed the industrial emphasis as a shelter for moderate whites and conservative Negroes, since it perpetuated the view that manual labor rather than intellectual ability was the strong point of the blacks. The decade of the 1890s would see this controversy increasing, especially after Booker T. Washington's controversial speech at the Atlanta Exposition of 1895, extolling the virtues of industrial education for Negroes. Among the more eminent dissenters was W. E. B. DuBois. Writing of this period, DuBois observed:

> Their own leaders decried politics and preached submission. All

[15] BMF, *Annual Report*, 1890, p. 6.

their efforts toward manly self-assertion were distracted by defeatism and counsels of despair, backed by the powerful propaganda of a religion which taught meekness, sacrifice and humility.[16]

Dr. Cowan felt that the industrial emphasis was a strong promotional device and played it up in the annual reports. But the organized church women were not in favor of an overemphasis on manual training. Dr. Cowan's point prevailed at most of the schools, although at a low level, because it was both an expensive and an unpopular idea at the schools.

Even though illiteracy was increasing with the rapidly increasing black population, in 1890 the Board found encouragement in the knowledge that Biddle, Scotia, Mary Allen, Brainerd, Wallingford, Ingleside, and other schools stressing the higher branches of learning were winning battles against illiteracy in their respective vicinities.

A dedicated individual who had been steadily at work but whose name had not appeared frequently in the Board's reports, was Miss Mary E. Holmes of Illinois. The Women's Department made mention of her services in its 1890 report—and also made clear the enormous contribution the women were making:

> Miss Holmes of Illinois, raised $774.14 for painting and furnishing the new buildings at Cotton Plant, Arkansas and Oak Hill at Indian Territory. . . . ninety-two full scholarships and eighty-two partial ones were sent through the Women's Executive Committee to twelve schools. . . . the small debt resting upon Cotton Plant has been entirely cancelled by the women of Illinois. . . . At Gainesville, Florida, a house for our school has been built and is now in use, the money having been furnished by a generous lady in New Jersey.[17]

There obviously was much more to be done, however, and so the report of the Women's Department continues:

> In Georgia, the Empire State of the South, the work has been greatly strengthened and pushed forward. The colored population in this State is rapidly increasing and numbers now probably not less than 900,000, and in no state, unless it be in Texas, are these people

[16] W. E. B. DuBois, *Black Reconstruction* (New York: Harcourt, Brace, and Co., 1935), p. 186.

[17] Presbyterian Church in the U.S.A., Board of Missions for Freedmen, Women's Department, *Annual Report* (Pittsburgh: Office of the Board, 1890), pp. 9–10. The Women's Department of the Board of Missions for Freedmen is the Freedmen's Department of the Woman's Executive Committee of Home Missions.

accumulating property so rapidly. . . . We may anticipate a marked advance by our Church in this state within the next few years. The same promising outlook is afforded us in Arkansas, where many of our colored people from the Atlantic states are settling. A Presbytery, White River, was organized there a little over a year ago, and is earnestly pushing the work in that state, and we may now regard Arkansas as one of our most hopeful fields. Two men have been put in the Indian Territory and we have the most encouraging reports of their good work in the Choctaw nation. The new Presbytery of Southern Virginia is doing good and efficient work . . .[18]

Despite these encouraging words, the report ended with regrets that the program had not been extended into Alabama and Mississippi. Because of the women, however, the Board of Missions to Freedmen could report that year that something had been done:

The ladies of Illinois proposed to raise $6,000 toward the founding of a boarding school for colored girls in that state to be known as the Mary Holmes Seminary . . . in memory of the mother of Miss Mary E. Holmes, through whose influence and that of the ladies of Illinois the building was erected at a cost of $16,000.[19]

Also in 1890, Ferguson Academy of Abbeville, South Carolina, was transferred over to the Board. This institution had been previously built and partly supported by friends outside the Board at a cost of $10,000, the sum at which the property was then valued. The board had aided in supporting the teachers at Ferguson Academy but had not owned the property. There were 115 pupils enrolled under the principalship of the Reverend E. W. Williams at the time.[20]

The rationale undergirding the philosophy of the board's policy was never more controversial than when it began to transfer the leadership of its major schools from white to black administrators in 1891. The board felt, however, that the time had arrived to test the validity of its original objective—to train leaders among the blacks to work toward their own full deliverance. The board had as a reliable justification for its position on this matter the success of those schools under its care that had been founded and executed under black leadership from the beginning. The Board remained firm on this policy in spite of strong opposition.

The transfer move began at Biddle University, the capstone of the Board's program. Despite widespread shouts of "unready," others dedi-

[18] BMF, *Annual Report,* 1890, p. 5.
[19] BMF, *Annual Report,* 1892, p. 5.
[20] BMF, *Annual Report,* 1891, p. 7.

cated themselves to making the adventure work, even though aware of possible consequences of this transfer. To this end, the Board appointed the Reverend D. J. Sanders to be president of Biddle University which had four Negro and four white professors. Three white professors resigned,[21] and several students withdrew from the institution.

President Sanders, a man of courage, sound judgment, and rich experience, assumed his duties with humility and dignity. His first faculty, one white and nine Negro professors, dedicated itself to make the transfer work. After one year, even the most skeptical dissenter acknowledged that the move had been a success.

Major changes in the Board's personnel also had significant effects on the program during this period of transition. The Reverend Richard H. Allen who had served the Board as corresponding secretary for thirteen years, died on September 27, 1892. This loss was felt keenly on the campuses of the Board's schools. The same year, the Reverend Henry N. Payne, after eight years as field secretary, made a detailed analysis of the work among freedmen as he saw it. After reemphasizing the continued need for the Board's parochial schools, he made this observation: "It will be many years before this feature of our work can be wisely discontinued. It is from them largely that the boys and girls in our higher schools come. It is to them chiefly that we must look for our future teachers and preachers."[22]

Apparently, the Board was so dazzled by the success of its expansion into the untouched regions that it failed to recognize the signs of the approaching economic crisis. Therefore, encouraged by the boost in funds, it raised its spending. At the end of 1894 this note was appended to its report:

> There was in prospect at the close of last year of a large legacy from the Mary Stuart estate of New York. The knowledge of its existence enabled us to contemplate our last year's deficit of nearly thirty thousand dollars with more calmness than we otherwise would have done. The receipt of the larger part of the expected fund in the latter part of May, not only enabled us to clear off all indebtedness, but put us in such good shape financially as to justify us in the feeling that we might safely venture on a reasonable and healthful expansion of the work. We began, therefore, almost immediately after the last General Assembly to make plans for advancement all along the line. . . .

[21] BMF, *Annual Report,* 1892, p. 18.
[22] BMF, *Annual Report,* 1893, p. 13.

Before we fully realized what was in store for us and the rest of the country, the financial crisis came and only by a prompt change of plans by the Board, aided by the approval and hearty cooperation of those who were to bear the brunt of the disappointment, were we able to avert disaster and escape general and serious embarrassment. We recalled promises, cancelled engagements, annulled contracts, and prepared ourselves for the worst. Our general line of policy was to stop every projected plan of improvement and extension that called for extra expenditure of money. This was carried out in all cases but with one exception. In the case referred to, the work was in such condition that the only course of economy was for us to go forward and not backward; and so, in spite of the money famine, we proceeded with the Rogersville building, which stands today complete as the only finished part of the extended advancement we had fondly dreamed of at the beginning of the year.[23]

Contrary to the general money famine, Mrs. C. E. Coulter of the Department of Freedmen, reported $1,356.16 had been raised in excess of the amount of the previous year. This surplus might have been because of increased industry and sacrifices on the part of the women to meet the emergency.

The Reverend Henry Payne described the situation as "precarious" and wrote of the reaction of the mission field:

> I have spoken of the financial embarrassment of the Board and a great deal of interest and sympathy have been expressed, not infrequently resulting in special collections being taken in presbyteries and churches to be forwarded to Pittsburgh. When I have said that the next year would probably be one of retrenchment, and that the Board would hardly be able to do as much for the various fields as heretofore, there has been a general disposition to accept the situation in the right spirit and to do all that is possible in the way of self-support.[24]

Added to the financial distress was the chronic fire and storm menace. Churches and schools at Columbia and Pine Bluff were destroyed by fire, and, on Wadmalaw Island, the Salem Church, used for worship and school, was swept away by cyclones.[25]

The general curtailment of operations continued during 1895. Teachers' salaries were reduced on an average of ten percent. The practice of

---

[23] BMF, *Annual Report,* 1894, pp. 4–5.
[24] BMF, *Annual Report,* 1894, p. 14.
[25] BMF, *Annual Report,* 1894, p. 15.

sending indigent boarding pupils home was continued. The Preparatory Class at Biddle University was discontinued, and additional parochial schools were closed.

Despite the drastic cutback in 1895, the Board still had seventeen boarding schools under its care: one each in Virginia, Georgia, Tennessee, Texas, and Oklahoma; three in Arkansas; five in North Carolina; four in South Carolina, and several parochial schools scattered along the way. There was a setback, however, when the entire plant of Mary Holmes Seminary at Jacksonville, Mississippi, was made a total loss by fire on January 31, 1895. The $27,000 loss was partially covered by a $15,000 insurance on the property.

In addition to the destruction by fire and financial shortages, the *Plessy v. Ferguson* decision was handed down by the Supreme Court in 1896. The Supreme Court took the position that the "separate but equal" policy did not necessarily imply inferiority of either race. This policy was accepted as just, but it protected the existing discrimination. The black child's public educational experience began under a deceptive system, and this substitute for quality education took its toll in the total public education system in the South and spread also to other areas of the country as the black migration North continued.

Ironically, the Board, of necessity, was forced to curtail its school activities at this time. The school terms were cut again in thirteen of its nineteen boarding schools. Twelve of them were allowed six months each, two academies only five months. After discontinuing twenty of its parochial schools the Board reduced those that remained to four months each. At the national level the services of the treasurer as a salaried officer were discontinued.

In 1897, the recession apparently began to lessen its grip on the economy and relief seemed in sight for the Board, at least temporarily. Mrs. Phineas N. Barber contemplated turning over to it a completed plant for the maintenance of a first-class boarding school capable of housing 150 girls at Anniston, Alabama. Mrs. Barber was the widow of the founder of the "Barber Fund." The fund was held in trust by the trustees of the General Assembly "for the benefit of the colored race."

The pathetic ruins of the burned Mary Holmes Jr. College were cleared away, and plans were made for a new structure, but not in Jacksonville. With money which had been contributed for enlargement before the burning and a gift of twenty acres of land, Mary Holmes was rebuilt on the outskirts of West Point, Mississippi.

The Women's Department was the organization that kept the awakened church active during this crisis. By its industry and influence among the women's societies, the program continued forward within a limited framework. The women's societies in Indiana Synod built a boys' dormitory at Oak Hill in Valliant, Oklahoma. The women of Warren, Pennsylvania church provided funds for the completion of a church and school at Newport News, Virginia. Special gifts from Indiana, New York, and California made possible a school at Sumter, South Carolina. With special gifts from the Chicago Presbytery, the Board bought additional land at Augusta, Georgia for Haines Institute and the church and school at Hot Springs, Arkansas. The Indiana women's societies also made possible the purchase of additional land and building a school at Chattanooga, Tennessee.[26]

Despite the lessening of the recession in the national economy, the difficulties were not over for the board. With the hope that this notice would fortify the teachers for the unpredictable future of the work, the following message was sent to all teachers in February 1897:

> . . . in the year to come such reductions will be made as shall bring our expenses within the limit of our income. It is now eight months before the school work of next year will begin, and this is thought to be ample time for preparation on the part of workers under our care to meet contingencies that may arise from the suspension of the support of the Board to any part, or to all of any particular work with which any of them may at present be connected. Our schedule for the new school year will be out as soon as possible after the close of the old one.[27]

As uncertain as this note left the matter of continuance, the faithful teachers remained at their posts. As an additional means of curtailing expense, the Board considered the possibility of closing the churches on the field but was swayed by the fact that in most cases the money had already been pledged for their support. The schools were reduced from sixty-seven to fifty-three in 1898. At the end of 1899 the Board made a detailed analysis of the 1890–1900 decade. It is quoted extensively here because it conveys so much of the emotion of the period:

> In 1893 our troubles began. Our income had reached its highest point, and our work its greatest expansion. Suddenly its progress

26 BMF, *Annual Report*, 1897, p. 10.
27 BMF, *Annual Report*, 1897, p.10.

had to be arrested. The momentum of its forward movement had to be overcome before we could begin the forced retreat which the exigencies of the time demanded.

The abandonment of many schools of lesser importance, the curtailment of others as to length of term and cost of maintenance, the reduction of the salaries of ministers and refusal to encourage the organization of new churches, all seemed of no avail. The debt steadily increased. Our resources steadily diminished.

Our darkest time was in the winter of 1898, when we reached the limit of our credit in bank and were nearing the payments of January, not only with absolutely no money in sight in any direction but with the largest interest-bearing debt we had ever carried. . . .

In our extremity we sent out a cry of distress to some of our best friends, ending with "Will you come to our help, or shall we give up the work." The cry was not in vain. Many friends wrote words of cheer, and sent us help and bid us keep our courage up. But best of all on the 2nd day of the New Year, the very day when over $9,000 should be sent out as salaries, and when we had not a dollar to send a modest letter came from one of God's noble-men, a man not personally known to any member of the Board containing a check for $10,000 "for our general work." Whether this came in answer to our direct appeal to men, as well as our prayer to God, we know not; but we do know that it was a Divine deliverance. It was the turning point in our struggle against debt. . . .

Other friends came later to our help, and by the close of that year we had paid all our bills and taken nearly $18,000 off our financial load. But we came to the Assembly with still a debt of $40,000.

There should be some record of how this burden was rolled away. The splendid loyalty of both ministers and elders to the whole Missionary work of our Church had such a striking exemplification in the heartiness with which one and all joined in our supreme effort to remove this last remaining debt of all the Boards of the church that some account of it should be preserved.

It having been learned before the Assembly met that none of the other Boards, would have any deficits, and that the Freedmen's Board, in this respect, stood alone, sympathy began to turn our way. Reverend Mead Holmes of Rockford, Illinois, through the religious journals, made the first offer of a thousand dollars toward the payment of our $40,000 debt, provided the rest was raised by a certain time. The time limit expired and the conditions were not fulfilled. But this generous sum was subsequently paid by Mr. Holmes in furtherance of another movement which had the same end in view.

A circular letter headed, Cleveland, Ohio, May 1, 1899 and

signed H. W. Hulbert, Chairman in behalf of the Committee, and sent to every Commissioner-elect to the approaching Assembly, stated that the Presbyterial Committee of Cleveland Presbytery had that day organized to clear off before June 1st the deficit of the Freedmen's Board—"this last vestige of debt upon the Presbyterian Church."

Mr. James A. Robinson, an elder from Cleveland, was treasurer of the Committee. Commissioners were asked to consult the brethren of their Presbyteries and come to the Assembly prepared to report pledges conditioned on the whole amount to be raised.

While no large amount was secured directly by this effort, the way was no doubt prepared for the finally successful effort of the Standing Committee on Freedmen, of which Rev. Charles Herr, D.D., of Jersey City, N.J. was Chairman.[28]

By the end of the Assembly the amount had been pledged, and a month before time to close the books of the Board $37,000 had been received; when the Assembly convened, excesses of receipts over expenditures enabled the Board to close its books out of the red.

The debt had been paid, but there had been a heavy price. The property throughout the entire mission field was badly in need of repair. While the Board was reporting the situation to the Assembly, news came over the wires that the new Margaret Barber Seminary had been consumed by fire. In this crucial moment, as had happened again and again, two unexpected gifts enabled the Board to apply them to their direst needs.

Mrs. Flora D. Palmer, who succeeded Mrs. Coulter following her retirement on October 1, 1899, gives this account of how the women helped the program through its crisis:

> The Treasurer of the Woman's Board has forwarded this year to the Freedmen's Board for this Department $55,736.27, which was contributed through auxiliary Societies, individual's gifts, and Sabbath Schools, contributing through Women's Societies. . . .
> Remembering "That it is the mind that guides the hand," the policy of the Board has been, and is, not to emphasize industrial training at the expense of the spiritual and intellectual, but to give to each department of training—each in its place—due emphasis.[29]

The daring and adventurous approaches of the women, their sense of detailed and methodical record-keeping, their observance of systematic

[28] BMF, *Annual Report,* 1900, pp. 5–7.
[29] Presbyterian Church in the U.S.A., Women's Board of Home Missions, Freedmen's Department, *Annual Report* (Pittsburgh: Office of the Board, 1900), pp. 154–155. Hereafter cited as Women's Board, *Annual Report.*

business practices, and their strict, organized approach were of particular significance in this otherwise dismal decade.

Industrial Emphasis, Expansion, War Years (1900–1920)

The dramatic liquidation of its harassing debt with the passing of the old century gave the Board of Missions for Freedmen a clean slate. The Board assessed the situation, took an inventory of gains and losses, and planned its approach into the new century. Fortified by past experiences, and better acquainted with the demands of the field and the techniques which brought desired results, the Board began with greater courage and confidence than it had before.

Its first concern was the faithful workers, many of whom had stuck to their posts with or without pay. Their salaries were modestly increased. Twenty-two new teachers were employed for six months each in the parochial schools, and ten were employed for the high schools. Terms of the larger schools were lengthened, and some of the parochial schools that had been closed were reopened. In addition, several new parochial schools were established.

Although the Women's Department and the mission field were wary about the increased emphasis placed on the industrial phase of the program at the beginning of the new century, the Board was insistent on this stress. This was prominently manifested in the "Farm Home Scheme," which had great social and economic potentials at schools with sufficient acreage to promote such a project. The scheme provided for the land to be divided into plots, ranging in size from ten to twenty acres, which were sold to reputable Negro men with families—Presbyterians preferred —at fair prices and on easy terms. Money was advanced to assist the purchasers in building homes, buying tools and seeds, to meet living expenses during the early years of occupancy. The loan was to be repaid at a fair rate of interest. Capable superintendents were employed to instruct in successful farming. The first year was a type of probation during which the land was rented, and the renter proved his good intentions or took advantage of the reasonable withdrawal provisions.

The Board's objective was to surround the schools with progressive communities that could be guided by the educational personnel and religious atmosphere of the campuses. This was attempted at Boggs Academy and Harbison Institute and will be described more fully in the stories of these schools.

At the end of 1901, the Board was able to close its books free of debt, and for the moment, at least, retrenchment was over. A modest advance toward expansion was launched, although with great precaution. By 1903, the Board's income was greater than in any one of the previous years. Eight new schools were founded, and with the aid of the "Jeans Fund" a number of sewing teachers were placed in some of the academies.[30]

At the close of 1904, the fifth successive year, the Board's books were closed free of debt and with a balance. The policy of operating the church and parochial school jointly was reemphasized, and ministers who were pastors of small churches were urged to open parochial schools in connection with their pastoral work, without expense to the Board. They were permitted to charge "a reasonable tuition fee . . . sufficient to meet expenses and possibly to remunerate the teacher somewhat for his additional labor." The plan seemed to work reasonably well as the number of schools increased from 91 to 113 by the end of 1905.

There were many losses at the administrative level which greatly affected the Board during this period. Dr. Henry Payne died in June, 1903, after eighteen years of varied services to the program. The Reverend H. T. McClelland, who had been with the Board for twenty years, including eleven as its president, was appointed field secretary; the Reverend Fisher was elected Board president and the Reverend E. P. Cowan became secretary-treasurer. The death of Mr. S. P. Harbison, who had been an energizing member of the Board since 1888 was a tremendous loss. A further loss occurred in 1906 with the death of Dr. Mary E. Holmes, who had contributed significantly in unsalaried but constant service.

One of the top program concerns in which the women were especially interested was the "Box and Barrel Project." They considered this project to be important to many destitute families who would not have been able otherwise to clothe their children adequately for school and church. In some cases the parents preferred to pay a small sum for the articles received. More often, however, missionaries at the schools, sensing individual needs privately, took a child and outfitted him or her. Some societies sent clothing, while others took special children as projects to keep comfortably groomed. Many touching and human interest stories

---

[30] Mrs. Anna T. Jeans donated over a million dollars to the education of black children. Although she gave additional sums of money to Hampton, and Tuskegee she was primarily interested in small rural schools and requested that Booker T. Washington and Dr. Hollis Burke Frissell determine how the funds should be distributed. Ullin Whitney Leavell, *Philanthropy in Negro Education* (Nashville: Cullen and Ghertner, 1930), pp. 71–73.

are told by the graduates who made their way through school out of barrels and boxes.

Late in 1908, the Board again was aware of a decline in income and included in its annual report a notice which had been previously sent to the workers on the field:

> The Board, with regret, will be compelled to adopt restrictive measures in order to prevent further serious financial embarrassment. Resolutions one and two: that no new schools were to be opened that would entail additional expense upon the Board. Three: No additional teachers would be employed at Board expense; Four: No extension of school terms; Five: No salary increases; Six: All schools and churches must assume responsibility for own local repairs.[31]

Despite this strict cutback in spending, schools increased during the year from 115 to 123, and buildings were erected as an emergency measure at some of the schools.

A highlight of 1908 was a giant mass meeting of all denominations and influential enterprises striving for progress among Negroes. The meeting was called to convene in Clifton, Massachusetts, by W. N. Hartshorn. The participants engaged in sincere and factual dialogue on the religious, moral, and educational development of the American Negro since his emancipation. Dr. Cowan was the Board's representative at this conference and made the following report to the Board:

> The conferees were frank and outspoken in their attempts to evaluate objectively the causes, describe effects, and map out plans for greater achievement. Efforts were made to solace the old sectional wounds and animosity. For the first time Negro leadership had an opportunity, on a large scale, to voice, unafraid, its opinions of the character of the Negro's plight in the South and basic needs for elevating it—without fear of repercussions.[32]

Many of the heads of the Board's schools attended the conference. Interested friends from North and South also attended and participated in the discussions.

The Board's schools continued to be plagued by fire. In 1910, the girls' dormitory at Alice Lee Elliott was burned. Three days later the main building at Harbison was destroyed by an incendiary bomb which claimed

[31] BMF, *Annual Report,* 1909, pp. 3–4.
[32] The source of the information referred to can no longer be located.

the lives of three students. Several persons were injured, and irreplace-able property was lost.

By 1910, the Board began to realize that the scope of its program was too wide and its specific needs too varied for the work of one person. It therefore appointed the Reverend John M. Gaston as associate secretary. In 1910 the Board had nine additional schools and thirty-two more workers than in the previous year.

Also in 1910, property in Knoxville and Chattanooga, Tennessee, owned by the American Missionary Association for school purposes, was sold to the Board. Schools under the Board's care had been operating in these buildings, but now the Board owned the property as well.

By 1914, the Board had 113 parochial schools and 27 boarding schools. Although this was the largest number ever operated by the Board at one time, the need remained great. In 1916, there were only 67 public high schools available to Negro students throughout the entire South.

There were other disturbing factors which affected seriously both the church and public schools at this time. World War I was beginning to take its toll of the school campuses. By 1918, 83,000 Negroes had been drafted, many of whom were from the campuses of the Board's schools. The church schools were kept alive, and, when the three-month public schools ended, their pupils went to the church schools for the remainder of the church school's longer term. The war and influenza depleted enrollment, but many of the *boys* who were drafted returned to the Board's schools as *men* with a purpose.

Significant changes were also occurring at the national level. On Friday, December 13, 1918, the Reverend E. P. Cowan, who had served the Board for thirty-five years, died. He began as a member of the Board in 1883; he continued as vice president in 1886; he was president in 1888; corresponding secretary in 1893, and in 1903 he held the combined office of secretary-treasurer which he continued to fill until his death. The associate secretary, the Reverend John M. Gaston, succeeded him and upon recommendation of the Standing Committee, was given the entire oversight and supervision of the Board's program.

At the close of this period, 1900–1920, the dual system of public education for the Negro at the elementary level in the South was increasing. Thus the board discontinued many of its parochial schools and placed its emphasis on higher level schools to meet the demand for more teachers.

Controversies and Curtailment (1920–1930)

Tensions were increasing in both North and South. The exodus of blacks from Southern rural areas to Northern cities increased. The revived Ku Klux Klan began to scatter terror through the land, and the Standing Committee of the General Assembly proposed that it take a stand against the ominous practice of lynching.[33] Migration almost depopulated some rural areas in the South necessitating the discontinuance of many of the parochial schools.

The Board began this decade with some gains, however. In 1921, the Harbison estate authorized the Board to purchase 2,402 acres of land at Irmo, South Carolina, to aid the Farm Homes Project there. The Board also continued to meet the demands of schools neglected during the war period.

The keynote of dialogue with changing situations is made clear in the report of 1925:

> As the law requires that Negro public schools be taught by colored teachers, properly prepared teachers are greatly needed and the states, of necessity, had to depend upon the Church's machinery for training these teachers.
>
> The state policy of maintaining dual systems of education in a section not yet fully given to the fairness of equity of education for all citizens justified the continued operation of the Board's program. There were some semblance of decency in this direction in North Carolina but most of the states seemed not to consider the wrongness or rightness of equality at this point.[34]

By 1926, it was obvious that the expansion of the Board's program for Southern Negroes was over. Clearly showing this was the action of the Board: "Twenty-one day schools in communities that seemed best able to take over this responsibility, were closed. That is to say, the Board withdrew from them all financial support. . . . In other instances, the terms were shortened from eight to six months."[35] In some cases, where funds were withdrawn and terms cut, the communities rallied and the teachers remained on duty—some donating their services while others accepted what their pupils' parents could afford to give them.

By 1928, the entire national economy was beginning to feel the effects of the approaching depression. The Board of National Missions explained its financial status during the years following the 1923 reorganization:

The uncertainty and confusion in the mind of the church incident

[33] *Minutes,* 1919, p. 170.
[34] BNM, *Annual Report,* 1925, p. 157.
[35] *Minutes,* 1928, p. 157.

to reorganization operated to reduce the income of the Board at a time when its obligations were being substantially increased. The steady upward trend of giving which had extended through fifty years was abruptly checked, and a forced policy of "no deficit" was adopted by the Board.[36]

This period may safely be said to have been the beginning of the gradual and final decline of the Board's program of education for Negroes.

Depression, Desegregation, and Decline (1930–1970)

At the beginning of this long period, The Division of Work for Colored People was operating 108 schools of which 80 were day schools and 28 were boarding schools. Twenty-one of these boarding schools were coeducational; 5 were seminaries for girls; 1 was a university for men, and 1 offered industrial work for men and boys. These schools faced an uncertain future, however, as the ensuing depression brought cuts in benevolent funds, philanthropy, and tuition income. The program had been overextended and undersupported.

The decline of the Board's work was greatly influenced by the Depression. The South's economy, already below the national norm, became paralyzed. Farm prices dropped; the new factory system on which the South based its hope for new strength began to shut down; its slowly rising public school system slipped back down the scale, and the schools for blacks lay neglected at the bottom. The South was in the impossible position of attempting to educate one-third of the nation's children in a dual school system which was supported by only one-sixth of the nation's school revenue.

In the midst of it all, the Board's schools were kept alive by curtailment and consolidation to provide increased efficiency without increased cost.[37] It was decided that the strong schools should continue to be supported although many weak ones would have to cease. And there were strong schools. In 1932, the Board reported:

> The development of our schools is due almost entirely to the efforts of the principals and presidents. We have but four schools under white administration. To the Negro, then, goes the credit for building up our mission schools from struggling, meagerly equipped, poorly housed, over-crowded makeshifts of the past, into institutions,

[36] The source of the information referred to can no longer be located.
[37] BNM, *Annual Report,* 1928, p. 157.

many of which compare most favorably with the best schools in the country.[38]

By this declaration it was obvious that the Board's original plan of turning over the execution of its schools to black leadership had been achieved. Curtailment continued, however, and black concern increased as they envisioned the educational plight of black children under the dual school system.

The moment of decision came in 1931 when the General Assembly requested a study of the work with Negroes. The machinery for this study consisted of two conferences, Northern and Southern, each of which included a board committee and representatives from the fields involved. The Southern Conference had as a consultant Dr. Arthur D. Wright, president of the Jeans and Slater funds and an executive of the Southern Association of Colleges and Secondary Schools. The Conferences began work immediately and Dr. R. N. Morse, secretary of the committee on the Study of Missionary Objectives, a subsidiary of the Southern Conference, made a temporary report to the Board in April of 1932 and to the General Assembly in May of the same year:

> Our Presbyterian work in the South is in 12 states but with the greatest concentration in Virginia, North and South Carolina and Georgia. 73 of these schools are classified as day schools, 35 of which, for financial reasons, are being discontinued at the end of the present school year. . . .
> 27 are classified as boarding schools, 10 of which could be listed as day schools as 80% of their enrollments are day pupils. . . . The Board submits the following recommendations:
> a. That the Board reaffirm the policy which it approved on October 28, 1931, on the recommendation of the Advisory Committee of the Division of Missions for Colored People of "closing all elementary schools and high schools where public school facilities are available with the explicit understanding that this policy applies not only to day schools but also to those schools now classified as boarding schools which draw the major part of their students from the communities in which they are located. . . ."
> b. That June 1, 1933, be set as the final date for the maintenance by the Board of day schools and of such boarding schools as are brought under the foregoing policy, except as particular schools may, prior to that date, be specifically exempt by the Board from the application of this rule. . . .

[38] BNM, *Annual Report,* 1932, p. 133.

d. That the boarding schools sustained be operated on a strict budget executed by the Board.

e. That Johnson C. Smith's Liberal Arts be made co-educational and that the Theological Seminary be strengthened and that a summer school for ministers be conducted.[39]

The black community was not only shocked but terrified by the reality of this manifesto. It seemed incredible that so great a loss could come to their communities at a time of such need. Neither the mission field, nor the supporting friends of the work, nor the administrative agencies that worked with the schools, were fully prepared for these swift and drastic changes. One year later, however, Dr. Gaston's report stated that four additional day schools had been closed and listed the agencies that would administer certain schools:

"Four day schools remain under the care of National Missions: James Island . . . Edisto Island . . . Due West, which receives the support and cooperation of a college for white students at that point under the Reformed Presbyterian Church; and McClelland Academy at Newnan, Georgia, which is earnestly recommended by the state board of education to be continued.

"As to the Boarding Schools: Mary Potter, Redstone and Albion, the schools at Franklinton and Lumberton are being continued by the public school board. Other schools within the bounds of this synod (Catawba) are: Johnson C. Smith University, with the University is affiliated Barber-Scotia Junior College. Johnson C. Smith University has an "A" rating and Barber-Scotia has a "B" rating from the Southern Association of Colleges and Secondary Schools. Gillespie and Selden merged June 1, 1933; Arkadelphia and Cotton Plant Academy were also merged.

"Atlantic Synod has within its bounds, Brainerd, Coulter, Harbison which absorbed the day school about a mile away from the campus. In the southern part of Georgia, Gillespie and Selden have been combined and located at Cordele. Boggs Academy, which is ten miles from any town is located in the midst of a 1,000-acre tract of land near Keysville, Georgia.

"In East Tennessee Synod, there are three boarding schools: Swift, Margaret Barber that absorbed the South Highland High School—located on the campus and thus becoming co-educational. Rev. A. W. Price, prin-

[39] Report of the Committee on the Study of Missionary Objectives to the Board of National Missions, April, 1932. This report is noted but not quoted in the BNM, *Annual Report*, 1932, p. 62.

cipal of the high school became assistant to Rev. H. M. Hossack, Principal of the consolidated school.

"Mary Holmes is the only school which we have in the state of Mississippi. About a year ago the Board added Teacher-Training courses there.

"In Kentucky, Bowling Green Academy is turned into a students' home, the pupils attending the city schools for their literary work and living in the dormitory where they receive their Christian training and contacts with home life. Also in Kentucky is located Fee Memorial Institute.

"An arrangement was effected whereby Haines Industrial Institute was kept partially alive. The local Trustee Board assumed responsibility for teachers amounting to $5,280; the Board for maintenance, $2,300; Miss Lucy C. Laney, founder and for 48 years principal, had the pleasure of seeing her work continue before she died in October, 1933."[40]

The following schools were discontinued June 1, 1933:
1. Hardin Academy, Allendale, South Carolina
2. Salem Industrial Institute, Anderson, South Carolina
3. South Highland High, Anniston, Alabama
4. St. Mary's, Blackstock, South Carolina
5. Harris Chapel, Brinkley, Arkansas
6. Good Hope, Brogdon, South Carolina
7. Camden School, Camden, South Carolina
8. Refuge Jr. H. S., Charlotte Court House, Virginia
9. Grandview, Chesterfield, South Carolina
10. Ebenezer, Dalzell, South Carolina
11. Wheeler, Drakes Branch, Virginia
12. St. Pauls, Greensboro, Georgia
13. Irmo, Irmo, South Carolina
14. John's Island, John's Island, South Carolina
15. Kersville, Lone Star, South Carolina
16. Mary Louise Esler, Louisville, Tennessee
17. Mt. Carmel School, Manning, South Carolina
18. Christian Light, Mannsboro, Virginia
19. Salem Wadmalaw, Martins Point, South Carolina
20. Grace, Martinsville, Virginia
21. Goodwill, Maysville, South Carolina

[40] John Gaston, "A Review of the Work," *Women and Missions*, vol. X, no. 11 (February, 1934), pp. 359–361.

22. Bethesda School, Nottoway, Virginia
23. Mt. Olive, Okmulgee, Oklahoma
24. Bethlehem Second, Oswego, South Carolina
25. Holmes Memorial, Ridgeway, Virginia
26. Lebanon, Ridgeway, South Carolina
27. Butler, Savannah, Georgia
28. Curry Institute, St. Charles, South Carolina
29. Westminster (Alcolu), Sumter, South Carolina
30. Mather-Peritt, St. Augustine, Florida
31. Church School, Tullahassee, Oklahoma
32. Pleasant Grove, Union Point, Georgia
33. Hodge Academy, Washington, Georgia
34. Thomas Steele Memorial, Wedgefield, South Carolina
35. Bethlehem First, York, South Carolina
    Schools that remained under Unit of Schools and Hospitals:
 1. Margaret Barber, Anniston, Alabama
 2. Arkadelphia and Cotton Plant merged June 1, 1933 (Arkansas)
 3. Monticello Academy—Discontinued June 1, 1933, Monticello, Arkansas
 4. Boggs Academy, Keysville, Georgia
 5. Haines Day School, Augusta, Georgia (under special arrangement)
 6. Gillespie and Selden, merged June 1, 1933, Georgia
 7. Bowling Green Academy, Bowling Green, Kentucky
 8. Fee Memorial Institute, Kentucky
 9. Mary Holmes, West Point, Mississippi
10. Mary Potter-Redstone—Albion Academy—merged June 1, 1933
11. Alice Lee Elliott Academy, Valliant, Oklahoma
12. Brainerd Institute, South Carolina
13. Coulter Academy, South Carolina
14. Harbison Institute, Irmo, South Carolina
15. Swift Memorial Institute, Tennessee
16. Mary Allen Junior College, Crockett, Texas
17. Ingleside, Burkesville, Virginia
    Under other Units:
 1. Johnson C. Smith University, Charlotte, North Carolina
 2. Barber-Scotia Junior College, Concord, North Carolina[41]

In the many communities where there was no evidence of state educa-

[41] *Women and Missions*, 1934, p. 359.

tion for blacks, the discontinuance of the church schools created tragic situations.

Another event of great importance was the appeal of Johnson C. Smith University for the status of an independent Presbyterian institution. The Board made the following announcement to the General Assembly in 1938: "Johnson C. Smith has decided to assume, with the assent of the Board of National Missions, the status of an independent Presbyterian College, reporting to the General Assembly through the Board of Christian Education as of October 1, 1938."[42] The appeal was granted and the institution which had been the capstone of the program for seventy-two years began its new independent career.

By 1938, the obvious decline in the educational phase of the Board of National Missions' program was emphatic, and the drastic cutback suggested that there would be for Negroes only state schools, which were sparse and of poor quality. Increasing black concern and pressure for a change in the public school system was becoming inevitable.

Between 1896, when the *Plessy v. Ferguson* decision involving the "separate but equal" policy was handed down, and 1930, only a few cases were brought before the Supreme Court questioning the inequities of the dual system. During the thirties, however, three major cases were brought to the Court. In each of these cases, the Court's position was evasive; whether it was to maintain "sectional peace and harmony" or whatever the reason, the Court failed to honor the black plaintiff's claim of injustices and took the position that the dual system did not necessarily imply inferiority of either race.

Between 1940 and 1950 more than a million blacks migrated to Northern cities. This altered the educational situation for blacks from a regional to national problem. Agitation spread and even the casual observer could discern that the time for the "separate but equal" myth was running out. The historic moment came in 1954 when the Supreme Court finally came to grips with the constitutionality of the dual policy in the case of *Brown v. Topeka*. This question was put bluntly by the Court: "Does segregation of children in public schools solely on the basis of race, even though the physical facilities and other 'tangible' factors may be equal, deprive the children of the minority group of equal educational opportunities? We believe that it does."[43] To implement

[42] *Minutes,* 1938, p. 137.
[43] Robert F. Cushman, *Leading Constitutional Decisions* (New York: Appleton-Century, Crofts, 1971), pp. 491–92.

the command to integrate, one of the methods employed was the busing of students outside their neighborhood to schools in order to achieve racial balance. Some states and communities were slow and erratic in enforcing this ruling, due to the strong opposition to this particular method of integration.

In the midst of this educational revolution, two Presbyterian churches made a move toward unification at the national level. In 1958, the Presbyterian Church, U.S.A. and the United Presbyterian Church of North America brought together their educational programs as they became the United Presbyterian Church in the U.S.A. To the schools sponsored by the Presbyterian Church, U.S.A., whose history has been followed up to this point, the United Presbyterian Church added Knoxville College, Henderson Institute, Jubilee Hospital, and several parochial schools which were scattered over the states of Tennessee, North Carolina, Virginia, and Alabama.

The new united church, however, continued the policy of curtailment. With the closing of Harbison in June of 1958, only five of the schools originally sponsored by the Presbyterian Church, U.S.A. were left. Three of these were boarding schools—Barber-Scotia, Mary Holmes, and Boggs; two were day schools—Goodwill and James Island. James Island was discontinued in June, 1961, and Goodwill was gradually phased out to the public school system. Of the 157 schools which had originally been sponsored by the merged churches only 4 remained active in 1970: Barber-Scotia, Boggs Academy, Mary Holmes, and Knoxville College. Johnson C. Smith University, having become an independent Presbyterian college, was not considered to be under the direct sponsorship of the church.

Black communities gradually began to realize that pitted against this step toward quality education were major losses: impressionable black children were placed under the instruction of dissenting white racists; black principals and teachers were frequently dispossessed, and many organizations and projects geared especially to the needs of the black community were absorbed and lost. Always integration seemed to mean the loss of the black school. Even more, many regretted the loss of the church schools that had been independent of the state and therefore of the surrounding white society. The black communities had built their homes and their lives around these educational centers sponsored by the church. Community life and activities revolved around them. Loved ones had been buried within the shadow of these schools, and the people had loved the church that had made the schools possible. Therefore, deep and mixed emotions characterized the temper of the black community at the closing of these schools. With the end of the schools, there had to be questions whether the church really did understand the situation and the great continuing needs of the black community.

THE VIRGINIA SCHOOLS 3

To visit the Board's schools in Virginia, one would follow the route of the Patrick Henry Highway where the echoes of "Give me liberty or give me death" vibrate. This historic trail is alive with memories including the ill-fated attempt of Gen. Robert E. Lee to escape from Generals Grant, Meade, and Sheridan just before the Rebel leader was surrounded at Appomatox Court House, Virginia. It was here in The Old Dominion that the Portuguese huckster bargained better than he knew in 1619 and began America's big business of a market-in-men; it was here that the pageantry of a great western aristocracy began. Nearly two and one-half centuries after slavery was established and near the sight of the surrender in Virginia, the Presbyterian church initiated its redemptive program.

Russell Grove School
Amelia Court House, Virginia

Whether driven by the energizing force of a faithful love or by an unseen power, Mrs. Samantha J. Neil, a pious Yankee from near Pittsburgh, searched in vain through the Virginia battlefields for the graves of her husband and three brothers. Though she did not find the graves she sought, she found a purpose to which she devoted her life.

Through loneliness and deep sorrow she had become readily responsive to the sufferings of others. The newly freed slaves, moved by her compassion and her prayers, were drawn to her. In the shade of an oak near an abandoned blacksmith shop on March 23, 1865, young and old gathered to listen as she opened the Book to teach them. The numbers increased day by day until her class extended beyond the shade of the spreading oak.

In 1866, she moved her class of 118 pupils into the dilapidated blacksmith shop and the Russell Grove School was housed for the first time. Despite this impoverished setting of clapboard roof, dirt floor, and benches hewn from logs, the school grew. In 1869 the Freedmen's Department of Missions erected for the school a two-story frame building near Amelia Court House, Virginia. Mrs. Neil spent sixteen years in this vicinity. The Russell Grove School made tremendous strides and later became known as Ingleside Seminary for girls. Its history as Ingleside will be discussed later in this chapter.

When one school seemed well established, Mrs. Neil moved on to another area of need. At Jetersville she established a parochial school in connection with the Allen Memorial Church. This elementary school enrolled seven grades and operated thirty-two weeks annually. In this work she was assisted by her sister, Miss Tillie Travis, and others. In addition, this school also served as an orphanage for destitute children of the freedmen. A devoted pupil recalls the fruitful days spent in Mrs. Neil's orphanage:

> I can see the small figure and greying hair of Mrs. Neil as she moved rapidly among the 35 or 40 pupils whom she fondly mothered in Jetersville. I was not an orphan but after mother died, father thought that it was well for me to spend my summers under her influence. It was there with her and her sister, Miss Tillie Travis, that many of the springs of my life began. Mrs. Neil was a small pretty woman with a wistful smile. Optimistic and sunny was her general manner but she could be firm if the necessity arose.
>
> She always took a sick child to her own home and nursed it back to health. I can recall the last conversation I had with her. It was almost time for me to go to Ingleside. She frequently said to me that she had something to tell me before I left. At last the moment came. That all-important something had to do with the change which a girl encounters during the period of puberty. She made me feel happy and honored to be a girl and approaching womanhood. Mrs. Neil remained at Jetersville until her death.
>
> I can recall the pall that hung over Ingleside that fall in 1909 when the news reached the campus in Burkeville that she was dead. She was buried in the north corner of the farm she left,—somewhere

in the vicinity of the graves she sought. Fittingly inscribed on her headstone is this phrase, "Mrs. Samantha J. Neil—1836-1909.— She lived for others."[1]

In addition to the schools and churches which she founded, her influence was multiplied through the lives she helped to mould. Dr. Floyd J. Anderson, a long-time professor at Biddle, was affectionately referred to as "Mrs. Neil's boy" because of her influence in sponsoring his education. Dr. Anderson honored her memory by christening his daughter Clara J. Neil Anderson.

Three other churches operated parochial schools in this vicinity: Big Oak, Mt. Zion, and Albright. The Reverend A. J. Henry was pastor and teacher of the school connected with each church in 1874. He also began the Oak Grove School in 1881.

Christian Light Mission
Mannsboro, Virginia

Another mission in this impoverished region was the Christian Light School. This school was founded in 1909 in Mannsboro, Nottoway County, Virginia, just across the county line from the Russell Grove School. Its founder was Mrs. Sarah Thompkins, a housewife and mother, who began classes in her home in 1909. The mission developed into an elementary school enrolling the first eight grades and running for twenty-four weeks annually. Christian Light School wielded a strong educational influence in its locality. Dr. R. Edwin Thompkins, of Charlotte, North Carolina, the son of the school's founder, says that the school operated in their home for about three years. About 1912 it came under the care of the Presbyterian Board of Missions and moved into a two-story frame structure erected for it.

Dr. Thompkins completed his early training at this school and he described some of the activities of his mother:

> Christian Light Mission was considered a very respectable "high" school in Nottoway County. The school building consisted of two rooms—one on top of the other. This made it higher than the average building in the vicinity, hence, "high school."
> When I entered the school there were two teachers including mother. I began in the first grade with Miss Hattie Mae Ward as my teacher. At the half-way mark of the first year, Miss Ward left and I finished the first grade under Miss Jennie Scott. Miss Addie Brown

[1] Interview with Mrs. Fannie Partee Dobson of Charlotte, North Carolina, 1944.

taught me through the 2nd and 3rd grades. After then I was my mother's pupil. I remained with her through the work of the eighth grade. I entered Biddle at the 9th grade level without deficiencies and finished among the honor students.

As I recall the work of those early years, I remember many of the molding and fashioning experiences at Christian Light Mission. Mother sang very well and led the devotional song-fests which were a source of spiritual strength for all.

The Shorter Catechism always supplemented the Scripture reading and the devotions closed with an inspirational talk. These talks were filled with the stark realities of life and the hereafter and are hard to forget.

Mother very rarely used physical punishment. She did, however, administer firmly hide-raising tongue lashings to the extent that her pupils preferred the "belt."[2]

After twenty-four years of educational and other services to Nottoway County the Christian Light Mission was discontinued in 1933. The program at this mission school was typical of the Board's schools at this level.

Winchester Normal School
Winchester, Virginia

Before the work was five years old in the Old Dominion, the Department had high hopes of operating a normal school in the Shenandoah Valley. From the very beginning the Department felt that the need for Negro leadership demanded the immediate establishment of schools of higher learning. Despite the low level at which these higher level schools began, they provided an accelerated and concentrated program of study for the promising pupil without neglecting the needs of the less promising ones. The work with the superior student, however, was unrelenting. Prepared leaders was the main goal. The establishment of Winchester Normal is summarized in the annual report of the Committee of Home Missions for 1870:

The Normal School at Winchester, Va., under the direction and oversight of our efficient Superintendent of schools for the Valley of Shenandoah, Mr. Oscar M. Waring, has increased in attendance and usefulness, and lacks but the expenditure of a few thousand

[2] Interview with Dr. R. Edwin Thompkins of Charlotte, North Carolina, 1943.

dollars to make it what it is designed to be, a first class educational
institution. There is a steady demand for good colored teachers. We
have here a good location, a superior lot in the very centre of the
town, and first class instructors; but the building upon the lot is inadequate to our use—for, although of brick and tolerable for a common school it is ill adapted for the purposes of a Seminary of high
grade.[3]

Although Winchester Normal School was well established on a beautiful lot in the center of town and had an efficient principal and staff, its
career was brief as is indicated in this Board report for 1871:

THE NORMAL SCHOOL, at Winchester, Va. Mr. O. M. Waring,
Principal, has a valuable lot; a building that answers for the present;
reports 95 pupils; and under its able principal, would be a school of
much promise, were it not for its indebtedness, which, if not soon
relieved, may probably prove fatal even to its existence, as, owing
to the pecuniary embarrassment of the property of this school, the
Committee have felt obliged to authorize negotiations for its sale.[4]

In all likelihood the property was sold since the Normal School does not
appear on the Virginia roll of schools for 1871.

By 1889, Presbyterian schools for freedmen in Virginia clustered
around four points: Chula Depot, Amelia Court House, Nottoway County, and Danville. These schools were fostered primarily by the churches
for their members and immediate communities. There were three church-
es with parochial schools around Chula: Albright, Mt. Herman, and Oak
Grove, under the supervision of the Reverend W. H. Shipperson in 1889.
Around Amelia Court House were also three: Russell Grove, Big Oak
and Mt. Zion, which were under the direction of the Reverend J. A.
Wright. In the Nottoway vicinity were three: Burkeville, Nottoway, and
Allen's Chapel, under the supervision of the Reverend J. M. Rittenhouse.
In Danville only one church and school developed, with the Reverend
Edward F. Eggleston in charge.

In some cases schools had been independently operated by individual
church members or even by individuals with the approval of a specific

[3] Presbyterian Church in the U.S.A. (New School), Committee of Home
Missions, Freedmen's Department *Annual Report* (New York: Presbyterian
Publication Committee, 1876), pp. 6–7.
[4] CMF, *Annual Report*, 1971, p. 186.

church for quite some time. The date such a school came under the care of the Board, however, was considered its official beginning.

The Classon School
Martinsville, Virginia

In 1890, The Classon School was established at Martinsville, Virginia and reported 247 pupils enrolled under the care of George F. Collier and Mrs. Anna R. Carter. Miss Sallie J. Harris joined Mrs. Carter in 1894 instructing 105 pupils in the basement of the church, where the school was housed for thirty-five years. The report for 1925 indicates the determination of the church to keep the school operating although no building had been provided. The Board's report for that year stated:

> Martinsville, Virginia, has a school of about two hundred taught in the basement of the church. The light is poor, the rooms are gloomy and there is nothing conducive to good cheer in these basement rooms.
> A lot has already been purchased through the principal of the school and his local friends and they are asking for a modest building to cost about $8,000.00. It should be granted.[5]

The Classon School was closed in June, 1933.

Great Creek School
Bracey, Virginia

The Reverend S. F. Young established the Great Creek School at Shaw's Store (later Bracey), Virginia in 1894 with fifty-two pupils enrolled. Mrs. S. F. Young was responsible alone for the instruction of the increasing enrollment until 1897 when she was joined by Miss Lelia A. Jackson. In 1899, the Board commissioned Miss Mary Beverly, a graduate of Ingleside, to teach at the school at twelve dollars a month for four months a year. For ten years she was teacher, janitor, Sabbath School teacher, and Missionary Society leader in the basement of the church. In 1909 a school building was erected. At the end of four months, her patrons, according to a rural custom, showered her with pounds of produce; also, they added a fifth month to the school term. She boarded with patrons during the sixth month and raised the money for her salary for the next school year, which was never over twenty-five dollars per month during the twenty-five years she taught at the Great Creek School.[6]

[5] BNM, *Annual Report*, 1925, p. 163.
[6] Mary B. Marks, "Personal Reminiscences: An Address Delivered at the Big Oak Presbyterian Church," *The New Advance* (May, 1946), p. 4.

One of the highlights of the school came in 1925 when the Southern Virginia Presbytery convened at the school. It was the twenty-fifth anniversary of the Presbytery, and the school felt honored to host the historic session. Despite the fact that the school had added the eighth grade and was running twenty-four weeks annually by 1929, the enrollment was steadily decreasing. The Great Creek School was one of the three-day schools discontinued in 1931.

Holbrook School
Danville, Virginia

The Holbrook School was begun as an educational adjunct to the Holbrook Street Church in Danville, Virginia, in 1886 by the Reverend Magager G. Haskins. He was a graduate of Biddle University and gave the school a good beginning before he left in 1887 to assume the pastorate of the Presbyterian church in Mebane, North Carolina.

No official report is made of the school until 1889 when the Reverend Edward F. Eggleston had charge of the school and reported 71 pupils under the instruction of two teachers: J. R. Barrett and Mrs. Ida B. Mebane. The school grew rapidly and in 1891 had 150 pupils enrolled. Administrative changes at this mission made the Reverend Barrett principal of the school and added Miss Emma Joy to the teaching staff, while the Reverend Eggleston remained as pastor of the church. The Board of Missions' report for this year (1891) stated: "The school work has also been enlarged by the erection of a building which is now being furnished at a cost of $3,000, the colored people of the church having donated and deeded to the Board a valuable lot for the purpose."

In 1892, Eggleston went to Grace Church in Baltimore and the Reverend William E. Carr became principal of the school with A. B. Fortune and Mrs. Carr as teachers in charge of the 200 pupils enrolled. In 1893, industrial courses were added to the curriculum and the name of the school was changed to "Holbrook Industrial High School." Beginning in 1895 several additional faculty members were added and by 1899 the 300 pupils enrolled were under the instruction of six staff members. In 1904 the enrollment reached 400; Miss Mary N. Holbrook was added to the staff and the Reverend Thomas A. Long, after four years of service, left to join the staff at Biddle University. The enrollment grew to an all-time high, 419, in 1905.

After developing the school into an influential factor in the Southern Virginia Presbytery, the Reverend William E. Carr terminated his twenty-eight years of service to the school and community and was succeeded by the Reverend Thomas B. Hargrave. The entire plant was destroyed by fire in 1921, and no further report of work at the school was made by the Board.

By the early 1890s, the Board's program was widely spread over the western part of the Old Dominion. In 1890, Central Church in Petersburg reported a school of eighty-three pupils under the instruction of the Reverend Yorke Jones and Miss Grace Clark. In Horse Pasture, two schools were reported: the Reverend H. M. Holmes reported seventy-two pupils being taught in the Martinsville community by George F. Collier and seventy-five pupils under the instruction of Miss Emma Galloway in the community around Stewart. By 1901, the Board was operating a total of sixteen schools in Virginia. Later this number was increased to forty.

The Wheeler Graded School
Drakes Branch, Virginia

The Reverend and Mrs. Legrande M. Onque began a church and school, the Wheeler Graded School, at Drakes Branch, Virginia, in 1915. The Reverend Onque, a graduate of Lincoln University in Pennsylvania, and Mrs. Onque, a graduate of Scotia Seminary in Concord, North Carolina, provided a concerted approach to the educational needs of this long neglected spot. Mrs. Onque had worked for the Board of Missions in several capacities: as matron at Harbison College at Abbeville, South Carolina; as matron at Monticello Academy in Monticello, Arkansas; and as matron and teacher at Cotton Plant Academy, Cotton Plant, Arkansas. While at Cotton Plant Academy she met Onque who was the assistant principal of the school, and after working together for three years they married, July 31, 1911, at Fargo, Arkansas, where Onque was stated supply. After five years there they went to Lima, Oklahoma, for three years. From Oklahoma they moved eastward to the Old Dominion and made a tremendous contribution to the Board's program in the Southern Virginia Presbytery.

The church, school, and manse, which they built in 1915, burned immediately upon completion. Undaunted, they started again and within six months had rebuilt the school and a larger manse and secured funds for rebuilding the church structure.

Mrs. Onque was an invaluable partner with her courage, sober advice, and inspiring personality. They quickly became involved in the life of the community. With the cooperation of the community the parochial school grew in three years from an enrollment of fifteen pupils to ninety-six. A room was set up for music instruction and another was equipped as a sewing room. An additional teacher was added, and the school term lengthened to eight months. After eleven years, however, Mrs. Onque's health broke under the strain, and upon doctor's advice, in 1926 they gave up the work and moved to Mocksville, North Carolina, Mrs. Onque's original home. The school continued, however, with an enrollment of eighty-five under the instruction of three teachers. It operated twenty-four weeks annually. The Wheeler Graded School was discontinued, along with five other Virginia day schools, in June, 1933.

One of the six closed in 1933 was the school at Charlotte Court House, Virginia. In 1902, the Reverend and Mrs. W. A. H. Abouy, along with Mrs. Maggie Hicks, were operating a prosperous school at the Refuge Church there. This grew to be an elementary and junior high school by 1918 and continued until 1933.

Ingleside Seminary
Burkeville, Virginia

The Board's program in Virginia reached its highest achievement in the establishing of Ingleside Seminary, an outgrowth of the Russell Grove School, founded in 1866 at Amelia Court House by Mrs. Samantha J. Neil. Ingleside was relocated in 1892 to Burkeville, high upon a hill commanding a fine view of surrounding country, about thirty miles west of Richmond, on a portion of the battlefield of the War Between the States. Its new site was in the vicinity of Burk's Tavern where Gen. Robert E. Lee surrendered to General Grant.

A flashback will place the origin and growth of the school in proper focus. While still at Amelia Court House, its name became Ingleside Seminary in 1885. Through the generosity of "a Pittsburgh lady" the Women's Committee of the Board purchased a house for a boarding department for the school in 1886. With Miss C. A. Carpenter as principal and Misses Sallie and Bettie Means as well as Misses Behard and McCreary as teachers, the Seminary graduated its first class in 1888. Miss Carpenter announced that each graduate was a Christian.

In 1890, the Reverend Graham C. Campbell became principal of the School and Mrs. Laura K. Campbell, his wife, the preceptress. The next year the cottage for boarding students was destroyed by fire on Thanksgiving morning and the Reverend Campbell received minor burns. This loss, however grave, stimulated the plans for growth. As early as 1889, the Board had recognized the need for expansion, both of the plant and of the curriculum at the school. To realize this, the school would have to be moved. The anonymous "Pittsburgh lady" again made this possible.

Sixteen acres of land were purchased at Burkeville. Burkeville was centrally located in the Presbytery of Southern Virginia and readily accessible to the entire region lying between Richmond, Lynchburg, Danville, and Petersburg. In this section the Negro population outnumbered the white five to three. The black Presbyterian church which had been established in Burkeville in 1882 was thriving. The Reverend J. M. Rittenhouse had established a parochial school in connection with the church there also in 1882 with fifty-seven pupils taught by W. L. Epes. This parochial school was active only when the pastor was able to secure a teacher. All these factors enhanced the value of the new location for Ingleside.

In 1892, the Seminary was moved into a four-story brick building erected on sixteen acres, although it was not completed until 1903. Also built was a heating plant. The total cost was about $12,000. The entire Ingleside plant was lost by fire in 1906. There were 150 girls enrolled at the time, May 23, 1906, but operation had to be suspended until October 1907 when a new building was ready for occupancy. By 1910 the excellent program of Ingleside was recognized by the state, and those graduating that year were given teachers' certificates which were good for one year. In 1911, Mr. Oscar L. Shewmaker, the state representative, delivered the commencement address and presented to each graduate a teaching certificate which was good for several years. This year also the curriculum was expanded by the addition of courses in sanitation and agriculture.

The curriculum cited below was typical of the course of study in the Board's seminaries and academies:

First Year
Fifth Reader
Spelling
Arithmetic
Descriptive Geography
Grammar and Composition
Bible—Old Testament
Writing
Vocal Music
Sewing
Cooking

Second Year
Fifth Reader
Spelling
Arithmetic
Descriptive Geography
Grammar and Composition
History of Virginia
Bible—Old Testament
Writing
Vocal Music
Sewing
Cooking

Third Year
United States History
Spelling
Arithmetic
Descriptive Geography Completed
Grammar and Composition

Bible—Old Testament
Writing
Vocal Music
Sewing
Cooking

Fourth Year
United States History
Arithmetic
Physiology
Rhetoric and Composition
Spelling

Sanitation
Bible—New Testament
Writing
Vocal Music
Sewing
Cooking

Junior Year
History of England
Arithmetic—Completed
Algebra
Physical Geography
American Literature

Bible—New Testament
Writing
Vocal Music
Sewing
Cooking
General History

Senior Year
Algebra—Part Year
Geometry—Part Year
British Literature
Astronomy—Half Year
Botany—Half Year
Pedagogies—Half Year

Agriculture—Half Year
Bookkeeping—Half Year
Civil Government—Half Year
Writing
Vocal Music
Sewing
Cooking[7]

The plant and grounds received special attention in 1911. The old church building was sold for public school use and a new lot, adjacent to the campus, was purchased for a new church site.

By 1912, 248 young women had graduated from Ingleside, a majority of whom became teachers in the public and parochial schools. One example of how these young women put their training into action was exemplified by three Ingleside graduates: Sallie Johnson, Susie Hopson, and Mary Miller Brown who erected a beautiful three-room school in Burkeville and began a school. Miss Johnson was principal and Miss Hopson was her assistant. Members of the local school board were generous in their praise of the work done at the school.

[7] See *Catalog of Ingleside Seminary* 1913–1916, Burkeville, Virginia, p. 17, for a similar course of study.

On December 2, 1915, a tragedy occurred at Ingleside which claimed the lives of the president and one student. By request, Mrs. Campbell reported the incident in detail to the Board. In her explanation, she related how President Campbell attempted to investigate a failure in the acetylene lighting plant while two students held a closed lantern to light the way. Nora French, from Amelia, Virginia, advanced too close with the lantern and the escaping gas ignited, causing an explosion which killed her and President Campbell. The other student was blown quite a distance but lived to tell the story of the incident. Momentary panic prevailed before order could be restored, as neighbors and alumni rushed to the scene. Dr. John M. Gaston arrived from Pittsburgh the next day and arranged for the continuance of the school under the guidance of Mrs. Campbell and one of her sons.

In July of 1916, the Reverend J. W. Dunbar was selected to take charge of the work and he remained for four years. From 1920-1927 the Reverend R. L. Bates was head of the school. The Reverend R. L. Alter succeeded him.

In 1935, Fee Memorial Institute of Kentucky was merged with Ingleside. The Board made this report to the General Assembly:

> Formerly each of these schools had been for girls only, but in order to render a greater service, it was decided to admit both sexes. Now the combined institution, Ingleside-Fee, is an accredited coeducational high school. It was also decided that the logical location of the combined school was at Burkeville, Virginia because Virginia has a Negro population almost six times larger than Kentucky. The New School under Rev. and Mrs. H. W. McNair, has a Negro faculty and the work is practically the same as that carried on at Nicholasville, Kentucky.[8]

Later, this additional statement was made concerning the progress of the school:

> Ingleside-Fee is accredited by the State and the Southern Association of Colleges and Secondary Schools. All the teachers in the high school department hold degrees from standard colleges. A commercial course has been recently added and recent improvements on the plant include new furniture in all rooms.[9]

Ingleside-Fee was discontinued in 1943 and the sixteen acres were

[8] G.A.M. Board Reports, 1935, p. 103.
[9] Pres. H. W. McNair's report to the Board, 1937.

sold, with the exception of a residence on a two-acre plot which was to be used by parish workers.

The United Presbyterian Church at Work in Virginia

Thyne Institute
Chase City, Virginia

The United Presbyterian Church of North America sponsored three thriving elementary and secondary schools in the State of Virginia. The first to be established was the Thyne Institute in Chase City, Virginia.

Thyne Institute was established in 1876 and for some time was the only high school for Negroes in the county. In May, 1876, the Reverend J. Y. Ashenhurst requested the Board of the United Presbyterian Church to establish a school for freedmen in Chase City, Virginia. That same year Mr. John Thyne, formerly of a congregation in Argyle Presbytery, proposed to donate to the Board his home surrounded by five acres of land if the Board would establish the proposed school in Chase City. The Board accepted Mr. Thyne's offer, and Mr. J. J. Ashenhurst, son of the Reverend J. Y. Ashenhurst, was commissioned to direct the proposed mission. The Thyne home was used to house teachers, except for one small room.

In 1877, the Board received a deed to the Thyne property with an offer to construct a suitable building for a school on the place. The new two-story building, containing a chapel and three classrooms, opened in the fall of 1878. The total cost to the Board was approximately eight hundred dollars. J. J. Ashenhurst was principal of the school until he resigned in 1880, and the Reverend Matthew Clarke, director of the Virginia missions, supervised the work for one year. In 1881, the Reverend John A. Ramsey was chosen to direct the mission. During the Ramsey administration, the teachers' home burned. When Ramsey was transferred in 1883, the Reverend J. H. Veasey filled the vacancy. During his ten-year tenure, the school made outstanding progress: a normal department was added, a primary training school was developed, industrial work was greatly emphasized, a "Girls' Industrial Home" was erected by the Women's Department at a cost of $3,000 to house girls from long distances. In 1893 the Reverend J. M. Moore, Ph.D., succeeded Veasey.[10]

[10] John Witherspoon, "Our Missions in Virginia and North Carolina, His-torical Sketch of the Freedmen's Missions of the United Presbyterian Church

The Institute was discontinued in 1946 when the county bought the property and continued Thyne Institute as a public high school.[11]

Bluestone Academy
Bluestone, Virginia

Bluestone Academy at Bluestone, Virginia, about sixteen miles from Chase City, was an outgrowth of the mission in that city. A small United Presbyterian church with a congregation of colonists largely from the North was located in Bluestone. In that congregation was a Mr. William McLeau, formerly of Jamestown, Pennsylvania, who deeded ten beautifully located acres to the Board for a school site. A forty by sixty foot, two-story frame building with a chapel and three classrooms was erected on the lot during the summer and winter of 1879, under the direction of the Reverend Matthew Clarke, who was in charge of the Chase City mission. The school opened February 16, 1880, with Dr. E. P. McLeau as principal. The freedmen contributed $150 and the white community about $200 toward the project.

That year, the Board reported to its Assembly, "This field is one of special interest, . . . located on a farm on which for many years the annual sale of slaves took place, for the market in the South or Gulf States. The ruins of the old jail in which the slaves, brought in from neighboring plantations for market, were shut up, are in full view from the house."[12]

Dr. McLeau resigned March 25, 1881, and Miss Helen McLeau filled the position until the end of the school term in May. The Reverend Clarke, who for so long had supervised the Virginia missions, retired in 1881, and Professor J. A. Little took over the work for two years, after which the Reverend J. A. Ramsey of Chase City replaced him.

The Board's spring report for 1889 called attention to the mass exodus of the freedmen from the area. School enrollment had dropped drastically, and for a while, the Board considered moving the school to Henderson, North Carolina, but finally decided to reorganize the mission. Three

---

—1862–1904, ed. Ralph McGranahan (Knoxville, Tennessee: Knoxville College, 1904), pp. 63–66.

[11] Archibald K. Stewart, *May We Introduce Negro Missions* (Pittsburgh, Pennsylvania: United Presbyterian Church of North America Board of American Missions, n.d.), p. 14.

[12] United Presbyterian Church of North America, Board of Freedmen's Missions, quoted by Witherspoon, "Our Missions in Virginia," *Historical Sketch*, ed. McGranahan, pp. 66–67.

small buildings for school purposes and housing teachers were constructed at Bluestone, but the large school building and teachers' home were moved to Henderson, North Carolina. Ramsey retired in 1890. W. M. Fowlkes and two teachers were commissioned to continue the work at Bluestone. Mr. Fowlkes remained until 1901 when he was succeeded by William G. Wilson. The Board's last report concerning the Bluestone mission merely stated that the school was prospering under Mr. Wilson's guidance.[13]

The Norfolk Mission College
Norfolk, Virginia

In December 1882, a few friends of the freedmen raised a sum of money and sent it to the Reverend Matthew Clarke, under the direction of the Department, to explore the educational needs of the freedmen in the Virginia area. Norfolk had a population of about 4,000 black youths with accommodations for about 1,000 in the public school system. Prevailing sentiment among both white and black citizens favored education for the freedmen. This made Norfolk a promising location. In addition, a friend in Chicago, who helped to finance the exploration of the Virginia field, sent a check for $400 to be used toward establishing a school for freedmen in the Norfolk area. The Board began work immediately. On January 15, 1883, Clarke, who had resigned from the Chase City mission, took over the work at Norfolk and at the end of that school year reported that 467 pupils had been enrolled. Because of this success, in July 1883, Board members visited Norfolk and with Clarke made a careful study of the field. It was decided that permanent buildings should be constructed immediately. A block containing five lots was purchased; contracts for a three-story building with a basement were let at a cost of $15,545. School opened in the new building September 1, 1884. For the school year 1884–1885, the enrollment in the day school was reported to be 986 and in the night school, 64. In 1886, a teachers' home was erected on a lot adjoining the school lot.

The Reverend and Mrs. Clarke, because of failing health, gave up the work at Norfolk in 1889, and Reverend W. L. Wallace succeeded him. Wallace's tenure at the mission was short, and the Reverend David R. McDonald was appointed his successor in 1890 but he remained only one year also. The Reverend J. B. Work directed the school from 1891–1896. Under this administration the school assumed a more permanent

[13] Witherspoon, "Our Mission in Virginia," *Historical Sketch*, ed. McGranahan, p. 68.

form. The primary training school was put under a principal and the curriculum organized to include subjects usually taught in a city high school. Industrial courses were emphasized; sewing and printing became special features with a teacher employed to devote his whole time to the work of printing.

When Work resigned in 1896, the Reverend William McKirahan became principal of the Norfolk Mission College.[14] When he took charge, the plant consisted of the college building, the teachers' home, and a workshop containing the printing department. Without cost to the Board a fourth building was erected which housed the domestic science department, the first to be established in the United Presbyterian schools. Later, the Board purchased a corner lot on Princess Ann Avenue and Chapel Street on which was standing a building "notorious for the wickedness done within its walls."[15] This building was moved to the back of the lot and equipped for dormitory use. In 1904, the Norfolk School was described in this way:

> The school has always maintained a high standard both in discipline and in scholarly excellence. And the religious work has from the beginning until the present received the earnest attention and united effort of all the workers in the mission. This has been our largest school and most largely attended mission, having a total enrollment for the twenty years of its service of 14,138, and an average of 706 for each year.[16]

[14] The school is referred to as a college by both Stewart and McGranahan. Both also call it a school and a mission. There appears to be no specific change in name or status.

[15] Witherspoon, "Our Missions in Virginia," *Historical Sketch*, ed. McGranahan, p. 72.

[16] Witherspoon, "Our Missions in Virginia," *Historical Sketch*, ed. McGranahan, p. 72.

THE NORTH CAROLINA SCHOOLS *4*

The Presbyterian Church was slow in developing a systematic approach to the situation of the former slaves who had been discovered in the Carolina section of the wilderness. In 1866, however, the Freedmen's Committee of Missions extended its operations across the stateline of the Old Dominion into the Carolinas. It was not obvious that this section would eventually become a Presbyterian stronghold among the freed slaves.

Fortunate for the Presbyterians interest in this section had not been solidly occupied by other denominations with stronger emotional appeal, as was the case in other regions. Also of great importance was the fact that many Presbyterian individuals, without official church sanction, had pioneered early in the Carolinas. These persons had made substantial progress in establishing the church-school combination in several Carolina towns, cities, and counties even before the Presbyterian foundation was securely established.

After the Committee's organized program began it spread rapidly in the Old North State immediately after the collapse of the Confederacy. Despite the shortage of funds, local hostility, and the nomadic movement of the freedmen, the receptivity by the freed slaves toward the Presbyterian program in North Carolina made speed possible, and the nature of their plight made haste a necessity.

The Reverend Sidney Murkland and the Reverend Amos S. Billings-

ley, concentrating around Statesville, established the following missions:
Freedom, Cameron, Pittsburgh, Mt. Tabor, Logan Chapel, Catawba, and
New Center. Concurrently, the Reverend Samuel C. Alexander, Willis L.
Miller, and Stephen Mattoon, assisted by Alfred Stokes and Robert M.
Hall, were busy establishing missions in the Charlotte area. They began
the black Presbyterian churches at Charlotte, McClintock, Mt. Olive,
Woodland, Miranda, and in other communities. Simultaneously, the
Reverend Luke Dorland with assistants went into the Concord area and
began the work at Bethpage, Bellefonte, Popular Tent and other places.
Licentiate Matthew Ijams was assigned early to the posts at Hamilton,
New Hope, Ben Salem, St. Paul, Murkland, Lloyd Caldwell, Lowes
Chapel, Fancy Hill, Duncan's Creek, and Swannona. The Reverend
James A. Chresfield established the work in the area of Greensboro,
Lexington, McClelland, Pleasant Grove, and Gold Hill. The Reverend
William J. Williams settled in the area of Mocksville, initiating the mis-
sion there and at Mt. Zion and Scranton. In the meantime, the Reverend
Lewis Nelson was establishing missions in the Raleigh locality and the
Reverend John C. Carson was initiating the work at Mills River and
Davidson's River.[1]

By 1878, the efforts of these pioneers and builders had been rein-
forced by graduates of Biddle and Lincoln Universities. The continuing
stream of graduates enlarged and brought new inspiration into the program. By 1877, the Reverend William R. Coles was located at Salisbury
and Licentiate Franklin Montgomery was at Fayetteville, Freedom East,
Friendship, and Anderson Creek. The Reverend Magager G. Haskins
joined the missionaries around Concord while the Reverend Daniel J.
Sanders worked in the areas of Wilmington, Wilson, Lumberton, Meb-
ensville, and Bainesville. The Reverend Calvin McCurdy went to Laurenburg and White Hall, and also joined the forces around Raleigh. Isaac S.
Stevenson began work at Mt. Airy.[2] By 1878 the Reverend Abner B.
Lawrence went to Lumberton. Moses A. Hopkins increased the services
at Franklinton and the Reverend Thomas B. Hargrave was added to the
workers around Carthage.[3]

North Carolina became central to the Presbyterian program in the
South. Within its borders were eventually to be found a theological
seminary, a senior college, a junior college, as well as a host of academies
and parochial schools. At its height there were forty-two schools in the

[1] *Minutes*, 1873, pp. 667–669.
[2] *Minutes*, 1877, p. 718 and p. 721.
[3] *Minutes*, 1878, pp. 249–250.

state under the sponsorship of the Board. By 1958, with the merger with the United Presbyterian Church, Henderson Institute and Jubilee Hospital, both of Henderson, were added to the schools then under the Presbyterian Church, U.S.A.

Albion Academy
Franklinton, North Carolina

Albion Academy evolved out of a parochial school which was established in Franklinton, North Carolina, in December, 1865, by Mr. J. H. Crawford.

In its report to the General Assembly the Committee on Freedmen announced:

> The school in Franklinton, N.C. is carried on, without assistance, by Mr. J. H. Crawford, a one-armed colored soldier. He organized the school in December last and it has been steadily improving ever since. It was closed during part of the summer but in six months this little school of 80 or 90 pupils has raised an average of $9.30 each month for tuition. This goes toward paying for their school house.[4]

Early in 1867, two white missionaries, authorized by the newly organized Committee on Missions for Freedmen, reached the field and threw their support toward developing the school. N. H. Downing, licentiate, J. H. Crawford, catechist, and Miss K. Gilfillan were among the teachers for the eighty-three pupils enrolled in the school that year. In 1878, the Reverend Moses Hopkins, the first black man to graduate from the Auburn Theological Seminary in New York, reorganized the school and was joined by the Reverend Henry Clay Mabry in 1879.

Mabry was graduated from Lincoln University in 1873 and was associated with the Reverend Chresfield at the Greensboro Parochial School before coming to Franklinton. He worked at Albion Academy for five or six years during which time the school made outstanding progress. In 1881, the school was chartered as a state normal school and remained so until 1903 when the state normal schools were consolidated. Albion Academy reverted to its original sponsor, the Presbyterian church, after this state action. In 1881, the enlarged program at the school was boosted by the erection of a new building. The Committee made the following announcement in its 1882 report to the General Assembly:

---

[4] The source of the information referred to can no longer be located.

At Franklinton, N.C. a large and elegant school building has been erected and paid for at a cost of $5,000 in which the district normal school is to be taught under the superintendency of one of our missionaries, the salaries of the teachers being paid by the State. The erection of this building will greatly increase our influence in that part of the State, as it will concentrate in it all the educational interests of the colored people in the whole region surrounding it.[5]

In 1883, the Reverend Hopkins had, in addition to himself and his wife, three other teachers to instruct the 335 pupils enrolled. In 1886, Professor S. A. Waugh, Mrs. William A. Alexander, and three other teachers joined the staff, and in 1887 Miss M. L. Lillson and J. N. Conyard were added. There was a decrease in the enrollment at the school over the succeeding two years: in 1887 there were 227 students and 247 were enrolled in 1888. In 1889, however, the Reverend S. S. Sevier and eight other teachers came to Albion to assist with the 375 enrolled pupils. In 1892, Sevier was succeeded by the Reverend John Anthony Savage.

Savage received his A.B. degree from Lincoln University in 1879 and the S.T.B. degree from the same institution in 1882. He organized the Shiloh Presbyterian Church in Goldsboro in 1882 and went to New Bern as head of the state normal school. In 1885, he became pastor and principal of the parochial school in Louisburg which had 250 students and five teachers. He built a new church structure in Louisburg before leaving for Albion Academy in 1892. At Albion he found diminishing enrollments caused by the developing state program of public education. Only twelve boarders and three teachers were there when Savage arrived.[6] The property consisted of two and one-half acres of land and one large school building. Savage, acquainted with Albion's former high quality of work, immediately began a campaign to restore Albion to its earlier years of prosperity, and the school rapidly developed its academic program as well as its physical plant. The property was expanded to include a sixty-acre farm, an administration building, dormitories for girls and boys, an industrial building, and a refectory. The course of study included grammar and high school work, with household arts for girls and manual training for boys, plus extension classes for teachers.

In 1914, the Board reported this unfortunately typical setback:

The work at Albion Academy under Dr. Savage, suffered tem-

[5] *Minutes*, 1882, p. 216.
[6] Hugh Victor Brown, *The Education of the Negro in North Carolina* (Raleigh, North Carolina: Irvin-Swain Press, 1961), pp. 35–6.

porary interruption by the recent burning of a boys' dormitory known as Carolina Hall. Plans are being worked out whereby the boys can be accommodated for the coming year, or until such time as we may be able after raising the money to give the school a well appointed Boys Dormitory.[7]

The President's wife, Mrs. Mary Dover Savage, died in 1920. She had been a tower of strength to the educational and religious program on the campus and in the community. On January 1, 1933, Dr. Savage died.

In that same year, Albion Academy, along with Redstone Academy, was merged with the Mary Potter School at Oxford, North Carolina, and the school's name became, "Redstone, Mary Potter-Albion Academy."

Redstone Academy
Lumberton, North Carolina

Redstone Academy, at one time known as Bethany School, was organized in 1903 in Lumberton, North Carolina, under the able leadership of the Reverend John H. Hayswood. In the same year and in the same town, he also became pastor of the Bethany and Panthersford Presbyterian churches. The Reverend Hayswood, a native of Louisburg, North Carolina, graduated from the college of liberal arts of Lincoln University with an A.B. degree in 1893 and from the seminary of the same university with the S.T.B. degree in 1896. His alma mater conferred the honorary degree of D.D. on him in 1912.

Dr. and Mrs. Hayswood started the school in an old building in east Lumberton. The material possessions of the school, then known as Bethany School, were meager. The rugged seats were limited; the blackboards were of stained planks; a potbellied, wood-burning stove provided local heat, and there was a distant privy.

During the first year of Bethany School's operation, forty-five students were enrolled in grades one through seven. They studied the Bible, arithmetic, history, geography, spelling, English, health, and reading. During the next school year, 1904–1905, the enrollment reached fifty-five. The first three years passed without significant changes at the Bethany School. In 1906, however, a plot of land adjacent to Bethany Church was purchased and a nine-room school building was erected. This frame structure included a dining room, kitchen, parlor, one bedroom for Dr. and Mrs. Hayswood, two classrooms, and three rooms that

[7] BMF, *Annual Report*, 1914, p. 10.

could be combined to make one large room for chapel activities or other large gatherings.[8]

After moving into the new quarters, the academy increased its enrollment until in 1910–1911 the students numbered 110.

During the school year 1911–1912, five additional grades were added to the program so that a complete educational course of study from the first through the twelfth grades was offered. New courses and equipment were added, and special emphasis was placed upon a liberal education for the secondary youth. Efforts were doubled on the fundamentals for the elementary pupils. The student enrollment for this year was 145.[9]

From its beginning until 1912, the Bethany Academy had been under the direct supervision of the Board of Missions for Freedmen. In 1912, however, the Redstone Presbyterial of Pennsylvania became interested in this school and was granted permission to take over its sponsorship. It was then that the school's name was changed to Redstone Academy. Two dormitories were built and a boarding department added to take care of students from other parts of Robeson County and northeastern North Carolina. The enrollment increased to 148 and a new teacher was added to the staff in 1913. For the first time Dr. and Mrs. Hayswood did not carry the entire teaching load unassisted. In 1914, the student body numbered 225, and another teacher was added, which brought the number of teachers to four. As enrollment rose, the number of teachers increased until in 1928 the teaching staff numbered fourteen.

Tragedy struck Redstone Academy in 1914 when its two main buildings and part of a third were destroyed by fire. In addition, the buildings of the two churches of which the Reverend Hayswood was the pastor were completely destroyed by fire. Although a loss of eleven years of planning, sacrifice, and materials, the downcast spirit of the community and the grief of Dr. Hayswood were soon solaced through the rebuilding support of the best citizens of the town.[10] From the insurance on the buildings and donations from friends, the Redstone Presbyterial assured Dr. Hayswood and the community that the academy would be able to reopen in the fall of that year and perhaps would be in a better condition than before the fire. The predictions were fully realized; the buildings

[8] Interview with Mrs. Mattie Hayswood, widow of the founder, March, 1958.

[9] George Clayton Shaw, "Seed Germination" and "A Glance Backward, A Present Meditation, A Forward Look," unpublished manuscripts, now in the possession of Mrs. G. C. Shaw, Oxford, North Carolina.

[10] BMF, Annual Report, 1916, p. 11.

were erected, the school reopened on schedule in the fall, and a new program of enrichment began at the school.

Extracurricular and curricular changes were made in the school's program between 1924 and 1926. Athletic teams participated in interscholastic competition and an industrial arts department was added in 1927 and home economics in 1928. Two years before this last addition the Board of Education of North Carolina accredited the academy as a standard high school, a notable achievement for Dr. Hayswood.

The fourteen teachers welcomed 368 students to Redstone Academy in 1920. In 1930, the enrollment reached 391 students and gave evidence of a growing dynamic institution. Enrollment had increased from 270 in 1916 to 391 in 1932, the staff had grown from six to fourteen, the campus had expanded from three to eight buildings, and the program had been enriched to include a vocational program in addition to the liberal program of general education. However, in 1933, Redstone Academy was merged with the Mary Potter School of Oxford, North Carolina.

Dr. Hayswood was given custody of the Redstone Academy property, and the city of Lumberton was given use of the school property as a public high school. Dr. Hayswood was employed as principal of the locally controlled high school which was named Redstone High School. Dr. Hayswood served in this capacity until 1940 when he retired with the title principal emeritus, a valuable tribute to his many years of service to the school and community. Later, a modern twenty-five classroom structure, complete with cafeteria and gymnasium, was erected and named the "J. H. Hayswood High School" in honor of the man who made such an indelible educational contribution to Lumberton and southeastern North Carolina.

Dr. Hayswood died March 31, 1958. He was buried from Bethany Presbyterian Church, one of the churches to which he gave so much of himself, his substance, and his service.[11]

Billingsley Academy
Statesville, North Carolina

Billingsley Academy was founded in 1889 on a six-acre plot within the city limits of Statesville, North Carolina, by the Reverend Samuel Farmer Wentz. The founder graduated from Biddle University with an A.B. degree in 1889 and received the S.T.B. degree from the same university in 1892.

The story of the development of Billingsley Academy is one of rugged

[11] Mrs. Hayswood interview, March, 1958.

beginnings advancing slowly through a maze of stiff opposition. The first sessions were held in the basement quarters of the Broad Street Presbyterian Church with a faculty of two, the Reverend Wentz and Miss Hall. A serious lack of funds was one of the basic blocks to the struggling school's progress. Wentz traveled North seeking to interest friends in the project. Mrs. A. S. Billingsley gave the first thousand dollars, out of which the first six acres of land on the east side of South Green Street were purchased from a Mrs. Fornlin. The lot stood vacant, however, until sufficient funds could be secured to build upon it. In the meantime the school continued operation in the basement, and in 1902 the Board commissioned Miss Fannie Bryant to assist the Reverend Wentz. In 1903, Miss Lillie Rankin was added to the staff to assist with the 102 pupils, and in 1904, Miss A. Rickens was employed. The enrollment reached 195 in 1905, and Miss H. E. Murdock was commissioned to assist with the overflow crowd. That year the Board made the following announcement:

> This year the Women's Department under the management of Mrs. V. P. Boggs as General Secretary, was asked to raise $1,000 to complete a fund of $2,500 for the erection of a school building at Statesville, to be known as the Billingsley Academy in memory of Rev. A. S. Billingsley, one of the earliest of our white missionaries to the Freedmen, who spent his whole life in that region in a faithful and willing service and to which object his wife, since his death, had already given the first thousand out of her scanty means. . . . The fund for the Statesville school has been fully made up this year and we are now ready to proceed with the erection of the new building.[12]

Professor Hunt, at Biddle University, had drawn up the plans for the building in 1904, and the new building was ready for the fall session of 1906. Statesville, and the Reverend Wentz in particular, felt that the one basic step so long needed had been taken, but Wentz did not rest after this accomplishment. He envisioned lofty achievements at the academy, and with the aid of four teachers he labored until 1913 when his staff was increased to five, consisting of himself, his wife, Miss A. M. Richardson, Miss M. E. Brown, and Miss H. E. Murdock. At the end of the school year in 1914, the Reverend Wentz, after twenty-eight years, accepted a call to the Grace Presbyterian Church in Winston-Salem, North Carolina. The Reverend Zander Adam Dockery became principal of the academy that year.

[12] BMF, *Annual Report*, 1905, p. 10.

The Reverend Dockery, who had received the S.T.B. degree from the theological seminary at Biddle University in 1902, brought a new faculty to the academy consisting of himself, his wife, Miss C. M. Dockery, and Miss A. L. Dunston. With his staff, the new principal began a career that was to prove difficult but rewarding. Getting the local people interested and involved was his ambition. This was realized, community pride was awakened, and a sense of ownership grew among the people, which was rewarding both for the school and the community.

The Board classified Billingsley Academy in 1929 as a day school which offered four grades at the high school level, six at the elementary level, and one at the primary level, with a staff of six teachers. The academy had added extraclass activities which included cultural clubs and athletics.

In 1930, the Board expressed high praise for Dockery's recreational activities for the students and the community. A tennis court had been constructed by the students, and the spacious academy grounds provided splendid opportunity for sports like football, baseball, and basketball.[13] In all likelihood the academy was discontinued after the 1931 school year, as it does not appear in the list of day schools dropped in 1933 nor does it appear on the list of schools sponsored by the Board thereafter. The Broad Street Presbyterian Church moved into the school building and later received from the Board a deed to the property.

Many of the parochial schools that had been established in the late 1860s and early 1870s were gradually discontinued. By 1889, however, new schools and churches were established in hitherto unreached communities. Some of these schools operated only a decade or so. This was true in Mocksville, Raleigh, Fayetteville, Winston-Salem, Chadburn, Salisbury, and in many other small towns where Presbyterian churches had been established.

Freedom Parochial School
Bethany, North Carolina

According to the Reverend William L. Metz, writing in the *Africo-American Presbyterian* in 1927 and confirmed by Mrs. S. C. Alexander, wife of the cofounder of the Freedom Church and Biddle University, the Reverend Samuel S. Murkland, a white minister, was preaching to Negroes in Bethany Township, Iredell County, before 1866.[14] Late in

[13] Interview with Elder Baker of the Statesville Presbyterian Church U.S.A., 1964. He also shared minutes of the Church Session and pamphlets.
[14] Letter from Mrs. Nannie R. Alexander to Professor J. D. Martin, Sr.,

1866 the Reverends S. C. Alexander and W. L. Miller associated themselves with Murkland and in October of the same year, these three met where Freedom Church now stands, set up a presbytery and called it Catawba.[15]

In this locality Reverend Murkland had discovered a typical postwar situation among the freedmen. A group of landed freedmen was enjoying a rather comfortable existence, but they were churchless and without educational opportunities. One particular freedman held in his possession a bill of sale of his father, a man named Ben. The new owner purchased "Ben" along with other slaves and gave them plots of land, in addition to their freedom.[16] This accounts for the situation found by Murkland when he arrived in Iredell County. This welcoming committee of one, Mr. Ben Bruner, served as a contact man for the minister and the widely scattered villagers and brought others under the influence of Murkland.

Murkland attempted to preach to two racial groups in the same sanctuary at the same time but failed. He then pitched a tent in order to preach "a separate but equal gospel." Negroes had worshiped from the balcony of the "white" church during slavery, but the situation changed radically after the surrender. The large "white" church became uncomfortable for the freedmen. Whether because of heat or fear, or the hostile atmosphere—no one seemed to know—but one of the freedmen died in the balcony during services one Sunday morning. After that incident none of the Negroes returned to the church.

In connection with his preaching, Murkland organized the Freedom Parochial School which was commonly called "The Murkland School." Associated with Murkland during the early developmental stages of the school work were John Graham, William L. Metz, and Henry Alexander. In this farming area, school was conducted mostly at night and accommodated both old and young. Blacks in Iredell County were industrious farmers and were interested in both the church and school activities, but they were scattered over large expanses of cultivated land which were separated by thick plots of forests. These conditions made church and school attendance difficult, especially when the weather was bad and the

---

of Johnson C. Smith University, December 6, 1910. (Copy in author's possession.)

[15] A more detailed account of this event will be found later in this chapter in connection with the founding of Biddle University.

[16] Interview with Mr. Ben Bruner, descendent of "Ben" at Freedom Church, Bethany, N.C., May 1963.

dirt roads were soft. During such times, however, it was not uncommon for large groups to walk, singing, from as far away as five miles to sing, learn, and pray.

Murkland stamped his image and principles deep in the memory of the community—both black and white. When he moved on to other nearby impoverished regions, the Reverend A. S. Billingsley continued the church and school work in Bethany. In 1875, the Reverend B. F. McDowell, who had graduated in 1872 from the Biddle Theological Seminary, was commissioned to take charge of the church and school at Bethany. There were forty-one pupils when he arrived, and he was impressed by their eagerness to learn. He guided the work of the church and school for three years assisted by Miss C. E. McGregar. McDowell left Freedom School to take over the work of the church and school in Lexington in 1878 and in 1879 moved on to the Mattoon Parochial School in Hamberg, South Carolina, where he remained for twenty-eight years.

In 1881, E. E. Summers taught the forty-eight pupils in Freedom School. Other teachers in the school were: Mrs. Gertie Stevenson, Mrs. Madie Alexander, Mrs. Maggie Pharr Morrison, Mrs. Addie Smith, Mrs. Hattie Harris and Mrs. Lottie Hall. After 1881 the Committee of Missions for Freedmen discontinued support of school activity at the Freedom Parochial School. The villagers, however, maintained that Mrs. Maggie Pharr Morrison and Mrs. Lottie Hall kept the school running "for a long time" after the Committee withdrew its support.[17]

Greensboro Graded School
Greensboro, North Carolina

Early collaboration between church and state in an effort to provide education for the recently liberated Negroes is illustrated by the history of the parochial school associated with the St. James Presbyterian Church in Greensboro, North Carolina. The school was organized in 1868 with a white couple, the Reverend and Mrs. James A. Chresfield, in charge. The Committee of Missions for Freedmen gives the following description of the origin and operation of the school in its annual report for 1878:

> This school is located at Greensboro, North Carolina where a good parochial school was opened in 1868, under the care of the General Assembly's Committee on Freedmen. This continued until 1874,

[17] Bruner Interview, May, 1963.

when the city commissioners proposed cooperation in getting up a graded school, to be known as the Greensboro Graded School, having two departments—white and colored. The commissioners requested Mr. Chresfield to take general supervision of the colored department, selecting the very best teachers to be obtained, those of the colored race to have the preference. Colored teachers were accordingly selected, and this department was organized during the same year—1874. The city has no school building, and feels unable to build at present, though anxious, we are told, to do so.

We take pleasure in adding—in regard to the union of this school with that of the city that the latter not only gives Mr. Chresfield the general superintendence of this department, but in no way interferes with his opening the school daily with reading the Scriptures prayer and religious instruction. The school is conducted in the colored Presbyterian Church, the city providing for about one-half the teachers' salaries and the necessary incidental expenses. It has reported during the past year as high as 350 pupils for three months in succession, and as the church—which cost less than $1,000—is by no means large, it must be readily perceived that a suitable school building is the great want here, the lack of which the superintendent as well as your committee greatly regrets, and all the more that the city is one of considerable importance and has a large colored population. The faculty for this year consisted of:

Rev. James A. Chresfield, Superintendent
Henry C. Mabry—Teacher (Received state aid)
Mrs. L. A. Chresfield—Teacher
Miss Julia A. Gilmer—Teacher (Received state aid)
Miss Chaney I. McAdoo—Assistant.[18]

The enrollment for this year as reported by Yadkin Presbytery was 224.

The receptive attitude of the Greensboro citizenry during the development of the school added much to its popularity in the community and surrounding vicinity. Both the city commissioners and the Committee seemed pleased with this cooperative approach to the problem of elementary education for Negroes in the vicinity as long as the Reverend Chresfield remained at the school. In 1879 the enrollment was 179 but the decrease did not indicate, in the opinion of the Committee, a decrease in local interest.

After seven successful years with this cooperative system, Chresfield resigned to go to a parochial school in Raleigh. The work at

[18] CMF, *Annual Report*, 1878, p. 26.

Greensboro was taken over by the Reverend L. R. Johnson who was assisted by C. M. Moore, Mrs. Julia A. Davis, and R. M. McKenzie.

After 1891, the Yadkin Presbytery made no further reports of the activity of the parochial school at Greensboro. It is assumed that after seventeen years of cooperative action the city took over the total responsibility.

The Charlotte Parochial School
Charlotte, North Carolina

In 1867, the Reverend Samuel C. Alexander, who had cofounded an institution of higher learning in Charlotte, North Carolina, organized the Charlotte Colored Presbyterian Church and established a school to be associated with it, the Charlotte Parochial School. The church and school were located in a section of the town known as "Log Town" because of the numerous log cabins in that area.

During the formative years of the parochial school, Alexander was pastor and superintendent of the mission and Mrs. S. C. Alexander, the Misses Margaret Miller, J. A. Brow, and N. C. Russell were the teachers of the sixty-five pupils enrolled. The early sessions were conducted in the audience chamber of the double-duty building which had been purchased for the church and school.[19]

In 1871–1872, the Catawba Presbytery, in its annual report, stated that a church building had been purchased at a cost of $1,900 and also a school building costing $600. The enrollment for that school term was listed at 113 and the Misses C. A. Lyon, C. R. Watt, and Lavinia were new teachers at the school. J. T. McMahan was working in the capacity of catechist. Jointly the church and school had raised $626.42 for self-support that year. The enrollment reached 147 during the school year 1873–1874, and with the exception of Miss Lavinia being listed as an assistant, the teaching staff remained the same.

The Misses C. R. Watt, A. J. Beach, and M. Davidson composed the teaching staff in 1875 with Alexander still superintendent. The school and church continued the local fund-raising drive and reported $426.11 for operational expenses. C. R. Oliver became licentiate for the church and school in 1876 and with Mrs. Oliver taught the 140 students enrolled. The self-support money raised by joint effort that year amounted to $419.57.[20]

[19] *Johnson C. Smith University Newsletter*, October, 1941, pp. 4–5.
[20] Alexander to Martin, Dec. 6, 1910.

Significant changes occurred in 1878. The Reverend C. R. Oliver became the new pastor of the church and superintendent of the school, and for the first time the position of principal at this parochial was created. John Edward Rattley, having taken first honors at graduation from Biddle University in 1877, was offered a position as tutor at the university which he declined in order to accept the principalship at the Charlotte Parochial School. Mr. Rattley held a deep sense of gratitude for early experiences which he had had as a student in this parochial. He had enrolled in the Charlotte Parochial School at age of fourteen in 1869 and remained until he was ready to enter Biddle University. In addition to the new principal, two teachers—Miss L. C. Mott, who received state aid, and Miss Sallie Hall—were added to the staff. The self-help fund which was raised locally that year was $591.50. There were no changes in the teaching staff for 1879, but the enrollment had increased to 164 pupils. The amount of money raised on the local level that year was $479.76.[21]

The Reverend R. P. Wyche, who had begun work at the school as licentiate, received the bachelor's degree from Biddle University in 1877 and the S.T.B. from the seminary of the same institution in 1881. He was commissioned pastor and principal of the station immediately after graduation. Miss M. J. Hayes was added to the instructional staff that year to help with the highest enrollment (349) in the history of the school.

After working about four years as a principal of the Charlotte Parochial School, Mr. Rattley was influential in merging the school with the City Graded School which had been recently organized for Negroes. He became the first principal of the combined schools in 1882. After eight years, he resigned to take a job as clerk in the Pension Office in Washington, D. C. The school does not appear in the Catawba Presbytery reports after 1882.

Some years later, 1927, John Edward Rattley wrote in the *Johnson C. Smith University Alumni Journal* the following observation.

> Few people, now living, know the extensive influence of that school in Charlotte and Mecklenburg County. It was not only filled with the very young but also had a large attendance of grown men and women not yet prepared to enter Biddle and Scotia.[22]

21 *Johnson C. Smith University Newsletter*, October, 1941, p. 5.
22 John Rattley, "The Early Days at Biddle as I Recall Them," *Johnson C. Smith University Alumni Journal*, vol. 1, no. 1 (October 1927), pp. 8–11.

The Charlotte Parochial School provides an additional example of the significant role played by the church in the development of a system of public education for Negroes in the South.

Calvary Parochial School
Asheville, North Carolina

The Calvary Parochial School was established in Asheville, North Carolina, in 1884 by the Reverend Charles Bradford Dusenbury. He was a descendant of a Christian family who put high values on education and who sent him to the Presbyterian Parochial School in Lexington. There he came under the influence and instruction of the Reverend James A. Chresfield. Charles Dusenbury made an excellent record at the parochial school and through Chresfield's influence was enrolled in Lincoln University in Pennsylvania. He graduated with honors from both the college and seminary departments of this institution. His first pastorate was at New Bern, North Carolina, where he received valuable experience for the tasks which awaited him in Asheville.

Dusenbury went to Asheville in 1881 at the insistence of the Committee of Missions for Freedmen to organize a Presbyterian church among Negroes. The way had been opened there for Negro church and school work through efforts made by some of the white people who had maintained both a day and Sunday school.

In 1884, three years after reaching Asheville, Dusenbury began the Calvary Parochial School and preached in the old Catholic Hill Church, while he and his family lived in cramped quarters in the back of the building. After a short lapse of time, however, a wooden church was built on Eagle Street. On the back of this lot was a small house where the Dusenburys lived with courage and self-sacrifice for several months. Later, however, a manse was built through the kindness of "a friend."[23]

Getting the Presbyterian system to work in the locality was not an easy task for the Dusenburys. To preach a gospel without undue emotional appeal but with Christian living as its aim and goal did not immediately arouse a great deal of enthusiasm. There was even opposition among fellow ministers to "the Dusenbury new ways." Especially was this true in the conduct of "Big Meetings" in which all denominations participated. The Reverend Dusenbury's courage, ardent piety, and good judgment, however, won the respect and good will of his fellow Chris-

---

[23] It was not always discreet to indicate openly a favorable disposition toward the Board's program. To prevent stirring up animosity, therefore, many valuable donations were made anonymously.

tians and citizens at large, whatever their denomination or race.

Calvary Parochial School grew until its enrollment of 150 pupils exceeded normal capacity. In addition to the ordinary graded school work, instruction was given in the Bible, the Shorter Catechism, and in practical lessons in cooking and gardening. The tuition fee ranged from ten to fifteen cents per month and was collected when and where possible. Dusenbury once remarked, "The pupils are taught to be honest and truthful, to be pure in thoughts and habits, to be kind and considerate, and also to be clean in their persons, for we believe in a soap and water gospel as well as the other kind and our efforts are to impress the virtues of each."[24]

After thirty-six years of devoted service, the Reverend Charles Dusenbury died during the summer of 1920, "not an old man but worn out by a life of unremitting work for his people and for his scholars."[25] The school was run by Mrs. Dusenbury until 1922 when the Reverend G. W. Hamilton became the new pastor of the church and principal of the school. Five years later the school was discontinued.

Sarah Lincoln Academy
Aberdeen, North Carolina

The Reverend William Jones Rankin was another Presbyterian who devoted years of his life to religious and educational leadership. He was born in Iredell County in 1862 while the Civil War was in progress. As a boy he was inspired while attending a parochial school in Iredell County. The Reverend and Mrs. W. H. Bryant, who had charge of the mission work there, saw great promise in young Rankin, and, when the Bryants moved to Salisbury, they took the ambitious youth with them. He was enrolled in the parochial school there and was later sent to Biddle. In 1889 he received the A.B. degree from Lincoln University and the S.T.B. from the same institution in 1892, along with the degree of Master of Arts. In 1911 Biddle University conferred the D.D. degree upon him.[26]

Immediately following his graduation from Lincoln University, he accepted the pastorate and principalship of the work in Laurenburg. In

---

[24] Francis L. Goodrich, *A Devoted Life and Its Results* (Pittsburgh: Board of Missions for Freedmen, Women's Department, n.d.)

[25] Goodrich, *Devoted Life.* Also, an interview with Paul Dusenbury, the founder's son, 1963.

[26] A. B. Caldwell, ed. *History of the American Negro*, vol. 4 (Atlanta: Caldwell Publishing Co., 1921), p. 433.

1894, he moved to Aberdeen to take charge of the mission there. The Rankins were distressed with the complete lack of educational facilities for Negro children in Aberdeen and began an educational project in their own home which grew into the Sarah Lincoln Academy. The school was first known as the Aberdeen Preparatory School. The name was changed to the Elizabeth School in honor of Mrs. Rankin whose indefatigable efforts made the school possible.

In 1903, the school, which had been taught primarily by the Rankins and Mrs. W. H. Byrd, was taken under the care of Board, and at the request of one of its benefactors the school's name was changed to the Sarah Lincoln School. Finally, by action of the Yadkin Presbytery, the school became permanently and officially the Sarah Lincoln Academy. The staff remained the same and shared the joy of the school's progress in size and usefulness. In 1911, Mrs. L. B. Cooper and Mrs. G. Lashley joined the staff, and in 1912 Mrs. H. D. Wood was added.

In addition to his school work, the Reverend Rankin was pastor of the Faith Presbyterian Church in Aberdeen and Emmanuel Presbyterian Church in Southern Pines. At each place he erected new church edifices. He was an industrious leader with creative imagination which kept both the church and school work alive and progressive. He was moderator of Catawba Presbytery from 1909 to 1910 and was chosen at three different times as moderator of Yadkin Presbytery. Twice he was a commissioner to the General Assembly, in 1898 and in 1918.[27]

In 1931, the Sarah Lincoln Academy was listed among the day schools under the supervision of the Division of Work with Colored People, offering five elementary grades and one primary grade. There were three teachers at the school and it was running twenty-four weeks.

The school obviously closed in 1932 as it does not appear in the list of schools after that date.

Yadkin Academy
Mebane, North Carolina

The Yadkin Academy of Mebane, North Carolina, was established in 1888–89 by the Reverend and Mrs. M. G. Haskins. Haskins, a graduate of the theological seminary of Biddle University in 1876, and his wife came to Mebane with a burning desire to enlighten and motivate the freedmen to strive for a better way of life. He and his wife challenged the 168 pupils who enrolled and also went out into the surrounding vicinity

[27] Caldwell, *History*, vol. IV, p. 435.

in search of other promising children. In his effort to prepare them for higher levels of learning, he attempted to instill in them a taste for reading, sound study habits, and the ability to communicate effectively. A higher grade was added to the curriculum as fast as the students were ready for it, until the eleventh grade was added and the school was classified as a boarding high school or academy. For eight years and nine months they labored diligently, realizing, here and there, gratifying responses.

After the Haskins resigned in 1900, the Reverend J. E. Tice was the next principal of Yadkin Academy. In his first report to the Board, he stated that the school was in a prosperous condition and the 138 students enrolled were eager to learn. In this locality, education for the freedmen was not a popular concept. The new principal, therefore, put to work everything that his training, experience, and energies could yield to educate the students and to end the prevailing attitude that education was dangerous or unnecessary. He worked courageously toward this objective for eleven years and resigned in 1911. The Reverend W. P. Donnell was his successor as principal of the academy.

Donnell graduated from the theological seminary of Biddle University and had amassed years of experience by the time he came to the school in 1911. The Reverend Donnell's emphasis was on program enrichment. In addition to the courses on religion required by the Board's program, the curriculum was also designed to meet state requirements. *The McGuffey Reading Series* and *Noah Webster's Elementary Spelling Book (The Blue-Back Speller)* were among the basic textbooks. Memory played a strong role in the teaching and learning process; the multiplication tables, historical dates, the Shorter Catechism, memory verses from the Scriptures, and poetry were stressed. The Friday afternoon "Spelling Bee" was a common and enjoyable activity at the academy.

The Reverend Philip John Augustus Coxe came to the academy as principal in 1916. He was a native of Chestertown, Maryland, born in 1872, in an area that had a history of free Negroes. He had completed the college course at Lincoln University in 1901 with the A.B. degree and earned the S.T.B. degree at the same university in 1904. After filling several small pulpits in the state of Pennsylvania, he taught at the Mary Potter School in Oxford, North Carolina. In 1916 he gave up the work at Mary Potter to accept the principalship of Yadkin Academy and the pastorate of the Presbyterian church for Negroes in Mebane.[28] In each

[28] Caldwell, *History*, vol. IV, pp. 658–660.

position his goal was to discover and inspire individuals who had a desire to learn and to grow.

Once when Coxe was asked for an expression on how the best interests of the Negro were to be promoted, he replied:

By Christian Education. Also a recognition of the fact on the part of race leaders that our rights are to be obtained, as history shows all subject races have; that agitation must be without bitterness; that the ascendant race must be educated into the fact that we are not the same people we were in 1619 or even in 1861. As men we want a chance to act, to live . . .[29]

After working at the academy for three years, Misses Lucy Webb and Annie Murry were commissioned to assist the teaching of 140 pupils, and they were still members of the teaching staff on the Board's last report which included it on its list of schools. The school, in all probability, closed at the end of the school year in 1931.

Mary Potter School
Oxford, North Carolina

The Mary Potter School was founded in 1889 in the county seat of fertile Granville County by George Clayton Shaw, a seminarian. It began as a small parochial school and held its early sessions in a church building which had just been completed through the persistent efforts of friends.

Shaw was born in Louisburg, North Carolina, on July 19, 1863. Missionaries had been sent to this field as early as 1866.[30] Misses M. V. Henderson and M. M. Miller were instructing 102 pupils there in 1866. Miss N. C. Russell reached the area in 1869, and in 1872, along with Calvin McCurdy, licentiate, she was instructing fifty-two pupils. Under these and other instructors, young Shaw completed a preparatory course and was carried by his deep Presbyterian inspiration to Lincoln University, Chester County, Pennsylvania, where he received the Bachelor of Arts degree in 1886. After one year in Princeton Theological Seminary in New Jersey, young Shaw transferred to Auburn Theological Seminary in Auburn, New York, where he completed the three-year theological course in 1890. The Timothy Darling Church and the Mary Potter School were founded while he was at Auburn Seminary. George Shaw so impressed Dr. Timothy Darling, one of his seminary instructors, that he

[29] Caldwell, *History*, vol. IV, p. 660.
[30] *Minutes* (Old School), 1867, p. 443.

arranged for him to meet Mrs. Mary Potter of Schenectady, New York, who was special secretary of the Freedmen's Board in Albany Presbyterial, New York Synodical. Mrs. Potter offered financial aid so that the young seminarian might spend the summer months of 1888 preaching in the South.

When school closed in May of that year he returned to the Old North State to preach. He was advised by the Cape Fear Presbytery to go to Wilson, North Carolina, where a small mission had been started, or to Oxford where there was no Presbyterian church for Negroes. On his way to Wilson he stopped by Oxford, which was about thirty-six miles from his birthplace. This was on Wednesday before the fourth Sunday in May, 1888. He spent Thursday surveying the prospects of beginning a Presbyterian mission there. After a hard unsuccessful day's work, he retired with a decision to continue to Wilson. The next morning, however, he spoke with the white minister before leaving. During the conversation the seminarian was advised to contact a Mrs. Harriette Howell who was the only Negro Presbyterian in the community. She was a member of the white church, attended regularly, and was greatly concerned about the lack of the Presbyterian faith among her people.[31] George Shaw walked the three and one-half miles to interview Mrs. Howell and was greeted in these terms: "Why certainly you can establish a Presbyterian Church here. That is what God sent you here for. That is what I have been praying for; you cannot go away."[32]

Dr. Shaw later wrote how he went about his work:

Saturday morning found me in search of a place to hold services. I found an old dilapidated building that had years before been used as a school house for colored children. I knocked together a few seats and spent the remainder of the day walking the streets and telling the people that I would preach in the old school house at eleven o'clock. I sent word to Mrs. Howell. She notified all the people in her section. Sunday morning found about seventy-five people to hear me preach.[33]

Services were conducted during the remainder of the summer months, and on the first Sunday in August, 1888, the church was established and

31 "Mary Potter-Redstone-Albion Academy" *Brevities* (New York: Presbyterian Church in the U.S.A., Board of National Missions, 1936), p. 2.

32 Owena Hunter Davis, *A History of Mary Potter School* (Oxford, North Carolina: no publisher given, 1944), p. 3.

33 *Brevities*, N.Y.: PCUSA, BNM.

given the name Timothy Darling Presbyterian Church, honoring the Auburn professor who had encouraged Shaw. By the second Sunday in September, the members had raised fifty-five dollars to help meet the expenses of continuing the services during the winter and spring months while Shaw continued his studies at Auburn.

At the end of the school year at Auburn in 1889, Shaw returned to Oxford, anxious to develop the small mission which he had started. Upon his arrival in Oxford, however, he found the doors of the church closed. Enemies and rivals of the new denomination were responsible for the closing. Repeated efforts to reopen the church failed. When his spirit was at its lowest ebb, he received a letter from Mrs. Mary Potter and Dr. Darling containing $300 and with the message to buy a lot and build a church. Shaw purchased a lot about two blocks from the center of the town for $225 from Dr. L. C. Taylor from whom three other large tracts were purchased later. The first Presbyterian church for Negroes in Granville County was constructed on this land. The small building stood as a monument to Dr. Timothy Darling, Mrs. Mary Potter, Mrs. Harriette Howell, and George Clayton Shaw through whose efforts this victory was won. The structure was used as a place of worship, a school house, and sleeping quarters for male students.

When Shaw returned to Auburn for his senior year, he left the parochial school in charge of his brother, William H. Shaw, who had recently received his degree from the Lincoln University Seminary. When Shaw returned after graduation, he brought with him a bride from Penn Valley, Pennsylvania, who was a graduate of the State Normal School of New Jersey and was a teacher in that state. Shaw married Miss Mary E. Lewis May 14, 1890, seven days after he graduated from Auburn Seminary.[34]

In September of 1890, Shaw relieved his brother of the mission responsibilities, and Mrs. Shaw became executive of the school work. The enrollment increased rapidly, and the small church was soon overcrowded with students ranging in age from five to forty-five. Each paid twenty-five cents monthly for tuition and was eager to learn to read and write. Mrs. Shaw's salary came from the tuition fees and her husband's salary, twenty-five dollars monthly, was paid by the Board. Miss Nevels of South Carolina was employed and was paid from funds raised locally.

In 1892, a boarding department was started and the Board agreed to pay Mrs. Shaw fifteen dollars a month for three months of the term. At this time roads were crudely constructed and conveyances for travel were

[34] Davis, *A History*, p. 5.

limited and poor. This posed a problem for rural students, especially during bad weather, and increased the necessity for boarding facilities. Dr. Shaw appealed to Mrs. Mary Potter and through her influence the New York Synodical Society contributed $2,000 to renovate the small church building. A three-story structure with two classrooms on the first floor was added. The monthly boarding fee of four dollars was frequently paid in produce. During the school year 1892, 132 pupils enrolled and $203 was raised for self-support by the mission.[35] The president's home, built adjacent to the church, was shared with five boarding girls, and the dining room with the ten boarders—five girls and five boys. In 1892 the school's name was changed from "Timothy Darling Field" to Mary Potter School.[36]

In 1893, the third floor was incomplete but was later finished as living quarters for boys, and the second floor was converted into an assembly hall. The average enrollment for the succeeding six years was 230. In 1896 Miss Eunice Dudley became the first regular music teacher. She was succeeded in 1898 by Mr. I. H. Buchanan, who organized the first school band. In this year also the faculty was increased to five and the first class graduated. Margaret A. Tucker was employed as teacher at the Mary Potter School in 1899 and remained there for forty-three consecutive years as organist, pianist, and history teacher.

After twelve years of operation, the Mary Potter School started an ambitious program of expansion. In 1900, a farm of about sixty-five acres was purchased at a cost of $960. Dr. Shaw made an appeal to the New York Synodical Society, revealing the need for more land for food production and wood for the wood stoves which heated the dormitories, and the Society sent him the money for the land. This year also, the principal's home and teachers' cottage were purchased at a cost of $900 each. A barn was constructed at a cost of $300, which was financed by the Women's Board and the New York Synodical Society. Miss M. B. Sullivan began a long career at the school as sewing teacher in 1900.[37]

In the spring of 1901 the second building was started on the campus. The Albany Presbyterial of the New York Synodical Society sent Dr. Shaw a check for $100 and later one for $200 for the purchase of building materials. The principal purchased the materials from a dilapidated tobacco barn near the campus. When the frame structure was completed it was named Albany Hall. The New York Synodical Society furnished

[35] Davis, *A History*.
[36] Davis, *A History*, p. 6.
[37] Davis, *A History*, p. 6.

$10,000 for furnishings and other costs involved in the erection of this building. Provision was made for a dining room, kitchen, and girls' parlor on the first and second floors, and living quarters for twenty-six girls on the third. Additional accommodations for boarding boys were also provided in 1906. Also in the interest of housing needs for boys, Dr. Shaw made an appeal to the Board for $1,000 to enlarge the first building to be erected on the campus, and near the end of the year $676.20 of the request had been raised. While completing this addition to the church to house thirty boys, the Hudson Presbyterial of the New York Synodical Society financed the purchase of two cottages: Lester Cottage, named for Miss Lucy Lester of Saratoga Springs, New York, and the Yeisley Cottage, named for Mrs. George C. Yeisley who was president of the New York Synodical at the time. These cottages were first used to house women teachers and girls but later were used for teachers only. The Yeisley Cottage was remodeled in 1938 for use as the principal's home.[38]

In 1906 the church was moved to a corner lot two blocks from the school. A new dormitory was also constructed for girls in 1906. It was named Wells Hall for Miss Helen A. Wells, secretary of the New York Synodical and Albany Presbyterial Society. The $10,000 required for constructing and furnishing Wells Hall was provided by the New York Synodical Society. The new dormitory contained a home economics room, kitchen, dining room with a seating capacity of about one hundred fifty on the basement floor, a teachers' parlor, and living quarters for eighty girls on the second, third, and fourth floors. The building, though frame, was much better than Albany Hall, which was finally torn down.

In 1908 Miss D. E. Peace began a thirty-four year career at the school. Special efforts were made to provide adequate library facilities; a marked increase was seen in the enrollment in 1910. Dr. Shaw's appeal to the Board for an administration building was granted in 1913 and the building was completed in 1914. It housed offices, classrooms, science laboratory, and auditorium.

In 1917 the school began to phase out the lower grades. The City Board of Education agreed to pay seventy-five cents per pupil per month to help provide high school training of local students at Mary Potter. This amount was increased to fifty dollars per month per student in 1920. There was a continuous increase in this amount and in addition, in 1931, the State Board of Education began paying teachers' salaries for undertaking the instruction of its high school students in the area. Beginning

---

[38] Davis, *A History*, p. 6.

in that year the state paid the salaries of seven teachers and gradually increased the number to sixteen. L. S. Cozart joined the staff as principal's assistant in 1919 and Miss Iola Branch was added as a teacher-training instructor.

The Reverend Hermon S. Davis, who had received the S.T.B. degree from Biddle University Theological Seminary in 1921, joined the Mary Potter staff in September of the same year. In 1922, Mary Potter received state accreditation, and in 1923 the curriculum was enriched by a facility for more trades courses; the Board constructed a brick trades building at a cost of $3,500.

In March of 1923, the boys dormitory was lost by fire, but without loss of life, and a new dormitory building, Pittsburgh Hall, was erected at a cost of $50,000. The building, with a capacity for 100, was so named because most of the building funds were collected in the area of Pittsburgh through the solicitation of Dr. John M. Gaston, Secretary of the Freedmen's Board. This fireproof brick structure became the pride of the campus. In 1927 the Mary E. Shaw Gymnasium was erected at a cost of $4,000 and named for the faithful and humanitarian wife of the founder. Mrs. Shaw contributed $1,000 to the building fund, and the remainder was raised through class projects and donations from alumni and friends. Mr. Thomas Hicks, instructor of manual arts, built the frame and the brick work was done by local artisans.

In 1928, Dr. George Clayton Shaw wrote a review of the thirty-eight years of his continuous service at Mary Potter. There were eight buildings in 1928 valued at $175,000. In 1932 he purchased the farm from the Board for his personal use, and in 1933 he retired at the age of seventy. The Reverend Hermon S. Davis, assistant principal, was chosen to fill the vacancy. In May of that year Albion Academy of Franklinton, North Carolina and Redstone Academy of Lumberton, North Carolina were closed, but to retain the interest of friends who helped to support the closed schools, the school names were added to that of Mary Potter, which became Mary Potter-Redstone-Albion Academy.[39] In 1934 the Mary Potter-Redstone-Albion Academy was accredited by the Southern Association of Colleges and Secondary Schools.

The gradual expansion of the physical plant ran parallel with and was a by-product of the academic innovations at the school. Courses of study

[39] "Mary Potter-Redstone-Albion Academy," *Briefly* (N.Y.:PCUSA, BNM, 1950), p. 1.

which had become traditional at the school underwent dramatic changes. Beginning back in 1910, the program had been divided into a primary department with A and B classes, intermediate and grammar department with like divisions, and a normal department which was divided into first and second year junior classes, middle class, and senior class. Continuing this expansion trend, a teacher-training course had been added in 1918 with the first instructor, Miss Mary O. Dent, paid from the Slater Fund. This department was under the supervision of the State Department of Education, and the graduates received elementary A and B grade certificates. The course was discontinued in 1929 when the state colleges took over this phase of the work. Near the end of this expansion and growth at the school, evening classes in carpentry and auto mechanics were offered for out-of-school youth. There were also classes stressing guidance to farmers and wider community services.

Wells Hall, the boys' dormitory, was partially destroyed by fire in February, 1946, and was replaced by the Board almost immediately from fire insurance funds.

Since 1931–1932, teachers' salaries had been paid from public funds, but in 1952 the city of Oxford assumed complete responsibility for the financial support and direction of the academic program, leaving the church to continue a small boarding department. Mrs. Mary E. Shaw died July 13, 1952 and at the request of the family was buried beside her husband in the small cemetery plot at the edge of the school property.

In 1953, the Board approved the sale of the school property to the city of Oxford for $75,000, except for a small corner burial plot to be deeded to the heirs of Dr. and Mrs. Shaw. The boarding department was closed, and the boarding students were given the opportunity to transfer to Harbison, May 31, 1953. The sale was concluded September 24, 1953, on the above terms with the understanding that the property would continue to be used for school purposes for Negro children. Student records were turned over to the local public school board.

Scotia College
Concord, North Carolina

Scotia College was founded as a seminary for girls in Concord, North Carolina, in 1867 by Dr. Luke Dorland. The first sessions of the school were conducted in the home of the founder and in a small room in the Westminster Presbyterian Church. The institution occupied these quarters for approximately three years. On December 13, 1870, a half-acre lot containing a small frame house was acquired. Two other small frame buildings were built later on this property.

When Dr. and Mrs. Dorland came South from Toledo, Ohio, in 1867, a small parochial school was being operated in connection with the program of the Westminster Presbyterian Church, and there was a supportive attitude toward the establishing of a stronger school in the town.

In connection with founding and developing the seminary, Dr. Dorland identified himself with the infant Catawba Presbytery and, judging from the records which he kept as stated clerk of the Atlantic Synod, he was a most careful, accurate, and painstaking recorder of actions and reactions. He was an active officer of the Atlantic Synod as long as he was president of Scotia, 1867–1886. In 1867, the General Assembly's Committee on Missions for Freedmen announced the beginning of the Concord mission for freedmen with Dr. Luke Dorland as minister and founder, a black catechist named Johnathan Harris, Mrs. Luke Dorland, and Miss M. Garrett, as teachers of 111 pupils. Dr. Dorland immediately began to execute the original concept of a seminary for the intellectual and religious development of Negro women.[40] The Committee's report for 1871 made the following announcement:

Scotia Seminary for colored girls at Concord, N. C., under the superintendence of Reverend Luke Dorland and opened but a few months since, reports 45 pupils in attendance. It has a small lot, and Manse or home with means enough to put up a small School Building for present use. This institution is the only one of its kind under the care of the Committee, and its success is esteemed of special importance, both for the training of teachers for schools, and for the proper cultivation of refinement and virtue among both sexes.[41]

It is not clear whether this last sentence refers to some very brief early coeducational phase, or, more likely, that it refers to the expected influence on both sexes of the education of women. The school received a charter from the state of North Carolina under the name of "Scotia Seminary." The name "Scotia" was in honor of Matthew Scott of Muskingum County, Ohio, who had made a liberal gift to the cause and preferred that name to his own.

In 1872, the report of the Presbyterian Committee of Missions for Freedmen stated:

[40] Interview with Dr. Leland Stanford Cozart, September 25, 1971. For thirty-two years he was president of Scotia College.
[41] CMF, *Annual Report*, 1871, p. 7.

> Scotia Seminary is located at Concord, Cabarrus County; Rev. Luke Dorland, Superintendent . . . it was designed, and its location selected by the General Assembly's Committee on Freedmen over three years ago: but funds were entirely wanting until eighteen months since, when chiefly by the liberality of Matthew Scott, Esq., of Muskingum County, Ohio, the present committee was encouraged to authorize the purchase of a half-acre lot, . . .[42]

Fifty-nine pupils were reported enrolled that same year in the seminary under the instruction of Dr. and Mrs. Dorland and Miss M. E. Scott. The parochial school in Concord had 115 pupils enrolled with Miss Jennie McNeil in charge. Miss M. J. McCree assisted in the parochial school until 1878. The Reverend M. G. Haskins was pastor of the Westminster Presbyterian Church and director of the parochial school until 1881. The Committee's major emphasis in North Carolina had always been on a higher level of training than the parochial schools offered. In view of this, the parochial school in connection with the Westminster Presbyterian Church, as was the case with other parochial schools located in communities where a center of higher learning operated, was often overshadowed in the Committee's records by the major school.

Though emphasis on education at the elementary level was a necessity, the goal of a program which was higher and more intensive than that was never lost. In the beginning, therefore, the curriculum included the usual elementary academic subjects and home economics with a view of creative and innovative additions as circumstances permitted. Because of the character and high quality of its staff, curriculum, and instruction, the seminary was called "The Mount Holyoke of the South." Later, Mary Allen Junior College in Crockett, Texas, would also be referred to in this manner.

The first frame building, mentioned in the Committee's report of 1872, was erected at a cost of $1,000. The total investment in the promising seminary in 1872 was estimated by the Committee to be $2,081.82.[43] In 1873, four acres of land were purchased as a site for a larger and more permanent building to be constructed as soon as funds were made available. By 1876, this ambition was realized in the completion of a three-story brick building at a cost of about $12,000, of which $5,000 was given by the Reverend George Morris of Baltimore, Maryland, his sister, Mrs. Ann Morris McDowell, of Glasgow, Scotland, and $1,000 by Mr.

---

[42] *Minutes*, 1872, p. 159.
[43] *Minutes*, 1872, p. 159.

Matthew Scott. The entire value of the seminary holdings, including a $1,000 endowment fund, was estimated by the Committee to be $16,000 in 1876.

By 1881, the seminary's enrollment had reached 181 and five additional teachers were assisting Dr. and Mrs. Dorland: Misses Mae Weagley, Jessie F. Harper, S. Ida Allen, and N. E. Latham. Previously the staff had consisted of: Mrs. Anna H. Logan, who had joined the staff in 1873; Misses T. S. Bausman and Blanche Dorland, who had been added in 1876; Misses M. W. French and Alice M. Luse, who joined the staff in 1878. Miss Kate Hearst, who was with the staff in 1879, was no longer with the faculty in 1881.

In 1882, the stem of the main brick building, completing the "T" plan, was erected. For this project a gift of $8,000 from the estate of Augustus Graves was made by his brother, E. A. Graves, and the building was then named Graves Hall. The enrollment was 202 this year, and the faculty consisted of nine members, including the Dorlands. The Scotia Choir was organized this year for local enjoyment and for promotional purposes. An industrial department was added to the curriculum in 1884, and the girls were taught to cut, mend, and darn. Two professional seamstresses taught them practical dressmaking.

Due to age and failing health, Dr. Dorland retired in 1886 and was succeeded by Dr. D. J. Satterfield. Mrs. Satterfield was elected principal. A school paper began publication this year. Dr. Satterfield was born in Pulaski, Pennsylvania, and received the A.B. degree from Princeton University in 1870 and the M.A. degree from the same institution in 1873. The honorary degree was conferred upon him by Hanover College in Indiana in 1873. He was also a graduate of the Western Theological Seminary in Allegheny, Pennsylvania. In 1885, he went to Biddle University in Charlotte, North Carolina as college pastor and general superintendent of the boarding department. As Dr. Dorland's successor at Scotia, he associated himself with a broader phase of the church's program. Though white he became a member of the Catawba Presbytery. He never resorted to the phrases, "you people" or "your people" but rather demonstrated a sense of oneness by preferring the use of "we" and "us."[44] In a like manner, Mrs. Satterfield made herself indispensable to the seminary. She died in 1900. Dr. Satterfield later married Mrs. A. Hatfield who had worked under his administration. The second Mrs. Satterfield likewise became a strong influence for good among the girls.

[44] William Metz, "Blazers and Chips," *Africo-American Presbyterian*, vol. XLIX, no. 36 (September 8, 1927), p. 1.

She was both their friend and a proficient instructor. In 1889, the enrollment was 234 with twelve persons on the instructional staff.

Faith Hall was erected in 1891. The name was inspired by the spirit which undergirded a fund-raising campaign. The campaign was launched on faith and a gift of five cents. The cost of erecting this building was $22,000; in Cincinnati, Ohio, $16,000 of this was raised, largely through the efforts of Mrs. D. J. Satterfield and Mrs. Sidney D. Maxwell. A library was started in 1892 and gradually became the center of the academic program. The industrial department was expanded in 1906, and other industrial arts were added to the home economics emphasis. Special cooking classes and a sewing department were added. A hospital unit was created for elementary training in fundamental nursing techniques and first aid. After the domestic arts and sciences were revamped, no girl could graduate from Scotia, no matter how high her scholastic standing, until she could make a suit of underclothes, one dress, and one man's shirt.[45] In 1909, the Reverend Satterfield retired and the Reverend A. M. W. Verner was chosen to fill the vacancy. Mrs. Verner had been commissioned as a teacher at Scotia in 1908. During the succeeding five years, a small-scale expansion program was executed at the institution. In 1912 a brick barn was erected and in 1915 a brick laundry house was built.

A major change in curriculum and administrative policy was effected at Scotia in 1916. A four-year college curriculum was inaugurated and three years later, in 1919, the institution's name was changed to "Scotia Women's College." The Board first referred to the institution by this name in its annual report for 1920. The lower grades were dropped in 1919.

Mrs. Verner's health began to fail in 1921 and Dr. Verner resigned. T. R. Lewis was elected to succeed him. In 1925 a three-story building was annexed to Faith Hall at a cost of $10,000. It contained rooms for teaching chemistry and provided space for bath facilities. One third of the construction cost was contributed by alumni, former students, and friends. The music hall was destroyed by fire that year, but plans for immediate reconstruction were made.

During the 1920s the institution's progress was accelerated. In 1926, it became a teacher-training school, and one staff member was paid by the state in recognition of Scotia's contribution to its program of teacher

[45] "Barber Scotia College," *Snapshots* (New York: 1931), p. 4. Presbyterian Church in the U.S.A., Board of National Missions.

education. The music hall was replaced in 1929 with a modern brick structure designed especially for the purpose. It was made possible through a gift from Mrs. Johnson C. Smith of Pittsburgh, Pennsylvania, who had been a strong supporter of Johnson C. Smith University of Charlotte, North Carolina. It was completed in October of 1929 at a cost of $25,000 and was named "Berry Music Hall" in memory of her mother. This year also Mrs. T. L. Lewis died and President Lewis resigned. Mr. Myron J. Crocker became the new executive of the institution.

Nineteen hundred thirty was a momentous year for Scotia. The college department of Barber Memorial College in Anniston, Alabama, was transferred to Concord, North Carolina and merged with that of Scotia. The name of the combined institution became Barber-Scotia Junior College. The curriculum of the merged institution was reorganized to meet accreditation requirements of junior colleges by the College Rating Board of North Carolina. This, however, did not complete the period of transition. The Board of National Missions convened in Pittsburgh and voted to affiliate Barber-Scotia Junior College with Johnson C. Smith University. A specific stipulation in this action provided that the first two years would be at Barber-Scotia and the last two would be at Johnson C. Smith University. It was also understood that Scotia could send graduates to any school of their choice for the final years of their college work. Home economics continued to receive special emphasis, but the value placed upon sound scholarship, mental and spiritual development, and exemplary character never waned. The affiliation between the two institutions became effective in 1932. Dr. Leland Stanford Cozart, the first Negro to head Scotia, was commissioned to succeed Dr. Crocker as dean of the Junior College, which was at the time under the executive administration of the president of Johnson C. Smith University.

Dr. Cozart, a native of Oxford, Granville County, North Carolina, was a product of the Board's program of education. He received his preparatory training at the Mary Potter School, in Oxford, North Carolina. Following this he entered Biddle University from which he received the A.B. degree in 1916. Following his graduation he joined the Mary Potter faculty in the fall of 1916. In July of 1917, he was granted leave of absence and volunteered for the armed service in World War I. He returned to Mary Potter in 1919 as teacher and administrative assistant to Dr. George Clayton Shaw and remained until 1926. It was Barber-Scotia's good fortune to become heir to Dr. Cozart's leadership qualities at a crucial period in its history. Dr. Cozart was sensitive and responsive to the needs of the institution and began an intensified program of strengthening expansion. In 1934, the high school department was discontinued, and the college was given "A" rating by the Southern Association of Colleges and Secondary Schools. It also became a member of the American Association of Junior Colleges this year. In 1935, a brick home was built for the dean and in 1938, a teachers' cottage and barn were erected, a central heating plant was installed, the health department was revamped and expanded, and a school nurse was employed.

When the affiliation between Barber-Scotia and Johnson C. Smith was terminated in 1940, the executive title at Barber-Scotia again became "president." Dr. Cozart, as president, rededicated Scotia to the high purposes for which it was founded: "pledged to the task of building fine Christian womanhood as reflected in sound physical and mental health and rooted in deep convictions born of religion."[46]

Barber-Scotia celebrated seventy-five years of abundant service in 1942. Alumni, former students, and friends from far and near gathered on the campus in remembrance of the many achievements in the institution's history. In April 1943, the Board of National Missions voted to develop Barber-Scotia into a four-year college by adding the junior year in 1943 and the senior year in 1944. A nursery school was started to provide practical experience for prospective teachers, and a "larger parish" was organized in connection with the religious life program to serve as a laboratory for prospective parish workers who were studying at Barber-Scotia and Johnson C. Smith. Barber-Scotia was approved by the Southern Association of Colleges and Secondary Schools as a standard four-year college in 1949.

The grounds also had been expanded. Miss Mary Daniel made a gift of property adjoining the campus, and in 1946 several additional lots, adjacent to the campus, were purchased by the Board. In 1949, the home management residence for prospective home economics teachers was completed at a cost of $13,105, plus $600 for equipment, provided by the Women's Missionary Society of the Second Presbyterian Church, Newark, New Jersey.

On April 22, 1953, the Board authorized steps to be taken to amend the Barber-Scotia charter to eliminate any reference to race or sex, and this was accomplished in 1954. Barber-Scotia became coeducational. Its first male student was also the first white student.[47] During the same year

[46] *Barber-Scotia Catalog*, 1942, p. 9.
[47] Cozart Interview, Sept. 25, 1971.

Barber-Scotia received the class "A" rating from the Southern Association of College and Secondary Schools' Committee on Accreditation. In 1955, a major plant extension was achieved with the erection of the dining hall and student union at a cost of $116,000. Funds for this addition were provided through the sale of the Mary Potter School property, gifts from alumni and friends, and several legacies. In 1956, the institution received a gift of $74,000 from the Ford Foundation to increase teachers' salaries, and in 1958 the school became a participating member of the United Negro College Fund.

Dr. Cozart retired in 1964 after devoting thirty-two years of service to Barber-Scotia College. He was succeeded by Dr. Lionel Hodge Newsom who remained two years and resigned. He was followed by Dr. J. L. Gresham, elected in 1966.

Biddle (Johnson C. Smith) University
Charlotte, North Carolina

Among the many pioneering individuals who preceded the organized church program were the Reverends Samuel C. Alexander and Sidney S. Murkland, members of the Concord Presbytery of the Presbyterian Church in the United States, who worked in and around the Statesville area. They were joined by the Reverend Willis L. Miller, a member of the Fayetteville Presbytery of the same church, who lived in Statesville. Their common goal was the evangelization and education of the newly emancipated slaves.

Establishing an institution for educating a newly liberated, illiterate, dehumanized, and poverty-stricken people was a strange concept in 1865. It was stranger still when its inception took place in the mind of a former slave master and Confederate soldier, Willis L. Miller. In such a time and place the idea of the Biddle University project began.[48]

According to a letter from Mrs. Samuel C. Alexander, wife of the co-founder, her husband had contemplated establishing a parochial school and gradually building up a collegiate and theological school for the education of preachers and teachers among the freedmen. The Reverend Willis L. Miller came to visit them in the winter of 1865 and discussed his church-school concept for the freedmen, one in which the college and theological school should be built immediately. This proposal, which was in reverse order of the Reverend Alexander's plan, seemed unrealistic to the Alexanders since only a few freedmen in the county could read and fewer still could write. Miller believed that funds for the project as pro-

[48] Alexander to Martin, Dec. 6, 1910.

posed by him would be more easily obtained from Northern whites and the federal Freedmen's Bureau. An agreement was finally reached on the Reverend Miller's proposal. The three pioneers pooled their creative imaginations and energies and began to work toward the fulfillment of the Miller proposal.[49]

The Reverend William Alexander, a brother of Samuel, knew of the existence of the General Assembly's Committee on Freedmen of the Northern Presbyterian church and through correspondence, after the interstate communication machinery had been restored, effected the acquaintance of the three Southerners with the Committee's secretary, the Reverend S. C. Logan.

In January, 1866, the three white ministers were commissioned by the General Assembly's Committee as missionaries and were thereby brought together under the sponsorship of the Presbyterian Church, U.S.A. These three and also the Reverend Amos S. Billingsley had previously organized several churches. This sanction of the Committee gave the ministers courage to redouble their efforts. They set high goals to be reached before the meeting of the General Assembly that year.

There were basic legal operational steps to be taken, and they were begun:

On the 17th of March an Act was passed by a two-thirds majority of both houses of the Legislature incorporating ten men by name as a Board of Trustees of the Freedmen's College in North Carolina. These Trustees are allowed to increase the Board to 48 members with the limitation that they all are to be members of some branch of the Presbyterian Church.[50]

The incorporated body met in Statesville, accepted the state charter, organized, and devised plans for further action. The Reverend Miller was appointed general secretary and financial agent and was also appointed commissioner to the ensuing General Assembly meeting. Through Secretary Logan's influence, he was placed on the agenda for the General Assembly meeting that spring. Miller took their cause to the floor of the General Assembly, in session at St. Louis, Missouri, on May 17, 1866. Although it had been the consensus of the reporting committee that the proposed freedmen's college in North Carolina might hinder the usefulness of the Ashmun Institute (later Lincoln University) in Pennsylvania,

[49] Alexander to Martin, Dec. 6, 1910.
[50] Presbyterian Church in the U.S.A. (Old School), General Assembly Committee on Freedmen (Pittsburgh Press of Jas. McMillin, 1866), p. 19.

Miller pointed to the expense necessary for poverty-stricken freedmen in the Southern area to attend the school in Pennsylvania. He further stressed the urgent need for an educational center, in the midst of the suffering field, that would educate leaders in the climate of the field in which they were to serve. After prolonged deliberation, the Miller proposal was adopted, and he was able to return to North Carolina with the Assembly's approval of the proposed institution in North Carolina.

There were ecclesiastical problems for the missionary trio. They were all members of presbyteries of the Presbyterian Church, U.S., the Southern church, and yet they were operating under the guidance and sponsorship of the Presbyterian Church, U.S.A., the Northern church. The Southern church did raise the issue very soon:

> As soon as the facts were known to the Presbytery (Concord) these brethren were required either to return their commissions and refuse all aid from the North or leave the Presbytery. They chose the latter alternative, and on the 4th of October, together with a member of Orange Presbytery, they organized a Presbytery which they called Catawba. The Presbytery on its day of organization (October 6, 1866) received and enrolled two churches: Freedom Church, six miles from Statesville, in North Carolina, organized by Reverend Sidney S. Murkland, who for ten years served the Scotch Church as missionary to the Freedmen of Demarara and McClintoch Church, ten miles from Charlotte, North Carolina, organized by Reverend S. C. Alexander. Reverend Willis L. Miller was appointed Evangelist. In December, the Presbytery met in Charleston, South Carolina, received a Reverend A. C. Gibbs from the Presbytery of Philadelphia, ordained two colored licentiates, licensed three others and revived the office of Catechist as a necessity for the peculiar nature of the work.[51]

With these successful milestones passed, the Catawba Presbytery met in the "Old Colored Presbyterian Church," now Seventh Street Presbyterian Church, in Charlotte, North Carolina on April 7, 1867 and devised the detailed system of operating the institution, which was still called "The Freedmen's College of North Carolina." Alexander and Miller were elected to be the teachers, associated equally in the "conduct and management" of the institution.

Miller was again elected commissioner to the 1867 General Assembly,

[51] Daniel J. Sanders, "Historical Sketch of Biddle University," *Biddle University Catalog*, 1893–1894.

and he was also authorized by the presbytery, with the advice and consent of the General Assembly's Committee on Freedmen, to act as fiscal agent for the projected institution during the summer following. In the meantime, Alexander was authorized by the presbytery to organize the school and erect a suitable building for housing it.[52]

There were circumstances which dictated each act of the presbytery. Alexander's work among the freedmen before and after the Civil conflict had won confidence of blacks, but many of the freedmen were skeptical of Miller's record as a slave master before the War and as a Confederate soldier during the conflict. On the other hand, Miller, writing in *The Presbyterian,* August 27, 1902, makes clear:

> Any man from the North doing the work I did would have been killed. But I had been the associate of the pastors of the white churches and they kept the "lewd fellows" from me. Rev. Eph. Harding of Concord, was especially kind, invited me to preach for him, called on me and received me at his house. He told me that I was doing right, that it was a grand work, but I was fifty years ahead of my generation.[53]

Both the Committee on Freedmen and the new Catawba Presbytery felt that it was necessary for a missionary to reside at the location of the work, and so the Reverend Alexander sold his farm in the Steele Creek settlement, reserving a site for the McClintoch Church, and moved his family to Charlotte in 1867.

Some white citizens opposed strongly the choice of Charlotte as a location for the school, thus making it almost impossible to find a suitable site. However, Henry B. Williams, a businessman of Charlotte who owned considerable real estate, was in dire financial difficulties and was forced to sell most of his property. Alexander bought for himself a square of the Williams' property on C Street, later Caldwell, and on one of the lots of the square he placed a building which had been given to the Committee by the Freedmen's Bureau of Washington, D.C. This building was transferred from the Fair Grounds, where it had housed the Union soldiers stationed there, and was renovated to suit the purpose of both the church and school programs. An audience chamber was constructed for

[52] Sanders, "Historical Sketch," *Biddle University Catalog,* 1893–1894, p. 43.

[53] Willis Miller, "The Founding of Biddle University," *The Presbyterian,* August 27, 1902, p. 20.

church and school activities, and rooms were arranged in the rear for students. The other two lots of this square were sold to the Committee and professors' homes were later built on them.[54]

In the meantime, the Reverend Miller was traveling throughout the North seeking funds and attending the General Assembly in Ohio. Facts relating to these preparatory steps toward a school were publicized in many of the church periodicals and were brought to the attention of Mrs. Henry J. Biddle of Philadelphia. She pledged $1,000 toward the project, later added $400 to the original pledge, and expressed a desire for the institution to be known as the Henry J. Biddle Memorial Institute in memory of her husband, who had died in 1862 fighting for the Union. The Committee on Freedmen accepted both the gift and the proposed name for the school. A few months later Mrs. Biddle added $500 to her earlier gifts.

On May 1, 1867, the first session of the school was held in the audience chamber of the reconstructed Union soldiers' hospital building on D Street, now Davidson, in a section then known as Log Town but later called Brooklyn. There were eight or ten students in attendance during that first session which lasted five months. Calvin McCurdy of Wilmington, North Carolina, was the first student to enroll. In June, John Sykes was admitted and in July Miles Caldwell joined them. From this small beginning the enrollment gradually increased. In the primary branches the students were under the instruction of the teachers of the parochial school, and instruction in the Catechism and Bible was the responsibility of the Reverend Alexander.[55]

Both Biddle and the Catawba Presbytery were taken under the care of the General Assembly's Committee on Freedmen in 1867, and the ministers along with their well-wishers received the sanction of the Assembly with great rejoicing. On September 23, 1867, Governor Jonathan Worth signed the charter of the Henry J. Biddle Institute.

Secretary S. C. Logan was not pleased with Log Town as a permanent location for the school and attempted to secure eight acres of green pastureland in the Charlotte area from Colonel W. R. Myers. The Civil War colonel was unwilling to sell, however, unless the Committee would purchase the entire 130 acres for $3,000. This amount exceeded the Committee's funds, and the offer had to be declined. Expansion on the existing site was planned. A Confederate navy building, located in the old Confederate Navy Yard, was purchased for $150 in 1868. This build-

[54] Alexander to Martin, Dec. 6, 1910.
[55] Alexander to Martin, Dec. 6, 1910.

ing was razed, and the salvaged lumber was loaded and readied to move eastward toward Log Town. When Colonel Myers learned that the lumber was to be used for the school for ex-slaves on D Street within the eastern part of the city he changed his mind. He made the Reverend Alexander a proposition stating that if the school would be constructed on the western outskirts of the town he would give the Committee the eight acres. Alexander acquainted Secretary Logan with the Colonel's proposal, and the Committee gladly accepted, as a gift, the plot which they had sought in vain to purchase. Anticipating the approval of the Committee, Alexander turned the loaded ox-drawn wagons westward toward the green pastures on Beatties Ford Road. This unexpected change in events added a new dimension to the Committee's planning. Mrs. S. C. Alexander, writing many years later, remarked that this gift was one of the best ever received by the Committee as it enabled them to sell the property in town and transfer their entire interest to the new location.[56]

Under the direction of General O. O. Howard of the federal Freedmen's Bureau, a contribution of $10,000, in several appropriations, was made to Biddle. This amount made possible the completion of the administration building, later known as Logan Hall; two professors' homes; three small frame structures, named Asia, Africa and Australia, which housed students; a stable; a fence around the grounds, and the sinking of a well on the premises. All were completed and ready in August of 1869. Biddle, therefore, after two years of operation in Log Town, moved out of the reconstructed Union army hospital building into the reconstructed Confederate navy building in September of 1869 and began its long and fruitful career on Beatties Ford Road.[57]

Events occurred rapidly at the institution in 1869. The Reverend William Alexander, brother of the cofounder, was elected president of the institution but declined in order to accept a call to a Presbyterian church in San Jose, California. The Reverend Willis L. Miller, cofounder, teacher, financial agent, and crusader for the cause of the school, moved back to Statesville on October 9, 1869, and in December of that year terminated his relations with Biddle. This action on the part of Miller left S. C. Alexander as the only teacher on duty at the institution.

During the first two years of Biddle's existence, it is obvious that no one had been designated as president. The cofounders had been authorized by the Catawba Presbytery "to be associated equally in the conduct

[56] Alexander to Martin, Dec. 6, 1910.
[57] "Johnson C. Smith University," *Brevities* (N.Y.: PCUSA, BNM, 1936).

and management of the Institution." On October 9, 1869, however, the
Reverend Stephen Mattoon was commissioned to fill the office of president at Biddle. He accepted and began a long, significant career there in
February, 1870. He found one teacher, the Reverend S. C. Alexander,
and a small number of pious students when he arrived at the school.
Alexander severed his relations with the school in May of 1871. In 1892,
when the institution was celebrating its twenty-fifth anniversary, he was
invited to participate in the activities and he wrote this note to the
administration:

> Five years of my life I gave to this work in its most critical and try-
> ing period, and especially to laying the foundation of your noble
> University. They were trying years, full of self-denying work and
> calling for constancy, patience, and prayer; but I was wonderfully
> supported by Divine Grace, and never for a moment lost faith in its
> utmost success. I never felt seriously the pressure of Southern white
> opposition or contempt. My conviction of the essential rightness of
> the work and of the Master's favor in it, rendered me proof against
> anything of that kind. I only deplored what seemed to hinder or
> retard the work and nothing more than the apathy and want of
> liberality on the part of its friends—North.[58]

The first president of Biddle was a man of learning and experience, having graduated from Union College in Schenectady, New York, in 1842
and studied theology at Princeton. His several pastorates included the
First Church of Bangkok, Siam and the Church of Ballston Spa, New
York. He was, therefore, well equipped to administer the work of Biddle.

The fruits and labor of President Mattoon's predecessors began to
mature and ripen in the early years of his administration. In 1872, Calvin
McCurdy of North Carolina, B. F. McDowell of South Carolina, and Eli
Walker, also of North Carolina, completed the course of study at Biddle.
In 1874, Matthew Ijams of North Carolina graduated, and in 1876 M. G.
Haskins of South Carolina increased the number of graduates to five.
These early graduates began a stream of workers into the fertile mission
field that gathered momentum and increased in dimension as the years
passed.

The school plant and grounds also received special attention at this
stage of progress. In 1873, the institution's land was extended to twenty
acres by the purchase of twelve acres at a cost of $1,200. Great emphasis

[58] Sanders, "Historical Sketch," *Biddle University Catalog*, 1893–1894, p.
45.

was placed on restructuring the curriculum, as is indicated by the following announcements:

> besides a Preparatory English Course of two grades; Higher and Lower, and an English Normal Department covering a four year course, it has also a Classical Department requiring the same time, and a Theological Department requiring a three-year course.[59]

In 1876, on the basis of these innovations, the institution's charter was amended and the name, "The Henry J. Biddle Memorial Institute" was changed to "Biddle University."

Among the many devoted persons who worked courageously during the school's early period of growth was the Reverend Sidney S. Murkland, who had returned to this country from Demerara, South America where he had been a missionary. When he returned, the Committee on Freedmen was attempting to gets its program of education for the freedmen launched in the Old North State, and he associated himself with it immediately.

As a charter trustee, he worked incessantly and intimately with the founders of Biddle Institute. Known affectionately by the students as "Father Murkland," he moved among them with a refined and understanding air which lent encouragement and inspiration. His home on Davie Avenue in Statesville, North Carolina, was a haven of welcome with Mrs. Murkland radiating the same humanitarianism as that which characterized her husband.[60]

The school had made amazing strides in its ten years of operation and was beginning to fulfill the dreams and goals of the founders. The curriculum was an obvious imitation, as far as the facilities and faculty preparation would permit, of Princeton, President Mattoon's alma mater and also the alma mater of a large number of the faculty members. In addition to the structure of the curriculum, there was rigid insistence upon securing well-prepared, dedicated, Christian teachers who held degrees from reputable institutions and could measure up to high standards in the academic world.

By the concerted efforts of President Mattoon and his wife, who was a teacher of English Bible, and an eminent faculty which included the Reverend Thomas Lawrence, later principal of the Collegiate and Nor-

[59] BMF, *Annual Report*, 1887, p. 22.
[60] George E. Davis, "Address on the Fiftieth (1917) Anniversary of the Founding of Biddle University," *Johnson C. Smith University Bulletin*, vol. 8, no. 3 (August, 1942), p. 43.

mal Institute of Asheville, North Carolina, the Reverend J. D. Shedd who was afterwards a missionary to Persia, the Reverend Robert M. Hall, later pastor at Plymouth, Illinois, and Professor George L. White, who had helped to build Fisk University, the school began its survival struggle. The theological department was constructed to consist of three divisions—the senior, the middle, and the junior; the classical department consisted of four classes; the preparatory department consisted of the higher division of three years and the lower division, also of three years. The English and normal department, which was primarily teacher education, consisted of a program of six years of study.[61]

In 1879 the enrollment increased to 141 students. But there was also loss in that year. The President's home was destroyed by fire. There were no fatalities, but an extensive library and valuable records and documents pertaining to the school's founding and early development were consumed. In addition, Dr. Shedd, who had been closely connected with the school's growth, resigned to return to Persia.

The report of Biddle University to the General Assembly in 1883 shows the growth of the school under Mattoon's administration. The faculty has been expanded greatly:

Professors: Rev. Thomas Lawrence, D.D.; Rev. R. M. Hall, M.A.; E. P. Semple, M.A.
Assistant Professors: William E. Hutchison and George C. Davis
English tutors: A. Robertson; H. S. Thompson; S. B. Pride; S. B. Young.[62]

The following year, Dr. Mattoon resigned as president but remained at the university as professor of theology and church government, as he was appointed to the chair of theology created by the Board in 1884. The Reverend William A. Holliday was appointed to fill the position of president. Holliday, of Paris, Kentucky, had graduated from Princeton Seminary in 1865. After one year at Biddle, however, he resigned and returned to the position as pastor of the Prospect Heights Church in Brooklyn, New York, of which he was the founder and first pastor.[63]

The Board was delayed in finding a successor for Holliday and asked Mattoon to return as interim president for the year 1885–1886. This he

---

[61] *Biddle University Catalog*, 1884–1885, pp. 6–7, 11, and 15 and Rattley, "The Early Days," *Johnson C. Smith University Alumni Journal*, vol. I, no. 1, pp. 9–11.

[62] BMF, *Annual Report*, 1883, p. 13.

[63] *Plainfield Courier-News* (Plainfield, New Jersey) January 21, 1924.

did, and he retired the second time in 1889. He died August 15, 1891, and was buried in a modest cemetery adjacent to the campus.[64]

The Reverend W. F. Johnson, elected president of Biddle University in 1886, graduated from Jefferson College in 1854 and from Western Theological Seminary in 1860. He had been a missionary in Allahabad, India, for twenty-five years and was well acquainted with the objectives of the new program which he was called to direct. He set out immediately to raise the scholarship standard at the institution. The appointment in 1886 of the first Negro, Mr. George E. Davis, to be professor of Natural Science, had significant and long-range implications, and foreshadowed future trends in the operational structure of the Board's activities among the freedmen. Professor Davis had received the A.B. degree from Biddle in 1883 and had spent three additional years at Howard University in Washington, D.C. as a student of medicine. Biddle awarded him the Ph.D. degree in 1890. He remained at Biddle for thirty-five years and demonstrated his executive ability as academic dean from 1906 to 1921. He impressed the administration with the potentials of black leadership.[65]

President Johnson, with the support of the Board of Missions and the Slater Fund, expanded the curriculum to include an industrial department.[66] Instruction was provided in carpentry, mechanical drawing, cobblering, brick masonry, and skills in the general use of machinery.

A concern of the president was the inadequacy of the library facilities. He said, "Our library, while well selected, is much too small for our needs, but we have at present no funds for its enlargement. About 150 volumes have been added to it during the year, mostly by gifts from thoughtful friends."[67]

[64] Both the Mattoon daughters, Misses Mary and Emma Mattoon, were devoted to this work of their father and in 1917, when the University was observing its fiftieth anniversary, donated fifteen acres of land valued at $30,000 to Biddle. This memorial to their father extended the school's acreage to 75 acres. Miss Emma Mattoon later married the Reverend W. E. Thomas and their son, Norman, was the Socialist Party nominee for the President of the United States six times. *Johnson C. Smith University Newsletter*, 1964, p. 1.

[65] *Johnson C. Smith University Bulletin*, 1927, p. 38. Under its first charter as a university, Biddle was empowered to grant both the master of arts and the doctor of philosophy degrees.

[66] BMF, *Annual Report*, 1888, p. 18.

[67] President W. F. Johnson's annual report to the Board of Missions for Freedmen, 1890.

The year 1891 was significant in the history of Biddle University. The resignation of President Johnson in order to return to Allahabad, India, terminated his five-year administration. It also ended a period of almost twenty-five years, 1867 to 1891, of administration by white leadership at Biddle. The Board had to weigh the wisdom of placing the administration of the institution in the hands of Negro leadership. The idea was attended with skepticism and misgivings by both black and white people whose loyalty to the school had stood many tests. Despite the fact that the Board had envisioned this day of change in its original planning, the loud cry of "not ready, not ready" was disconcerting. Finally, the Board concluded that the change was both opportune and sound and justified its decision in the following excerpt which, because of its significance, is quoted at length:

In the very outset of our work and as necessary to its complete success, it was felt that, if we expected to prosecute and build up a permanent work among the Freedmen, colored men should be educated and trained as preachers and teachers for the race. Not that white men were to be excluded from the work, but that colored men and women might be qualified to fill equally responsible positions along side of our white laborers. For this purpose a college known as Biddle University, was established in Charlotte, North Carolina, some 20 years ago, and in these years it has educated and trained a number of preachers and teachers who have done honor to their Alma Mater. Heretofore, the college has been entirely under the control and direction of white professors, except one colored professor, who was appointed some years since, and whose services have proved entirely satisfactory both to the Trustees of the college and the Board. Last year the Board felt that there should be a reorganization of the faculty of the college.

The Synods of Atlantic and Catawba, composed largely of Negro men, though they did not express it in so many words, yet, evidently felt that this was due them. True, they were inexperienced in the duties of professors in colleges, but how were they ever to gain such experience unless they tried and opportunities were offered them in this line? It was certainly expected that they should ultimately fill such positions along with their white brethren, and the time seemed to have come when they should be given the opportunity at least to try of what stuff they were made.

The Board hesitated for a while, but the more the question was considered the more it was impressed upon the mind of the Board that the experiment should be made, and the doors open to them.

It was not, however, merely an experiment, for we had some knowledge of the capability of colored men in the management of some of our schools and Seminaries. . . . In view of these facts, the Board felt that it could safely nominate three additional colored men as professors in Biddle University, making four with the one previously elected, and retaining four white thus securing, as we hoped, the cooperation of all the friends of the Institution both white and colored. The white Professors, however, for reasons satisfactory to themselves, resigned, though urged very earnestly by the Board to remain. Three other colored men were then nominated together with one white, Rev. Dr. Bissell, professor of Hebrew, a ripe scholar and a man who has the confidence of his brethren. The colored men elected as Professors in the college are men of good scholarship, of high standing and having the entire confidence of both their colored and white brethren. Of course at this date we cannot judge of the success of our colored brethren as professors, and of the success of the college under their management as their first term has not yet closed. So far, however, they have given satisfaction both to the Board in Pittsburgh and the Board of Trustees of the college, and the success of the college has been as marked as any year of its previous history, and in the way of students, more so, having enrolled 203 against 175 last year. Of course we expect mistakes to be made in the management of the college under this new and untried administration but let us not be too ready to attribute their mistakes to incapacity because they are made by colored men. In opening the way for our colored brethren . . . [we] not only place before them the best motives to prove themselves workmen who need not be ashamed, but before the young men of the race . . . the noblest incentive to seek for higher attainment in education and learning.[68]

The Reverend Daniel J. Sanders, seventeen years a slave, was elected the new president of Biddle University. Fully aware of the ramifications attending his appointment, President Sanders girded himself to meet the challenge. Reminiscing about the rocky path over which he had to go to reach this position of honor, the president later wrote:

I learned a few letters of my alphabet from my more favored associates. Signs, advertisements, and any letters or figures, in whatever combinations, were utilized and all were made textbooks. It was required that these studies be carried on unobserved by persons outside the household. At the age of nine, I was put to learn the

[68] BMF, *Annual Report*, 1892, pp. 16–19.

Shoemaker's trade and served an apprenticeship of five years. . . .
I took to the trade and made phenomenal progress; In three months'
time I was making children's shoes. At the end of three years, I was
considered as having finished the trade and my master began to
collect pay for my services. . . . In some way a little book called,
"Crown of Thorns," came into my hands. I made a pocket in the
inner side of my shirt. Here the book was carried many months. For
quite a while it served as a speller. Later on, an old mutilated copy
of the "Blue Back Speller" (Noah Webster's Elementary Spelling
Book) was secured. Thus at the time of the Emancipation, I had
learned to spell and read some.[69]

There is also to be found in the president's remembrances a narrative
of how, in early March, 1866, on a Friday at three o'clock in the morning he secretly left his home in Winnsboro, South Carolina, where he had
been born February 15, 1847, for Chester, South Carolina. Here he
found work and a white tutor, Mr. W. B. Knox, who instructed him over
a long period. Studies in the *Blue-Back Spelling Book* and the *McGuffey
Graded Reader* were pursued religiously by Sanders and his progress was
rapid. Daniel Sanders later entered Brainerd Institute under the presidency of Dr. Loomis and studied under his personal instruction. He remained at Brainerd, studying, practicing his trade, and teaching until he
was prepared to enroll in a theological seminary. He was licensed in 1870
by the Fairfield Presbytery and enrolled in Western Theological Seminary
in 1871. He graduated with honors three years later with prizes in
Hebrew and Sanscrit. Immediately after graduating in 1874, he went to
Wilmington, North Carolina, and began a career of church and school
work which Lincoln University rewarded with honorary degrees of
Master of Arts and Doctor of Divinity. After fifteen years as pastor of
the Chestnut Presbyterian Church in Wilmington, he resigned to go
abroad in the interest of the educational program of the Board of Missions for Freedmen. He spent more than a year in Scotland and England
raising funds for the Board. This trip netted much for the program, both
in friends and finance. In addition to the sizeable sum of money which
resulted directly from his efforts, he impressed and motivated the theological students of Scotland in their collection of more than six thousand
dollars for an African Scholarship Fund at Biddle University.[70]

[69] *Johnson C. Smith University Alumni Journal,* 1928, pp. 2–11.
[70] Davis, "Address on the Fiftieth," *Johnson C. Smith University Bulletin,*
vol. 8, no. 3, p. 45.

When he was called to the presidency of Biddle University in 1891, he had been for fourteen years a member of the Board of Trustees of the institution. His previous administrative experiences included principal of the public school for Negroes in Chester, South Carolina. He had also been principal of the city school for Negroes in Wilmington, North Carolina, from 1875 to 1890. He had begun the publication of a religious journal which he named *The Africo-American Presbyterian* and he took this journal to Biddle University with him in 1891.[71]

Sanders, as the new president, realized that more than ordinary tact and diplomacy were needed in handling the administrative machinery of the school in this new situation. Sagacious discernment, tolerance and understanding, patience and wisdom, therefore, characterized his approach to the challenge which he faced. His fine qualities of poise, dignity, caution, forebearance, and integrity merited the respect that made the transition surprisingly smooth and satisfying. Despite the efficient operation of the program, some skepticism lingered, in diminishing degrees, as to the wisdom of the change. When the white faculty withdrew and the Negro president was appointed, some students withdrew with them. Following their departure only one white professor, Dr. Bissell, professor of Hebrew, was left on the staff. The new president, however, went about his duties with devotion and diligence while the student enrollment steadily increased. The black professors felt the pressure of the challenge and tapped all their energies, skills, and endurance to implement the solid planning of the administration.

In 1892, personnel was also changing at the Board level. The Reverend Richard H. Allen died, and the Reverend E. P. Cowan succeeded him as Corresponding Secretary of the Board of Missions for Freedmen. In Cowan's administration there was a stronger emphasis on the industrial phase of the Board's work among the freedmen. At Biddle, however, the industrial emphasis in no wise threatened its original goal of academic excellence. Frequently Board reports highlighted industrial training while the university catalogs placed emphasis on the religious and classical phases of its program. The industrial stress strengthened the Board's promotional efforts, however, since many white supporters felt this was the most sensible approach and more willingly financed it.

The early 1890s not only marked the change from white to black

[71] Dr. Daniel Jackson Sanders, *Down Through the Years*, ed. Arthur Henry George (Charlotte, North Carolina: Johnson C. Smith University, 1961), p. 24.

leadership at Biddle; they were also years of severe economic crisis in the whole program. Biddle went forward, however, under President Sanders' administration, and in 1893 the Board's annual report indicated that it was gratified with the progress being made at the institution.

Miss Mary A. Carter of Geneva, New York, gave funds for the erection of a boys' dormitory in 1895 at a cost of $15,000. The structure, named "Carter Hall" in honor of the donor, was considered one of the most substantial buildings on the campus at that time. It consisted of three stories above a basement and housed about one hundred fifty students. Subsequently, Asia, Africa, and Australia, the first three crude, whitewashed structures used for housing students, had served their purpose and were no longer used for dormitory buildings.

In 1896, the total value of Biddle's thirteen buildings and sixty-acre campus was estimated by the Board to be $125,000. At that time 260 students were under the instruction of thirteen professors. On the basis of its bright promise the Board made an earnest plea for a generous endowment for the school. Biddle continued to be the beneficiary of affluent friends, and its scholarship fund rose to $48,500. The Board's second plea for an increased endowment for the institution was granted in 1901, and $250,000 was added to the 20th Century Fund Movement for the purpose.

Soon after Dr. Sanders arrived on the campus he recognized the serious need for better and additional library facilities. Earlier presidents had striven to supply this need, especially after the president's home was destroyed by fire in 1879, consuming his extensive library which had been at the disposal of the students. President Sanders took definite steps to relieve the situation and in 1904 and 1905 made contact with his personal friend, Booker T. Washington, who was acquainted with and had the confidence of Mr. Andrew Carnegie. President Sanders solicited Mr. Washington's cooperation and aid in winning the interest of the generous philanthropist in Biddle University's library needs. Mr. Washington not only consented but also accompanied President Sanders to Pittsburgh and secured him an introduction to Carnegie. So convincingly did the President present the Biddle case to Andrew Carnegie that when he left Pittsburgh, he carried with him a provisional offer of $12,500, which was later confirmed through correspondence. The proviso stipulated that an equal or greater amount should be raised to guarantee the enrichment, expansion, and continuous growth of the proposed library. The Board accepted Mr. Carnegie's offer, expressed its gratitude and set up a fund-raising campaign to meet the stipulations in the offer. The Board announced these actions to the General Assembly as follows:

> Biddle University at Charlotte, North Carolina has on hand at present some 16,000 volumes which is the beginning of the much larger library the University hopes some day to possess. These volumes are now kept in one of the classrooms of the Main Building. The room is at the same time used as a class room. The double use to which the room is put reduces its value for either purpose for which it is constantly used. Dr. Sanders, President of the University, seeing that an arrangement of this kind cannot long continue for the good of the school and noting that many towns and institutions in various parts of the land were receiving libraries from one of the leading philanthropists of this country made bold to lay his cause before Mr. Andrew Carnegie and received from him last December that he would be glad to pay for a library building at a cost of $12,500 provided a similar amount as new endowment were raised 'toward the upkeep and carrying of the library . . .'
>
> The raising of this required amount—$12,500—has been referred to our Field Secretary, Dr. McClelland.[72]

Dr. Sanders communicated his own intellectual inquiry to the campus. This is seen clearly in the all-student activity known as "March Ex," an exposition which was one of the earliest all-student functions on the campus, combining art, music, oratory, and social festivities. According to the memory of old Biddle men, this activity was truly a rare exhibition of culture, charm, fine literary tastes, and the height of social graces. The following is the description of the 1908 event:

> One of the greatest events in the life of a Biddle boy is the "March Ex." It is the beautiful green oasis that suddenly dawns upon his vision as he treads the dull routine of his classroom work; the ray of sunshine that dispels the social darkness; the charming melody that breaks the silent monotony and cheers his lonely heart.
>
> Promising indeed is the outlook for this year's exhibition. The energetic and businesslike chairman of the Committee of Arrangements, Mr. I. E. Wilson, promises to have a banquet that will delight the most fastidious Epicurean taste. The Choral Society, under the skillful direction of Prof. Thomas A. Long, is preparing for this occasion veritable "gems of sweetest music" and in nightly dreams and daily visions the performers are visiting the Elysian Fields and

[72] BMF, *Annual Report*, 1906, p. 9.

communing with the departed shades of Demosthenes, Burke, Cicero, Webster, et al.[73]

During President Sanders' administration the school catalog listed "Affiliated Schools of Biddle University." These secondary schools geared their curricula to prepare students to enter Biddle without deficiencies. The list grew and by 1932 there were eighteen schools on the list with Barber-Scotia in a featured position. This official sort of relationship gave the feeder schools stimulus and motivation for higher academic achievement at the secondary level.[74]

After sixteen years of epoch-making leadership at Biddle, President Sanders died in 1907. His mission had been accomplished. The theological department had evolved into a specialized part of the institution's program. Under his administration the transition from white to black leadership was smooth and successful, to the gratification and complete satisfaction of the Board and all seriously concerned about the school's well-being. The Board was highly pleased with the progress of the school. As early as 1893 the Board had reported:

> Of all our schools, Biddle University stands at the head. It is the only institution under our care in which a young man can receive a thorough college education. Its eleven Professors, from the President down, are all colored men save one. It is just finishing its second year under the present regime and all friends of both the race and the College rejoiced in its prosperous condition and the signs of its growing usefulness.[75]

It was not uncommon for the Board to refer to Biddle as the "Capstone," or the "Hub" of its program which was indeed a tribute to its 1891 decision.

The Reverend Henry Lawrence McCrorey was elected in 1907 to fill the position of president at Biddle. President McCrorey was the first graduate of Biddle to become its chief executive. He had received the A.B. degree from the college division of Biddle in 1892 and the S.T.B. degree from the seminary in 1895. For twelve years he had taught under Dr. Sanders' administration and was, therefore, well acquainted with the university's program, its needs, and the previous administration's un-

[73] *The Argus*, vol. VIII, no. 3, March, 1908 (Charlotte, North Carolina: Biddle University), pp. 1–4.
[74] Johnson C. Smith, *University Catalog*, 1930–31, pp. 111–112.
[75] *Minutes*, 1893, p. 341.

finished business. The lean years of the nineties were subsiding and benevolence was on the increase. Much of the racial tension was waning, and the "experiment" of black leadership was proving to be sound. The new administration revitalized the library fund, and in 1911 it was successful in the complete library building plus $2,500 beyond the stipulated goal. Thus, six years after the originator's death, the campaign ended in success.[76]

Nineteen seventeen was a great year for the institution. During this year the high school department, which had been a part of the program from the beginning, was given an "A" rating by the North Carolina State Board of Education. This year also, the grounds were extended by a gift of fifteen acres, which increased the acreage from sixty to seventy-five acres. This gift, estimated at $30,000, was from Mrs. Emma Mattoon Thomas and Miss Mary Mattoon, the daughters of Biddle's first president. The gift was made during the institution's celebration of its fiftieth anniversary.[77] During this year, Dr. Willis L. Miller, cofounder of the institution, died in Oklahoma.

Biddle University began operating a summer session in 1919. North Carolina raised its qualifications for certification of public school teachers and, in view of the state action, many of the teachers who held provisional certificates as normal school graduates began to seek further training during the summer. To meet this need, Biddle University, in collaboration with the state, organized a summer curriculum. W. C. Donnell directed this phase of the institution's program over an extended period. In addition, those students who had suffered difficulties in courses during the regular session also made use of the summer session.

The 1920s were a new period of expansion and enrichment. One of the most substantial causes for this was the appearance on the scene of a new benefactress, Mrs. Johnson C. Smith of Pittsburgh, Pennsylvania. Mrs. Smith made sizeable donations to the institution from 1921 through 1929. During these years, Mrs. Smith donated approximately $400,000 for buildings and equipment and $302,500 for endowment. With the money designated for buildings, the following structures were erected: two massive memorial arches of stone marking the entrances to the campus; the Hartley Woods Memorial Gymnasium; a memorial theological dormitory for about eighty students; a science hall; a dormitory named Berry Hall to accommodate about one hundred students; the Uni-

[76] *Biddle University Catalog*, 1912–1913, p. 16.
[77] *Johnson C. Smith University Bulletin*, August 1, 1942, p. 44.

versity Church, of an attractive colonial design; three teachers' cottages, and a bungalow for Mrs. Smith's campus home. All buildings were constructed of brick except her stone and stucco home. Each building was well equipped for its purpose.

In deepest appreciation for Mrs. Smith's benevolence, the Board of Trustees of the university voted on March 1, 1923, to change the name of the institution from Biddle University to Johnson C. Smith University.[78] The Administration Building was given the name "Biddle Memorial Hall," thus keeping the memory of the original donor alive. This tremendous plant expansion strengthened the school and also made it possible for the school to serve more widely and more effectively. As part of this campus renewal, the General Alumni Association installed a chime clock in the tower of Biddle Memorial Hall at a cost of more than six thousand dollars. In 1924–1925, the school received recognition as a four-year college from the North Carolina State Board of Education. During this year also it benefitted from the generosity of a new benefactor, Mr. James Buchanan Duke, a highly successful industrialist and organizer of the Duke Power Company. Mr. Duke gave approximately $1,300,000 for the endowment of Johnson C. Smith University, a gift which added substantially to the school's security.

On January 1, 1924, Dr. William A. Holliday, second president of Biddle University, died.

During the decade of the twenties, the theological division was restructured. Until 1921 the president of the institution had held the combined title of president of the institution and dean of the seminary. This year, however, the first official dean of the Seminary, Dr. Charles H. Shute, was appointed. At the same time Dr. Arthur H. George was appointed professor of Church History and Homiletics and Dr. Algenon O. Steele was elected professor of Religious Education.

Wednesday, October 3, 1928, was proclaimed a day for manifestation of gratitude to Mrs. Johnson C. Smith for her deep devotion and extensive generosity. Dr. John M. Gaston of the Board of Missions, President H. L. McCrorey, Dr. Charles H. Shute, and Professor Robert L. Douglass spearheaded the all-out celebration. During the program George Newell, president of the senior class and representing the entire student body, presented to Mrs. Smith a sterling silver loving cup lined with gold. *The Johnson C. Smith Alumni Journal* tells the story in these words.

[78] Henry Lawrence McCrorey, "A Brief History of Johnson C. Smith Uni-

At the close of the usual devotional service, President McCrorey spoke words of thanks and appreciation and the appropriateness of the occasion in honor of Mrs. Smith.

Dr. C. H. Shute, Chaplain, and Prof. R. L. Douglass, one of the professors in the college department, followed with appropriate tributes of gratitude and appreciation. Some of those who had heard them many times previously said they "spoke as never before."

Those who knew what was next on the program were eager in expectation when Mr. George Newell, President of the Senior Class, stepped forward from among his fellow students and in manner and words that touched all that listened, presented Mrs. Smith, in behalf of the faculty and student body a handsome sterling silver loving cup, lined with gold.

Then, immediately following, Mr. A. E. Fortune, of the Senior Theological Class, presented a beautiful floral offering of roses and ferns.

The truly inspirational moment came when Mrs. Smith, herself arose to acknowledge the gifts. With her heart too full to speak at length, she expressed in a few endearing words, her deep gratitude and appreciation.

Then, Mr. Chavis began the college yell and the students broke forth as only they can for Mrs. Smith.[79]

One year and fifteen days later, this moment of great joy turned to sorrow as Mrs. Smith died at twelve noon, October 18, 1929. She died holding the hand of Mrs. Teressa Powell Underwood, who was the mother of two of the school's graduates.[80]

On June 29, 1929, the third president of Biddle University, Dr. William F. Johnson, died in Landour, India, where he had resumed his missionary work after leaving Biddle in 1891.

The high school department at the university, which had been for years the prime feeder for the college department, was discontinued inasmuch as public high schools for Negroes were approaching a level of respectability. Although the church-operated academies and high schools

versity," *Johnson C. Smith University Bulletin*, vol. I, no. 4 (May 30, 1935), p. 17.

[79] *Johnson C. Smith University Alumni Journal*, vol. II, no. 1 (October, 1928), p. 1.

[80] Teressa Powell Underwood, "Reminiscences of Mrs. Johnson C. Smith," *Johnson C. Smith University Bulletin*, 1942, pp. 47–48.

were producing better students, the Board felt justified in dropping the department with the 1929 graduating class.[81]

The new buildings brought many changes. Because of the construction of the new chapel building, a Presbyterian church—The University Church—was organized on the campus by the Catawba Presbytery. Between 1867 and 1929 students were required to attend religious services such as: midweek prayer meeting, young people's organizations, and Sunday school and church services on Sunday, across town in the Seventh Street Presbyterian Church, the mother church of the institution. A $10,000 pipe organ was installed in the University Church a few years after its dedication. Students and faculty were now expected to attend and support this church on the campus.

Music had always been a strong feature in student activities on the campus, and the new church provided an additional motivation for its expression. As early as 1907–1908, Dr. Thomas A. Long, music director, had organized the University Quintet, which made its first significant appearance before the 1909 General Assembly of the Presbyterian Church, U.S.A., in Atlantic City, New Jersey. For more than thirty years following that initial appearance, the Quintet sang before the General Assembly during its annual sessions.

The new gymnasium also had a great impact on the campus. In 1924 Johnson C. Smith joined the Central Intercollegiate Athletic Association. The first Biddle football team had been organized in 1890 and given the name "The Golden Bulls." According to "Ace" (Thomas M.) Martin, one of the early Golden Bulls of considerable fame, the first intercollegiate contest began in 1892. Interested students had met in 1890, organized a team, and elected L. B. Ellerson as captain. After two years of intramural activity they met the Rams of Livingstone College on December 27, 1892, in the first intercollegiate football contest to be staged between predominantly Negro colleges. This game, the Methodists versus the Presbyterians, was played in Salisbury, North Carolina, during a heavy snowstorm, and when it ended, the scoreboard read: Biddle 4—Livingstone 0. Forty-eight years later this event was commemorated by the National Capital Classic, while convening in Washington, D.C. in 1940. A plaque was presented to both schools at that time which was inscribed as follows:

First Negro College Football Game
Livingstone—0   :   Biddle—4

[81] McCrorey, "A Brief History," *Johnson C. Smith University Bulletin*, vol. I, no. 4, p. 18.

Dec. 27, 1892
Presented by
National Capital Classic
Dec. 15, 1940
Washington, D.C.[82]

Dr. R. P. Wyche and "Perk" Williams were two of the early football coaches. In 1938, Smith won its first Central Intercollegiate Athletic Association (CIAA) football championship. Norman Pettis of the Dallas Cowboys, Freddie Neal of the Harlem Globetrotters, and Vincent Matthews, Olympic Gold medalist in track (Mexico 1968), were among the Smith alumni to enter professional and international sports contests.

When Dr. Sanders became president of Biddle in 1891, he brought his publication, *The Africo-American Presbyterian,* with him. He built a printing press, equipped it with up-to-date apparatus, added a printing course to the curriculum, and took over the business of campus publications, and a large portion of the printing for the Negro community. Mr. W. E. Hill, a quiet, unassuming person, highly skilled in the printing business, was Dr. Sanders' associate editor. Mr. Hill had begun working with *The Africo-American Presbyterian* as a boy in Wilmington, North Carolina and, with the exception of a few months, remained with it continuously for fifty-two years. He was affectionately referred to as "Mr. Africo-American Presbyterian." Another outstanding personality connected with this publication was the Reverend William L. Metz, "The Sage of Edisto Island," a scholar, a wit, and a gentleman, well versed in the matter of Presbyterian involvement in the uplift of the freedmen. His column, "Blazers and Chips," made him famous in the circulation area of *The Africo-American Presbyterian.*

In view of these vigorous religious, intellectual, athletic, and cultural activities, the McCrorey administration was characterized as the renaissance period in the history of the institution. In 1931, the university received "B" rating by the Southern Association of Colleges and Schools, and in January of the same year the institution became a member of the Association of American Colleges. In 1932, Barber-Scotia was affiliated with Johnson C. Smith University. This arrangement, however, lasted only a brief period. In December 1933, Johnson C. Smith University was given an "A" rating by the Southern Association of Colleges and Schools,

---

[82] The writer witnessed the presentation of the plaque which now stands in the Display Case in the New Hartley Woods Gymnasium on Johnson C. Smith University campus.

and in 1934 it was elected to full membership in the American Council on Education.

The major reorganization of the boards and agencies of the Presbyterian Church, U.S.A. in 1923 produced some conflict between the former Board of Missions for Freedmen and the Board of National Missions with which it was to be merged. Administrative procedures regarding the schools and colleges which had been under the sponsorship of the Board of Missions for Freedmen were placed under the newly created Division of Work for Colored People, and from this Division they were switched to other church agencies in rapid succession. Fear for the schools was engendered in the hearts of those intimately affiliated with the work, causing much unrest among the Negro constituency of the Presbyterian Church, U.S.A.

With this turmoil as a background, Johnson C. Smith University appealed to the Board of National Missions for the status of an independent Presbyterian college. In reply to this request, the Board took the following action:

> That the Board of National Missions after September 30, 1938, relinquish any and all control over the financial support of the Johnson C. Smith University and assent to the University attaining the status of an independent Presbyterian University reporting directly to the General Assembly through the Board of Christian Education.
>
> That the Board of National Missions express to the Trustees of Johnson C. Smith University, Incorporated, its deep satisfaction of the progress of the University to date, its recognition of the contribution which the University has made to the Negro race and to the Presbyterian Negro Churches, and its hopes and prayers for the continued progress and the usefulness of the University in the work of the Kingdom; and the hope that under the arrangement now to be in effect the University will continue in the closest possible relations of cooperation and of mutual helpfulness with the Negro Presbyterian Churches and with the other Negro schools maintained by the Board of National Missions.[83]

This change to autonomous status did not represent a consensus at Smith or elsewhere and was, therefore, met with some misgivings throughout the constituency of the church. Barber-Scotia Junior College had been affiliated with Johnson C. Smith University since 1932, and this change at Smith placed Barber-Scotia in an uncertain position in its rela-

[83] *Johnson C. Smith University News*, January 1943, p. 4.

tions to the Board of National Missions. Therefore, as Jesse Barber states astutely:

> It was agreed that the best interest of the two colleges would be more effectively served by permitting each to proceed separately. As a result, Johnson C. Smith University became coeducational, while Barber-Scotia expanded its program and work to become a fully recognized four-year college for women.[84]

Duke Residence Hall for women was erected and dedicated in 1940 on the campus of Johnson C. Smith University and was named for its generous donor, Mr. James Buchanan Duke. Prior to this date women students had been housed off campus. In 1941 women were admitted to the freshman and sophomore classes. By this action the seventy-four-year-old institution became fully coeducational in all its branches.

On May 15, 1942, Johnson C. Smith University celebrated its seventy-fifth anniversary with fitting ceremonies. During this Diamond Jubilee celebration many distinguished alumni and friends gathered on the campus and this celebration revitalized slumbering loyalties and motivated a new consciousness of the need for active and generous support by alumni and friends.

In 1942, President McCrorey began to speak of retirement, and the Board of Trustees of the university created the position of executive vice-president. On September 1, 1943, Dr. Hardy Liston gave up his work as dean and coordinator of the program of Knoxville College, which was sponsored by the United Presbyterian Church, to accept this newly created position at Johnson C. Smith University.

Tragedy struck the campus in 1944 when the president's home was destroyed by fire, claiming the lives of the president's wife, Mrs. H. L. McCrorey, and the university nurse, Mrs. Emma Mathews. The fire was started by an undetermined cause in the basement of the brick structure and trapped the two women in the upper story, preventing their escape or rescue. President McCrorey retired in 1947 and was succeeded by Dr. Hardy Liston, who was inaugurated on October 20 of the same year.

Dr. Liston received his early formal training in the parochial school in Fairfield County, South Carolina. He spent six years in the preparatory department at Biddle, went on to the college division, and in 1911 received the B.S. degree. His graduate work was at the University of Chicago from which he received the Master of Arts degree in 1928. He continued advanced study in mathematics and education at Chicago.

[84] Barber, *Climbing*, p. 66.

Honorary degrees were conferred on him from Johnson C. Smith University, Maryville College, and Lincoln University. With thirty years of experience as teacher, dean, and administrative assistant, he returned to his alma mater in 1943 with a wealth of experience and training.

Dr. Liston was the first layman and second alumnus to become the chief executive of Johnson C. Smith University. He was a sincere humanitarian and a man of wisdom and vision, creativity, sound value judgment, and high ethical principle. Liston assumed the executive position at an extremely difficult period in the life of the school. The university was eighty years old and much of the plant and many of the personalities who had rendered services of inestimable value to the institution over a long period of time were beginning to show the inevitable signs which the passage of time creates. In addition, the effects of a devastating national depression, plus the toll of World War II, were to be seen and felt on every hand.

Dr. Liston was a mathematician by nature and training, as well as a shrewd administrator. With these qualities in his favor, he set to work immediately after assuming his new post to make disorderly operational machinery more efficient; certain positions were reactivated, and new ones created. In 1947, he initiated a campaign to salvage, reclaim, and renovate the degenerating plant and grounds and to revitalize the curriculum and increase the instructional staff.

Within Carter Hall, built in 1895, was erected an entirely new, modern structure at a cost of $65,000. By this means, Miss Carter's gift of $15,000 for the construction of the first substantial men's dormitory retained its historic identity. A committee consisting of faculty and students was appointed by the administration to explore the campus and make recommendations for utilizing wasted space and equipping the plant according to reasonable demands. Upon the recommendation of this committee, Biddle Memorial Hall, erected in 1883, the science hall, and residence halls, erected during the 1920s, received complete renovation. Biddle Memorial Hall's basement and fourth floor, which had been used previously for storage, were transformed into classrooms and office spaces. Along with other improvements, a local post office branch was installed on the campus.

Dr. H. L. McCrorey, president from 1907 to 1947, died on July 13, 1951 and was buried in the cemetery adjacent to the campus, near the grave of the first president of the institution.

Continuing his efforts to reclaim the plant, President Liston had Carnegie Library restyled, expanded, equipped with additional furnishings, and restocked with badly needed volumes. Adjacent to the library an annex was erected which provided needed room for expansion. From 1953 to 1955 a self-study program was launched to reassess the strength and weaknesses of the curriculum. Many sound and forward-looking changes were made at the general education level. The State Department of Education and the Southern Association of Colleges and Schools furnished guidelines for this study, and both were highly pleased with the results. Some limited grants for summer school study encouraged faculty members to resume study in their special fields. Also, in the interest of faculty development a system of tenure became effective, and retirement benefits were made more adequate.

The George E. Davis property adjoining the campus was purchased and renovated, thus relieving a serious housing shortage and bringing to the campus several professors and their families who were living in undesirable housing projects far removed from the campus. In addition, the science hall was completely renovated and named "The George E. Davis Science Hall." To help finance these ambitious changes, President Liston launched in 1950 a "Redevelopment Campaign." In connection with this project he published a brochure entitled, "An Overlooked Element of Community Prosperity and Well Being." The needs of the university were listed: a gymnasium-auditorium, estimated at a cost of $300,000; a central heating plant; a seminary building, and a student union building. With the aid of trustees, a host of sponsors, and an advisory committee consisting of men and women, black and white, the campaign was successfully launched.

The campaign began fulfilling its goal immediately, and campus transformations took place rapidly. The fund-raising had almost reached its goal for the erection of the gymnasium-auditorium when on October 20, 1956, Homecoming Day, Dr. Liston died. His death was a sudden and great loss to the campus. He was a keen scholar and an honest and warm person. Through his nine years of administration more than a million dollars worth of improvements were carried out.

Dr. James Ward Seabrook, a man of unusual intellectual power, a successful administrator, an alumnus and trustee of the university, was persuaded to accept an interim position until the vacancy could be permanently filled. He reluctantly came out of retirement—he had formerly been president of Fayetteville State Teachers College—to answer the call of his alma mater. His preparatory education was received at the Presbyterial parochial school at Sumter, South Carolina, where he was born. Seabrook's education was continued at Harbison Institute, Abbeville,

South Carolina, and, after completing the course there, he enrolled at
Biddle University and graduated with the A.B. degree in 1909. In 1923,
he became dean of Fayetteville State Normal School and later its president. He received the M.A. degree from Columbia University and pursued further graduate work there.[85]

At the first chapel service as interim president, he likened his new
adventures to that of Alfred, Lord Tennyson's *Ulysses*. The final six lines
of the poem[86] typified the life and ambition of the speaker so well that no
further challenge was necessary to unify the campus personnel during the
interim. After stating emphatically his philosophy of education, his
policy, and what he expected, Dr. Seabrook moved cautiously until his
successor was chosen. That occurred soon. Dr. Rufus Patterson Perry
was elected president on July 1, 1957, following the declination of Dr.
Matthew Whitehead, who had been unanimously chosen previously.[87]

Dr. Perry was born in Brunswick, Georgia, and attended the Board's
Seldon Institute there. He later enrolled in Biddle University and received the Bachelor of Arts degree in 1925. His graduate work was done
at the University of Iowa where he received the M.S. degree and in 1939,
the Ph.D. degree. From 1927 to 1943, he was professor and chairman of
the Department of Chemistry at the Prairie View College in Prairie View,
Texas. In 1943, he went to Langston University, Langston, Oklahoma as
administrative dean and vice-president and remained there until he was
elected president of Johnson C. Smith University in 1957. Dr. Arthur H.
George, writing in *Down Through the Years,* speaks of Dr. Perry in
these words:

> His warmth and quiet manner have endeared him to the Church,
> alumni, and people in all walks of life. With a fresh and undiscour-
> aged outlook, he has set himself to the task of elevating the college
> to a more lofty position in the academic field. With a dedication
> stemming from a robust Christian faith, he is striving to make the
> Christian image of an educated person meaningful at the Institu-
> tion.[88]

Dr. Perry came with a wealth of experience to guide him in the new
work and was acquainted with the school's purposes and goals. He had

[85] Dr. James Ward Seabrook, *"Down Through the Years.* Arthur George,
ed. (Charlotte, N.C.: Dowd Press, 1961), p. 35.
[86] Alfred, Lord Tennyson, "Ulysses," in *Anthology of British Poetry*
(Englewood, New Jersey: Prentice-Hall, 1960), p. 1160.
[87] "Dr. Rufus Patterson Perry," *Down Through,* ed. George, p. 35.
[88] *Ibid.*

kept contact with his alma mater. In 1942 he had brought greetings from the General Alumni Association during its Diamond Jubilee celebration, and in 1956 he had returned to his alma mater to receive the honorary degree of Doctor of Laws.

He assumed the position with a feeling that the plant should be greatly expanded. In 1961, a new gymnasium-classroom building was constructed to replace the outgrown Hartley Woods Memorial Gymnasium. The old gymnasium had been constructed in 1928 for a student body of about five hundred and, at the time, was one of the few regulation-size gymnasiums for participation in CIAA contests. The new gymnasium made provision for a regulation size basketball court and a swimming pool in its west wing to meet all state and CIAA specifications. With Dr. Jack S. Brayboy as athletic director and swimming instructor, swimming was added to the general education requirements for graduation, and swimming contestants were entered in CIAA competition.

In 1964, under the direction of Professor C. W. Kemp, the University Choir was chosen the official broadcasting choir for the Protestant Hour series during that year by the United Presbyterian Church, U.S.A.

A woman's residence hall was erected and named Liston Hall, honoring the late President Liston. The half-million-dollar structure was dedicated in April 1963. His widow, Mrs. Estelle Hoskins Liston, a Scotia woman who was an influential and dedicated churchwoman, returned for the dedication. Her children stood by her side while her granddaughter Charlene Muse unveiled the pictures of her grandfather as a part of the ceremony. Liston Hall was an airconditioned, modern three-story brick structure designed to house 152 women.

President Perry had initiated a self-study program to reassess the university's total structure—its curriculum, its students, its plant, its staff—and to project with a fair degree of certainty its future course. The study was rewarding, and implementation of its findings and recommendations were beginning when another change of administration came in 1968.

The celebration of the school's centennial began in October, 1966 with the lighting of the Centennial Candle—a one-hundred-inch-high candle, symbolic of the institution's one hundred years of service. The year was highlighted by an address by Martin Luther King, Jr., the 1964 Nobel Peace Prize Winner. These events culminated on April 7, 1967, with the formal Centennial Convocation.

Dr. Perry resigned near the end of 1968, and Dr. Lionel H. Newsom was elected to succeed him as the eighth president in 1968. He began his executive career at the university on January 1, 1969, liberally equipped with a rich background in many areas of education, community relations, military service, and social organizations. Newsom was born in Wichita Falls, Texas, and reared in St. Louis, Missouri. His intellectual curiosity motivated his matriculation at Lincoln University in Missouri, where he earned the Bachelor of Arts degree in history, *cum laude*, in 1938. Continuing his education at the University of Michigan, he earned the Master of Arts degree in sociology in 1940. He did further study at the University of Ohio and in 1956 received the Doctor of Philosophy degree in social pathology from Washington University in St. Louis, Missouri. Dr. Newsom had held many significant appointments in the educational field.

The impact of the unfinished business of the university's ambitious building program, which demanded immediate attention and needed changes in curriculum and staff, greeted the new president upon his arrival.

The Board of Trustees took steps to ease the pressure on the president's office when Dr. Newsom was elected. The office of vice-president of Academic Affairs was created, and Dr. Jack S. Brayboy was elected to fill the position. In a second action by the trustees the office of vice-president of financial affairs was created, and Mr. Harvey R. Alexander was chosen to fill the position.

There was a strong, emotional reaction on the part of many when the members of the University Church, with the approval of the Catawba Presbytery, voted to discontinue the church. Limited attendance and heavy operational costs were among the reasons for this move.

There was one other major change early in this administration which caused far greater reaction, however. In 1969, the General Assembly of the United Presbyterian Church, U.S.A., approved its Advisory Council's recommendation to relocate the Johnson C. Smith University Theological Seminary so as to become affiliated with the Interdenominational Theological Center in Atlanta, Georgia.

Only a few knew about the Seminary's brewing problems which came to light in 1961 when the General Assembly's Council on Theological Education appointed two committees to study the conditions at the seminary and make recommendations. The committees carried out their charge and made the following recommendations: the institution should work with all haste to have the seminary accredited; the faculty should be upgraded and increased to at least seven; the enrollment of twenty-four should be increased to at least fifty, and the library holdings should be increased. The administration agreed to strive to meet the committees' proposals. The faculty was increased to seven full-time, degreed professors; the library holdings were substantially increased and separately housed; the student enrollment, however, continued to decrease despite concentrated efforts to recruit seminarians. The annual operational deficit also continued to increase.

In view of the financial crisis of the whole university, the trustees voted that it could no longer assume the operational cost of the seminary and appealed to the General Assembly to finance this phase of the program. The final decision of the General Assembly was instead to merge the seminary with the Interdenominational Theological Center in Atlanta. The seminary moved to Atlanta in 1970, taking with it its library, including invaluable manuscripts and reference books upon which the university had relied heavily. Eleven seminarians were enrolled at the time.

The United Presbyterian Church at Work in North Carolina

Henderson Institute
Henderson, North Carolina

The General Assembly of the United Presbyterian Church of North America decided at its 1889 session to establish a mission in Henderson, North Carolina. In the early fall of 1890, the Board of Freedmen's Missions of the United Presbyterian Church purchased for $1,700.00 a thirteen-acre plot just beyond the city limits of Henderson as the initial step toward the establishment of the mission. A six-room dwelling with an orchard and shrubbery and a fine spring of running water was on the plot. The Reverend John D. Irons, who was spending some time in the area, supervised the enclosure of the plot with fencing and the preparations for the opening of the mission. A large school building and a teachers' cottage at the Bluestone Mission in Virginia were razed and reconstructed on the grounds in Henderson in 1890.[89]

The formal opening of Henderson Institute was held September 1, 1891, under the superintendence of the Reverend J. M. Fulton. During the first year of operation 586 pupils enrolled, and the principal requested an increase in his staff and additional buildings—one for sewing and housekeeping classes and two dormitories, one for boys and one for girls. The Board responded to the request.

The Reverend Fulton established himself in the community, and communicated the purposes of the mission to the people; thus, by the end of the second year, the institution was the genuine concern of the citizenry.

[89] Witherspoon, "Our Missions in Virginia," *Historical Sketch*, ed. McGranahan, p. 72.

The superintendent wrote to the Board that year: "in the day school we have 702 enrolled: 425 of them are regular attendants; the night school, for five months, reached 200.[90] Because of poor health, Dr. Fulton reluctantly had to resign after the second term. The Reverend C. L. McCracken filled the position September 1, 1893.

The Reverend McCracken's administration was church-oriented, and he rendered a service by eliminating appearances of competition between the two Presbyterian branches that were operating in Henderson and effecting a congenial relationship which was lasting. He was successful in purchasing from the Board of Missions for Freedmen of the Presbyterian Church, U.S.A. a small, neat church building and parsonage for $1,700. He died on June 28, 1898, and the Reverend A. N. Porter was appointed to fill the position.[91] Porter served the institution for one year and his successor, the Reverend D. A. W. Johnson, also served for only one year. At this time the Board decided to place the administration of the school in the hands of black leadership, and the Reverend J. L. Cooke, who had directed the mission at Athens, Tennessee, was chosen to make the transition. His prosperous administration was cut short by his death in 1903; however, the Board continued its policy of black leadership at the institution, transferring Dr. John A. Cotton from the Cleveland, Tennessee, mission to Henderson, in August of 1903. Under Dr. Cotton's administration the school grew rapidly. A new dormitory was completed in 1906 at a cost of $9,500, and in 1908, the McCracken Memorial Library was arranged and equipped in one of the rooms of the main building. There were also this year 400 students enrolled under the instruction of twelve teachers.[92]

Dr. Cotton was an executive of great influence, and he formed congenial relationships with the citizens. Toward the erection of the new dormitory, businessmen—black and white—along with other friends of the institution, contributed $1,000 and other valuable services. Although there was no official connection between Henderson Institute and the Mary Potter School, which was about twelve miles away under the care of the Presbyterian Church, U.S.A., the two schools coexisted for approximately sixty-one years feeling that they were sister institutions. The two schools rose to great heights in the affections of the people and in the high

    [90] Witherspoon, "Our Missions in Virginia," *Historical Sketch*, ed. McGranahan, p. 73.
    [91] Witherspoon, "Our Missions in Virginia," *Historical Sketch,* ed. McGranahan, p. 74.
    [92] Stewart, *May We Introduce*, p. 15.

regard of the state Board of Education. They became the strong mainstay for respectable high school education for freedmen in Granville and Vance counties.

After thirty-one years of an exceedingly successful administration, Dr. Cotton retired in 1934 as principal but continued to serve as superintendent of the United Presbyterian work in Henderson and Vance County which included, in addition to Henderson Institute, Jubilee Hospital and the United Presbyterian churches in Henderson, as well as Townsville, about fourteen miles from Henderson. Mr. Oliver T. Robinson succeeded Dr. Cotton at the school.

Mr. Robinson, as the new principal of Henderson Institute, worked diligently for several years. When North Carolina upgraded its high school system for Negroes, Vance County helped support Henderson Institute. In 1951, the Board turned the school over to the county and sold the property to the county. The Board's parochial school at Townsville was also turned over to the public school officials. Therefore, when the two Presbyterian branches merged in 1958, there were no United Presbyterian schools operating in the state.

Jubilee Hospital
Henderson, North Carolina

The Jubilee Hospital was established by the United Presbyterian Church of North America in Henderson, North Carolina, in 1911. Dr. J. A. Cotton, principal of Henderson Institute, after seeing one of the students die of appendicitis because there were no hospital accommodations for Negroes in the vicinity, resolved to build one. He donated a lot adjacent to the campus and began a fund-raising campaign for the building. He posted on the lot a sign which read, "This lot is waiting for a hospital." Two members of the Women's Board of Missions of the United Presbyterian Church saw the sign, were impressed, and their concern influenced the addition of the project to the Jubilee Movement, a fund-raising campaign of the United Presbyterian Church of 1911–1912. Sufficient funds for the erection of the building were collected through this movement, and the building was named "Jubilee Hospital." This building was soon outgrown, and in 1928 the Duke Endowment Fund donated a small maintenance fund. In 1929, the Duke Fund increased its appropriation to $1,579 and gave an extra $10,000 for expansion. The Women's Board provided a matching sum to this gift in order to have wings added to the building.[93]

[93] Stewart, *May We Introduce*, p. 20.

For several years the hospital maintained a nurses' training department, but it was discontinued when standardization requirements became too exacting financially. On the basis of its fine record, the hospital was permitted to remain in operation until a $400,000 hospital building was completed in January of 1959. Between 1928 and 1959, the Duke Fund contributed over $33,794, in addition to the expansion money, to Jubilee Hospital.[94]

[94] Stewart, *May We Introduce*, p. 21.

THE SOUTH CAROLINA SCHOOLS 5

At the same time that the Presbyterian Church in the U.S.A. was becoming strongly involved in North Carolina, there were several people across the border in South Carolina who were also developing schools and churches for the newly freed blacks. These pioneers, however, were significantly different from those in North Carolina, since they were predominantly freedmen. Among them, two, Ishmael S. Moultrie and Paul Campbell, are of particular interest.

Writing in the August 27, 1902 issue of *The Presbyterian*, the Reverend Willis L. Miller, cofounder of Biddle University, tells how these two men were officially brought into the Presbyterian program. In 1868, the Reverends Samuel C. Alexander, Willis L. Miller, and Sidney S. Murkland had been directed by the Committee on Freedmen to go to Charleston, South Carolina and organize the presbytery there. During the first scheduled session of the Atlantic Presbytery, Paul Campbell requested that the churches he had organized be brought into Atlantic Presbytery. Paul Campbell, as a slave, had been brought from Virginia to the islands off the Charleston coast by his master during the Civil War and was left stranded on James Island when the war was over. Like many other house slaves of wealthy planters, Campbell had learned to read and began preaching and teaching his people in the surrounding vicinity. Miller describes Campbell as being well-dressed, gracefully formed, nearly as fair as an Englishman, cultured in speech, and with the polished manners of the aristocratic South. Conversely, Ishmael S. Moultrie, who also came to the meeting of the new presbytery with his request for ordination, is described by Miller as a jet black, full-blooded Negro, broad shouldered, heavyset, and speaking a jargon that was hard to understand. Moultrie had also been deserted by his master at the close of the Civil War. His leadership ability had been demonstrated when he guided a band of slaves from the place where they had been deserted in the inland part of the state, over a 150-mile journey through the swampland back to their island home. The two freedmen preached to the presbytery audience and not only captivated the audience but also made a lasting impression upon the officers of the presbytery. Both men were received by presbytery; Moultrie was ordained and Campbell was licensed. There was great rejoicing among the people of the missions which had been started by these two freedmen. Some of the other pioneering freedmen in this impoverished region were the Reverend and Mrs. A. A. Jones, the Reverend and Mrs. W. R. Coles, and Mr. and Mrs. Emory Williams.

There were also white Presbyterians pioneering in South Carolina at an early time. Some of the Board's more effective and long-lasting schools were either established or developed by them. Coulter Academy, Fairfield Institute, and Brainerd Institute are outstanding examples. The Reverends Samuel Loomis, Stephen A. Mattoon, Willard Richardson and family, associated with these schools and others, made unforgettable contributions toward the establishment of Presbyterianism in this section.

In South Carolina, the major educational emphasis was placed on having numerous parochial schools, a few academies and institutes, and for a few years two junior colleges. When the program reached its peak, there were seventy-eight schools in the state of South Carolina. A more detailed history of some of these is given on the following pages.

Wallingford Academy
Charleston, South Carolina

The first solid footing by the Board's educational program in South Carolina was in Charleston. In 1867, Mrs. E. G. Wallingford of Pittsburgh, Pennsylvania, made a gift to the Committee on Freedmen to purchase a site for a school that would be a memorial to her late husband. The Committee purchased the site and constructed the building in Charleston, South Carolina, the commercial center of the state. In 1869, the Committee reported that the academy was the only school of its kind that it had attempted in the state of South Carolina. The grounds consisted of a city block, and the main building was used for both school and church. There was also a teachers' cottage on this lot. The Freedmen's Bureau of Washington, D.C. contributed about seven thousand dollars toward the total cost.

It was reported to the General Assembly in 1869 that the Reverend J. H. Bates was the principal, and the average attendance was 380 pupils.[1] The academy was chartered by the state of South Carolina in 1871–72. Bates' health failed after three or four years of conscientious endeavor, and he died May 10, 1871, in Glenn Springs, South Carolina, among strangers, except for a small Negro boy who had accompanied him.[2] Bates was succeeded by the Reverend William A. Patton in 1871.

At this early stage, the Committee held Wallingford in highest esteem, along with Biddle in Charlotte, North Carolina, Quindaro High School in Kansas, and other schools of higher levels which were under its care. The Reverend Patton spent nine fruitful years directing the continuous progress of the school and was succeeded by the Reverend Thomas A. Grove in 1880. By 1889 the enrollment had increased to 650.

In the fall of 1888, two graduates of Wallingford Academy were admitted, without deficiencies, to Biddle University's senior preparatory class. It may be said that the academy reached its highest peak of expansion during Grove's administration. It was during this period that the Board classified the academy as one of its most influential schools for freedmen along the coastal border of South Carolina.

The Reverend Grove was succeeded in 1897 by the Reverend David Brown at a time when the school's continuous progress was abated by a decrease in the Board's operational funds. Increased sacrifice and dedicated services of the workers at Wallingford, however, prevented a decrease in the caliber of the program it offered. When Miss M. A. Delesline, a former faculty member, became the first female executive at the academy in 1908, the enrollment had dropped to 189. She remained only a year and in 1909, the Reverend J. R. Pearson, another faculty member, succeeded her. This rapid administrative turnover continued. Miss R. A. Middleton, a member of the first Wallingford faculty, assumed the principalship in 1914 and in 1918, when the Reverend C. H. Uggams became principal, only 130 pupils were enrolled. Assisted by the Reverend Gorden, Uggams attempted to restore the academy's former prestige. In 1929, the Reverend W. J. Frasier assumed the principalship and made an urgent appeal to the Board, pointing up the dire need for the continuation of the academy:

[1] *Minutes* (Old School), 1869, p. 990.
[2] CMF, *Annual Report*, 1872, p. 5.

A survey was made with reference to the number of Negro children for whom no educational provision was made, and it was found that in our own community, there were five thousand children of school age running the streets, lanes and alleys. I have been here for eleven years and in that time no additional school buildings have been provided. Hence the crying need for Wallingford Academy to live and expand. It seems almost incredible that in the midst of this modern civilization such conditions could exist.[3]

Wallingford Academy continued its struggle to wield an effective influence. It had the machinery and the personnel to transform the undesirable situation in the area, but was held back by insufficient funds, which resulted in its discontinuance in 1933.

Larimer High School
Edisto Island, South Carolina

Off the coast of South Carolina and very near Charleston are located three islands: Edisto, James, and John. When its program was organized in the Charleston area, the Board's attention was drawn to the grave needs of the inhabitants of these islands. The situation was described in this excerpt:

After the Civil War, the islands off the coast of South Carolina, once prosperous plantation areas, were generally neglected. Many owners were killed, others moved to more promising regions. The ex-slaves were left to get along as best they could. As early as 1869, the Presbyterian Church began school work on Edisto Island.[4]

Edisto Island is a tract of land eight miles long and is located fifty miles south of Charleston. It is bounded by the North and South Edisto rivers and the Atlantic Ocean. The population was unlearned, poor, and superstitious. The terrain was profusely covered with tropical vegetation with expanses of fertile farmland in between.

In addition to the slaves on the lucrative plantations during the slave period, Edisto Island had been one of the corralling places where slaves waited the auction block in Charleston. Slave customs were deeply instilled in the folkways of the primitive dwellers and, when the church program reached the area, the inhabitants had to be "untaught" and "retaught." Before the organized program of the church was initiated there, however, individual pioneers were making valiant efforts to arouse and enlighten these islanders.

[3] BNM, *Annual Report*, 1931, p. 126.
[4] *Briefly* (N.Y.: PCUSA, BNM).

Ishmael S. Moultrie, a freedman, had been pioneering on the island, teaching and preaching and laying an early foundation for those who followed him. One island legend states that a Reverend P. P. Hodges, a freedman, served as pastor of the preaching stations; a J. Charles Moultrie taught the schools, and I. S. Moultrie went along before them as organizer and founder. During the slave period the church for whites had permitted the slaves to worship in the balcony of their church, but when the war ended the white congregation scattered and left the ex-slaves using their church building. When the white pastor returned and assembled his congregation, however, the freedmen were dispossessed. Hodges secured the Baptist church to house his congregation. The Baptist minister, also a freedman, assisted with the school work. Some of these black congregations may have been established by Moultrie before the end of the war, since many requested to be taken into the Atlantic Presbytery in 1869.

Larimer High School was the first school to be taken under the care of the Presbyterian Committee on Freedmen in this island region. It had been started about 1865 and was taken under the Committee's care in 1869. By 1875 both a church and a school building had been erected. The Reverend and Mrs. Moultrie continued the work there until 1893.[5] Several ministers directed the work of the church and school between 1893 and 1907, including the Reverends H. H. Hunter, Adam Frayer, and J. C. Carlyle. In 1907 the Reverend J. W. Mahoney took over both the church and school program on the island. For fifteen years he launched a vigorous fight against ignorance and superstition, and in 1912 the school was given a much needed school building, erected at a cost of $1,500.

The Reverend and Mrs. William Lee Metz were commissioned to take charge of the Larimer High School and the church on the island in 1918. Metz, who later became known as "The Sage of Edisto Island," had refused offers to go to Harbison Institute and to the St. James Church in New York City in order to accept the work among the islanders.

When the Reverend and Mrs. Metz arrived on Edisto Island, February 16, 1916, only twenty pupils came to enroll. These attended only when there was no work to be done on the farm. Most of the time there were only ten students in attendance, and four of them were the Metz children. The Reverend Metz was a warm humanitarian, scholarly without sophistication, keen intellectually, wise and witty, courageous and unafraid. He

[5] *Africo-American Presbyterian,* August 27, 1902.

had a deep insight into matters, material and spiritual. Along with his talented and industrious wife, he moved among the islanders, touching their lives and winning their confidence and affection. The Metzes walked and talked with the inhabitants at work and at play, casually teaching as they moved among them. The community became involved, and the school gradually became the community center for all progressive activities on the island. Far and near, the school was reputed to be a preparatory school of distinct quality, offering grades one through twelve. The diligent and persistent labor of the Metzes had been rewarded.

Journalism was another medium through which this preacher-teacher publicized the program at Larimer High School and other schools sponsored by the Board of Missions. Metz possessed unusual skills as a journalist and was eagerly sought by the *Africo-American Presbyterian* as a columnist. "Blazers and Chips," a series of articles highlighting the work of the Board's schools, was published in 1927 by this paper and is recognized as one of the most authentic records of the school work.

After thirty years of dedicated service to a people he came to love, the Reverend Metz retired in 1946, and Mrs. Metz succeeded him. Following her sudden death, the Reverend U. L. Brewer became principal of the Larimer High School in 1946 and remained with the program until it was discontinued by the Board in 1955. Concerning the closing of the school, the Board made the following report to the General Assembly that year:

> Larimer High School, established in 1869 on Edisto Island, and now one of the last of the major Board day schools of the southeast, will close at the end of the present school year. New schools and good transportation make this step possible. The Secretary of the Department of work in ABC Synods and committees of presbytery and synod are planning to unify work in the Charleston area. Part of the Larimer plant will be used to implement the public school program. Some of the present teaching staff will assist local pastors in a community-centered program of Christian education, medical service, library, and perhaps pre-school play center for children of working mothers.[6]

Goodwill Parochial School
Mayesville, South Carolina

There was a cluster of eight rural churches and schools established in the adjoining counties of Sumter, Lee, and Claredon in South Carolina: Goodwill, Ebenezer, Friendship, Congruity, Melina, Mt. Sinai, Trinity,

---

[6] BNM, *Annual Report*, 1955, p. 34.

and Westminster. The Committee considered the Goodwill Parochial its banner school of its type. It was the largest, with 371 pupils enrolled, and exerted a wide influence over old and young in the surrounding communities.

In 1872, the Goodwill Parochial School, Wallingford, and Ebenezer were listed as being the three most active parochials which were supported by the national committee in the Atlantic Presbytery.

Emma J. Wilson, a pupil of Goodwill, exemplified the kind of high aspiration and noble ambition which the school instilled in its students. While walking seven miles to and from school daily for three years, she became obsessed with the idea of being a missionary to Africa. Upon completing the course of study at Goodwill, she was encouraged and aided financially to enroll at Scotia Seminary. After three months at Scotia she had so impressed the administration that she was awarded a scholarship to complete her work there.[7]

The school was expanding in all areas of its program when the Reverend I. D. Davis began his long and prosperous career there in 1895. A sketch of him and his work is given by A. B. Caldwell in 1919:

> Rev. I. D. Davis, A.B., A.M., D.D., of Sumter, is said to have the largest Negro Presbyterian county congregation in the South. While he looks like a man of forty, he was, as a matter of fact born June 18, 1858.
> He decided to take up the work of the ministry in 1880, and was, the next year, ordained by the Catawba Presbytery in Charlotte, N. C. His first pastorate was at Lincolnton, N. C., where he remained six years, teaching in connection with his church work. From that point he went to Winnsboro, S. C., where he taught and preached for four years. He then moved to Sumter, where he has since resided, and has charge of a splendid religious and educational work at Mayesville.[8]

Miss Kate Moorehead, who had been principal-teacher in the school for fifteen years, gave up the work temporarily because of poor health. She was a tireless and dedicated worker in church school and civic activities and taxed herself beyond endurance. During the interim the school work was conducted by Misses Ashley and Boyden and Mrs. M. E. Fister. At the end of the Reverend Davis' tenure at the school the Reverend W. J. Nelson took over the administrative phase of the work, and Mrs. Nelson and Mrs. Hanna became teachers in the school.

[7] Caldwell, *History*, vol. III, p. 460.
[8] Caldwell, *History*, vol. III, p. 320.

Ebenezer Parochial School
Dalzell, South Carolina

The other parochial school of wide influence in this cluster was the Ebenezer Parochial School at Dalzell. It apparently began at the same time and fostered a program similar to that of the Goodwill School. According to the Board's annual report in 1930, the school filled a vital community need in organizing the black community even beyond denominational lines.

Goodwill and Ebenezer schools were discontinued in 1933, but the churches became members of the Goodwill Larger Parish in March of 1948. The Goodwill Parish consisted of the seven Presbyterian churches which were still active in the area. It provided recreation, promoted health protection, stimulated community consciousness, revealed the need for education, encouraged home ownership, strengthened community and individual resources, drew the ministers into a needed fellowship with one another and with their people, and helped interpret the church's program.[9] This partially filled the void created by the closing of the parochial schools.

St. Mary's Grade School
Blackstock, South Carolina

During the early days of the pioneer period, the Reverend Samuel Loomis was preaching and teaching the freedmen in the area of Blackstock, South Carolina. In 1866 he established a mission there in a farmhouse. Mr. and Mrs. Christopher Elder, a white couple, were the first teachers in the new school. They taught from 1866 to 1878, at which time the Reverend B. F. Russell of the third graduating theological class of Biddle Theological Seminary assumed the teaching responsibility.

As the school grew, it became necessary to have a principal operating under the supervision of the pastor-superintendent. During these years of getting established, the school shifted from farmhouse to farmhouse. The second farmhouse was adjacent to the church, which had become known as the Mt. Tabor Church. A more stable location was hoped for when the Reverend Russell began a building fund. Miss Mary A. Hemphill was one of the first contributors to the fund. The school was finally permanently housed, and by 1889, the Reverend Russell had two assistants helping with the 170 pupils enrolled.

In 1907, Russell secured the services of Mr. William Hemphill as prin-

[9] BNM, *Annual Report*, 1949, 48–49.

cipal of "The Russell School," as it was then called locally. After one year Miss Mary A. Hemphill succeeded Mr. William Hemphill as principal and began a fourteen-year career at the school in that position. The Board discontinued its operation of the school in 1922, but retained the Reverend Russell as pastor of the Mt. Tabor Church. The school also continued operation, although no longer supported by the Board, with the Reverend Russell superintending its activities. Two principals served the school under his guidance: Mrs. Alcia Wynn and Mrs. D. W. Parratt. Russell continued in his post until 1933. In 1936 the Reverend L. J. McRae, a Biddle Theological Seminary graduate, succeeded Mrs. Parratt and remained for eighteen years. At the beginning of the new school year in 1954, Mrs. F. G. Mays became the new principal of St. Mary's Grade School and remained until it was closed in 1956. The buildings and grounds were sold back to the people from whom the ground was originally purchased.[10]

The state had made some gestures toward taking over the educational phase of the mission, but the caliber of the state program in no wise met the educational needs of the Negro community as had St. Mary's Grade School.

Fairfield Institute
Winnsboro, South Carolina

Fairfield Institute was founded in Winnsboro, South Carolina in 1867, by the Reverend Willard Richardson, who was ably assisted by his wife and their children, Clara and Oscar, both of whom were strong contributors to the success of the institution. Clara Richardson was an educated and experienced teacher, though still a young woman, when she came to Winnsboro with her parents. Because of her dedicated services in and beyond the classroom, she was held in highest esteem by the students. Her knowledge and love of music greatly enhanced her usefulness to the developing institution. She organized a music ensemble called "The Carolina Singers" which were the delight of black and white audiences. Miss Richardson was assisted by her brother, Oscar, whose resonant bass voice was a great addition.

The institute was established on a city lot of more than an acre. On this lot were erected a home, a church, and a school building. This little acreage was, in every sense of the word, dedicated to religious education

---

[10] Interview with Mrs. Cora Russell Young of Columbia, South Carolina, December, 1963. She is the daughter of the Reverend B. F. Russell.

with great emphasis on preparation for the ministry. The institution soon became an educational center in Fairfield County and the surrounding vicinity. Its greatest disadvantage was the lack of adequate facilities to accommodate properly the large numbers that flocked to the school. During the early days of the school's development, nine young men lived in one of the classrooms, and nine girls occupied the old "Negro Quarters," a light frame shell.

The school was temporarily suspended in 1873 so that the Reverend Richardson could solicit funds. The school was soon reopened, however, and in 1878, Richardson reported 390 pupils in attendance. In 1879 Miss Julia Tripp joined the teaching staff, and in 1884 the Reverend J. C. Walkins was added. "In 1883 the Board reported five buildings, a dwelling house, a boarding hall, two dormitories, and a school building."[11]

During its twenty-one years, Fairfield Institute was in the top rank of the Board's preparatory schools in its production of prominent leadership among the Negroes. It was, however, located within twenty miles of Brainerd Institute at Chester, and the Board contemplated consolidating it with Brainerd since the two schools, very similar in character, were so near to one another. The Fairfield property was sold and the proceeds, after settling some old claims against the property, were transferred to Brainerd at Chester. The brilliant career of Fairfield Institute ended, and the Richardson family returned to their home in Delaware in 1888.

As a postlude to this closure, the Reverend William Metz, writing in the *Africo-American Presbyterian* in 1927, paid the Richardson family and the school this compliment:

> Some of our best constructive work in the State of South Carolina, in those early days of Home Mission work among Negroes by early pioneers who blazed the way for greater service among a people just emerged from slavery, was at Winnsboro and in and about Fairfield County, by Rev. W. Richardson. Some of our strongest men and most active women in Christian service are products of the once famous Fairfield Institute, which was organized by Rev. Willard Richardson when he came south from Houston, Delaware in 1867. He suggested and organized the first graded school system in Winnsboro among the colored and white people. He established and maintained this school, Fairfield Institute, for over twenty years for Negro youths. He organized eight churches of the Presbyterian Faith in Fairfield County, besides assisting in the organization of Baptist and Methodist churches. . . . No groups of northern white

[11] *Minutes*, 1883, p. 801.

teachers ever worked harder and with more brilliant success than
Rev. Richardson and his family.[12]

Blufton Institute
Beaufort County, South Carolina

The Committee of Missions for Freedmen made few efforts to extend
its program in South Carolina during the early days of the Reconstruction
period. In instances which were deemed critical, however, some attempts
were made to meet the challenge. Such was the situation which motivated
the establishment of the Blufton Institute in Beaufort County on March
18, 1877. It was considered by the Committee to be a promising location
at which to try its combined church-school policy in order to alleviate the
undesirable conditions there.

The Reverend J. Douglas Robertson had initiated and operated a
church and school at Blufton, and in his urgent appeal to the Committee
reported 171 pupils in attendance. He also explained in this appeal the
character of the problem he faced. There were, according to Robertson,
30,000 black people in an area of more than twenty-four hundred square
miles without a Presbyterian church. There were about one hundred
thirty schools and more than a thousand families who owned their homes
and farms. Rev. Robertson issued this evaluation:

> The field is ripe for harvest. The people crave instruction. The
> religious instinct is strongly developed in them, it leads to a species
> of fetishism. Under proper training it will become a devoted Chris-
> tianity. Under Presbyterian training it will become an enlightened
> Christianity as well. The intellectual training of our parish school
> system is admirably adapted to hold in check the impassioned
> temperament of the African. His ardent nature needs the curb. Our
> schools will be the curbs to control, to direct, to guide. The school to
> save and cultivate; the Church to reap. The State schools are of
> comparatively little advantage. They are open only three months out
> of twelve. The other nine months give plenty of time to forget what
> has been taught in the three. Result: no progress.
> With Blufton as a centre, Mr. Robertson names seven outposts or
> stations for primary schools and aggressive church work combined,
> at most, if not at all of which some colored Presbyterian element is
> found. He also names two other points in the same county, as
> centres for a like work, and with each seven outlying stations to be
> connected—each station ten miles from the centre and nearly as far

[12] William Metz, "Blazers and Chips," *Africo-American Presbyterian*, vol.
XLIX, no. 37, September 15, 1927, p. 1.

from each other. Of his own, he says, "In my immediate field, the people are poor and ignorant, but anxious that their children shall be taught. They rejoice that your Committee has commenced the good work here. They pray for your success and will cooperate in every way in which they can."[13]

The Committee's annual report for 1879 described favorably the location, enrollment, and needs of this community but attached this final note in conclusion, "But for reasons entirely satisfactory to your Committee, it has—for the present, at least—suspended its work at this point, the same to take effect from and after April 15, 1879."[14] Blufton's short-lived career paralleled that of several parochial schools in rural South Carolina.

Immanuel Institute
Aiken, South Carolina

The Committee accelerated its program in South Carolina during the 1880s by establishing or taking under its care one or more schools per year during the decade.

Immanuel Institute was established by the Reverend W. R. Coles in Aiken in 1881. Its beginning was in a rented house containing about six rooms. When Coles arrived in Aiken with the ambition of establishing a school and church, there were only two Presbyterians in the community, a Mr. Green and his mother, both ex-slaves. Coles was faced with the problem of recruiting members as well as of location and housing. After all the legal steps were taken, Coles found a suitable plot three miles from town and bargained successfully with the owner. He immediately launched an intensive fund-raising drive to purchase the property. The Greens gave the first ten dollars, and at a prayer meeting held at their home urged the people to contribute generously. The campaign ended successfully and the property was purchased.

The first building owned by the mission, after renovation, was used for school, church, parsonage, and boarding department, from 1882 to 1886. A church building was erected in 1886 with a seating capacity of 250. The third building acquired was Derby Hall, a distinctive building with a mansard roof and thirty-five rooms for boarding students and teachers.

The school was taken under the Board's care in 1889 and a new building was erected. By 1901, the school had an enrollment of 206, a staff of

---

[13] CMF, *Annual Report*, 1878, p. 23.
[14] *Minutes*, 1879, p. 717.

11 and a program consisting of a boarding school, with a normal and industrial department, a church, and a Sunday school.

During a celebration of progress at the school in 1896, testimonies of praise were given concerning the services of the institution to Aiken and the vicinity. In the messages of these representative citizens, however, was an overtone of anxiety concerning the school's future.[15] The Board of Missions, in its annual report of 1906, wrote ". . . the Immanuel School is doing its part towards the uplift of the backward race in that section. . . . [There is] urgent need of improvement and better facilities if it is to continue to compete with other schools in that section."[16] Coles and his staff continued the work for three more years. Then he resigned and the school was closed for two years.

The school reopened in 1911, with the Reverend James E. Jackson as principal. Jackson, writing in the *Home Mission Monthly*, said: "Old things have passed away and all things have become new. The New Immanuel again takes her place among the schools under the care of the Board of Missions for Freedmen, with new management, new equipment and new ideals."[17]

The Reverend Jackson reorganized the work at the school and began a campaign to reestablish its former prestige. In 1913 the Board reported:

At Aiken, S. C., after some years of patient waiting we have come into possession of a valuable piece of school property, in which we formerly maintained a school for a number of years, but which we had to abandon in order to preserve our own good name. Contrary to our general policy we had been induced to take under our care this school where we did not absolutely own and control the entire property. Our only course was to close the school, as far as we were concerned, and wait. The waiting came to an end within this last year on terms exceedingly favorable to our Board. The property had been in the meantime sadly neglected and it required the expenditure of $1,280 to put the dormitory in good condition. Everything is now in good shape and with a good man at the head, we are now only waiting the return of public confidence to make this school one of the best in its class.[18]

[15] Interview with Mrs. H. C. Dugas of Charlotte, North Carolina, by the author, in December, 1964. She is the daughter of Dr. W. R. Coles.
[16] BMF, *Annual Report*, 1906, pp. 165–166.
[17] James E. Jackson, "Good Cheer at Immanuel School," *Home Mission Monthly*, vol. 27, no. 6 (April, 1913), p. 141.
[18] BMF, *Annual Report*, 1913, p. 12.

One of the Board's problems at Immanuel was a matter of clear title to property ownership. This problem was solved during the period between 1909 and 1911. Obviously there were also other serious but unspecified problems. In 1914 the school was given a new name, "Andrew Robertson Institute," with the same principal and faculty operating it. Jackson remained at the school as principal until 1924. The Reverend L. E. Ginn became principal of the school in 1924 but the school was closed in 1930–1931, and the property sold to a Mr. G. K. Toole.[19]

Brainerd Institute
Chester, South Carolina

The taproot of Brainerd reaches back into the years where it is lost in legends. The most reliable of these legends reveals that in 1866, a Mr. Harris of Chester, South Carolina, requested the Freedmen's Committee of the Presbyterian Church, U.S.A. (New School branch) to establish a school for former slaves on the Brawley plantation. During that same year, a Miss Richmond from New York established a school there and lived and taught in a log cabin during the summer and spring of that year. In the fall the school was moved five miles away to Chester, South Carolina, and Miss Richmond was joined in the relocated school by Miss Caroline Kent from New Jersey. They established a day and night school, as well as a Sunday school, on the second floor of a large storage building. Here preaching services by invited Negro ministers were also held at frequent intervals.

In the fall of 1868, the Board of Home Missions of the New School branch of the divided church sent the Reverend Samuel Loomis to explore upper South Carolina with a view to establishing churches and schools among the blacks at such points as seemed advisable for beginning the program. After pioneering through the designated section, he arrived in Chester, South Carolina, in December of 1868 and chose it as a most promising beginning point. Soon after his arrival, he established a church, and the existing school being operated by Misses Richmond and Kent was reorganized. Miss Richmond terminated her services at the school, and Mrs. Loomis and Miss Kent became the teachers of the reorganized school.

The school grew rapidly, and in 1869 both the school and church were moved into another building, known locally as "The Old Commissary." Until this time the school was referred to as "the County Parochial School at Chester," but soon after going into this building the name was

[19] Dugas interview, Dec., 1964.

changed to "The Brainerd Mission School" in memory of David Brainerd, the revered missionary to the Indians who pioneered in Massachusetts and along the Delaware and Susquehanna rivers during colonial days. Miss Kent, being acquainted with the local character of the situation in and around Chester, had been indispensable to the mission, and her resignation at the end of that school year was accepted with deep regret. In describing the mission, the Board made this comment: "The County Parochial School at Chester, S. C., Rev. Samuel Loomis, Supt., is well located at the end of Chester, upon a lot containing one acre and a quarter. Upon this it has a neat two-story frame building, 24 x 44 ft., combining schoolrooms and rooms for a missionary 'Home,' the former on the first floor and the latter on the second."[20] The Board felt that the school had great promise and solicited funds for the completion of the school building. The report for that year also stated that a church had been erected at a cost of $1,000, a donation from Mrs. A. C. Brown of New York City.

The years passed; the enrollment increased rapidly and the influence of the school spread, attracting students from miles around. All of this necessitated expanded quarters. Proportionate with the expansion was the increase in the services of the Reverend and Mrs. Loomis. Their varied services involved training and supervising catechists, training teachers for the newly established public schools for Negroes, and revising and updating the curriculum to meet the demands.

Upon the recommendation of Loomis, the Board of Missions for Freedmen purchased a twenty-acre plot on which was a "fine old mansion." The new location struck a sharp contrast with the former quarters. The school made the move to its permanent location, redesigning for its own use the lawn and mansion of an affluent pre-Civil War aristocrat. By the end of 1869, the entire plant had been transferred to the Board of Home Missions of the Presbyterian Church, the Freedmen's Department.[21] The influence of the Loomises spread to York and Chester counties, and by 1873 the school had two additional cottages in use. The fine old mansion served as a girls' dormitory until 1925 when it was greatly damaged by fire.[22] The name of the school became "Brainerd Institute" in 1873.

[20] *Minutes*, 1872, p. 158.
[21] "A Brief of Pertinent Facts of the Founding, Growth, and Progress, of Brainerd Institute, Chester, S. C." (New York: Presbyterian Church in the U.S.A., Board of National Missions, n.d.), p. 2.
[22] BNM, *Annual Report*, 1925, p. 159.

In 1878, the Reverend Loomis made the following report to the Board:

> In the four counties: Chester, York, Lancaster, and Union, Brainerd Institute is the only school for the colored people above the grade of primary. The state is providing primary schools, and the law has just passed the Legislature to open for them also a university. But for *training schools for teachers* and those affording academic and high school facilities *nothing* is done. The state is working at the top and laying good foundations at the *bottom* but the necessary work—intermediate—is wholly neglected. Whatever of this work is being done, the Presbyterian Church is doing it.[23]

The report that year also described in detail the nature of and the need for the following departments at Brainerd: a department for training catechists; a department chiefly for training teachers for the public schools; a high school department with Presbyterian influence, and a department for training the best students for advanced studies at the college and university levels. He added that a "town parochial school" had always been a part of the school's work.

In 1879, there were two public schools connected with Brainerd, both under the Reverend Loomis's supervision. The public school authorities eventually gave to Loomis the responsibility of supervising the entire public school work for black children in Chester.

Brainerd expanded faster in many areas than did many of the Board's other schools. One reason was that it was not hampered by the intense hostility that was present in many other localities. In a later report, Loomis announced the addition of an industrial department to the curriculum, and in 1882 the report included the following description of the school:

> The Institute buildings are beautifully situated on nearly two acres of ground, not far from the centre of town, and near the three railroad depots. These comprise the chapel, Institute building and two cottages containing dining room and kitchen with rooms for students . . . a large two-story mansion, 50 x 80 feet, with extended piazzas, airy, well-furnished rooms and ample accommodations for a large number of students. This building has attached to it about ten acres of ground, and is situated on a level plateau on the range of hills east of the town, two sides pointing on main streets.[24]

[23] *Minutes*, 1878, pp. 201–202.
[24] *Minutes*, 1882, p. 214.

This was the first report containing a specific description of the estate on which the "fine old mansion" was located.

In 1889, a large recitation building was added to the plant, which provided living quarters for the boys. The superintendent stated that generous contributions had been made by students and alumni.

Loomis retired in 1892 after twenty-four years of broad and constructive services to Brainerd, Chester, and the surrounding areas. Near the conclusion of his tenure, he made the following statement:

> The years between the little parochial school and Brainerd Institute were fraught with hills of difficulty, sloughs of despond, and labor abundant—a recital of which would make a volume of itself as heart stirring as Livingstone's letters from Africa. The Lord's presence lighted the gloomy surroundings, as favoring providences were intermingled with discouragements.[25]

In September of 1892, Professor and Mrs. John S. Marquis of Washington, Pennsylvania were commissioned to direct the work at Brainerd, and with a devoted staff of workers they continued the school's rapid progress. In 1913, they suffered a temporary loss as the boys' dormitory and a teachers' cottage were burned. Three years later, Kumler Hall was built in memory of the Reverend Dr. Kumler by his daughter, Mrs. William M. McKelvey of Pittsburgh, Pennsylvania.[26] The new administration became deeply involved in the Board's program in and around Chester, and the Marquises remained at Brainerd for thirty-six years. Marquis resigned in 1928 when his health began to fail and was succeeded by Professor J. D. Martin, Sr., a professor at Johnson C. Smith University. When Professor Martin took charge of the school, the first all-Negro faculty was introduced at Brainerd.

During the seven-year tenure of Professor Martin, Brainerd experienced significant progress. At the opening of the fall term of 1930, junior college work was added; the teaching staff was increased to fourteen, and there were twenty-two graduates at the end of that school year. Professor Martin retired in 1934 and was succeeded by Professor and Mrs. L. S. Brown, of Charlotte, North Carolina.

The operational plan of the Board of National Missions was restructured in 1932, and the majority of the work with Negroes was executed by the Unit of Work with Colored People. Professor Brown came to the executive position at Brainerd under the new system and sensed the deep

[25] *Brainerd Institute Catalog*, 1901–1902, p. 1.
[26] *Brainerd Institute Catalog*, 1934–1935, p. 2.

concern of the black community about the possible ramifications of the reorganization for the black Presbyterian schools. There was a prevailing fear that the change threatened both the prestige and longevity of Brainerd. Professor Brown strove for five years to establish with the Board that there was no adequate substitute in the near vicinity for Brainerd. Despite all his efforts, the school was discontinued in 1939. According to the Board, the closure was due to budgetary conditions which made necessary rehabilitation of the plant impossible. The portion of the Brainerd Institute property located on Lancaster Street was sold to R. E. Hamrick of Chester, South Carolina, August 27, 1940.

Bethany Parochial School
McConnellsville, South Carolina

The Board continued its expansion in South Carolina with the establishment of the Bethany Parochial School at McConnellsville in 1878, with the Reverend and Mrs. A. A. Jones in charge. While pioneering in Georgia, Jones received the following letter from H. N. Payne, Field Secretary of the Board of Missions for Freedmen:

Rev. A. A. Jones

Dear Sir:—

How would you like to move to South Carolina and take charge of an important work under our Board? The field is now vacant but there are several applications for it. It is not very far from Mrs. Jones' former home—Spartanburg, and I have thought, on that account, it might be pleasant for you both to go there.

I have written the Board suggesting it, but haven't as yet had a reply; and I will not be more specific to you until I learn how the matter strikes you.

Yours — — —
H. N. Payne, Field Secretary
Board of Missions for Freedmen[27]

During the same year, Elder McCleave of the McConnellsville Church attended the meeting of the Synod in Macon, Georgia, and urged the Joneses to come to McConnellsville. His impassioned plea was, "If you

[27] Letter from H. N. Payne to Rev. A. A. Jones, September 24, 1887, quoted in Charlotte Cooper, "Story of Mary M. Jones Life" (unpublished manuscript copy in the possession of the writer). Charlotte Cooper was the daughter of the Reverend and Mrs. A. A. Jones.

would most serve your race, go where no one else will go and do what no one else will do." This challenge haunted Jones and he went to the McConnellsville post in 1887 as stated supply and principal and remained there until his death in 1929.[28]

The Joneses had been told that the church had 173 members who had recently separated from the white church which had ministered to them during and after slavery. When they arrived early in December, they found four elders, eighty-five members, and sixty in the Sunday school. The building was dilapidated; a wood stove without a door heated the building. A pipe extended from the stove through the roof and, in the absence of a flue, the wind frequently brought more smoke back into the building than it drew out. The manse was an old log schoolhouse which stood in the woods. It had no windows, and light and fresh air came through the two doors which were opposite each other. The chimney was made of mud and sticks. The people of the community rejoiced in the arrival of the Joneses and later built for them a two-room house with glass windows and a brick chimney.

The new principal-pastor and his wife were disappointed when they arrived but not discouraged. In less than a month they saw possibilities of a growing school and an enthusiastic church program. The Board reported to the General Assembly in 1888 that the Reverend A. A. Jones was actively engaged as stated supply at the Bethlehem Church at McConnellsville and also at the Hopewell Church at Kings Creek, thirty-five miles away, and at each post the school work was prosperous.

At McConnellsville, a school building was erected adjacent to the new church during the year 1913–1914. The new school building was much larger and contained a small platform in one of two rooms with sliding doors, which provided a type of auditorium. Later, a kitchen was built and home economics was added to the course offerings, which was not only a help to the girls but was also an added incentive for better living in the community. Mrs. Mary M. Jones, one of the sixteen women who participated in the founding of the Atlantic Synodical, was an asset to the educational phase of her husband's work. The Joneses were active and influential in all phases of the Board's program for Negroes. Especially were they motivating factors in the Workers' Conference, the annual gathering of all Board educational workers, which was initiated in 1914.

When the Joneses left the work in 1929, the Board discontinued operating Bethany. The county took over the operation of the school and, for the most part, employed former students of Bethany as teachers in it.

[28] Payne to Jones, Sept. 24, 1887, quoted in Cooper, "Story."

Mattoon Parochial School
Greenville, South Carolina

Several parochial schools were established in South Carolina during the 1880s, under the direction of the Reverend Stephen A. Mattoon, while he was still president of Biddle University. The Reverend B. F. McDowell, one of the first three men to graduate from the theological seminary of Biddle University, was sent to take charge of the school called "the Mattoon School" and the church in Greenville in 1882. Mattoon was greatly concerned about the contribution which these graduates from the seminary would make, thus he had a particular interest when McDowell began his career at the school.

The community at Greenville was in great need of Christian leadership, and the recent graduate accepted the challenge and worked tirelessly to meet the people's needs. He remained there twenty-eight years. Another graduate of the Biddle Theological Seminary, the Reverend T. J. Harris, took over the principalship at Greenville in 1909 and found the school progressive with 103 students enrolled in the day school and several adults who attended the night sessions. The Reverend Harris remained with the work there for six years and was relieved in 1915 by the Reverend J. W. Pennington, who worked with the people of the community on practical matters in addition to his extensive efforts in the pulpit and classroom. The Reverend McAdams was commissioned to take charge of the work in 1919, and under his administration the enrollment reached 226 in 1921.

The Mattoon Parochial School was discontinued at the end of the 1929 school term.

Lincoln High School
Due West, South Carolina

Continuing its expansion in South Carolina, the Committee of Missions for Freedmen established Lincoln High School of Due West in 1882, under the supervision of the Reverend A. G. Davis, a native of the West Indies. The school operated in connection with the Mt. Zion Presbyterian Church and was called the Mt. Zion Mission School. The school sessions were conducted in an old lodge hall near the permanent school site.

After nine years at the school, Davis was succeeded by the Reverend F. L. Broadie in 1891, who had just received the S.T.B. degree from the Biddle Theological Seminary. For the next decade or more the school and church work at Due West was directed by graduates of the Biddle

Theological Seminary: the Reverends N. N. Gregg, E. J. Gregg, and M. B. Spann. Spann named the school the "Mt. Zion Parochial School," increased the faculty and began a campaign for a greater community interest in the values of education.[29]

The Reverend Suder Quilerford Mitchell, a product of Goodwill School and also a graduate of the Biddle Theological Seminary, came to take charge of the church and school in 1915. He advanced the work of this elementary school to include the first eight grades, increased the enrollment from 194 to 240 by 1916, increased the faculty, and named the school the "Lincoln High School" with the hope of adding the other three grades. Before his plans were complete, however, he accepted a commission at Selden Institute in Brunswick, Georgia, in 1919.[30] The stream of Biddle Theological Seminary graduates to Lincoln continued with the Reverend J. H. Toatley assuming the principalship of the school in 1919. He was successful in raising the level of the work at the school to that of a junior high school, which became responsible for the county school work at that level for a number of years. The county school building was finally condemned, and Lincoln High School assumed the entire educational responsibilities for Negroes in the county, with the Board and the county collaborating in paying teachers' salaries.

The faculty was increased from three to nine, and, when the enrollment reached five hundred, twelve faculty members were employed. Some of the students came a distance of ten miles. Some walked, while others came by horseback, buggies, or wagons. Soon students were entering Biddle, Scotia, and South Carolina State College from Lincoln High School without deficiencies.

The Reverend Toatley's brilliant career at Lincoln High School ended in 1936 when the Board discontinued the school. With the closing of Lincoln High School, the Board had only two day schools left under its care in South Carolina.

Emerson Industrial Institute
Blackville, South Carolina

Emerson Industrial Institute began in the late 1880s and was maintained for several years as an independent, nondenominational enterprise. Records are not available to identify officially the names of the origi-

[29] Interview with Dr. A. H. George of Charlotte, North Carolina, 1963. Dr. George was an early student at Lincoln High School.
[30] Interview with the Reverend S. Q. Mitchell and his daughter, Dr. Mildred Mitchell in Charlotte, North Carolina in 1956.

nators. These unknown persons, however, made several appeals to the Board to be admitted under its care. It was not until 1904 that the Board considered it feasible to grant the request. In that year a generous ruling elder, whose interest had been enlisted in the work, proposed that if the Board would take the school under its care, he would donate $3,000 toward its improvement and also guarantee $1,200 a year, for five years, toward its maintenance. The Board apparently was impressed by the proposal and felt justified in departing from a rule regulating such transactions. The Board accepted the deeds to the property; required the employment of Presbyterian teachers; placed the school on its list, and undertook to manage it according to Board regulations.

The property consisted of nearly one hundred acres of land and several buildings, worth between four and five thousand dollars. Sixteen acres of the land, including the buildings, were deeded to the Board, and the donor held the rest of the land in his name for the use of the school.[31] Mr. and Mrs. Pomeroy had charge of the school when the Board took over and remained until 1912. At that time the Reverend and Mrs. E. W. Coberth were commissioned to take over the church and to teach the 192 pupils enrolled in the Emerson Industrial Institute.

The Women's Department of the Board of Missions for Freedmen wrote in the *Home Mission Monthly* for April, 1913, that the institute was making a good record and was establishing a reputation for thoroughness highly satisfying to the Board.[32] In its annual report for the same year the Board made the following announcement: "The Board has recently received the deed to a farm containing a little more than 73 acres at Blackville, S. C., from the estate of the late Mr. E. O. Emerson of Titusville, Pa."[33] The Board does not identify Mr. Emerson as the ruling elder who made the original proposal, but it seems possible that he was.

The Reverend J. M. Miller, a graduate from the Biddle University in 1905, was commissioned to succeed the Reverend Coberth in 1914. He was a man of rich experience, having taught in several places including the parochial school in Chesterfield. When he assumed the principalship at Emerson Institute, 200 pupils were enrolled under the instruction of a staff of seven. Miller lived an active and busy life, rendering community

[31] BMF, *Annual Report*, 1904, p. 7.

[32] "Echoes from a few Freedmen Schools," *Home Mission Monthly*, vol. 27, no. 6 (April, 1913), p. 138.

[33] BMF, *Annual Report*, 1913, p. 13.

services in addition to the work of the school and church. He also directed the work on a 108-acre farm in connection with the school. In 1918 the Reverend Miller was made chairman of the Food Conservation Committee of Barnwell County, a distinction which brought prestige to both the principal and the school.

In 1916, the Board considered the school a thriving institution and gave it high praise in its annual report for that year. During this year the inscription in the school's letterhead was: "I shall endeavor to live in peace with all men." This, apparently, was the school's motto during the administration of Miller.

Emerson Institute was classified by the Board as an elementary school offering the work of the first eight grades and running twenty-four weeks annually.

The school was discontinued June 1, 1933.

Coulter Memorial Academy
Cheraw, South Carolina

In addition to the numerous parochial schools which the Board of Mis sions for Freedmen established in South Carolina during the 1880 period, it also brought under its care two of its most prosperous higher level schools: Harbison Agricultural Institute and Coulter Memorial Academy.

From 1881 to 1908, the parochial period of Coulter, factual records concerning the founding and development of the school are scant and, in some instances, quite different in approach. This is evidenced by two quotes from Board records. The introductory paragraph of the story of Coulter in the files of the Unit of Work with Colored People stated:

> 1881—Coulter School founded at Cheraw, S. C. Rev. J. P. Craw-ford, pastor of the church, built the first school building and started and organized the first parochial school. Rev. W. R. Cole, acting as colporteur for the Board of Missions for Freedmen had effected the first organization preparatory to the organization of the church. Dr. Cole tells the story of the hostile attitude of some members of the Baptist and Methodist churches who one night chased him with rocks because he was seeking to organize what they called the "Church of the Devil." But within five months after the organiza-tion, the leaders of the hostile gangs came and joined the church and were ordained the first elders—one from the Methodist church and one from the Baptist. One of them served from 1881 until 1929 and was most loyal and faithful.[34]

[34] Card File on Negro Schools.

The story of the beginning of Coulter as recorded in *Brevities*, a publication of the Board of Missions, carried a slightly different account:

> The history of Coulter goes back farther than 1908. In 1880 Rev. W. R. Coles, a young theological student from Biddle, had been sent to establish the first little mission school and church in that part of South Carolina. It was Mrs. C. E. Coulter of Hanover, Indiana, secretary of the newly-created women's department of the Board of Missions for Freedmen, who gave him the first twenty dollars for his project, and the school has made her name live. The work flourished and then declined, so that when Dr. Long began his task of reviving it, he found a dilapidated place with not a whole pane in the building.[35]

Twenty-seven of the formative years of Coulter, 1881–1908, therefore, have been without official records of its early development. As in many other cases with the Board's schools, factual records were either not kept, or were lost in the many fires encountered by the schools, or were misplaced during the changes which the schools experienced. Information from contemporaries or their descendants, together with tombstones, church windows, and obituaries, have frequently yielded valuable information. This dearth of records at Coulter changed in 1908 when Dr. George Waldo Long was commissioned to take charge of the work at Cheraw.

Dr. Long had just completed his work at the theological seminary at Biddle University after a long experience with financial difficulties. He was, therefore, thoroughly conditioned to face realistically the plight of boys and girls who came to Coulter without funds craving an education. He arrived in Cheraw during the summer of 1908, mostly on an exploratory mission, and remained for thirty-five years.

Dr. John Gaston, representing the Board of Missions for Freedmen, visited the Cheraw field with the expressed purpose of discontinuing the work there because he thought it hopeless. Dr. Long, young and courageous, begged for a chance. The chance was given, and Dr. Long came to realize that his life's work was centered in Cheraw—to do or to die.

The very next year after his arrival in Cheraw, long-range changes began to take place at Coulter. Following the death of Mrs. Caroline E. Coulter in 1909, the name of the school was changed to "Coulter Memorial Academy." The school became a coeducational boarding school that year; a lyceum program was started, along with other programs of a

---

[35] "Coulter Memorial Academy," *Brevities* (N.Y.: PCUSA, BNM, 1936).

cultural character, and the run-down physical plant underwent significant repairs. Dr. Long dedicated himself to the hard work involved in bringing about the desired transformation and never broke his covenant with the cause.[36]

Dr. Long attended a meeting of the Atlantic Synod convening in Jacksonville, Florida in the fall of 1908. While there he was impressed by Miss Lillian Bull, a teacher at Bethune-Cookman College, Daytona Beach, Florida, who read a paper at the meeting. He laughingly said, "I got my teacher." She came to Coulter as his wife on December 29, 1909.

Home for the bride was an "executive mansion" in the most rustic sense. She and her husband and four boarding students shared a dilapidated manse of four rooms in which the classroom work was also done. There was no ground space other than that on which the building stood. Grateful for the hard lessons which he had learned under the instructions of the Joneses at the parochial school at McConnellsville, Dr. Long put past experiences into immediate practice. In 1911, the home economics course was added to the curriculum, and the first mission school in the Pee Dee River section of South Carolina began a new chapter in its history. Mrs. Long devoted a great deal of her time to the new course, which, at first, consisted of making old articles usable and attractive. For this purpose the mission barrels and boxes were used.

Seven rooms were added to the manse in 1912 with $900 from the Board of Missions for Freedmen and local gifts. The manse was further expanded in 1913 with funds amounting to $1,200 from the same sources. After the last additional rooms were added to the manse, additional land became a necessity. In 1914, an adjacent lot was purchased for $500, and five additional rooms were added for dormitory purposes with funds raised locally. Another adjoining lot was purchased in 1915 for $700, $300 of which came from the Board, with the rest contributed locally. The manse now consisted of twenty-eight rooms and was used as a home for the principal and his wife, living quarters for students and teachers, dining room, kitchen, and classrooms.

The extension of the physical plant and grounds continued into 1917 when another lot was purchased from a Mr. Pratt for $1,000. A two-room house, which was formerly an undertaker's shop, stood on the lot. The Board contributed one half of the cost and the other half was donated locally. The Board's annual reports frequently stated, concerning

[36] Grover Dwight Nelson, "The Life and Works of George Waldo Long" (S.T.B. dissertation, Johnson C. Smith Theological Seminary, June 1, 1949), p. 11.

the local funds, "Amounts raised locally—unknown," or "The cost of brick—unknown." Dr. Long observed, "We became attached to forgotten boys and girls, men and women; we were filled with the desire to build an institution." [37]

The grounds were further extended in 1918, and an administration building was constructed on the new lot at a cost of $2,000. The Board sent $800 toward the cost, and the students, teachers, churches, and local friends contributed the balance. The undertaker's shop was converted into a cottage for boarding boys in 1921, and two rooms were added to it for primary work. Dr. Long related an experience of a boy with two dollars for tuition who roused him at 1:30 one morning and greeted him with, "They told me in Jacksonville that you never turned anybody away if they really wanted to get educated." The boy stayed, and he and other boys with similar stories found the converted undertaker's shop to be an oasis.

The construction of the administration building in 1924 united the black and white citizens of Cheraw. All the brick, apparently ten carloads, was furnished by the Palmetto Brick Makers' Association for the construction of the $45,000 building. The manual training department was added to the curriculum because of job opportunities offered by these brick makers and the desire of the boys to learn the trade. The concerned boys joined the construction crew in laying the brick for the administration building. During the same year, the skills developed by the boys in helping with the administration building were put to good use as the citizens of Cheraw pooled their efforts to build a new church edifice.

Nineteen hundred twenty-five was an important year for Coulter Memorial Academy. The first high school class graduated, and shop work was added to the curriculum. The year 1927 was equally important. A gymnasium-trades building was built for $4,000, which was raised by the Coulter P.T.A., Alumni Association, teachers, and students. This year, also, the Frederick lot on the corner of Second and Kershaw Streets was purchased. A one-room brick store building on the lot was converted into a workshop for boys and later into a library. A six-room, dilapidated house was also on this lot, which cost $3,200. The Utica Presbyterial Society of New York donated $1,000 toward the purchase; the Unit of Work for Colored People donated $2,000, and the balance was raised locally.

[37] Nelson, "The Life," p. 11.

Many student activities were started during this period, especially in music and sports. These activities helped in promotional ways as well as in building pride in the school.

In 1928, white friends of the community donated a lot for the permanent location of the new church, and the boys helped to roll the church onto the new lot. Utica Cottage was built the same year with a gift of $1,000 from the Utica Presbyterial Society of New York and donations from local friends. In addition to the expansion of the plant and grounds, progressive steps were being taken to enrich and upgrade the academic program.

In 1928, the Laney Mission, a one-teacher day school, was maintained in the county, and in 1929 another school of the same type was established and was called "The McDonald Mission." The teacher-training course was added in 1933, and Coulter became a junior college this year. Health education courses were added in 1934, and in 1940 grades one through five were taken over by the public school system. Library extension courses were added in 1943.[38]

At the climax of this continuous stream of expansion and enrichment, Dr. Long died suddenly, August 3, 1943. Henry Louis Marshall, the dean, was appointed acting principal and Mrs. Long became dean of women. In commenting on the work of Dr. Long, the Unit of Work with Colored People had this to say:

> One generation has seen the extraordinary growth of Coulter from an inactive, run-down little church and parochial school, to a thriving establishment of a church with 268 members, a school with five hundred students, two organized preaching stations, four other mission points, and Sunday Schools at each place. One man and his wife have the satisfaction of knowing that it is their vision and their creative energy which have made the thing possible, though many people have contributed to its success.[39]

Dr. Long had lived long enough to be comforted by the realization that he had not labored in vain. The school had grown numerically from 87 in 1908 to 509 in 1943; from one building in 1908 to 8 in 1943; from a five-month elementary school in 1908 to an accredited junior college in 1943. Beginning with a faculty of two in 1908, the school helped to awaken within the community a willingness by its members to work, pray and give.

[38] *Ibid.*, pp. 12–13.
[39] "Coulter," *Brevities.*

When Dean Marshall took over the work at Coulter in 1944 it was the only high school and junior college for Negro girls and boys in the county, so this made it mandatory for Coulter to prepare Negro students of the area for participation in higher level schools and for the public school classrooms. Marshall added a guidance program through which each student received personal counseling geared to his specific problems and ultimate goals.[40]

The retrenchment trend which began at Coulter in 1946 created concern in Cheraw and vicinity. The sixth grade was dropped in order that greater emphasis could be placed on the high school program and, in 1947, the junior college department was discontinued because of the small enrollment and inadequate facilities. The anxiety of the community was increased in 1948 when the city school board held a meeting with the Board of National Missions regarding Coulter's future. Events that followed are continued in this report of the Unit of Work With Colored People:

> Coulter Memorial Academy was by vote of the Board at its meeting 4/21/49 turned over to the public school authorities of Cheraw for administration and support, the school board to rent the central school building, the gymnasium, the library, and the Chapman Training School Building with the stipulation (1) that the school be maintained on a par with local schools for white children, (2) that the boarding department be discontinued, and (3) that plans be developed in cooperation with the church and parents for a community recreational program. The rent paid for the property, approximately $5,500 a year, was used for operating expenses of the school according to a budget agreed to by the Board of National Missions and the city.[41]

The rental agreement was renewed in 1952, and Marshall's salary was taken over by the school board on September 1, 1952. The girls' dormitory, having been condemned in 1951, was demolished. In 1955, the lease with the school board was cancelled, and the public school moved into a new building which was named "Long High School," honoring Dr. George Waldo Long. Marshall continued to occupy Frederickson House in return for oversight of property. Academic records and student transcripts were to be retained by the public school. In 1956, the Board voted to deed the Second Presbyterian Church of Cheraw, without cost, that part of the Coulter property which adjoined the church property

[40] BNM, *Annual Report*, 1944, p. 78.
[41] Card File on Negro Schools.

and contained the old gymnasium. The Board also voted that proceeds from the sale of the balance of the property be devoted to some object related to education of Negro youth. On December 12, 1956, the property was sold for a total price of $48,580. This transaction terminated the seventy-six years of cultural, religious, and educational services of Coulter Memorial Academy to Cheraw and the surrounding vicinity.

Harbison College
Irmo, South Carolina

One of the higher level schools taken under the Board's care during the 1880 period was Harbison College. The development of Harbison College began in Abbeville in 1885 when the Reverend and Mrs. Emory W. Williams established a coeducational institution to promote the industrial, literary, musical, and religious advancement of their people in that section. The institution was named Ferguson Academy, honoring the Reverend James A. Ferguson of New Jersey, who was one of the first contributors to its founding. The Reverend and Mrs. Williams of Washington, D.C., educated in Northern schools, came to Abbeville, saw the conditions, and resolved to do what they could. From the beginning their efforts were met with unexpected difficulties.

The Board of Missions for Freedmen was attracted by the efforts being made in Abbeville, and it rendered some small assistance. In the board's report for 1889, comments were made on the situation at Abbeville, in particular the works of the Williamses there and the optimistic hope for their efforts in the future. A large four-storied brick building for school, teachers' home, and boarding hall had been partially completed but stood almost useless for the lack of $2,000 needed to complete it. Before the new building could be completed, however, the school was completely destroyed by fire in 1890. The Board made a definite effort to relieve the situation in Abbeville and made this report in 1891:

> Ferguson Academy at Abbeville, S. C., has been transferred and made over to the Board during the year. This institution was built and partly supported by friends outside of the Board, at a cost of $10,000, at which sum the property is now valued. The Board has aided in supporting the teachers but it did not own the property, but on the Board's assuming a debt of $1,631 the property has become the Board's by deed. It is a flourishing school with 115 pupils under Rev. E. W. Williams, Principal.[42]

[42] BMF, *Annual Report*, 1891, p. 7.

The Williamses terminated their services at the institution at the end of that year, and in the Board's 1892 annual report it announced that the Reverend Thomas A. Amos was the new executive at Ferguson. With him was an all-Negro faculty of five who were instructing 134 pupils. For five years this staff concentrated on renovations and innovations that would lay the foundation for achieving the school's great potential. Their efforts were rewarded in many ways.

Ferguson's vacillating fate, however, seemed to swing in shorter frequencies than at other Board schools. The school building was condemned as unsafe for use in 1899, but it was immediately reconstructed at a cost of $2,750. At last the friendships which the school had won began to pay dividends. Samuel P. Harbison of Pittsburgh, a member of the Board, gave twenty acres of land in the suburbs of the town. The school moved into new buildings at this new location in 1901 and was renamed Harbison College. The school benefitted from intense interest and support by the Harbison family. The school in reality became the Harbisons' foster child. This observation will be increasingly substantiated as the history of the school unfolds. During the same year, Mr. Harbison added to his original gift of twenty acres a tract of forty-seven adjoining acres. On these sixty-seven acres, Mr. Henry Phipps, a generous friend of Abbeville, had a boys' dormitory erected at a cost of $3,800, which was called Phipps Hall. The dormitory was furnished by the Women's Missionary societies of New Jersey and was ready for occupancy by the fall of 1902.[43] At last, there was a span of quiet, comfort, and progress in this new location, and the Board considered its largest advances in the school work for 1902 to be at Harbison College.

Two hundred acres of farmland were added to the 67 acres in 1903 by Mr. and Mrs. Harbison and were put under cultivation immediately by the principal and students. They also had a building erected at a cost of $5,000 for the 327 students enrolled that year. Other gifts of a different nature also came to the school that year. Mrs. Ira Condit, wife of the Reverend Ira M. Condit, superintendent of Chinese and Japanese Presbyterian work in the United States from 1870 to 1903, presented a gift of five hundred volumes to the school. Three hundred volumes were designated by Mrs. Condit as the beginning of a library for ministers regardless of denomination. This was the nucleus around which the school's library developed.

In 1905, Harbison Hall was built, at a cost of more than $10,000,

[43] BMF, *Annual Report*, 1902, p. 8.

financed by Mr. Harbison. This building, which housed a chapel, class-rooms, and rooms for student religious activities, greatly increased the facilities and widened the influence of the institution.[44]

A local political campaign during the summer of 1906 stirred up strong racial antagonism, and President Amos was caught in the middle. Animosities caused him to resign after fourteen years of dedicated serv-ice to the institution.[45] The school was closed from September 12, 1906 to February, 1907. The Reverend Calvin M. Young, who graduated from Biddle Theological Seminary in 1894, became executive of Har-bison following Amos's resignation, and began a twenty-four-year career at Harbison when it reopened. Soon after the school reopened, Mrs. Harbison visited Harbison College. She saw the president's family of eight living in three rooms in the girls' dormitory and resolved to build a president's home.

Ferguson Hall, the girls' dormitory, was completely destroyed by fire in January of 1907 and, after being closed for four months, the school reopened with a much smaller attendance. President Young, though perplexed and stunned by this experience, began to revitalize the school program. A choir was organized in 1909. School choirs had proved to have both valuable promotional factors as well as campus benefits. A ministerial club was organized, which enriched religious activities and took the school program to the community. Most of the members of this club who had ambitions for entering either Biddle or Lincoln theological seminaries, proved to be excellent seminary students.

The greatest tragedy at any of the Board's schools occurred at Harbi-son on March 17, 1910. The main building, which was the administration building and the boys' dormitory, was in its entirety destroyed by an incendiary bomb. Three students lost their lives in the fire and three others and a teacher were seriously injured. The loss of property was severe but was almost forgotten in view of the more serious human losses in this destructive conflagration. The act was severely denounced by the leading Abbeville citizens and state authorities. Citizens of the town of-fered a reward, which was matched by the Board of Missions, for the detection of the person responsible for the bomb, but to no avail.

Despite a petition by representative citizens of Abbeville to have the school rebuilt there, the Board began negotiations for removal. The

[44] *Minutes*, 1905, p. 352.

[45] "Harbison College: Statement of Conditions which led to Resignation of President Amos," *Press & Banner* (Abbeville, South Carolina), Sept. 12, 1906.

Board stated that for many reasons Abbeville would have been its choice, but "the culprit who did the burning, was unapprehended and presumably still living in the community, and might in an evil hour, be tempted to repeat his wicked deed."[46] While still in a state of indecision, the Board was presented with many tempting proposals. One of these proposals came from the small town of Irmo, South Carolina, about ten miles out of Columbia. A Board committee visited Irmo and strongly recommended it for the new location. There was a suitable tract of land containing about four hundred forty-five acres for sale on reasonable terms, and a forty-seven-acre adjoining tract was offered as a gift if the location was selected for rebuilding. The proposition was accepted, and the Board came into possession of nearly five hundred acres at Irmo. The Board immediately agreed to a plan for the construction of a $20,000 building, $10,000 of which was advanced by the Harbison estate. The Board also made another important decision in addition to the removal:

> There is, however, to be one important change in the character of the new Harbison College at Irmo: It is to be distinctly an Agricultural College and it is to be only for Boys and Young Men. The students are to be thoroughly trained in modern, scientific and intensive farming, and other industries are to be added, as the way opens for expansion of the work. The literary course, as previously maintained, is not to be abandoned or neglected, and above all, the religious influence of the school is to be emphasized, with the hope that no young man may leave the institution without having learned that the fear of the Lord is the beginning of wisdom. Such is the plan of the future Harbison College at Irmo, S.C., as it lies in the minds of the members of the Harbison family and as approved of by the Board. The building plans are already agreed upon, and it is hoped the new building will be ready for occupancy in the early fall of this year.[47]

The name of the school was changed to Harbison Agricultural College. The new administration building was a brick four-story structure with a basement and contained classrooms, dormitory rooms for boys, kitchen, dining room, and chapel. The top floor was left unfinished. A specifically trained teacher of agriculture was employed and a blacksmith shop was set up. By these transactions Harbison began a new career at Irmo.

[46] BMF, *Annual Report*, 1911, p. 10.
[47] BMF, *Annual Report*, 1911, pp. 10–11.

The generosity of the Harbison family continued to flow to the institution. In 1913, $3,000 was contributed by the Harbison estate to build a president's home, and the top floor of the administration building was completed and furnished as a boys' dormitory, at a cost of $1,500. In 1913, the Harbison estate added 762 acres contiguous to the college, which motivated the beginning of a Farm Homes project at the school. This year also a suitable church building, belonging formerly to the Negro Baptists at Irmo, was purchased, and the Irmo Presbyterian Church was organized in connection with the college.

The continuous trend of expansion and enrichment continued at the college, and in 1914 the Harbison estate extended the acreage of the college with a gift of 36 additional acres of land. Seventeen of these acres formed a part of the campus, and the other 19 were to be subdivided into town lots of one-acre each and sold for homes. The Harbison estate continued the expansion of the plant by financing the building of a boys' dormitory, extensive repairs on the main building, and the enlargement of the heating plant at a cost of $33,783. In 1921, the Harbison interest was extended further into the community by authorizing the purchase of 2,402 acres of land to be sold in small tracts of 25 acres each. The money from sales was to become a permanent fund for the endowment of Harbison. At that time the college owned 500 acres in college farmland, 3,600 acres in the "Farm Home Community," plus the expanded campus area.

Nineteen hundred twenty-nine was a year of change at the college. Once again its name was changed, from the Harbison Agricultural College to the Harbison Agricultural and Industrial Institute. This all seemed to imply progress in the direction of industrial training, which was, in nature, terminal. Many Harbison students, however, desired preparatory work toward advanced study. This desire on the students' part was evidenced by a continuous decrease in the institution's enrollment. In an annual report the Board made this relevant observation:

> At first it was set up as a boarding school for boys only, and an effort was made to instruct the boys not only in farming but in trades as well, along with their regular academic work. There never was adequate equipment for teaching trades, since for this an expensive kind of equipment is needed. Consequently, while the boys are taught to turn their hands to many kinds of repair and construction work around the school and while they are given some practical instruction in automobile mechanics, there is no claim made that the

school offers a full trades course. Instead, more and more of the pupils are in search of a regular high school academic course and prepare to go on after graduation.[48]

There were changes in the administrative staff in 1929. The Reverend Calvin M. Young resigned and the Reverend James L. Hollowell was appointed president. He, however, became ill suddenly and died on the seventeenth of October. A few days later the former president, the Reverend Young, also died. Dean R. W. Boulware, who was well acquainted with the Harbison program, was appointed interim president.

A community development which had direct bearing on the school's activity also began in 1929, when a two-million-dollar dam was constructed nearby. A small town grew up around it, and new job opportunities were offered skilled and industrious students. The project also furnished a new market which provided additional revenue. The Harbison farm furnished one to two truckloads of vegetables to this town daily. A new well was drilled on the campus, and additional water facilities were provided at a cost of $5,000, contributed by a Pittsburgh "friend."[49]

The Reverend John G. Porter, a graduate of Biddle Theological Seminary in 1910, was appointed president of Harbison in 1930. Another year which was packed with significant changes was 1933, when the school became coeducational again. The girls were housed on the top floor of the administration building; home economics courses were added to the curriculum. The Irmo Parochial School, which was maintained by the Board on Harbison property about a mile away, was merged with Harbison. In 1935, the practical work in mechanics was strengthened and added to the curriculum with academic credit.

Harbison was again harrassed by fire on March 18, 1941, thirty-four years after the burning of Ferguson Hall in 1907 and thirty-one years following the tragic fire of 1910. This fire consumed, without loss of life, the main building which housed classrooms, girls' dormitory, dining room, and kitchen. By action of the Board in April of that year, the school was closed for the school year 1941–1942 to permit an extensive building and remodeling program.

When the school reopened it offered a varied vocational training course

[48] "Harbison A & I Institute," *Brevities* (N.Y.: PCUSA, BNM, 1936).
[49] "Harbison Junior College," *Briefly* (N.Y.: PCUSA, BNM, 1951), p. 1.

for promising Negro students from all over the South. It remained coeducational but accepted only boarding students, since Lexington and Richmond counties were expected to provide for local pupils of high school age. Harbison again seemed to be moving progressively ahead. In 1942, four workers' cottages, a barn, and a new water system were added to the plant at a cost of approximately five thousand dollars, which was realized from the sale of property of closed Negro schools and miscellaneous sources. In addition, two buildings were erected: a one-story school building which cost $25,000 and a one-story dining hall at a cost of approximately fifteen thousand dollars, funds received as insurance and miscellaneous gifts. A two-story girls' dormitory, accommodating twenty-eight girls and five staff members, was built for $31,000 from the Sage Legacy Fund. This building was called the Olivia Sage Memorial Building for the Negro Field. Equipment and heating installations for all three buildings, costing $11,000, were provided by the sale of timber from the Harbison Forest.

Following this program of rebuilding and remodeling, the school reopened in September of 1943 with a new president. Dr. T. B. Jones, a Biddle graduate, ex-president of Mary Allen Junior College, a shrewd administrator with wide experience in the area of education, was appointed the president of the new Harbison. For his wife, Mrs. Vivian Young Jones, a Scotia graduate gifted in music, returning to Harbison was equivalent to returning home. Her father, the former president of Harbison, the Reverend Calvin M. Young, Sr., had brought his family with him when he moved with the school from Abbeville to Irmo in 1905. Twenty-four of her early years had been spent on the campus, and she had sentimental as well as humanitarian reasons for devoting her talents wholeheartedly in helping her husband make Harbison live again.

A new administrative building was erected in 1944 and was named The Byrd R. Smith Building as a memorial to the late president of Mary Allen Junior College of Crockett, Texas. A dining hall was built and named the Lucy Laney Memorial Hall after the magnificent founder and builder of the Haines Institute of Augusta, Georgia, at a cost of $9,254 from the sale of the Haines property. These buildings were the beginning of the process by which the Harbison campus became, as the other schools were closed, a living monument to some of the late executors of the Board's program of education for Negroes.

In 1945, an agreement was reached with the state Forestry Commission of South Carolina in which the Board transferred to the

Commission 2,100 acres of forest land and received $21,000 for it. Approximately eleven thousand dollars of this amount had been previously earmarked for furnishing the new buildings built in 1942.

The name of the school was again changed in 1946 to Harbison Junior College, by official action of the Board, and the boys' dormitory was named Calvin M. Young Building in honor of Dr. Young, president from 1905 to 1929. With $10,000 secured from the sale of Fee Memorial property in Virginia, Dr. Jones remodeled and enlarged the existing plant; in 1949 a new church structure was financed by a grant of $20,000 from the Charles K. Smith Fund. The grant was supplemented by donated labor and gifts, which were valued at approximately ten thousand dollars. Before dedication, however, the church was destroyed by a fire of suspicious but undetermined origin, on October 2, 1952. A little more than one year later the C. M. Young Dormitory for girls went up in flames. The girls were housed in the boys' dormitory and the boys in the gymnasium for the remainder of the year.

Again, progress and restoration seemed in the offing at Harbison when in 1956 a new dormitory was erected to replace the C. M. Young dormitory, at a cost of $60,000. The girls were housed in the Sage Memorial Dormitory, which was renovated and completely refurnished for $16,000. Other repairs and renovations were made where needed throughout the campus. These 1956 transactions, however, which seemed to be signs of progress and longevity, were in reality the beginning of the end for Harbison.

As a result of the general field study of the work for Negroes by Dr. Milton Brown, the Committee on Education and Medical Work recommended to the Board that Harbison be discontinued. The Board voted to do so, as of August 31, 1958. The reasons given were the small enrollment, the lack of accreditation, and the large financial investment that would be necessary to secure accreditation. Student records from the junior college program were sent to Barber-Scotia, and those from the high school program were transferred to Boggs Academy. By these transactions, Harbison's seventy-three years of promise ended.

The loss of this school was particularly keen to the black community, since it had become the final memorial to so many of the great figures in the history of the Presbyterian schools for Negroes. The sense of loss was made more bitter when, in 1964, the Harbison property was leased to the South Carolina Department of Correction as a prison or correction camp for felonious women. Harbison graduates who might want to revisit their *alma mater* are greeted by a sign which reads: "Stop. Do not enter. Blow Horn Twice. Officer will come. South Carolina Department of Correction."[50]

Grant Academy
Spartanburg, South Carolina

The Presbyterian Parochial School in Spartanburg, South Carolina, was organized with 139 pupils by the Board of Missions for Freedmen in 1889, with P. G. Hammett as principal and Miss P. E. Bomar the teacher. The Board's program in the state of South Carolina had reached an all-time high by 1889. The Bethel Church in Spartanburg became the fifth in the McClelland Presbytery. The school and the church were highly esteemed by the townspeople, who rallied in conscientious support of both. School enrollment increased steadily; in 1891 there were 164 pupils and in 1894, there were 206 enrolled. The school was named Grant Academy in 1894. In 1897, Grant Academy was listed with Kendall, Salem Industrial, Mattoon, and Goodwill as academies of the larger sort that were destined to wield a strong influence in their respective communities. In that year, the school moved into a new building and the faculty was increased.[51]

Mr. Hammet resigned in 1899 after the school had been well established and the community deeply involved in its development and progress. Mr. Hammett had splendid cooperation during his tenure at the school, and he received ovations at his departure. He had witnessed many desirable changes in the vicinity: crowded cow paths and wagon trails winding to the school building had been transformed into good highways with improved means of transportation; the awareness of the values of education had been stimulated, and higher standards of living were evident in the community.[52]

The Reverend H. M. Stinson, a graduate of the Biddle Theological Seminary in 1895, became principal of the school in 1900 with 146 pupils enrolled. By 1903, however, the enrollment had reached 229 pupils. Signs of progress characterized both the academic program and the physical plant during Stinson's administration.

[50] *Charlotte Observer*, 8 August 1964, sec. E., p. 1.
[51] BMF, *Annual Report*, 1897, p. 14.
[52] *Johnson C. Smith University Bulletin*, 1927, p. 82.

The Reverend J. M. Johnson, another graduate of the Biddle Theological Seminary, class of 1901, succeeded Stinson in 1913, and the work continued to advance under his wise guidance for eight years. In 1921, he was succeeded by the Reverend B. H. McFadden, and in 1928 Mrs. Dollie A. Weston became the first woman to be chief executive of Grant Academy. The community appreciated her feminine concerns, enriched program, and industrious approach to the demands of community needs and supported her for the seven years of her tenure. She was succeeded by the Reverend J. W. Smith in 1933. Smith remained at Grant until the Board discontinued the work in 1940.[53]

Calhoun Falls Mission
Calhoun Falls, South Carolina

The momentum of the Board's 1880s expansion in the state carried over into the 1890s before the impact of the financial crisis curtailed its progress. Among the parochials established or taken under its care during the new decade were: Calhoun Falls, Kendall Institute, New Hope, and Harden Academy.

The Calhoun Falls Mission was apparently started in 1890 by the Reverend and Mrs. S. D. Leak. The parochial school was soon adopted by the Presbytery of Baltimore and became an invaluable asset to the Bellway Presbyterian Church and the community at large. With the Reverend Leak supervising the entire mission, Mrs. Leak taught the school and extended the influence of both the school and the church into the community and beyond. Descendants of the charter members of both the church and the school still relate stories of Mrs. Leak's mingling with the people, teaching as she went from house to house and from field to field throughout the county.

Mrs. M. S. Norwood came to the mission in 1916 and Miss A. Ritt in 1921. Both made lasting contributions to the school work and to the worship at the Bellway Presbyterian Church.

The Board did not include the Calhoun Falls Mission in its reports to the General Assembly after 1923. The fate of the school after that date, therefore, is not known.

---

[53] Interview with Mrs. Katie Barksdale 1965. She was an instructor in the school after it was taken over by the public school system. Interview with the Reverend J. W. Smith, 1965.

Kendall Institute
Sumter, South Carolina

Kendall Institute was founded in 1891 and sustained by the Board of Missions for Freedmen from the beginning. The school was named for Mrs. Julia B. Kendall, the late wife of the Reverend Henry Kendall, who was secretary of the Board of Home Missions from 1870 to 1892.

This school was destined from its beginning to become a recognized center of training for Christian education at the secondary school level by the Reverend J. C. Walkins. Walkins once observed that the work at Sumter was a hard but rewarding endeavor. He labored at this mission for eleven years and was succeeded by the Reverend A. U. Frierson in 1903.

Frierson, a product of the Goodwill School, received the bachelor's degree from Biddle University in 1885, the master's degree in 1888, and the D.D. degree was conferred on him in 1892. He resigned a professorship at Biddle University to acccpt the pastorate of the Second Presbyterian Church in Sumter and the principalship of the Kendall Institute. At this mission his administrative ability was outstanding, and the splendid progress of every phase of the school work amazed those who had labeled him "a college professor" and, therefore, probably administratively inept. After thirteen years, Frierson had seen eleven classes with an average of eleven young men and women graduate, many of whom had continued their studies at a higher level. Dr. Frierson resigned in 1916, in order to accept the principalship at Salem Industrial High School in Anderson, South Carolina, and to become pastor of the Salem Presbyterian Church there.

In 1908, the Board proposed to build a girls' dormitory for $5,000, but a shortage of funds delayed construction. A three-story frame structure was built later, however, with the money contributed mostly by the women's societies of Indiana.

The Reverend John Peter Foster assumed the responsibility of the executive work at Sumter in 1916. He began his academic work at Ferguson Academy in Abbeville and in 1887 completed a theological course at Howard University. At the age of twenty-five he began his professional career in Anderson by establishing the Salem Industrial High School and organizing the Presbyterian church for Negroes there in 1888. It was after twenty-eight years there that he came to Sumter in 1916 as principal of the Kendall Institute and pastor of the Presbyterian church.

Because of this training and experience, he created a revitalized morale and a progressive academic atmosphere at Kendall Institute. In 1918, the total enrollment was 272 with a graduating class of 10 pupils. In addition to the enrichment of the academic courses, practical crafts and athletics were added to the school's program. After twelve years Foster resigned, and the Reverend I. P. Pogue became principal of Kendall in 1928. A cottage was built for the boys, and athletics became a major activity at Kendall.[54]

In 1932, Kendall Institute was closed, along with other parochial schools under the board's care.

New Hope Parochial School
Camden, South Carolina

The New Hope Parochial School was established in 1893 by the Reverend Samuel Calvin Thompson, who received the bachelor's degree in 1890 from Biddle University, and the S.T.B. degree in 1893 from the same institution. His many-sided accomplishments at Camden within eight years were gratifying to the Board. He not only succeeded in the church work but also left the school and its purposes deeply embedded in the hearts of the people of the community. A deep sense of what education meant to them and their children was shown in their support of the work. When he was relieved by the Reverend F. J. Anderson in 1901, a foundation for progress had been laid.[55]

Anderson, a graduate of the theological seminary at Biddle University in 1900, took charge of the school with enthusiasm. Parents began sending their children to school in larger numbers, and the enrollment increased from 58 to 108. Anderson resigned and was succeeded by a Biddle man from the seminary class of 1901, the Reverend W. R. Muldrow. One of the accomplishments of Muldrow during his short stay at the school was the erection of a new school building, with money donated largely by friends in Quoque, Long Island. Prior to getting the new building, school had been conducted in two rooms connected to the manse.

This continuous flow of Biddle graduates paid important dividends. At the university, they had been instilled with the fact that there was an

[54] Letter from Mrs. I. P. Pogue, 1963. Interview with Mrs. Lou Benson of Charlotte, North Carolina, 1970. Mrs. Benson is the daughter of the Reverend and Mrs. I. P. Pogue.
[55] *Johnson C. Smith University Alumni Journal*, 1927, p. 32.

urgent need for Christian leadership among Negroes. With this need in mind, the graduates launched an intense campaign to recruit promising young men in the schools they now led. They attempted to inspire these students, through teaching, preaching, and example, to go on to Biddle with this same ambition in mind.

The Reverend H. W. Cooper was commissioned to work at the New Hope School in 1910, at which time Mrs. S. C. Thompson and Mrs. W. E. Boykin were teaching there. The Reverend C. H. Uggams succeeded Cooper in 1914, but remained only one year; he was followed by the Reverend M. T. Wash, a graduate from the seminary of Lincoln University in Pennsylvania who served as principal for two years. In 1917, the Reverend J. H. Toatley, a Biddle Seminary graduate of 1916, became the principal. Toatley's tenure at the school was also of two years' duration as he left in 1919. The line of Biddle men continued at the school with the arrival of the Reverend M. A. Sanders, Sr., who was later to make history among the deprived on James Island. He worked in Camden for two years, and his staff at New Hope was increased by one, Miss Mae Jones, in 1921. Even though there was no adequate substitute for the services being rendered by the school, the Board felt justified in closing out the work at Camden that year.[56]

Harden Academy
Allendale, South Carolina

One of the last parochial schools to be established by the Board in South Carolina was Harden Academy. It was founded by the Reverend W. H. Mitchell in 1898 in Allendale, located 104 miles from Charleston in the midst of a dense Negro population. The black population outnumbered the white in 1910.

The academy was located near the suburbs of the town in the center of a five-acre plot. The students came largely from the county and frequently traveled from one to eight miles to reach the school. Before a school building was erected, the Reverend and Mrs. Mitchell stored their household goods and conducted the school sessions in their home. After this first "schoolhouse" was destroyed by fire, the Board built an elementary school building consisting of five rooms.[57]

[56] Interview with the Reverend M. A. Sanders, Jr., the son of the former principal of New Hope School, and with Dr. Arthur H. George of Charlotte, North Carolina, who attended the New Hope School.

[57] BNM, *Annual Report*, 1929, p. 145.

Although Harden Academy was classified by the Board as an elementary school offering eleven grades and running twenty-four weeks annually, in reality its curriculum was devised to meet the state requirements for certification to teach in the public schools for Negroes. Seventy-five percent of the teachers in the Barnwell County Schools for Negroes received their training at Harden Academy.

As far as available records reveal, during Harden Academy's thirty-five years of service, it had only three principals: the Reverend W. H. Mitchell, 1898–1915; the Reverend Orlean Reid, 1915–1919; and the Reverend H. McFadden, 1919–1933. Harden was discontinued in 1933.

St. James Parochial School
James Island, South Carolina

By the beginning of the new century, the pace of the Board's advances had slowed down permanently. However, the Board did resume activity in the sea islands off the coast of South Carolina. In 1926, it took under its care a parochial school which had been established previously on James Island.

The fourteen-mile long James Island begins two miles outside of the Charleston city limits and is five miles wide at its broadest point. It is surrounded by the Ashley, Cooper, and Stone rivers, and the Atlantic Ocean. This island is replete with rich legends regarding the origin and development of its church and school. One of the most reliable tells of the pioneering of Paul Campbell, the ex-slave who began preaching and teaching soon after the close of the Civil conflict. As revealed earlier in this account, he was licensed to preach during the first session of Atlantic Presbytery in Charleston, South Carolina. At that time, Campbell and the church he organized became related to the Northern Presbyterian church. Earlier accounts also show the general condition of the sea islands at that time.[58]

According to legend, Paul Campbell constructed brush arbors in this tropical setting and held regular prayer meetings and other services. His prayer meetings attracted the attention of local white sympathizers, and they helped him make plans for organizing a church and constructing a building to house it. The church was organized under the auspices of the Southern Presbyterian church, but the building did not materialize. The white congregation's church structure burned, and their financial efforts

[58] Mrs. M. A. Sanders, "The Workshop—James Island," *The New Advance*, vol. 4, no. 2 (October 15, 1941), p. 4–5.

were now directed toward rebuilding their own church. A member of the white congregation, however, gave the freedmen the site where the prayer-meeting arbor stood for a church-school location. Through free labor and a great deal of sacrifice, the building was eventually erected and was called the St. James Church and School. Later, after the death of the original donor of the land, his son demanded $500 for the land on which the church building stood. Since no deed or clear title had been given to the black congregation, the money had to be raised and paid.[59]

In 1926, when the mission was taken under the Board's care, the Reverend H. H. Hunter, who was already there, was retained. He had worked faithfully at the school for many years and was succeeded by the Reverend Adam Frayer. Frayer died in 1931, and St. James was without an executive for ten years. During this interval, the people lapsed into their former folkways and began speaking a language that was familiar only to themselves. When the Reverend M. A. Sanders, a Biddle Theological Seminary graduate, was commissioned in 1941 to take charge of the mission, the challenge was equivalent to that encountered by the early pioneers more than seventy-five years before. The people who gathered to greet the new minister presented a pathetic scene. The church-school building was badly in need of repairs; there were no steps to the front entrance; the porch was falling, and the floor was gone. Progress was gradual, however, as the building was repaired, and orderly worship services were restored. Mrs. Sanders' friendly house-to-house visits brought about many desired changes. Irregular school attendance was improved. Age was not used as a criterion for classifying students, and most of them were placed in first or second grade.[60] Sanders appealed to the Board of National Missions for a new building with the hope that it would be an incentive for greater educational concern. When the Board became aware of the nature of the situation, the appeal was answered favorably.

After the Sanders had commuted from Charleston to James Island for five years, the Board built a manse for them on the island. This became both a home for the minister's family and other mission workers and a center for the islanders, regardless of denomination.

The Board's report for 1936 is indicative of the growth which had been made at the St. James Parochial School. It was described as an elemen-

[59] Sanders, "The Workshop," *The New Advance*, p. 4–5.
[60] Sanders, "The Workshop," *The New Advance*, p. 5.

tary school with an enrollment of 230 pupils and offering extension courses for adults. In 1953 six persons, including the Reverend and Mrs. Sanders, comprised the staff, the largest in the history of the school. In 1959 the eleventh grade was added and enrollment stood at 219.[61]

In addition to the regular academic work, the girls were taught sewing, cooking, and canning, and the boys were given instruction and practice in upholstering, woodworking, and other skills. These practical courses were beneficial in a truck-farming community with a very stable market.

Within the twenty-year tenure of the Reverend Sanders at the St. James Parochial School, many achievements were realized, including the improved living standards and an enlightened attitude toward education and worship.

When the St. James Parochial School was discontinued in June of 1961, it marked the final step toward eliminating all day schools under the Board's care.

Mary A. Steele Memorial
John's Island, South Carolina

The Board constructed a school building costing $754 on John's Island in 1917. This was made possible by a legacy that came to the Board through the Women's Missionary Society of the South Bend Presbyterian Church of Chilicothe Presbytery in Pennsylvania. The Society requested that the money be used for the building on John's Island.[62]

Ishmael Moultrie, another former slave whose entrance into the Presbyterian Church, U.S.A. has already been mentioned, pioneered in these small islands off the coast of South Carolina.

The Reverend and Mrs. S. D. Thom, who had been preaching and teaching in the original structure, moved into the new building and continued their fight against the primitive folkways of the islanders. Customs were strong and deeply imbedded, thus progress was slowly made. There were lessons in the sanitation and beautification of their homes, economy, and preserving perishables for later use. The values of education and the benefits of a more intellectual and less emotional worship service were among the basic lessons they taught. The Thoms dedicated themselves to these varied services until they were relieved of the work on John's Island in 1921 by the Reverend Daniel Campbell.

[61] Sanders, "The Workshop," *The New Advance*, p. 5.
[62] *Year Book of Prayer For Missions* (New York: Presbyterian Church in the U.S.A., Board of National Missions, 1953), p. 29.

Even a short period without leadership in the church and school on these islands caused the inhabitants to lapse back gradually into what was customary. Thus, each successive pastor and teacher commented on the undesirable discoveries which they made at the beginning of their services. Conversely, they also commented on the many promising potentials which were discovered among the island dwellers.

The Reverend S. H. Scott, who relieved Campbell in 1922, wrote the following statement in 1931:

> A canning factory here would do more immediate good than the new six million dollar bridge which connects James Island with Johns Island and cuts the distance from Charleston in half, ever will. To see the nearby resorts that cost ten thousands of dollars you would think that all was well on the Island, but such is far from the case.[63]

Two years later, however, Mary A. Steele Memorial was among the other day schools which the Board discontinued in 1933.

Salem Industrial High School
Anderson, South Carolina

A small "Pay School" founded in the home of the Reverend and Mrs. John Peter Foster in about 1887 was, in all likelihood, the beginning of the Presbyterian church's program of education in Anderson, South Carolina. The beginning of the school is narrated by Mrs. Eula E. Jefferson as follows:

> Shortly after my father began his work in Anderson, the world over was a bit gloomy but he was determined to fight for success. Because he could not get help from the Board of Freedmen, he went to Pendleton, S. C., a few miles away, to teach in the public school. Mrs. Susan Foster, my mother, opened a pay school. This was the beginning of the Anderson Industrial School. This school grew to be the largest in the town. Through the founding of this school, the young people, as well as the adults of all denominations really cemented the fellowship and love for the Presbyterian Church.[64]

This account of the formative years of the school is substantiated by a biographical sketch of John Peter Foster, which states that he was about twenty-five years old when he went to Anderson, after completing a theo-

[63] BNM, *Annual Report*, 1931, p. 128.
[64] Letter from Mrs. Eula E. Jefferson, daughter of Rev. John Foster, 1961.

logical course at Howard University. He remained at the Anderson
school to see the work which he and his wife had established grow and
many of his pupils fill a variety of useful positions in the community and
beyond. After twenty-eight years, Foster resigned in 1915 to accept work
at Kendall Institute in Sumter, South Carolina. This move on the part of
Foster was equivalent to an exchange, since Dr. A. U. Frierson, who had
been at Kendall for thirteen years, resigned his position there to fill the
one created by Foster's resignation.[65] While the Reverend Foster was at
Anderson, however, the Board of Missions for Freedmen had taken over
the school and expanded its physical plant, as is evidenced by the following Board report in 1905: "A farm has been purchased in connection
with our school work at Anderson, S. C., for $1,800 . . . the purchase
money having been sent to us by a good friend of the work."[66]

Although there are no available records to establish the exact date
when the school came under the Board's care, a rather reliable conjecture
can be made from dates that are given. The school was not listed in the
Board report for 1903. It does, however, appear in the 1904 report. It
seems reasonable to conclude, therefore, that the school was taken under
the Board's care sometime between May of 1903 and May of 1904.

Apparently a change in location and the construction of a new building brought about inactivity at the school between 1918 and 1919. In
1917 the Board made the following announcement in its report:

> At Anderson, S. C. we have maintained a church school for some
> years but have felt that the locality in which the school is situated
> was unfavorable. Having a small farm on the edge of town, not
> bringing us any income, we bargained with a real estate man to
> secure for the $2,500 of the farm price, five acres in a desirable
> locality in Anderson and on this site erected a new school building
> at a cost of $5,449 including $2,100 of the farm money. . . .[67]

Between 1918 and 1919 the Board made no report of activity at
Anderson, but in 1919 the Reverend Benjamin H. McFadden is reported
actively engaged at the school. Turnovers were swift during these postwar
years, and the Reverend Charles W. Francis was commissioned to take
charge of the school in 1922. Francis remained with the school until it
was discontinued by the Board of National Missions June 1, 1933.

---

[65] W. N. Hartshorn (ed.), *An Era of Progress and Promise* (Boston: The
Priscilla Publ. Co., 1910), p. 154.

[66] *Minutes*, 1905, p. 352.

[67] BMF, *Annual Report*, 1917, p. 10.

Irmo Parochial School
Irmo, South Carolina

In 1912, the Board of Missions for Freedmen established the Irmo Parochial School to meet the serious educational needs of blacks in the little town of Irmo, South Carolina. This school not only served as a feeder school for Harbison, located about a mile away, but it also aroused and awakened the people to a realization of their spiritual and intellectual needs.

Mrs. C. B. Johnson, of the Johnson family who made tremendous contributions to the educational and spiritual needs of Negroes in Irmo and Columbia, opened the school in 1912 with sixty-one pupils. In 1913, Mrs. R. H. Boulware joined Mrs. Johnson and helped to raise the enrollment to 96. Thereafter, the enrollment never dropped below 100 and rose to a high of 231 in 1917, when Mrs. G. L. Hardy joined the workers there.

The Board erected a new building for the school in 1920. It was financed by a gift of $2,500 from "a friend" and housed 300 pupils. A report from the school in 1926 describes its program:

> We have eight grades and the children who finish from the eighth grade are able to make first year high school wherever they go. Our forty boys and girls who are now in high school, are studying with the intention of becoming teachers, preachers, farmers, doctors, trained nurses, music teachers, dress makers, etc. Many other boys and girls have finished from our Colleges and Seminaries. Last year, we had two of our own girls back as teachers and we are very proud of them.[68]

Mrs. J. G. Porter, wife of a former president of Harbison, after joining the staff in 1918 made this report to the Board of National Missions. She continued her description with an explanation of the splendid effects of the Spiritual Emphasis Week on the campus and community. Negro Health Week was also stressed in this report. She explained how each day of the week was devoted to some particular phase of health and how the 210 pupils were requested to launch a cleanup campaign. The report also announced that the Division of Work for Colored People, under which the school was then operating, because of a shortage of funds had cut the term from eight to six months, and that the school raised $100 toward its own support. One teacher was paid for two months out of the sale of clothing from missionary barrels and boxes.

[68] BNM, *Annual Report*, 1926, p. 132.

The Board of National Missions was operating the parochial school on Harbison property about a mile away from the campus and in 1933 merged it with the college program. That year 174 students were enrolled.

Frasier Excelsior School
Bamberg, South Carolina

The Board of Missions for Freedmen was still establishing small day schools in South Carolina in 1916. A day school was established in Bamberg, South Carolina, that year with the Reverend and Mrs. W. A. Robinson as directors of the 125 pupils who enrolled for instruction.

In 1921, the Board's annual report made the following announcement:

> At Bamberg, S. C., we erected a new school building at a cost of about $5,000. This is a large and flourishing day school . . . known as the Frasier Excelsior School already they have over 232 pupils in attendance.[69]

The establishment of the Frasier Excelsior School answered a serious need in that rural section of South Carolina. One pastor of the town wrote to the Board when the General Assembly began to feel that the Southern states were beginning to upgrade their elementary schools: "The removal of the school would be a death blow to the intellectual, moral and spiritual growth of the people in this locality."[70] The Board, however, reiterated its original policy concerning the maintenance of day schools in the Southern states, "It is the well established policy of the Board to close these elementary schools as rapidly as it becomes possible for the different Southern States to provide education for the Colored children."[71] It is obvious that the school only lasted a few more years, as it was not in operation when the Board of National Missions executed the mass closure of day schools in 1933.

[69] *Minutes*, 1921, p. 344.
[70] BNM, *Annual Report*, 1926, p. 132.
[71] BNM, *Annual Report*, 1926, p. 132.

THE GEORGIA SCHOOLS   6

Allen Augustus Jones and Mary Magdeline Bomar Jones laid the foundation for the Board of Missions for Freedmen's program of education for the liberated slaves in Georgia. In 1867, the Bomar[1] family moved to Dalton, Georgia, where there had never been a school for Negroes. Mary Bomar's mother was persuaded to open a school for the freedmen, and Mary, age eleven, having a better education than her mother, became her assistant. The Reverend G. S. Thompson, a graduate of Lincoln University, discovered the school operated by the Bomars and wrote appreciatively of it to the General Assembly's newly appointed Committee on Freedmen. His communication was received and in the spring of 1869, Mary received her first check, for thirty dollars, for services at the school. With or without pay, the Bomars continued their earnest endeavors among those who were still dazed and groping for a clearer understanding of their newfound freedom.[2]

The union of two mission-minded persons in Dalton, Georgia, strength-

[1] When their emancipation came, Mary and her mother took the name of Mary's father, Bomar and moved into a house which he leased for them, according to the Reverend J. T. Jones, youngest son of Allen Augustus and Mary Magdeline Jones. J. T. Jones, "The Life and Works of Allen A. and Mary M. Jones" (S.T.B. thesis, Johnson C. Smith University, 1953), p. 6. This thesis is now in the library of the Interdenominational Theological Center, Atlanta, Ga.
[2] Jones, "The Life and Works," pp. 7–10.

ened the Bomar project in that section of Georgia. Allen Augustus Jones and Mary Magdeline Bomar were married on July 10, 1875, and spent some ten years thereafter pioneering in church and school work in the state of Georgia. Allen Augustus Jones was born near Macon, Georgia, and when General William T. Sherman passed through Macon on his famous "March to the Sea," Allen followed the soldiers more than a hundred miles until he was halted by cold weather, hunger, and fatigue. He returned to Macon, and the Reverend David Laney discovered him wandering about the streets looking for work. Laney helped him secure work, taught him basic academic fundamentals, and in 1866 Jones entered Maryville College in Maryville, Tennessee, where he spent five years. In 1868, he was licensed to preach by the Presbytery of Kingston and was ordained in 1872 by the Presbytery of Knox. He began his ministerial career in Dalton, Georgia.

After their marriage, the Joneses remained in Dalton through 1877 and went to Atlanta, Georgia, in 1878, teaching and preaching until 1884, when they moved to Madison with their three children. While in Madison, they organized a church and school and purchased three acres of land on a road leading to Oglethorpe. They later built a home on this lot and a church and school nearby. Still later, they pioneered in Greensboro, Georgia and built a church and school there.[3]

When the Joneses left Georgia to begin their work in South Carolina, they had established a total of eight church-school plants in various sections of the state. Mrs. Jones spoke specifically about their numerous activities in the state of Georgia:

> I taught mission schools at the following places in Georgia and my husband came along with me and established preaching stations and later these grew into churches: Oglethorpe, near Union Point, Rome, Dalton, Greensboro, Atlanta, Madison, Decator [sic], and Macon, Georgia. Many of these small beginnings grew into thriving well established churches and schools. Allen was known as the "Father of Presbyterianism in Georgia."[4]

When they left Georgia the Joneses went to the state of South Carolina and continued their services at McConnellsville.

As late as 1889, the Board of Missions had only three schools operating under its care in the state of Georgia: Midway, Rome, and Macon.

---

[3] J. N. Robinson, *Presbyterian Ministerial Directory*, 1898, p. 34.
[4] Jones, "The Life and Works," pp. 9–10.

The Pleasant Grove Parochial School
Liberty County, Georgia

The Pleasant Grove Parochial School, located in Liberty County, Georgia, was in connection with the Pleasant Grove Church. It is said to have been founded in 1866 by the Reverend Joseph Williams, "Uncle Joe," who was pioneering in that section immediately following the close of the Civil War. The church is also said to be the oldest church in Liberty County.

The narrative of "Uncle Joe's" work in Liberty County is similar to that of Ishmael Moultrie and Paul Campbell pioneering among the deserted slaves in South Carolina sea islands and "Parson" Charles Stewart, the pioneer circuit rider among the Choctaw freedmen in the Indian Territory. There were countless other unnamed freedmen, with little learning and a great deal of native ability and compassion for their fellow sufferers, who became self-appointed preachers to show the way to a better life, long before an organized approach to the problem was effected. Descendants of early Liberty County freedmen still remember with deep affection the stirring appeals of "Uncle Joe."[5]

The missionaries who came to Liberty County later found the visible signs of Williams' work, revamped and pushed it on toward the fulfillment of his dreams.

The Reverend H. N. Payne, field representative of the Board of Missions for Freedmen, with headquarters in Atlanta visited the area. He reported two parochial schools being operated from the Pleasant Grove post, which were located about six miles south of Riceboro. It was apparent to him that the Reverend Joseph Williams laid the groundwork for the Presbyterian program in Liberty County, beginning at Midway and Pleasant Grove, while he was sponsored by the Knox Presbytery.[6]

The Pleasant Grove section of Georgia, from the standpoint of population, literacy of the freedmen, and their economic achievements, compared favorably with that at Midway, which will be described in detail in the narrative of the Midway school.

It is obvious that "Uncle Joe" was not a trained man and, though he gave full measure of his ingenuity to bring the freedmen to a state of awareness of the meaning of their freedom, a planned program for progress was necessary. In 1889, the Reverend A. M. Caldwell took over the work at St. Paul and Pleasant Grove and remained with those posts

---

[5] William Metz, Study for the Catawba Presbytery, 1927.
[6] Metz, Study.

until 1905. He had received the S.T.B. degree from the theological seminary of Biddle University, and between 1889 and 1905, his devotion and
industry created the necessary planned program.[7]

When the Presbyterian work in Georgia was divided between Knox
and Hodge presbyteries in 1903, Pleasant Grove went under the care of
Hodge Presbytery and the guidance of the Reverend Italy Le Conte, who
greatly stimulated the progress of the school and church. By 1916 the
enrollment of the Pleasant Grove Parochial School had increased to 203,
and there were five teachers on the staff. The continuous growth and
services of the school were reflected in its steadily increasing enrollment.
In 1921 the enrollment had increased to 225. The Pleasant Grove Parochial School, however, was discontinued with thirty-eight other day
schools in 1933.

Haines Normal and Industrial Institute
Augusta, Georgia

The formative period of the Haines Normal and Industrial Institute is
inextricably interwoven in the struggle of an ex-slave girl to see a dream
come true. The institute was founded in Augusta, Georgia, in 1886 by
Lucy Craft Laney, daughter of the Reverend David Laney, co-organizer
of the Presbytery of Knox in 1867. He had been ordained a Presbyterian
minister by the Hopewell Presbytery of the Southern church but withdrew later and was received by the Old School Assembly of the Presbyterian Church, U.S.A., in 1868. During the slave period, Lucy's mother,
Louise, belonged to the Campbell family. When she married she was permitted to live with her family in their own home.[8]

Lucy was taught to read and write by Miss Campbell, her master's
sister, who chose her books and in 1869 made it possible for her to enroll
at Atlanta University at the age of fifteen. Lucy was one of the four students comprising the first graduating class of Atlanta University in 1873.

Her teaching career began in a public elementary school in Savannah,
Georgia, where she rose to the principalship of that school. When her
health began to fail, she went back to Augusta hoping that the climate
would be more suitable. When she grew stronger, however, she returned
to her work in Savannah, but not until she had promised the Reverend
W. J. White, pastor of the Harmony Baptist Church, that she would re-

[7] Metz, Study.
[8] Sadie Iola Daniel, *Women Builders* (Washington, D. C.: The Associated
Publishers, 1931), p. 10.

turn to begin a school for Negro youth. In the meantime, Dr. Richard H. Allen, who knew her parents and who at that time was corresponding secretary of the Board of Missions for Freedmen, convinced her of the need for a day nursery for the daughters of black working mothers. Miss Laney liked the proposal and moved back to Augusta at the end of the school term in Savannah. On January 6, 1886, she rented the lecture room in the basement of the Christ Presbyterian Church on Cummings and Telfair Streets and began a small school. She had envisioned a school for girls only but on that first rainy morning, three girls and two boys came to the school, and Miss Laney enrolled them all.[9]

Within two months her quarters were overflowing. She went to J. F. Davidson, an attorney who owned a large, vacant, two-story building on Calhoun Street and asked to rent the building. He was astonished and told her that the pupils would not go to school in it since it was reputed to be a haunted house. Miss Laney insisted and the lawyer replied, "All right, I'll let you have it to use; all you have to do is pay the taxes. But I tell you, they will not follow you in it."[10] Miss Laney converted the building into a home and dormitory and turned an old barn on the lot into schoolrooms. By means of ropes and pulleys the separate compartments could be converted into an assembly room for devotional exercises and concerts. Seventy-five pupils enrolled the first year, and by the end of the second 234 had enrolled.[11] Miss Laney supplemented her personal savings with donations and paid the teachers who came to help her after the first one or two years.

The school was clearly growing, and Miss Laney was persuaded to appeal to the General Assembly in behalf of the school. The General Assembly convened in Minneapolis that spring of 1886.[12] Despite the fact that she only had daycoach fare one way, she went to Minneapolis. Exhausted from the harrowing trip by way of a Jim Crow coach and spiritually hurt by the jealousy encountered over the possible influence her speech might wield at the expense of other phases of the work, she fell asleep in the Assembly Hall. Aroused by hearing her name called, she stood and, in sincere and simple eloquence, addressed the Assembly in the interest of "my people," asking only for return trip fare back to

[9] Daniel, *Women Builders*, p. 10.

[10] Daniel, *Women Builders*, p. 5.

[11] G. F. Richings, *Evidences of Progress Among Colored People* (Philadelphia: George S. Ferguson Co., 1902), p. 166.

[12] Richings, *Evidences*, p. 166.

Augusta. This was the extent of financial aid which she gained from the experience.

Some of the commissioners were in favor of aiding the school in Augusta, but the men in charge of the freedmen's schools objected and the available money went to the general program. The Board of Missions for Freedmen did, however, pledge its moral support and commissioned Miss Laney without pay.

Through courage and determination, the old "Haunted House" began to buzz with activity and youthful enthusiasm until it was struck by typhoid fever. Miss Cora Freeman, who had been teaching at the school for three years, became a victim of the epidemic. A druggist sent morphine instead of quinine and only quick action averted a mass tragedy.[13]

Miss Laney's trip to the General Assembly, though discouraging at first, began to bear fruit in 1889. She had made staunch friends while in Minneapolis. One of these friends was Mrs. F. E. H. Haines of Detroit, Michigan, secretary of the Women's Executive Committee of Home Missions. Her influence was a strong factor in favor of the school, and the Board of Missions took the school under its care in 1889. In addition, tourists staying at the Bon Air Hotel in Augusta were told about the school, and a Mrs. Marshall visited Miss Laney and gave money to purchase a site for the school. Later her daughter gave $10,000 to erect Marshall Hall on the lot between Phillip and Robert streets facing Gwinnett Street. Marshall was a four-story, brick structure with classrooms on the first floor and girls' dormitory facilities on the upper floors.[14]

The following report of the Board to the General Assembly in 1891 differs from this history, leaving out the total independence of Lucy Laney from the Board during the first years of the school:

> We now have a most interesting work at Augusta, Georgia. Some five years ago, Miss Lucy Laney, a colored girl, went there under commission of the Board, but without a salary, as she requested, to open a school. The school succeeded beyond all expectations. Miss Laney was re-inforced by other teachers, and the school taken under the care of the Board, and it became necessary to build a house for them. By the generous gift of a friend in Pittsburgh, Pa. of $10,000, the Board was enabled at once to erect a substantial building at a cost of about $20,000 which was completed and occupied last fall, and has enrolled this year 525 pupils. The School is the Haines Industrial Academy, named in memory of Mrs. F. E. H. Haines of

13 Daniel, *Women Builders*, p. 11.
14 Daniel, *Women Builders*, p. 12.

Detroit, the late efficient Secretary of the Women's Executive Committee of Home Missions.[15]

Despite the different elements in the reports of these early years, Miss Laney finally won tangible endorsement of the Board and substantial financial support of friends, making the school more secure.

Dr. Richard H. Allen, a staunch friend favoring the development of Haines, died September 27, 1893, and the Reverend E. P. Cowan succeeded him as director of the freedmen's work. Reflecting on Miss Laney's fruitless trip to the General Assembly in 1886, Cowan made the following confession in 1893:

> Equipped for work and fired with a dauntless zeal for the elevation of her race, of whom she always speaks as "my people," she entered Augusta, single-handed and alone and began teaching the few children she could at the beginning draw around her. As she taught, her school increased. No one stood by her at the first. The Freedmen's Board was back of her, but we scarcely knew her value at the time, commissioning her for the work, but giving her only what she could collect for her services on the field. On this point her success brought us the information we needed. We did not help her at the first as we would now. Her courage, patience, self-forgetfulness, and withal her good common sense, attracted attention. She began with a few and at the end of the first year reported 75 scholars under her care. At the end of the second year she reported 234. The progress of her work was so satisfactory that when the opportunity to place $10,000 in some particular educational work in the South came to the Board, the unanimous opinion of the members was that Miss Laney's school had merited the proposed help.[16]

In 1897, the Savannah River overran its banks and Haines Industrial Institute was marooned for three days. Professor J. N. Tutt's father, one of the rescue crew carrying drinking water, food, and other supplies, stuck a nail in his foot and died of blood poisoning. Thus Haines' early years continued to be struck by epidemic, floods, and fire.[17]

The Board made the following announcement in its 1898 report to the General Assembly:

Haines Academy was one of the special projects brought before

[15] BMF, *Annual Report*, 1891, p. 7.
[16] E. P. Cowan, article in *The Church at Home and Abroad*, August, 1893, cited in Richings, *Evidences*, pp. 165–166.
[17] Daniel, *Women Builders*, p. 12.

the ladies last year. The flood of September last, which over flowed
the building now occupied, makes it more imperative that a house
be provided for the school. A lot in a most desirable part of the city
has been bought and paid for, and we are now ready to receive
donations for the building. It would be a shame to leave this school
of more than 300 pupils without suitable accommodations.[18]

Miss Laney's budget frequently exceeded that approved by the Board.
She refused, however, to cut back her staff, her term, or turn away pupils.
She maintained that good teachers could not be expected to remain at
Haines for less than they could get elsewhere. She, therefore, often used
her own salary to supplement teachers' salaries when she could not beg or
borrow the amount needed.

Despite the temporary setback by the loss of a dormitory by fire, the
school's growth was phenomenal, beginning in 1886 with 75 pupils and
one teacher; by 1901 it had an enrollment of 512 pupils under the instruction of fourteen instructors. When McGreger Hall was erected in
1906, the enrollment had reached 703. Mrs. Tracey McGreger of Michigan contributed $15,000 toward the erection of this administration build-
ing, the total cost being $18,000.[19] Mrs. Anson Phelps Stokes, after visit-
ing the school and observing its needs, contributed to it an entire city
square, with the exception of one corner which the school already owned.
Another timely gift came from a friend of Mrs. Stokes in the form of a
beautiful and costly organ.

After twenty years of amazing personal sacrifice, firm faith, and un-
swerving courage by the founder, Miss Mary Laney, her vision began to
take shape. Her brother Frank L. Laney and Mrs. James Smith, along
with Miss Mary McLeod Bethune, joined her staff. Miss Mae Belcher,
one of the first five students to enroll in 1886, also joined the staff and
gave many years of valuable service to her alma mater.

During the long struggle to get the school properly housed, the academic program was not neglected. The word "Industrial" in the name
was misleading, since the school was, at all times, typically academic or
classical. Although some thought it foolish, Miss Laney continued to require the students to decline Latin nouns and conjugate Latin verbs, and
algebra and the classics were stressed. The literary department of Haines
consisted of college preparatory courses, higher English, grammar school,
primary, and kindergarten. There was a well-planned normal course and

[18] G. A. Board Reports, 1898, p. 16.
[19] *Minutes*, 1905, p. 369, and BMF, *Annual Report*, 1906, p. 9.

more than a dozen young women had graduated from it by 1908. Before the kindergarten was recognized as an important phase of education in the South, Haines had a well-equipped kindergarten with a trained teacher. The employment of Miss Irene Smallwood, the first kindergarten instructor, and the furnishings in the kindergarten department were made possible through generous gifts from friends in Buffalo, New York.[20] It was later supported by the Lucy Laney League of New York City, an organization which consisted of Haines graduates who decided in 1900 to express their lasting devotion to the school in a material way.

In 1908, shortly before his inauguration as president of the United States, William H. Taft visited Haines. Speaking of Miss Laney, he said to the friends with him:

> That a colored woman could have constructed this great institution of learning and brought it to its present state of usefulness speaks volumes for her capacity. Therefore, I shall go out of this meeting, despite the distinguished presence here, carrying in my memory only the figure of that woman who has been able to create all this.[21]

The addition of a teacher-training program necessitated a building specifically for the purpose. A bequest of $10,000 from a Mrs. Wheeler made this possible in 1924. The Lucy Laney League of New York City provided a cottage for Miss Laney, which she did not use until after her health began to fail. With an enrollment of between seven and eight hundred, Haines became the largest school under the Board's care in 1926 and its only school with a woman executive.[22]

In May of 1932, the General Council of the General Assembly classified Haines as a day school since 409 of its 446 pupils were day students. With few exceptions, the deadline for closing all day schools was set for June 1, 1933. Dr. John M. Gaston, Secretary of the Division of Work for Colored People, wrote in *Women and Missions* for February, 1934, that seventy-two workers had been dismissed and thirty-nine schools had been discontinued.[23] Pertaining specifically to Haines, he wrote:

> At the beginning of the year, it was felt that on account of a reduced budget we would have to close Haines Normal and Industrial Institute of Augusta, Ga. The local Board of Trustees, with other

---

[20] Richings, *Evidences*, pp. 166–167.
[21] Hartshorn, *An Era*, p. 207.
[22] Daniel, *Women Builders*, p. 13.
[23] Gaston, "A Review," *Women and Missions*, vol. X, no. 11, p. 359.

friends of the institution, held a conference and proposed that the local Board of Trustees would pay all the salaries of all the teachers, amounting to $5,280 if the Board of National Missions would allow $2,300 for maintenance. This group, has to date, sent in over $2,100, and the school is operated under this mutual agreement. Miss Lucy C. Laney, the founder and for forty-eight years the principal, thus had the joy of seeing the work continue before she passed on to well earned reward last October.[24]

By this mutual agreement Haines was continued as a day school. Dr. August Cummings Griggs, a teacher of history and chaplain of the institution from 1913 to 1925, with the A.B. and S.T.B. degrees from Lincoln University, was appointed principal and treasurer of Haines. The school was closed in 1952.

Midway Parochial School
Midway, Georgia

The Midway Parochial School was established in Midway, Georgia, in 1874 by the Reverend James Thomas Hamilton Waite. The Reverend William L. Metz wrote in the *Africo-American Presbyterian* in September, 1927:

The first white man, according to record, to labor in Georgia among the Freedmen after the Civil War was The Reverend James Thomas Hamilton Wait[e], who was commissioned to labor as a missionary among the Freedmen, in Brunswick, Ga. . . . Rev. James Thomas Hamilton Wait[e] was born in New York City, February 17, 1825. He graduated from Columbia Theological Seminary, North Carolina, '52. . . .[25]

In 1872 and 1873, the Committee of Missions for Freedmen had reported to the General Assembly that Mrs. R. A. Grimes was teaching thirty-eight pupils at Midway, Georgia, near Dorchester in Liberty County. How long she worked with Reverend Williams, "Uncle Joe," is not known. She was, however, there in 1874 when Waite arrived. It is not known whether Waite built upon this earlier work or whether his way was a new beginning.

Liberty County, Georgia, did not present the appalling conditions which other missionaries encountered in other sections of the Wilderness. Waite was pleased with the caliber of the freedmen and the temper of the

[24] Gaston, "Review," *Women and Missions*, vol. X, no. 11, p. 361.
[25] William Metz, "Blazers and Chips," *Africo-American Presbyterian*, vol. XLIX, no. 39 (September 29, 1927), p. 1.

Liberty County community. He attributed the more favorable conditions
to the influence of the early settlers who had migrated there from the New
England section. The 1878 report of the Committee stated that:

> This school is located in Liberty County, Georgia,—the first county
> settled in the State. The original settlers were Pilgrims from New
> England. They have left the impress of their manliness, intelligence
> and piety on their descendants. In the County, slaves were long a
> majority, and by the death and emigration of the whites, the Freed-
> men are much more so.[26]

As was customary in the South during the slave period, the slaves
attended the church of their masters. This had been the case in Midway
as explained by Waite:

> Medway [sic] Church (white) was, nominally at least, Congrega-
> tional up to the time of the late war, but for 100 years previous, had
> been served by Presbyterian ministers; many of these colored people
> were members of it, and at the close of the War, were united as a
> Presbyterian Church under the care of Rev. Joseph Williams, famili-
> arly known as "Uncle Joe."[27]

Waite described the economic uniqueness of the Liberty County freedmen:

> The lands within a radius of five miles around the Church have
> been mostly bought by the Freedmen who having built their cabins
> and provided their implements, are still struggling under many dis-
> advantages to pay for their homes. The entire district (the 15th) is
> largely held by Presbyterian Freedmen, who ever since emancipa-
> tion longed for a school. The Medway [sic] colored Presbyterian
> Church is large reporting 665 members, 15 ruling elders, and 13
> deacons. The Freedmen of Liberty County are in power, as the gov-
> erning majority. Georgia does not and will not for many years, pro-
> vide public schools for more than three months in the year.[28]

Waite's detailed report continued with a statement regarding the liter-
ate level of the pupils; the attitude of the black community toward education, and the organization of the school:

> In 1874, when the school was first organized, most of the scholars
> knew the alphabet and a few could read blunderingly. But now, if,

[26] Minutes, 1878, pp. 203–204.
[27] CMF, *Annual Report*, 1878, p. 24.
[28] *Minutes*, 1878, p. 204.

as wise men have often said, correct spelling, proper reading, legible writing, and thoroughness in the four processes of arithmetic constitute an excellent education, Medway [sic] School has been very successful. There has been a regular advance from division to division, and nearly 100 who began in the third Department have risen to the First: nearly all in this department can write with positive beauty. Seven out of the First Department have each obtained a teachers' certificate from the white Board of County Commissioners, and have taught with commendation.[29]

This review describes specifically the founders' concept of the situation in Liberty County as he found it. He spoke of "the fortunate purchase of a huge old building" which was in the process of being renovated and the comfort which should follow its completion. He also had hopes of receiving stoves from a friend in New Jersey, which should complete their comfort.

The Waites were joined by their son Paul, in 1878, and their daughter Roxie, in 1879. Mrs. A. L. Lyons also joined the staff that year and by 1881, the enrollment had reached 200. In 1889 Miss I. Lambright was added to the staff, and in 1890 another son James, joined the family in its work.

Apparently, the Waites began a parochial school in connection with the church work within the town limits of Dorchester, also in Liberty County, in 1894 with 87 pupils enrolled. This increased to 100 students in 1895. While the Waites were in Dorchester proper, Mr. and Mrs. C. C. Cassels were out in Liberty County at the Midway Mission with a limited enrollment in 1894. In 1895, Mr. S. L. Stacy had charge of the work at Midway. The following term the school was under the guidance of Miss Effie Stevens with 50 pupils under instruction, while Mrs. Waite had 55 under instruction in Dorchester.

The Board does not include the Midway School as under its care after 1896. Therefore, it was either discontinued or operated outside of the Board's program. In 1897, however, Mrs. Waite is listed as instructor of 40 pupils at the Dorchester Parochial School. Following this date no further mention is made of the Dorchester Parochial School. Although the school is not mentioned, the church at Midway was reported to be very active, with 537 members in 1898. According to a study made by the Reverend William L. Metz for the Catawba Presbytery in 1927, the Reverend Waite was still the pastor in 1898. Metz's study also revealed

---

[29] *Minutes*, 1878, p. 204.

that the school operated by the American Missionary Society enrolled the students who had attended the Waite school and the county took over the Midway property.

After twenty-nine years of missionary services in this rather isolated but unique section of the state, the Reverend Waite died in Savannah and was succeeded as pastor by the Reverend N. N. Gregg, who had received his A.B. degree from Lincoln in 1899 and the B.D. degree from Auburn Theological Seminary in 1902. The Reverend Gregg was pastor at Midway for six months, after which time the church does not appear on the Board's roll of churches.

Ebenezer Parochial School
Rome, Georgia

The Ebenezer Parochial School, established in Rome, Georgia, in the early 1880s, exemplifies several such schools that were founded by individuals or the Board which struggled for a decade or more and then ceased. Their impermanence was often caused by the inability to get a supporting church operating in the vicinity, the monopoly of other denominations, or the migration of the freedmen away from the area.[30]

The Reverend and Mrs. Calvin McCurdy arrived in Rome, Georgia, between 1883 and 1884, and began the groundwork for establishing a church and school in that town. McCurdy was one of the first three men to complete the theological course at Biddle University, Charlotte, North Carolina. He received the S.T.B. degree after President Stephen Mattoon had thoroughly instructed him in theory and the actual nature of the mission field to which he was being sent. He accepted the president's proposal to go to Rome, Georgia, evidently after some time in Macon.

As stated in a study made by Metz for the Catawba Presbytery, the Reverend McCurdy as pastor, and Messrs. Ned Huggins, T. A. Attaway, Stephen Allen, and W. A. Jackson, as elders, petitioned the Georgia legislature for a charter establishing the Ebenezer Church and School. The charter was granted. On this basis, a double-purpose edifice was constructed and dedicated in 1887.

The Reverend McCurdy spent several years founding and developing

[30] Schools which probably had fairly similar histories in Georgia, judging from the scanty records, were: St. James (Decatur); Columbia (Columbia); Day Memorial (Arcadia); Washington (Macon); Antioch (Dalton); Butler (Savannah); Alamo (Alamo); Allen Memorial (Milledgeville); Olgethorpe (Union Point); Radcliff Memorial (Atlanta); Bethany (Conyers); Riceboro (Riceboro); Center (Center); Dorchester (Dorchester); Ebenezer (Fleming).

the school and church and retired in 1890 because of ill health. He was succeeded by the following persons: the Reverend R. H. Blunt, 1890; the Reverend C. S. Hodges, 1895; and lastly, the Reverend W. W. Walker, who was in charge of the school when the last report was made in 1905.

McClelland Academy
Newnan, Georgia

McClelland Academy was established in Newnan, Georgia, in 1889 by the Reverend and Mrs. B. L. Glenn. The Board of Missions reported that year that the Glenns were operating two churches and a parochial school with 45 pupils enrolled. A new church building was erected in 1894, and the parochial school had developed into an academy with 90 pupils enrolled, which increased to 117 by 1899. In 1900 the Board made the following observation: "The McClelland Academy, located at Newnan, Georgia, under the care of Reverend B. L. Glenn and his wife, with the long-prayed-for teacher and the attractive new school building, reported 135 pupils, ranging in age from 6 to 38, has attained good results."[31] The "long-prayed-for teacher" to whom the Board referred was Miss Sallie E. Jones. Miss Mary E. Smart joined the staff in 1901. There were 148 pupils enrolled that year under the instruction of four teachers, including Glenn.

After the first school building was erected the enrollment increased annually: in 1902, 191 students were enrolled; in 1903, there were 213; and in 1904, enrollment reached 221. The following year the Women's Department of the Board of Missions for Freedmen announced that the Women's Department had been asked to raise $3,500 for another school building at McClelland.[32] The Reverend Glenn never lived to see the proposed building erected:

> Rev. B. L. Glenn, who was known to so many of our societies by correspondence as Principal of the McClelland School at Newnan, Georgia, and who came to the Assembly last year to plead for a new and larger building for his school, was on the 27th of September called suddenly and unexpectedly without a moment's warning to the Heavenly Home.[33]

The Reverend Glenn's sudden death left his wife, an expectant mother, with five small children to rear. He also left an active church, a three-

---

[31] Women's Board, *Annual Report*, 1900, p. 158.
[32] *Minutes*, 1905, p. 65.
[33] Women's Board, *Annual Report*, 1905, pp. 161–162.

room school building which was packed with students, and a small amount of money to be applied to a building to house the proposed high school. The Reverend Lawrence Miller, who had been associated with the work in Macon, Georgia, was commissioned to succeed the Reverend Glenn.[34]

Mrs. Miller was familiar with the new post, since she had been connected with the earliest work of the Board in Newnan. Although the much-needed new building had not materialized, 182 students and a faculty of five greeted the Millers upon their arrival. By 1911, the faculty had increased to six, with the addition of Miss Estelle Hoskins, a Scotia graduate. Highly qualified and dedicated, Miss Hoskins was immediately engaged in the new administration's revamped program for the McClelland Academy.

The Reverend Franklin Gregg was commissioned in 1912 as assistant to Miller. Gregg, widely known for his keen intellect and scholarly approach to academic matters, was a product of Kendall Institute, Sumter, South Carolina, where he completed his preparatory work in 1901. He received the bachelor's degree from Lincoln University in 1905 and the S.T.B. degree in 1908. Miller died during the Christmas recess in 1912, and Gregg was chosen as his successor.

The academy's growth was gradual but substantial. Beginning as an elementary school, with grades added periodically until the tenth was added, the Academy became a junior high school operating eight months annually. McClelland Academy survived the drastic cutback of 1933 and continued as a day school by virtue of an urgent appeal made by the officials of the public school system. With Gregg as principal, the McClelland Academy remained active three additional years and was discontinued in 1936.[35]

Selden Institute
Brunswick, Georgia

To the roster of Presbyterian pioneer women who ventured out on faith to help the liberated slaves—Mrs. Samantha J. Neil in Virginia, Miss Lucy Craft Laney in Georgia, and Mrs. Mary Magdeline Jones in Georgia and South Carolina—must be added the name of Miss Carrie E. Bemus. On October 6, 1903, Miss Bemus, of Pennsylvania, founded Selden Institute in Brunswick, Georgia. She had traveled extensively

[34] *Minutes*, 1905, p. 406.
[35] Interview with Mrs. Hardy Liston, formerly Estelle Hoskins, in Charlotte, North Carolina, 1963.

through the state of Georgia to become acquainted with the situation and settled in Brunswick. With two freedmen to help her, she began what she called "The Normal School," for the correct training of black young men and women.[36] Working against great odds, she achieved success because of her courage and efforts.

By 1908, there were 103 students and 9 teachers. A printing office had been established, both for the use of the school and for the black community. After six years at the school, Miss Bemus died in June of 1909. In a memorial service for the founder, Mrs. F. B. Bohannon, a teacher at Selden under Miss Bemus's administration, described her after this fashion: "She was a pioneer Christian worker in the field of education; a friend of humanity, regardless of race, color or creed; one who gave the full measure of her life in service to others, and one who for many years gave sacrificial service to the education, welfare, and spiritual needs of Negro young men and women at Selden."[37]

Miss Bemus had won many friends for her work in Brunswick, and they continued to support the school. The Board of Missions for Freedmen paid a tribute to these friends in its 1914 report:

> But for their help during the past five years the school would probably not have been able to maintain itself.
> Their interest in the work is more likely to increase rather than diminish, now that it is brought wholly under Presbyterian auspices. It had been previously maintained as an undenominational school. They furnished this last year $1,500 toward the salaries of the teachers.[38]

Among the continuing friends, following the death of Miss Bemus, was the Selden family—E. P. Selden of Erie, Pennsylvania, Dr. Charles C. Selden, missionary to China, and their sister—who aided the school's operation until substantial support came to it. The Board made an exception to its general rule and took Selden under its care in 1914 when forty-seven acres of land were turned over to it in addition to $8,500 for the erection of a new building. In describing the school's progress after it came under the Board's care, the following announcement pointed out the industrial emphasis:

> Printing, nurse training, millinery, fancy needle work, domestic science and agriculture are taught daily by competent instructors.

[36] Daniel, *Women Builders*, p. 24.
[37] *The Atlantan* (Atlanta, Georgia: Atlantic Synod, December, 1961).
[38] BMF, *Annual Report*, 1914, p. 13.

Each male student is given one half acre of land to cultivate. The school furnishes each young planter with the seed plowing, fertilizer and the experienced instructor, and is allowed one third of the profit of his labor.[39]

The industrial emphasis helped in the solicitation of financial support for the mission schools. In many cases, however, as at Selden, the rich academic phase of the school's program received the major emphasis at the local level.

The institution was named "Selden Institute" in 1914, honoring the Selden family. In 1915, a new girls' dormitory, including recitation rooms, was completed. In addition, arrangements were made for kitchen facilities separate from the main building, and adequate water connections were provided at a total cost of $10,519, most of which was furnished by the Selden family.[40]

The Reverend H. A. Bleach, who had been principal since 1912, died in 1917, and Mrs. Bleach ran the school successfully for more than a year. The Reverend S. Q. Mitchell, a graduate of Biddle University and Seminary, was chosen to succeed her in 1919. He arrived at the school, wearing a first lieutenant's uniform from World War I, and found a very modern plant located between two cemeteries—one for blacks and the other for whites. The main school building was a long, two-story brick and concrete structure, which provided space for classrooms and an auditorium with folding doors for smaller enclosures. Dormitory provisions for women teachers and students, a music studio, and a private apartment for the president were located on the second floor. The dining hall and kitchen, in which home economics was taught, were in a one-story frame building. A second frame building, two-storied, housed male students and single male faculty members.[41]

The curriculum consisted of English, social studies, Spanish, Latin, Greek, physics, general science with laboratory work, arithmetic, algebra, and plain and solid geometry. In addition, for the women students were cooking, sewing, and millinery classes; men students studied printing. Typing, shorthand, and bookkeeping courses were open to both men and women. The commercial courses were taught by an efficient young woman, Miss Beatrice Monroe from Kansas.[42]

[39] *Minutes*, 1914, p. 103.
[40] *Minutes*, 1915, p. 439.
[41] Interview with Dr. R. P. Perry, an early student of Selden, in Charlotte, North Carolina, September, 1965.
[42] Perry interview, Sept., 1965.

In the area of extraclass activities, the school had an excellent mixed choir and a male quartet, which provided music for school activities and for promotional purposes. In 1919 the school had teams competing in baseball, basketball, and track. As a result of these activities, Selden became the center for community gatherings—cultural, recreational, religious, and educational. Enthusiastic people came from miles around, walking and riding, to attend these events. The Sunday evening vespers and commencement always drew large crowds.

Selden owned a bus for transporting students to and from town—the school being three miles outside of the city limits—for personal purchases, programs, and other activities. The "Red Path Chatauqua" made its annual circuit through Brunswick, and Selden students always planned far in advance to attend.[43]

One former student related this personal experience:

> During the senior year at Selden, all senior students were required to live on campus. I lived within walking distance from the institution but I packed my trunk and went away to school at Selden. It was wonderful—going away to school and becoming accustomed to boarding school life. The students serenaded city homes at Christmas and we were invited in and often were served punch, cookies, and sometimes hot chocolate. Those were great days—being away in boarding school.[44]

The enrollment ranged between 150 and 200 students during the 1920s, and the curriculum and plant underwent modest renovations. The boys' dormitory was brick veneered, and its capacity increased to twenty rooms, at a cost of $6,750.[45]

The principal, Mitchell, was a product of the Board's parochial and higher schools of learning, having received his early training at the Goodwill School and later at Biddle University. When he arrived at Selden, the students from Brunswick were either Baptist, Methodist, or Episcopalian. Mitchell was anxious to arouse interest in Presbyterianism, but he was unable to establish a functioning Presbyterian church in Brunswick. Although the Episcopal church was operating a school there, many of the Episcopal young people came to the Presbyterian school.[46]

In 1933, the doors of Selden were closed in Brunswick but reopened in Cordele, Georgia, as part of the Gillespie-Selden Institute. Its thirty years

[43] Perry interview, Sept., 1965.
[44] Perry interview, Sept., 1965.
[45] *Minutes*, 1921, p. 344.
[46] Perry interview, Sept., 1965.

of educational, spiritual, and cultural uplift of the Brunswick community were abundantly rewarding, as is evidenced by the success of its graduates in leadership positions across the nation.

Gillespie-Selden Institute
Cordele, Georgia

Gillespie Institute was established at Cordele, Georgia, September 1, 1902, by the Reverend A. S. Clark. Thirty-seven years after the Presbyterian program of education for freedmen was launched, the Reverend and Mrs. Clark traveled through southwest Georgia looking for a locality which seemed to them to have the greatest need for a school for Negro girls and boys. Unlike South Carolina, where the Presbyterians established their largest number of schools, Presbyterian strongholds were few in the state of Georgia. The Clarks' search ended at Cordele, where the St. Paul Mission Church had been established in 1898.

In a meeting called to consider the possibility of beginning a school in the vicinity, W. M. Bryant gave the first money, five dollars, toward the project. Jack Porter, the first elder in the St. Paul Mission Church, assisted in securing the lot on which to erect the school building, and James Crowley did the first actual work on the grounds.

In 1902, when the project began as a primary day school in the chapel of the St. Paul Mission Church, it was called the Converse Normal School, in honor of John H. Converse of Pittsburgh, Pennsylvania, who had contributed $500 toward its establishment. Converse, however, did not feel that the amount merited the honor. In 1904, therefore, the name was changed to Gillespie Normal School with the permission of Mrs. Nannie J. Gillespie of Pittsburgh, Pennsylvania, with whom Mrs. Clark had established a friendship during a speaking engagement in that city.

The first substantial building was erected on the campus in 1904 and was named the Converse Hall. Some senior citizens of Cordele maintain that the first name of the church established there for Negroes was the Portis Memorial Church, and that it was changed to St. Paul Presbyterian Church in 1904.

Gillespie Institute's beginning was small, consisting of two frame buildings, a faculty of three, and an enrollment of 28 boys and girls. "Leaps and bounds" is the phrase used by the Board, however, to describe the growth after its establishment. There was a steady increase in enrollment: in 1903 there were 140 students enrolled; in 1904 the enrollment consisted of 190 students, and in 1905 the student enrollment was 210. In addition to the increasing enrollment, there were other signs of growth.

In 1905, the instructional staff had been increased to five and a school chorus had been organized. The institute's library was begun in 1910, and a band was organized for the 388 students then enrolled.

During these formative years, each addition carried more than its normal weight in influence and goodwill for the school in the community. The second story of the teachers' home was completed in 1914; an orchestra was organized, and a health center was started. By 1920 shop and agriculture courses were added to the curriculum.

The Clarks were cheerful even when things looked doubtful and at all times were tireless workers. One student admirer described the Reverend Clark: "I remembered him as a man of polish and refinement, philosophical, intelligent, and maintaining at all times a high scholastic bearing that overshadowed the slightly disfiguring scar-tissue on one side of his face. His beautiful daughter became the wife of Reverend S. Q. Mitchell, principal of Selden from 1919–1933."[47]

Miss Eula Burke, a graduate of Gillespie and the University Hospital of Augusta, became head nurse of the new hospital department which had been installed in 1925. Five rooms were set apart on the second floor of the main school building for the new department which was named the Charles Helm Hospital in memory of a young leader in the Northern church who provided the funds. Eight girls enrolled for nurses' training, and both Negro and white physicians cooperated in the training program. No health facilities available to Negroes were in the vicinity, and the nearest hospital accessible to blacks was 160 miles away.[48]

The physical plant was expanded in 1927 with three frame buildings, and in 1929 a girls' dormitory, David L. Gillespie Hall, was constructed for about sixty thousand dollars. Of this amount $50,000 was given by Mrs. Gillespie after the death of her husband. In 1931–1932 a brick structure was built as a home economics kitchen.

A historic event occurred in 1933 when Selden Institute of Brunswick, Georgia, was transferred and merged with Gillespie to become the Gillespie-Selden Institute. The Gillespie family which had supported Gillespie Institute through the years continued its support, and in 1936, Mr. William J. Gillespie left the bulk of his estate for the continuing growth and development of the Gillespie-Selden Institute. The consolidated school was also fortunate that year as it narrowly escaped the damaging effects of a devastating tornado that cut a swath down the street

[47] "Gillespie-Selden Institute," *Briefly* (N.Y.: PCUSA, BNM).
[48] Mrs. A. S. Clark, "The Hospital at Gillespie," *Women and Missions*, vol. IV, no. 1 (April, 1927), p. 25.

on which it was located. The hospital, school, and church served as relief headquarters for Negroes who were homeless or injured. The church was also the living quarters for the state militia. Fifty-three patients, all seriously injured, were cared for under the direction of Red Cross nurses. Classrooms were converted into emergency wards, and the school became a refuge for every black who needed help. Gillespie-Selden boys were sent through the damaged area to assist with rescue and cleanup work.

Gillespie-Selden launched an ambitious expansion program in 1937: an administration building, containing nine rooms and a large chapel was built; the Gillespie Hospital, with a capacity of twenty-five beds, was named for Mr. William L. Gillespie. The administration building and a frame home for the superintendent of the hospital were also built through funds from the Gillespie family. In 1936, thirteen white doctors were giving their services to the patients, and some of them were soliciting funds for an ongoing program at the hospital. Drs. McArthur, Sr., Welchel, and Ward were active influences in the organization and development of the hospital.[49]

In the academic area, some major changes took place at the institution. The city public school system assumed responsibility for the first five grades but left them under Dr. Clark's direction and in Board-owned buildings. The funds released by this transaction were used to improve the high school work. The boys' dormitory was damaged by fire in 1940 but was rebuilt and surfaced with brick.

After thirty-nine years, Dr. Clark retired September 1, 1941, and L. S. Brown, who for five years was an executive at Brainerd and had served one year as principal of Harbison, was elected to fill the vacancy. In 1942, at the Board's request, the city took over the responsibility of housing the first five grades since the two buildings on the Gillespie-Selden campus were badly in need of repair. A vocation building was erected as a student project in 1943, and a building constructed from army barracks was equipped for courses in agriculture and auto mechanics for the fifty-eight veterans enrolled at the school. The institution was accredited by both the Georgia Accrediting Commission and the Southern Association of Colleges and Secondary Schools in 1949. The sixth grade was transferred to the public school system, and the city and county boards of education began transporting county high school students to Gillespie-Selden during this year.

Gillespie-Selden added the twelfth grade to its high school curriculum

[49] "Gillespie-Selden Institute," *Brevities* (N.Y.: PCUSA, BNM, 1936).

in 1950 in order to conform to the revised state program for high schools. In addition, the school offered limited adult vocational courses in home economics, agriculture, shop work, business, beauty-culture, practical nursing, and brick masonry.

The Board of National Missions approved a plan in 1951 for studying uses of the Gillespie Hospital in view of a proposed nonsegregated hospital in Cordele. In October, 1953, the Gillespie Hospital was closed when the new, modern, well-equipped, biracial Crisp County Hospital replaced its services. As soon as the Board learned that the county had applied for federal Hill-Burton funds, thus forcing plans for biracial accommodations, it announced the closing of Gillespie Hospital. Mrs. Eula Burke Johnson, head nurse at Gillespie Hospital for twenty-five years, was called to the new hospital as chief nurse in the Negro wing.

In keeping with the opening and closing trends during this period, the city and county announced plans for erecting a modern elementary and high school building for Negroes, at a cost of $335,000, that would be ready for occupancy by September 1954. As a result of these two developments, the Board approved the sale of the school and shop buildings, with the stipulation that the proceeds would be used to provide a day care center, adult education facilities, recreation, boarding facilities for high school students, and many other services for the black community.

The formal opening of the new day care center was held on February 15, 1954, in the old Gillespie Hospital building. There were thirty-five children enrolled that day, ranging in age from one to five years old. A biracial advisory committee was set up for the day care center and the school of practical nursing. This new school of practical nursing was opened with five students in the old Gillespie Hospital building on January 3, 1955. The student nurses got their clinical experience at Phoebe Putney Memorial Hospital in Albany, Georgia. On January 10, 1956 the first class, consisting of four persons, graduated. In 1957, the clinical experience was transferred to the General Hospital in Macon, Georgia.

The closing phase of Gillespie-Selden's educational program was accompanied with greater compassion than was the case in many of her sister schools. The development of new areas of work carried on the good intentions of the founders and the benefactors of the mission work.

Boggs Academy
Keysville, Georgia

Through Burke County, Georgia, about thirty-five miles south of Augusta, runs a roadway called Quaker Road. Over this path General

William Sherman marched from Atlanta to Savannah during the Civil War. One stretch of Quaker Road winds through a piney grove, not far from Keysville, and emerges upon an expansive, cleared plateau which is dotted with low, modern, red brick buildings. This is Boggs Academy. It was founded in 1906 by the Reverend Dr. John Lawrence Phelps, at the suggestion of Mr. J. S. Reynolds, solicitor general of the Augusta District. In the midst of this green setting—deep in the heart of the "Black Belt" of Georgia, where superstition and ignorance gripped the minds of the inhabitants, and where the seeds of discord between the house slaves and field slaves had germinated and taken deep root—the Presbyterian Church, U.S.A. established the academy on a two-acre plot donated by a Baptist elder. The school was named for Mrs. Virginia P. Boggs, at that time corresponding secretary of the Board of Missions for Freedmen.[50]

Reynolds had told the Board of the need for a boarding school for blacks in the vicinity and had promised his assistance, even though some in the vicinity felt that it would be impossible to establish and maintain such a school in the area. The Reverend Phelps, however, was chosen to make the attempt. He felt that similar transformations as those which occurred at Haines Institute could be accomplished in Burke County.

During Phelps's frequent visits to the Haines Institute in Augusta, he met Miss Mary Price, attended the Christ Presbyterian Church with her, and married her. He was a graduate of the normal course at Paine College, and soon after his marriage he went to Biddle University. After three years at Biddle, studying, serving as supply pastor, and operating a shoe shop, he received the A.B. degree while Mrs. Phelps continued teaching at Haines Institute. He returned to Paine College and in 1906 received the B.D. degree.[51]

When he was commissioned to make the experiment in Burke County, Georgia, he was well prepared for the task. Dr. Phelps started out on foot for the designated plantation area but reached the Walker Grove community by mistake and stopped in the home of Mrs. Martha Boyd, who had two nieces attending Haines Institute. This chance acquaintance proved to be a fortunate coincidence as the years passed. Mrs. Boyd was well acquainted with the temper and character of the Burke County community. Through her and others, the prospective builder learned that the community was largely populated by mulattoes, quadroons, and octoroons—many of whom had inherited or purchased from their landed

[50] "Boggs Academy," *Briefly* (N.Y.: PCUSA, BNM).
[51] Howard Givens, "An In Depth Study of Burke County, Georgia," (S.T.B. thesis, Johnson C. Smith Theological Seminary, 1935).

forebears large plots of land—and that there were those who rented and still others who were domestic workers and sharecroppers. The community was one in which the Baptists and Methodists had a strong influence. There were other things to be learned from this willing teacher, such as techniques to be used in soliciting aid from the business community and how to deal with the varied black community. He learned his lessons well.[52]

Phelps won the friendship of the Horace Gresham family, who furnished him with a horse and buggy. In all, he won the support of seven people in the beginning who were willing to join him in the crusade for a church and school in the community—Horace and Lizzie Gresham, Martha Boyd, Sylvia and Lucy Ware, Giles Glasock, and Mozella Griffin. They were acquainted with the character of the locality and accompanied him to confer with Mr. Reynolds and others. Although Mrs. Phelps was still teaching at Haines, she was her husband's constant comforter, encouraging him to keep faith in his ultimate objective.[53]

When plans were well laid, Dr. Phelps with his seven friends attended a church, known locally as "Noah's Ark" and spoke to the congregation concerning starting a school in the community, like Miss Laney's school in Augusta, Georgia. Some liked the idea while others expressed strong opposition. These were the days of rugged resistance and inertia. Thoughts of no money, no church, no school, and limited friends coursed through Phelps's mind, yet he was steadfast in his ambition for those who did not realize what it meant to be without the benefits of education. Through his rugged determination and persistence, favorable events began to happen, however. A Baptist elder donated the two acres of land on the old "Dunn Place" on which Phelps built a brush arbor.[54] In the fall of 1906 he began teaching a class of eight pupils—three boys and five girls. Mrs. Phelps joined him, and they lived in the home of a friendly family in the community.

Through the influence of Mrs. Virginia P. Boggs, two frame buildings were built on the plot. One building was used for both church and school and the second, the principal's home, provided for kitchen, dining room, and dormitory space. Mrs. Boggs also helped to secure funds toward the purchase of additional land and the erection of another building which bore her name.[55]

[52] *Ibid.*
[53] *Ibid.*
[54] *Ibid.*
[55] *Ibid.*

Opposition spent itself in the wake of compassion, patience, and tolerance. Those who had once opposed the concept of a community school began gradually to perform neighborly functions in its interest, and genuine friends began to support the Presbyterian project.

In 1910, the Boggs Memorial School building was completed, shop work was added to the curriculum, and a farm was purchased. Boggs became deeply involved in community interest and needs, and a farmers' institute was started. This activity increased in benefits and popularity and became an annual affair. The best agriculture consultants, black and white, were secured for the institute's program. Continuing the interests of this project, in 1911 the Board of Missions purchased an old plantation of 1,000 acres near Keysville, Georgia, for use in a farm-home scheme, with the Reverend Phelps, principal, in charge. In 1912, the farmland was divided into tracts of forty acres, and in a very short time all the acreage available was rented to desirable tenants, who had the privilege of purchasing the land after a year of probationary occupation. According to terms, the renter was to prove himself an honest, industrious farmer before being allowed to buy.

In 1915 a girls' dormitory and three cottages were on the farm-home site. The following four or five years were devoted, to a large extent, toward increasing the school and community relationship, using the farm-home scheme as a major device to that end.

Adams Hall, a brick dormitory for girls put up in the fall of 1920, at a cost of $25,000, was donated by George H. Adams of Latrobe, Pennsylvania. This building contained a dining room, kitchen, reading room, music room, teachers' lounge, and dormitory facilities. The expansion of the plant continued with the complete renovation of an old store building for a library and office space. In this effort to expand the plant, a new home was built for the president, and a boys' dormitory was completed. The Virginia P. Boggs Memorial Hall, which in 1910 replaced the brush arbor, the school's first home, was destroyed by fire in 1920. Following this disaster, church and school were conducted in the basement of the new dormitory and the principal's home. The Virginia P. Boggs Memorial Hall was replaced by a one-story brick veneered structure in 1924.

In 1921 a young physician, who desired to remain unnamed, gave his tithing money to furnish two rooms, one for music and the other a hospital room. These rooms made a tangible contribution to the comfort of the campus personnel. Another anonymous friend of Boggs financed half the cost of a laundry building in 1925.

Mrs. Boggs, who had been for so long the energizing factor promoting the funding and building the academy, died in 1931 after twenty-five years of service. Her death, however, did not end her influence, and the momentum which she had initiated at Boggs gained lasting support for it. Five years later on November 15, 1936, Phelps, the founder and builder of Boggs, retired after thirty years in Burke County, moved back to Waynesboro and became pastor of the Westminster Presbyterian Church. The Reverend Charles W. Francis of Anderson, South Carolina, succeeded him.

Francis had received the S.T.B. degree from the theological seminary of Biddle University in 1915 and had the advantage of twenty-one years of rich experience in the program at Boggs. This made a smooth transition from one administration to another.

A public grade school near Boggs consolidated with the elementary department of the academy in 1938, and the state provided free textbooks, in keeping with a law which the state legislature had passed in 1937.

Tragedy struck Boggs in 1940 when Adams Hall was destroyed by fire, claiming the life of one girl and injuring several other students and some teachers. The institution was stunned by this tragedy, but although the program was slowed down, it still moved forward. An agriculture building was built the same year and, through the cooperation of the Smith-Hughes Fund, Burke County, and the state, a teacher for the new course in agriculture was provided.

A new program of expansion and remodeling was launched at Boggs in 1941. Adams Hall was rebuilt on the old foundation at a cost of approximately twenty-four thousand dollars. Also during this year, Dr. Francis was granted sabbatical leave following a period of serious illness. T. E. Ross, the principal, was appointed chairman of an executive committee of three to administer the work of the school. In 1942, however, Dr. Francis resigned and Ross was appointed executive as well as principal of Boggs. After filling the position for one year, Ross resigned, July 1, 1943. In anticipation of Mr. Ross' resignation, Harold N. Stinson, a science teacher at Boggs, was appointed principal, May 1, 1943. Stinson, though thought to be very young for the demanding responsibilities of such an executive position, proved to be a capable administrator.

Mr. Stinson was born, reared, and educated in the Presbyterian tradition. His preparatory training was at Cotton Plant Academy in Cotton Plant, Arkansas, during the administration of his father at the school. With a solid foundation received at the Arkansas academy, he enrolled in Mary Allen Junior College in Crockett, Texas, and, to complete his college training, he entered Johnson C. Smith University and received the

B.S. degree in 1941. The 1943 appointment was a challenge to which Stinson devoted his youth, talents, and experience. After the work at Harbison was discontinued, Mrs. H. M. Stinson, Sr., his mother, was transferred to Boggs and her experience helped fulfill her son's dream for the institution.

Boggs Academy was the only four-year high school in the immediate vicinity of Keysville to be accredited by the Southern Association of Colleges and Secondary Schools in 1943. In 1947 and 1948, various land transactions concentrated the Boggs' holdings and paved the way for providing recreational facilities and other extra-class activities.

In 1949 a new trades building, housing courses for veterans, was completed. The Board approved the raising of funds locally to erect a gymnasium and community building and, as a challenge, set up a fund to be matched by the community. This year, also, the academy received "A" rating by both the state High School Accrediting Commission and the Southern Association of Colleges and Secondary Schools and, in keeping with the state's new policy, added the twelfth grade.

At a time when it seemed that its program of education for black Presbyterians had spent itself, the Board of National Missions took action in 1951 to improve the plant and program at Boggs. Accepting a proposal from the state, the Board added a canning unit to the vocational offerings. The Board, in September 1951, agreed that it had valuable investment at Boggs Academy and was convinced that the services of the school were still needed in the church's program of Christian Education and Leadership in the South. It expressed intentions of continuing the school as part of its educational program. In 1952, the Board approved the project of enlarging the Boggs plant as the object of Women's Special Building Giving for 1953, and a great series of new buildings were added in the next few years.

Dr. Harold Stinson resigned in 1968 in order to accept the executive position at Stillman Institute. Mr. Calvin E. Thornton was appointed superintendent of the academy. In 1970 Boggs, with a staff of thirty-six, was one of the four remaining schools of the Board's education program for black Presbyterians.

THE TENNESSEE SCHOOLS 7

Although the Presbyterian Church, U.S.A. got an early start among the hills of Tennessee, in 1866, its program progressed slowly in that section of the mission field. Two years after its inception, the Committee on Freedmen had only been able to establish two somewhat stable missions in Tennessee. One of these schools was located at Columbia and was under the supervision of the Reverend and Mrs. S. S. Potter, who, with the aid of four teachers, had 289 pupils under instruction. The other parochial school was located at Clarksville where the Reverend E. M. McKinney, with the assistance of two teachers, was instructing 169 pupils.

Twenty-four years after the church's program was initiated in the state of Tennessee, however, pastors and their congregations were operating seven mission schools under the care of the Board of Missions. Two of these schools were under the supervision of the Reverend and Mrs. C. B. Ward, in connection with the programs of the two churches of which Ward was the pastor. At Rogersville, the Reverend W. H. Franklin was also operating two parochial schools in conjunction with the two churches of which he was the pastor. As an adjunct of the Salem Church program in Columbia, the Reverend and Mrs. D. Murry had 160 pupils under instruction. At the St. Luke Church in New Market, Mr. Gillette was teaching 46 pupils, and Miss Flora F. Scott was instructing 49 pupils at the Calvary Church in Knoxville.

By 1910, the number of parochial schools under the Board's care reached ten and remained constant until the decline began in 1920.

Mt. Tabor Graded School
Columbia, Tennessee

The Mt. Tabor Graded School was, perhaps, the first of the parochial schools established by the General Assembly's Committee on Freedmen. It is said that the Committee commissioned the Reverend S. S. Potter to establish the school in 1866. One year later, the Committee reported that Potter had 289 pupils enrolled in the school. Between 1872 and 1875, the Misses M. E. and N. E. Anderson conducted the school with an average enrollment of 200 pupils.

In 1875 the Reverend and Mrs. W. R. Polk were commissioned to conduct the program at the Mt. Tabor School. Three years later the Committee's report revealed outstanding progress at the Mt. Tabor Graded School:

> The building is a two-story, frame structure, 35 feet wide by 60 feet long, containing a chapel, two school rooms, and three rooms for the missionaries. One acre of ground belongs to the property. It is suitably located in the edge of Columbia, county seat of Maury, Tennessee. This property is valued at $3,000, and is free of debt. Tabor Church, with which the school has always been connected, was organized in 1866 and worships in the chapel of the building. The colored population of the place and vicinity is large. The school reports 118 pupils. . . . Latin and Algebra are among the higher branches taught here. Mr. A. F. A. Polk is a graduate of Lincoln University and says, "I am trying all I can to advance the cause of education and Christianity. I want to add to the studies Greek and geometry but not at present, and make the course four years. One of the Elders thinks it would add to the Church if we could build a boarding department to the school, large enough for 25 or 35 pupils. The students boarding now pay $7 to $8 per month. Do you think we could get a little aid? I have some warm *white Presbyterian* friends here trying to advance the work."[1]

For unstated reasons Polk resigned as superintendent of the school, and the Reverend D. Gibbs and Mrs. Polk continued the work. Following this, there were annual increases made in the staff: R. P. Wyche in 1880, W. L. Lewis in 1881, and a Mr. Maxwell in 1882.

[1] CMF, *Annual Report*, 1878, pp. 26–27.

In 1889, the Board of Missions for Freedmen reported the Reverend D. Murry as superintendent of the school in Columbia in connection with the Salem Church, but there is no further report of the educational phase of the Mt. Tabor Graded School, which was related to the Mt. Tabor Church in Columbia. In all probability, the work at both the school and church had been discontinued.

Mayers Parochial School
Knoxville, Tennessee

Shortly after the Reverend Richard Mayers and Mrs. Ellen Toole Elons were married, February 12, 1902, in Sumter, South Carolina, they went to Knoxville, Tennessee, to the East Vine Avenue Presbyterian Church to fill the vacancy created by the resignation of the Reverend John D. Paul, who had been at that church since 1890.

Mayers was born, educated, and reared in Barbados, an island of the West Indies. He was scholarly, spoke several languages, and his British training was pronounced. Mrs. Mayers was born in Maryville, Tennessee, and attended the Presbyterian parochial school there. She later completed the teacher-training course at Scotia in Concord, North Carolina. She was compassionate and greatly concerned about the needs of Negro youth. One day she saw children playing on East Vine Avenue and invited them to her home. This was the beginning of the Mayers Parochial School.

There was also a parochial school, the Slater School, located in Knoxville, which was operated by the Congregational church. When the Slater School closed in 1904, the Mayers persuaded the Board of Missions for Freedmen to purchase the building on Payne Street, and the Mayers School moved into it. Mayers was appointed principal of the relocated school. Because of the school's community oriented program, the Mayers school gradually became the preferred school for elementary training. By 1908 the enrollment had reached 170 pupils. The Misses Cora Goodner and M. Dickerson were added to the staff in 1911. In 1925, the faculty had increased to six full-time teachers and one part-time instructor who taught carpentry.

In 1928, however, the Board of National Missions decided that the city schools of Knoxville were beginning to improve educational opportunities for black children and that the Mayers Parochial School was an unnecessary expense. The feeling of the black community was different from that of the Board, for it knew from experience that the public school program for Negro children could not be depended upon as an adequate substitute for the mission school as long as the "separate but equal" policy prevailed. After the death of the Mayers in 1931, however, the Board's approach led to a final decision to discontinue the school.

Rendall Academy
Keeling, Tennessee

The Rendall Academy, in all likelihood, was founded prior to the year 1918, since in the Board's annual report for that year, the following observation was made: "We expended $1060.00 on a new school building at Keeling, Tennessee, in charge of Reverend M. J. Nelson with whom we had an understanding conditionally. His compliance with the conditions obligated the keeping of the agreement."[2] In 1922 Rendall Academy had 287 pupils enrolled, and the promise of its future progress was very encouraging. Rendall's closing is as vague as its opening or founding. Its name was not among the thirty-nine day schools closed on June 1, 1933, and in 1932 there were three schools under the Board's care in Tennessee—Rendall Academy was not one of them.

Newton Normal Institute
Chattanooga, Tennessee

The Newton Normal Institute was founded as a day school in connection with the Leonard Street Presbyterian Church in Chattanooga in 1903 by the Reverend and Mrs. Charles H. Trusty. It was so named because the Newton Presbyterial of New Jersey agreed to support a teacher there. The school became known later as the Newton Normal Institute.

The Birmingham Presbytery, in summarizing its work for 1906, listed the following persons working at the school: the Reverend and Mrs. C. H. Trusty and Mrs. L. P. Perry. In the change of boundary lines of presbyteries, frequently a school might appear in one presbytery one year and the next year in another. Such was the case of the Newton Normal Institute in 1908. That year the Levere Presbytery reported ninety-one pupils enrolled at the school under the instruction of Mrs. M. A. L. Wilson, Mrs. M. S. Lewis, and Miss Emma Fletcher. Available records do not reveal when the Trustys gave up the work at the school, but senior citizens in the community recall that the Reverend Trusty was there in 1916.

Between the Trustys' administration and that of the Reverend O. E. Williams, Mrs. M. S. Lewis, a long-time teacher at the school, kept the school operating. In 1913, Mrs. Mary L. Wilson wrote the Women's

[2] BMF, *Annual Report*, 1918, p. 10.

Board of Home Missions expressing happiness in being able to open school in the new school building with everybody comfortable and happy. According to her report the school was full, with 185 pupils enrolled.[3]

The Reverend and Mrs. O. E. Williams were commissioned to direct the work at the school in 1917. Four teachers composed the staff and 165 students were enrolled. When the Workers' Conference convened on its campus in 1921, the school's progress was viewed as outstanding. The Reverend C. E. Tucker, who had been connected with the school for some years, resigned in 1908 to accept the presidency of Swift Memorial College in Rogersville.

During the decade between 1920 and 1930, the public schools for Negro children were being upgraded and expanded. In view of this, the Board of National Missions decided that the Newton Normal Institute was no longer a necessity and began to focus on what it termed "other grave social needs." Dr. Jesse B. Barber had both the Leonard Street Church and the Newton Normal Institute under his supervision at this time. In 1932 a change in program was made. The parochial school, which had grown to be a respectable normal institute, was replaced by a community center called the "Newton Community Center" which provided care and training for preschool age children of working parents. The dense population of low-income families was increasing in the area, and small children of working mothers had less than half a chance of escaping numerous hazards. A day care and clinic program, therefore, became a special emphasis at the new center. When the city finally assumed a greater part of its responsibility for meeting the health needs of the people, the clinic was discontinued and a varied program for teenagers was developed. Dr. Barber resigned in 1943 and accepted a position at Lincoln University. Miss Mary L. Wilson, who had been with the work over a long period, became the new executive of the center.[4]

The center's frame building was destroyed by fire in August, 1953 but, fortunately, the fire broke out in the early morning hours when the center was vacant. Within a year, the Chattanooga community, recognizing the great need for the center's program, matched funds given by the Board for rebuilding. With the addition of the funds given anonymously, the center was assured of a continuing day-care program. While the new all-purpose Newton building was under construction, its program continued in the basement of the nearby Leonard Street Presbyterian Church.

[3] "Echoes," *Home Mission Monthly*, vol. 27, no. 6, p. 138.
[4] "Newton Community Center," *Briefly* (N.Y.: PCUSA, BNM).

Swift Memorial College
Rogersville, Tennessee

In the northeastern section of Tennessee, along the Appalachian Mountain range is located Rogersville, Tennessee. In the range and on a foothill of the Clinch Mountain, Swift Memorial College was established as a parochial school in 1883 by the Reverend William H. Franklin.

After graduating from Maryville College, in Maryville, Tennessee, Franklin was ordained, commissioned, and sent to establish a school for children of the freedmen. He began a small parochial school which was named "Swift," honoring the Reverend Elijah E. Swift, pastor of the First Presbyterian Church in Pittsburgh, Pennsylvania. Swift was president of the Board of Missions for Freedmen from its inception in 1883 until his death in 1888; however his association with this work started in 1865 as chairman of General Assembly's Committee on Freedmen; in 1870 he became chairman of the Presbyterian Committee of Missions for Freedmen.

Franklin's quest was hampered by numerous duties and many hardships: preaching, teaching, building, and persuading his people that education was desirable. The original plan was for the school to be a seminary for girls but instead Swift became coeducational. In 1884, there were twenty-five pupils enrolled in the school, but Franklin, along with his pastorate at the St. Marks Presbyterian Church, increased the staff by the addition of Mrs. M. J. Woodfin. The Board announced in 1889: "At Rogersville, East Tennessee, a desirable property of seven acres with the buildings thereon has been purchased and converted into an institution to be known as the 'Swift Memorial Institute,' in memory of the late lamented President of the Board."[5]

The enrollment continued to increase: 1890—198 pupils; 1892—205 pupils. Miss L. N. Netherland and J. S. Cobband were added to the staff, and the plant was also being expanded. In 1893, a three-story brick building was erected to serve as an administration building and girls' dormitory, at a cost of $14,000. This was done through the efforts of the Reverend Franklin and "friends." The work on the building was completed in 1894, and by 1897 the enrollment reached 255.

Racial feelings subsided slowly in Tennessee and, in some instances, grew more intense as conflicting opinions developed regarding "the Negro's place" in the scheme of the Reconstruction Period. The Tennes-

[5] BMF, *Annual Report*, 1889, p. 13.

see State Legislature passed a law in 1901 prohibiting the instruction of black and white students in the same institution. This action ran counter to the Maryville College policy and posed a serious problem that had to be faced cautiously. Maryville College, a Presbyterian U.S.A. institution, had opened its doors to the freedmen at the close of the Civil conflict, and several Negroes, including William Franklin, had graduated from it. In addition, some funds had been left to the college with the distinct understanding that both races should have equal privileges in the use of the funds. The legislature's new law closed the doors of Maryville College to nonwhites. Mrs. Mary R. Thaw, daughter of the donor of the funds and a trustee of Maryville College, came to the rescue of the Board of Trustees and requested that the Board turn over to Swift $25,000 of the $100,000 endowment which her father had given to the college. The Board of Trustees voted its approval. In addition, Mrs. Thaw gave to Swift an additional $1,000 toward the purchase of land on which the boys' dormitory was built later.

This transaction made it possible for Swift to make some vital advances. In 1904, both a high school course and a four-year college course were added to the program of study; Franklin became the first president of Swift Memorial College. Out of the funds turned over by Maryville College and the fruitful efforts of Dr. Mary E. Holmes of Rockford, Illinois, and friends of Swift, the boys' dormitory was built and dedicated in 1905. The total cost of the dormitory was $11,000. Including the Franklins, the staff that year consisted of ten persons and the enrollment was 272. During the following years the increases were gradual but continuous. By 1911 there were twelve staff members and 284 students.

The expansion of the physical plant and grounds was also indicative of the institution's growth. The dormitory facilities for girls were increased in 1913 by the additions of new wings at the ends of the main building. Five acres of land adjacent to the school grounds were purchased at a cost of $2,000, covered by a gift sent to the Board by Mrs. E. E. Swift of Colorado Springs, Colorado. Another valuable gift which the institution received during this period was a laundry and a home economics building, donated by President Franklin. A series of innovations and additions greatly enhanced the general program at the institution: the dining room capacity was increased; living quarters for teachers and girls were extended; accommodations for the library and music and sewing classes were provided.

Also completed was a new structure for the St. Mark's Church which stood on the corner of the campus and was first used on Thanksgiving Day of 1912. The president's cottage was constructed in 1925, but before the rejoicing subsided over its completion the boys' dormitory was consumed by fire. Restoration began immediately. The year 1926 marked the retirement of the founder, the Reverend W. H. Franklin. The Reverend C. E. Tucker, pastor of the Leonard Street Presbyterian Church of Chattanooga, Tennessee, succeeded him.[6] The founder and builder had served the institution and community for forty-three years.

Since the public school system had made token advances toward providing elementary education for Negro children, the elementary grades at Swift were dropped. This enabled the new president, in 1928, to restructure and enrich the high school course. The college curriculum was reorganized to conform to standards set for junior college recognition in 1929. This step followed the discovery that the Tennessee State Board of Education would grant Swift graduates only one year's college credit. Dr. Tucker discovered solutions to other problems at the school:

> One of the major problems which faced Dr. Tucker was the reconstruction of a dormitory for men; the first dormitory having been destroyed by fire in 1926. However, through the gracious and genial influence of Mrs. Agnes B. Snively, Field Representative of the Unit of Work for Colored People, the Ladies Missionary Society of the First Presbyterian Church of Hollywood, California, voted a legacy, which was bequeathed to it by Mr. Nelson E. Woodward and his wife, Mrs. Minnie G. Woodward, to Swift in order that the new dormitory might be furnished. A modern two-story brick building as a dormitory for men was erected. The building was dedicated and named "The Franklin Dormitory" by the Synod of East Tennessee during its sitting in Rogersville, Tennessee, October, 1932.[7]

After ten years of dedicated service and relentless labor at the institution, Dr. Tucker resigned in 1936, having reached retirement age. The new Swift, however, had met the requirements for the standardization of its high school and college departments and had greatly expanded its plant. The Tuckers were succeeded by the Reverend and Mrs. W. C. Hargrave.

Reverend Hargrave was a graduate of Biddle University, having received the S.T.B. degree in 1903. He had been connected with the

[6] William H. Franklin, "Hopes Realized," *Home Mission Monthly*, vol. 27, no. 6 (April, 1913), pp. 134–135.
[7] *Swift Memorial Junior College Catalogue*, 1954, p. 5.

program at Swift as chairman of the English and education departments for some time during Dr. Tucker's administration. The program of enrichment and expansion continued, and in 1939 a commercial course was added to the curriculum, the grounds were further extended by the purchase of a lot in front of the Franklin dormitory, at a cost of $7,000, which was provided from the school budget.

Dr. Hargrave retired in 1941, after five years of service at Swift. R. E. Lee, dean and teacher at Swift since 1926, was commissioned to fill the vacancy. The Board of National Missions sold a plot of the school property to Hawkins County in 1948 for the purpose of erecting a $20,000 gymnasium on it. It also sold an additional plot of the school property for $4,000, which it considered no longer necessary in the school's program. The funds received were to be used to erect a home economics cottage.

Hawkins County completed the erection of the gymnasium-auditorium in 1949. This year, also, the high school department received a "B" rating by the Tennessee State Department of Education. The "B" rating was based on its limited enrollment of fewer than one hundred but the institution maintained its "A" rating with the Southern Association of Colleges and Secondary Schools.

President Lee's administration was characterized by outstanding signs of progress. But there were also distinct hints that the school's future was insecure, especially in the sale of property. By 1950, the signs of decline in the program at Swift were becoming more apparent. State requirements for teacher certification were being increased, and classes were being overloaded by teachers seeking advanced courses required by the new regulation. Swift was unable to adequately provide the necessary personnel to respond to this new situation. Badly needed individual attention, which had been the practice with smaller classes, was no longer possible. As a result, many students began losing interest and dropping behind in their work. This situation increased and there was no relief in sight.

The expected Board ultimatum came in 1952 when its intentions were made unalterably clear. Increased cost of maintaining the institution, combined with little potential for increased missionary services due to the size of the Negro population, prompted the Board to discontinue Swift at the end of the school year 1952.

Rallying to the support and continuance of the school in June, 1952, a group of seven local professional and business men formed a board and became incorporated under the laws of Tennessee as "Swift Memorial

Junior College, Inc." This board appointed five advisory members and assumed responsibility for maintaining the school. For the school year 1952–1953, this incorporated board leased the Swift plant from the Board of National Missions at one dollar a year and sought state support for the maintenance of Swift as a state junior college for eastern Tennessee. These developments occurred during the summer months and the treasurer, acting for the Board of National Missions, approved the lease of the property, since the proposition was similar to that which the Board had approved at Mary Potter and Gillespie, where local units had leased Board property for school use.

In 1953, the newly incorporated board requested the resumption of support of Swift by the Board of National Missions, but the Board did not see its way clear to guaranteeing funds for this. It would, however, continue the rental policy of one dollar per year. This rental policy continued through the school year 1954–1955, at which time the Board of National Missions requested the local incorporated board to purchase the property or pay reasonable rent. The board did not think the proposal feasible and requested the Board of National Missions to cancel the existing lease and lease the property to the county for high school use. In concurrence, the Board of National Missions leased the property to the county at $2,000 per year, beginning September 1, 1955. The Board also voted to make the $2,000 available to cover the expense of closing the college and moving its equipment to other schools.

The Swift Alumni Association, still clinging to a ray of hope following the Supreme Court's 1954 decision which dealt with desegregation in schools, had its national president, James L. Martin, write to the Board of National Missions requesting its resumption of the operation of the school as of September 1, 1954, on an integrated basis. The Board of National Missions voted its regrets, stating that it was unable to accept the proposal, since the conditions which were factors in the Board's withdrawal in 1953 still prevailed, and that Warren Wilson Junior College in western North Carolina, which was operated on an integrated basis, was near enough to serve Tennessee.

In 1956, the Board of National Missions approved the sale of the Swift property to the Board of Education of Rogersville, Tennessee, for $100,000, and voted "that the proceeds be set up to be voted later by the Board for some object or objects related to the education of Negro youth."[8]

[8] W. E. McCulloch, *The United Presbyterian Church and its Work in*

The United Presbyterian Church at Work in Tennessee

Knoxville College
Knoxville, Tennessee

The United Presbyterian Church of North America entered the mission field early to minister to the freedmen. Its first missionary to Tennessee, Rev. Joseph G. McKee, reached Nashville in September, 1863. He was sent to this location by the Second United Presbyterian Synod in answer to an appeal of the Union army, which had been swamped by hordes of suffering freedmen who congregated around its camps.

When the Reverend McKee arrived in Nashville, he was faced with a situation of misery and depravity, which he described as "incredible and unbelievable." The church rushed additional personnel and supplies to the area.

McKee was born in County Down, Ireland, and came to this country when he was about fourteen years of age. After graduating from Westminster College in New Wilmington, Pennsylvania, and completing the theological course at Xenia Theological Seminary, he entered the ministry of the United Presbyterian Church and eventually went to Nashville, Tennessee.[9]

In September, 1863, one month after his arrival in Nashville, he organized a church with Negro elders, the first in the denomination. On October 13, 1863, he established a parochial school in the Baptist Church in northwest Nashville which was the first free school for Negroes in the South. In November and December of the same year, his teaching force was increased. The Reverend M. M. Brown and the Misses M. Dougherty, Sarah McKee, and Aggie Wallace were employed in November. In December, Miss Ada Arbuthnot joined them. All taught in the Baptist Church for a short while but, at the request of the director of the school in Caper's Chapel, they divided their forces and conducted the schools in both places. The winter months of 1864 were exceedingly severe and there was great suffering. Smallpox broke out and one of the teachers caught the disease. The times were very difficult:

America (Pittsburgh: United Presbyterian Church of North America, Board of Home Missions, 1925), p. 92.

[9] James McNeal, "Biographical Sketch of Rev. Joseph G. McKee, The Pioneer Missionary to the Freedmen in Nashville, Tenn.," *Historical Sketch of the Freedmen's Missions of the United Presbyterian Church, 1862–1904.* Ralph W. McGranahan, ed. (Knoxville College, 1904), pp. 9–10.

This work every way was exceedingly hard upon all the teachers, and made such a demand upon the sympathies and strength of Mr. McKee that he was unable to engage afterward in the duties of the school room. His place there was taken in February, 1864 by Miss Mary Hudelson. Mr. McKee's health, continuing to fail, he went North the latter part of March, and presented to the Church the necessity for a building in which to carry on the school. Not gaining in strength as he had hoped, he sailed for Europe but his heart was in his work at Nashville, and his prayers were earnest and frequent for its success. . . .

The schools were also turned out of the Baptist Church and the basement of Caper's Chapel, as the latter was taken for government use. In a few days, however, the audience chamber of Caper's Chapel was kindly given and the schools resumed. A new teacher, Mr. Hutchinson, came and opened another school in the contraband camp. These schools were kept open until the last of June when the teachers returned North with the exception of two who proposed remaining to keep up the Sabbath School, but taking sick, all left the field.[10]

On July 7, 1865, Brigadier General Clinton B. Fisk wrote McKee, "I cannot half enough thank yourself and your most excellent and efficient corps of teachers for industry, perseverance and patient faith with which you have steadily through storm and sunshine prosecuted your labors of love among the Freedmen of Nashville."[11]

The Reverend A. S. Montgomery and some of the teachers arrived in Nashville in September to open the fall sessions of the schools but found themselves again dispossessed. McKee arrived about the last of September, much improved in health, and resumed his work with the same enthusiasm. Messrs. J. R. McCullough, T. R. Andrews, and T. A. Clark were added to the teaching staff of the five women who had kept the schools running when Montgomery gave up the work.

McKee pulled his forces together for a renewed approach to their problems and became involved in the life of the community. His services to the community and particularly to the program of education were soon recognized, and he was elected to the position of county Superin-

[10] J. W. Wait, "The United Presbyterian Mission Among the Freedmen in Nashville," *Historical Sketch*, ed. McGranahan, p. 2.

[11] Letter from Brig.-Gen. Clinton B. Fisk, Ass't Com. for Kentucky and Tennessee, to Rev. J. G. McKee, Supt. U.P. Mission in Nashville, July 7, 1865, cited by Wait, "The United Presbyterian Mission," *Historical Sketch*, ed. McGranahan, p. 4.

tendent of Education. In his efforts to find a permanent location for the mission school, he purchased a lot on Ewing Street. The construction of a building, however, was delayed because building materials were hard to buy in Nashville. To offset this local handicap, lumber was purchased in Cincinnati; after much difficulty and delay, it finally reached Nashville. The carpenters Messrs. Graham and Robb went to work immediately and, within a few weeks, the McKee school house was ready for partial occupancy. McKee wrote, "As we look back upon the times when we were tossed from place to place, sometimes our school thrown out without a day's notice, with no place where we could go, we, with our fond and faithful adherents, looking around upon a large audience rejoicing in our own chapel, sang with a heart almost too full to sing."[12]

McKee failed to receive the support he had expected from the government through the Freedmen's Bureau, and his health began to fail. During the closing exercises of the school that year, 1867, it was obvious that his health was rapidly declining. He resigned his positions of alderman, county superintendent, and superintendent of the McKee School; turned the leadership of the school over to his faithful workers; returned with his family to his home in Ohio, and died in 1868. There were 670 pupils enrolled in the McKee School when his leadership came to an end that year. The school was temporarily closed in 1871 but reopened again in October of 1873. James McNeal, who had been sent as a missionary to that section, announced that year: "As the associations that have been successfully engaged in the work are enlarging and improving their facilities, the Board has decided to remove the school to a more needy location and resume the work with renewed vigor."

Dr. J. W. Witherspoon became secretary of the Board of Freedmen's Missions in 1870. At that time other denominations were establishing schools for freedmen in Nashville and vicinity and, in addition, a local system of public education at the elementary level for Negro children was being established. In view of these and other developments, in 1872–1873, the General Assembly of the United Presbyterian Church of North America directed Dr. Witherspoon to appoint a committee to survey the mission field in order to ascertain where the need was greater. What was sought was a suitable location for a normal school for the freedmen. The committee was appointed and, as a result of its survey, Knoxville, Tennessee, was selected as the most desirable location for the renewed endeavor. After eight or more years of serious concentration in the Nash-

[12] Wait, "The United Presbyterian Mission," *Historical Sketch*, ed. McGranahan, p. 4.

ville area, therefore, the McKee School was closed, and the Board's resources and energies were transferred to Knoxville in 1875.[13] The United Presbyterian Church had laid a foundation here before this time:

As early as May, 1864, a school was opened under the super-intendency of Mr. R. J. Creswell. It was in operation both by day and night. It enrolled more than one hundred pupils. In the fall of 1864, it was taken under the care of the United Presbyterian Church, it having been an independent school till that time. A second teacher was provided at that time, Miss Lizzie G. Creswell, sister of R. J. Creswell.

The first months found it housed in the Baptist Church on Gay Street. After being compelled to vacate here an old blacksmith shop was utilized for a time and the handsome rental of $20 a month was paid. In the fall of 1865, the Board purchased a government build-ing for $180, but before the school was opened the building was set on fire and burned to ashes. In 1866, there was erected the building that was sometimes known as "The Long School House" and some-times as "The Creswell School House." It was located on the corner of Pine and Lee Streets and stood till 1884. . . . The mission was closed in 1869.[14]

The fire was not the only harassment. "Certain lewd fellows of the baser sort" had tried to break up the work by ordering Superintendent Creswell to "close up his nigger school and go north."[15] With the aid of Governor William G. Brownlow and others, the culprit was appre-hended and he apologized.

When the new start was made in 1875, those who were leaders in the work, however, were more and more convinced of the necessity of starting again, this time uniting the educational and church work closely by establishing the school and church together.

In 1875, therefore, Knoxville College opened in the "Long School House," which was still the Board's property. The college was to con-vene there until the new brick building was erected on "the Hill." The proposed new brick building was completed in time for the fall opening in 1876 and was dedicated on September 4 of that year. The Reverend J. P. Wright was elected principal, and three teachers were employed to assist with the instruction of the pupils. Dedication day was a great

[13] "Early History of Knoxville College," *Historical Sketch*, ed. McGrana-han.
[14] "Early History," *Historical Sketch*, ed. McGranahan, pp. 22–23.
[15] "Early History," *Historical Sketch*, ed. McGranahan, pp. 22–23.

occasion for the black community of Knoxville. They came out in a body, having nearly a thousand persons in line. The Freedmen's Board sent a delegation consisting of Drs. J. W. Witherspoon, W. H. McMillan, R. B. Ewing, D. S. Kennedy, and J. S. Sanders.

Although Knoxville College's major emphasis was on the elementary branches of education at the beginning, the long-range view of establishing a normal school and college was never abandoned. With this ultimate objective in mind as a guideline, the courses of study were rapidly upgraded; standards of scholarship were raised, and material resources were increased. The institution attained the rank both of a normal school and a full college in 1877. The Reverend Wright resigned in 1877, and the Reverend J. S. McCulloch was commissioned to fill the vacancy as president. Miss Eliza B. Wallace was commissioned principal at the same time. This executive combination proved to be a most fortunate administrative partnership in the progress of the school. The lady principal was received by the blacks as "one of the truest and best friends that the colored people had in the trying times when freed from physical slavery, they were endeavoring to emancipate themselves from the bondage of ignorance and superstition."[16] It was Miss Wallace who made the first attempt to provide boarding facilities in 1877, but with little or no success. She was convinced, however, that the desired rounded education for Knoxville students could be achieved to greater satisfaction in a boarding school. Her industrious and prayerful efforts were eventually achieved. President McCulloch gives this analysis of their opposite yet complementary dispositions:

> I never knew how Miss Wallace came to be appointed to Knoxville but for a long time I have had no doubt that God's hand was in it. It was my privilege to be intimately associated with her for more than twenty years. In many respects we were unlike. She thought nothing of making changes, I was for holding onto old things and old ways. She could flank a difficulty with a humorous remark. I became more serious the more I looked at it. She excelled in going for the main thing, taking the short cut over obstacles; I was too often occupied with details when I ought to have been driving ahead at the main thing, but I was comforted by this thought, that God designed that we should work together, and thus accomplish his purposes. We never had a serious disagreement in all those twenty years, and when we could not agree in any thing that might be proposed we learned to have respect for each other's opinion. . . .

[16] "Early History," *Historical Sketch*, ed. McGranahan, p. 29.

Above all else she was entirely consecrated to the task of up-lifting those whom she was called to serve. She was always planning for larger and better things and her splendid faith looked forward to the redemption of a whole race through the gospel of Jesus Christ taught and preached and lived by those trained in distinctly Christian schools.[17]

The history of Knoxville College, for practical purposes, may be described in four periods, with a transition between the third and fourth periods. The beginning years between 1877 and 1899 were under Dr. J. S. McCulloch's administration. Under his guidance, courses of the most elementary sort were, of necessity, initiated. From this basic beginning, the institution "on the Hill" grew from a single building on three acres of land to a plant of nine buildings on twenty-two acres, valued at $100,000. When Dr. McCulloch began his administration the teaching force numbered seven. When he resigned in 1899, there were twenty-four members of the teaching staff, and the school had become a college.[18]

The second period was one of expansion under the administration of Dr. R. W. McGranahan, 1899–1918. The campus increased from twenty-two to one hundred acres, and twelve additional buildings were erected. In 1908, there were 507 students enrolled under the instruction of thirty-three teachers. There was an agriculture department, which was being conducted in connection with a ninety-acre farm. Dr. McGranahan resigned in 1918, leaving the institution greatly expanded educationally and physically.

A period of standardization was under the administration of Dr. J. Kelly Giffen, 1918–1935. Through the New World Movement the endowment of the college was increased. The faculty numbered thirty-seven, and the average student enrollment was more than four hundred. After the curriculum was studied and restructured, the following departments were established: college, normal, academy, music, domestic arts, and grammar.[19] It was during this administration that the school developed its music department to rival that of the nationally famous one at Fisk.

The period which followed the Giffen administration was one of more rapid turnovers and can be seen as transitional. Dr. S. M. Lang succeeded Dr. Giffen in 1936 and resigned in 1940. Dr. J. A. Cotton,

[17] "Early History," *Historical Sketch*, ed. McGranahan, pp. 27–29.
[18] "Early History," *Historical Sketch*, ed. McGranahan, p. 29.
[19] McCulloch, *The United Presbyterian*, p. 98.

formerly principal of Henderson Institute in Henderson, North Carolina, came out of retirement to become the first Negro president of the institution in 1940. Dr. Cotton's failing health, however, forced him to give up the position in 1942. To fill the vacancy, an interim committee was appointed, chaired by Hardy Liston, Sr. In 1943, Dr. Liston was called to Johnson C. Smith University as executive vice-president, and Dr. William Lloyd Imes, who at the time was pastor of St. James Presbyterian Church of New York City, became president of Knoxville. When Dr. Imes resigned in 1947 the Board of National Missions once again returned to a white administrator in the person of the Reverend John Reed Miller, who at the time of his election was the pastor of the First United Presbyterian Church of Wheeling, West Virginia. In 1950, at the end of the Miller administration, the Board elected Dr. R. D. Chase as interim president. In 1951, Dr. James A. Colston was elected to the presidency.[20]

James A. Colston, Ph.D., the third Negro president of the institution, immediately launched a campaign to reclaim the prestige which the college had enjoyed before the depression years. This period, therefore, may be described as a period of reconstruction. The curriculum was restructured; the faculty's rank and salary were raised. Dr. Colston's thrust for restoration was made effective throughout the Knoxville community, and the student enrollment, which had decreased during the transition period, made an outstanding increase. The physical plant was greatly expanded by the addition of Young Memorial Fine Arts Building, Faculty Residence, Colston Hall, and the A. K. Stewart Science Hall, as well as by major renovations. All of these improvements on "the Hill" began once more to attract admiring friends from across the nation. Dr. Colston resigned in 1967 to accept an assignment in Africa, and Dr. Robert Owens became his successor. After four years, however, he resigned and in 1970, Dr. Hardy Liston, Jr., a University of Tennessee professor, was chosen interim president.

[20] Stewart, *May We Introduce*, p. 13.

THE ARKANSAS SCHOOLS   *8*

Getting a permanent footing in the state of Arkansas was a difficult task for the Board. Even though Presbyterian pioneers were establishing missions in the Indian Territory northwest of the Arkansas borderline as early as 1866, penetrating to reach the needs of the freedmen in Arkansas was delayed until twenty-three years later. Despite sporadic individual efforts in the state, it was not until 1889 that the Board of Missions became confident that it would be able to operate in the state. There was an encouraging note in its report for that year:

> In Arkansas a new Presbytery has been organized with 7 churches and 6 ministers, with the most promising outlook, as just now there is a large emigration of colored people from the Atlantic States to Arkansas. One community that went from these States has erected a house of worship and sent for the minister who served many of them in their old home and promising to support him entirely after the first year. This brother has been commissioned and is now on the field. At Cotton Plant in this State a large and substantial building has been erected during the year at a cost of $2,000 for our academy located at that place, which has opened with 182 pupils. Another has been completed at Pine Bluff at about the same cost, and known as Richard Allen Institute and has now over 200 pupils.[1]

[1] BMF, *Annual Report*, 1889, p. 12.

Advances in Arkansas were slow but gradual, and by 1908, the Board had established ten schools in the state, which was the maximum number to be operated by the Board there at any one time. Some of these schools were discontinued early, but others were moved to other areas of the state which were considered to be more needy. This system of discontinuance and relocation kept the peak number more or less steady until the recession began in the late 1920s. The cutback in Arkansas was much more rapid than the buildup. By 1932, the Board was operating only five schools in the state, and two of these were the Brinkley and Monticello academies, which were closed in 1933. These closures left only one school, the merged Arkadelphia and Cotton Plant Academies, under the Board's care in the state.[2]

Mount Herman Parochial School
Fordyce, Arkansas

Mrs. Myrtle McCrarey, daughter of one of the early teachers in the school, told the story of how Mount Herman Parochial School began and operated. According to her, the school was founded by the Reverend G. S. Turner at Fordyce, Arkansas, in 1898. Mrs. Ida Bradley, wife of one of the deacons in the Mount Herman Church, superintended the school, and at the same time taught many of the courses. The Board, however, did not mention this school in its annual reports until 1908, at which time it was under the guidance of the Reverend A. L. Tolbert, who had eighteen pupils under instruction.

Mrs. McCrarey described the methods and activities sponsored by the school. Memorization was a popular teaching technique during the early days of the school. Multiplication tables, historical dates, Scripture verses, poems and orations were memorized for classroom and public performance. The "Spelling Bee" was one of the most popular activities.

The students and faculty assembled in the chapel basement and were seated by classes with their respective teachers in different sections of the room. The classes were generally grouped by reading ability. For this method of classification, the following textbooks were common: McGuffey's *Reader and Spelling Skills*, Webster's *Blueback Speller*, Webster's *Elementary Spelling Book*, and the Shorter Catechism. The school day began with a devotional period which consisted primarily of catechism lessons, singing, and prayer. To miss this phase of the school program was a serious offense, seldom, if ever, overlooked by the teacher, the principal, and the pastor. Despite the fact that many students had

[2] Gaston, "A Review," *Women and Missions*, vol. X, no. 11, p. 359.

to walk from three to four miles, they were expected to be there for the opening devotion.

Mrs. McCrarey does not state when the school was discontinued, but it was not listed among the thirty-nine schools dropped in 1933. Mount Herman Parochial School, like many of the other small parochials, was merely an extension of the church program.

Monticello Academy
Monticello, Arkansas

The beginnings of Monticello Academy were closely related to the pioneer work of Dr. Mary E. Holmes in the midwest and northwest section of the Board's mission field. Dr. Holmes of Rockford, Illinois, was the talented and scholarly daughter of Dr. Mead Holmes, who for so long had faithfully served the Board of Missions for Freedmen. She volunteered her services, unsalaried, to the Board in 1886 and as volunteer secretary of the northwest, she traveled many miles speaking directly to people in the interest of the Board's program of education for Negroes.

In 1891, the Board announced: "Another Academy has been built and opened in Monticello, Arkansas, under Reverend C. S. Mebane, at a cost of a little more than $2,000 and was paid for by contributions mostly from the ladies of Illinois." There were sixty-two pupils enrolled when this announcement was made, and they were under the instruction of Miss Sallie Means. This parochial school was connected with the program of the Holmes Chapel, of which Reverend Mebane was pastor.[3] The school's enrollment increased annually; in 1893, 152 students were enrolled under the instruction of Miss Lizzie Dennis and Mr. T. M. Oglesby; in 1894, the enrollment had increased to 210 and the faculty to 5, including the pastor.

The school was considered by many to be a blessing to the community, but biracial understanding was at a very low ebb. Dr. Mary E. Holmes, a white woman, was the Board's appointee to guide the development of the Monticello project. Mebane was the black minister commissioned by the same Board as pastor of the Holmes Chapel and principal of the Monticello Academy. Both apostles were devout, dedicated, and enthusiastic about the prospects of a center of learning in that impoverished region of the state. Their business was education and evangelism, and they went about their work unmindful of the local temper. A small, horse-drawn carriage was their means of transportation in the conduct of their assigned tasks. Because of its size, they sat together. The white

[3] BMF, *Annual Report*, 1891, p. 7.

community was intensely displeased with this apparent disregard for the proper decorum of a white lady and her black driver. Agitation increased and hostility was inflamed; the life of the pastor-principal was threatened by a labeled casket placed on his porch at his front door. The black community was aroused and all efforts at conciliation failed.[4] The Board's reaction was quick and it described the situation to the Assembly in these words:

> Money was raised last year for an additional building at Monticello, Arkansas, and plans were drawn for a moderate structure costing about $2,300, containing a Chapel, dormitory rooms, and other needed conveniences for the school. The supervising of the work of erecting this building was placed in the hands of Miss Mary E. Holmes, but serious opposition was encountered and antagonism developed which compelled us, for the time being to suspend operation, and made it advisable for the principal of the school not only to close the institution but also to leave the town.
>
> A committee from the Board subsequently visited the field and from personal observation and inquiry were led to believe that possibly if the work were put under different management the existing opposition would disappear. We are not entirely sure this will reach the root of the trouble, but we have sent a new man to the field to look after our property, to make himself acquainted with the general situation, and determine the advisability of our resuming work at that place in the fall.
>
> It is too early to report the outcome of our plans in this case and further information as to our success or failure in endeavoring to handle wisely a difficult situation will have to go over until next year.[5]

The "new man" to which the Board referred was the Reverend O. C. Wallace, who with his wife went into the troubled area in search of a means of restoring peace and continuing the work of the school. Wallace was soft-spoken, patient, and moved cautiously among the townspeople as an ambassador of good will. Bewildered patrons concurred with the Board's opinion that a change in management might produce the desired results and urged the complete restoration of the school in the community. The school was reopened on a modest scale in the fall; and the Board's report for 1906 made this clarification:

[4] Interview with Dr. Richard Allen Carroll, son of the Reverend R. H. Carroll, who was principal of Monticello Academy from 1920 to 1933.

[5] BMF, *Annual Report,* 1905, pp. 7–8.

The School at Monticello has been conducted as a parochial by the minister in charge of the church at that point, assisted by his wife. The work has been most encouraging. In reply to an inquiry, "Is the Board justified in continuing the school at Monticello?" the answer came "If need and desire on the part of the pupils and patrons justify the work anywhere, they certainly do here. The school has been full to its utmost capacity with no effort on our part to secure pupils." While the boarding department has been discontinued until the new building is erected, a number of pupils at the earnest request of their parents have been received into the minister's home.[6]

Once the school was again in operation, Wallace tried to keep the morale of the school and community high and the interest of the Board lively, but a degree of unrest and frustration lingered in some quarters of the town, posing a constant threat. The Board spent the year studying the situation and made its intentions known in the following statement:

We have thought it wise and best to move our school site at Monticello, Arkansas, to a more acceptable part of the town. To this end the Board has purchased on reasonable terms 16 acres of land, where a new school building will be erected as soon as the old one can be disposed of at its fair market value. The new minister in charge of our little church at that place has been favorably received and with his wife, has maintained a successful parochial school during the winter. He has attempted no boarding school this year in connection with his work but with the sale of the old building and the erection of the new one, there is no discernible reason why a great and good work cannot be done at this place. Many of the former patrons of the school are making inquiries as to the opening of the Boarding School. . . . We are hoping it may be accomplished this year.[7]

By 1909, the Board had sold the old building and the sale price helped defray the expense of rebuilding the academy on its suburban plot. It was felt that the larger acreage would offer greater possibilities for expansion, the tension would be lessened, industrial training would be possible, and the isolation which had proved helpful in other cases would be conducive to greater security.[8]

In 1911, the 90 pupils enrolled were under the instruction of the

[6] Women's Board, *Annual Report*, 1906, p. 167.
[7] BMF, *Annual Report*, 1906, pp. 8–9.
[8] BMF, *Annual Report*, 1910, p. 10.

Wallaces and Miss E. L. Bamfield. The enrollment reached 121 and remained rather constant until 1918 when a gradual decline began.

Wallace resigned in 1920, and the Reverend and Mrs. R. H. Carroll took charge of the work at Holmes Chapel and instructed the seventy-seven pupils. When the Carrolls took over the work in 1920, Miss Carrie Means was still a member of the staff and Miss Hattie Westbrook was added. By 1926, the school was offering three grades of elementary work and four high school grades; in addition, it was, by far, the Negro youth's best opportunity for quality education in that section of the state.

Although the Board had announced that the school was active and growing in 1931, it was discontinued in 1933. After a forty-year struggle to survive all manner of opposition, the closure left deep feelings of regret and dismay in the black community.

Mebane Academy
Hot Springs, Arkansas

Located among the southwestern foothills of the Ozark Mountains is a thriving resort town, Hot Springs, Arkansas, an early stronghold of the Quawpaw Indian tribe. Its name originated from the clear, continuously flowing hot mineral waters from the mountain's interior. The uniqueness of this town is that it has a dual system of operation. In the valley between two mountains, the Reservation and the East, Central Avenue divides the city into the federally operated west side and the municipally run east side. At the peak of Reservation Mountain is located the Federal Lookout Tower; along its side is a veterans hospital and at its base, extending the length of Central Avenue, is the government's bathhouse row. On the east side of the avenue, with the exception of its bathhouses and convention halls, the town is operated as the average resort mountain town.

Early during the 1890s the Reverend A. E. Torrence established a parochial school on the east side of the avenue for the children of freedmen. He conducted it independently over an extended period of time. It was never under the complete care of the Board of Missions but received Board aid. As early as 1895, however, the Board reported 100 pupils enrolled there under the instruction of Torrence, pastor of the Second Presbyterian Church, with the assistance of Miss Addie Robinson.

The school was never a large one but was highly regarded locally for its program of culture and quality education. Its religious emphasis also made a distinct contribution to the life of the community. When the Reverend C. S. Mebane left the Monticello Academy in 1904, he replaced Torrence as director of the parochial school in Hot Springs. By 1911, however, enrollment had dropped to forty-five pupils.

Dr. John M. Gaston explained to the Board its relationship to the school, stating that the Board did not own anything at Hot Springs, Arkansas, and that the property and contents of the building were all owned by the Reverend C. S. Mebane and his wife.

Locally, the school was known as "The Mebane Academy" but Mebane chose to call the school "Hot Springs Normal and Industrial Institute." The school's main building was a three-story structure, which sat high on a hill off Whittington Avenue overlooking the northern section of the town. Its high elevation made it appear twice its actual height, and to the young people in the community this was a symbol of importance. Many craved to go to the "high school on the hill."

There were sixty-eight pupils enrolled in the school in 1916, and Miss M. J. Onque was assisting the Mebanes with the instruction of them. Paradoxically, though, the enrollment decreased to fifty-five, and the teaching staff increased to four during the waning years of the school.

In the early 1920s the public school authorities erected a one-story, frame building to house a school for Negro girls and boys on an adjacent hill, but the Mebane Academy school building and its program dwarfed that of the public school. Although fewer in number, the academy students mingled in the community with a certain dignity and respect that set them apart.[9]

During the late 1920s the Mebane Academy became the Hot Springs Community Station, without Board aid. It was never completely under Board control.

Arkadelphia Presbyterian Academy
Arkadelphia, Arkansas

The Arkadelphia Presbyterian Academy was founded in Arkadelphia, Arkansas, in 1882 by a man of that town whose name is unknown. He began teaching black children under a tree which stood in the northwest corner of what was later the campus.

The school operated independently until 1889 when it was taken under the care of the Board of Missions for Freedmen. The Board purchased a thirty-eight acre plot of land with a frame building on it and housed the school in it. This latest adoption of a school by the Board came just before the financial crisis of the 1890s, and little mention is made of the school's progress during this period of stress. In 1900,

[9] Interview with Miss M. J. Onque, 1936.

however, the Reverend W. H. Smith was reported as pastor of the West Bend Church, and Mrs. Smith, his wife, was instructing 135 pupils in the parochial school there. The Smiths only remained with the school until April of 1901.

After a lapse of five years, reports concerning the progress of the school were resumed. In 1906, the Reverend B. M. Ward was reported as pastor of the West Bend Church and Mrs. Ward, his wife, was the instructor of the seventy-seven children enrolled in the parochial school. Ward built the first building to house the school, which was a two-story frame structure providing space for classrooms and boys' living quarters. The Wards' stay at the school was also brief. They were succeeded by the Reverend and Mrs. W. D. Feaster in March of 1906.

During the Feaster administration the school was revitalized and began a long career of commendable services in the community. Within two years the enrollment increased to 127, and Mrs. Feaster and Miss A. Nelson had charge of instruction. A new building was erected in 1910 at a cost of $4,820, including furnishings. For a decade or more, progress was evident in all phases of the school's program. The enrollment was 287 in 1913, and in 1914 there were 313 pupils enrolled under the same administration and a faculty of eight.

The Black Memorial Hall, a gift from C. W. Black, was erected at a cost of $25,000 in 1920. This building contained the dining room and kitchen in the basement, recitation rooms on the first floor, and dormitory rooms for girls on the second and third floors. One room on the second floor was equipped for hospital use. The administration building, providing classroom space and housing for boys, was destroyed by fire in 1922. This building was replaced in 1924, primarily by student labor. The principal's cottage was also built this year, and the school had apparently reached its mature stature, offering twelve grades, thirty-two weeks annually.

Dr. Feaster, industrious, courageous, and determined, was successful in guiding the school to a point of respectability, locally and at the national level of the church. Suddenly his administration came to a tragic end. He died on March 25, 1926, after twenty years of unusual dedication to the school and community. Within six months his successor, the Reverend Elmo C. Hames, died on September 23, 1926.

The Reverend L. W. Davis, who had been a teacher at the school, was commissioned to fill the executive position at the school October 1, 1926. Between March 22, 1926 and October 1, 1926, the Arkadelphia Presbyterian Academy was directed by three different executives. During this period the temper of the campus and community was tense and filled with many misgivings. The uncertainty of coming events was too frustrating for the mission to thrive in a town the size of Arkadelphia, yet Davis strove valiantly to restore a normal atmosphere at the school. His efforts, however, were to little or no avail. In 1931, the main building and Black Memorial Hall were destroyed by fire of undetermined but suspicious origin.

This final incident apparently left the Board with two alternatives—to close the school or to transfer it. The Board chose the latter and in 1933 transferred the school to Cotton Plant, Arkansas, and merged it with the Cotton Plant Academy. Thereafter the consolidated school was known as the Arkadelphia-Cotton Plant Academy. Davis, principal of the Arkadelphia Academy, was retained as principal of the consolidated school. Beyond a doubt, the Board's education program rose to its highest stature of permanence and effectiveness in the state of Arkansas at the Arkadelphia-Cotton Plant Academy.

Richard Allen Institute
Pine Bluff, Arkansas

From the very beginning the Richard Allen Institute gave promise of developing into a permanent institution with wide influence. It was founded in 1886 by the Reverend and Mrs. Lewis Johnston. Miss Anna E. Grenage, an educated Negro woman, began assisting with the program there in 1887. There were 200 pupils enrolled in the school in 1889, and Miss Ella Jarvis was added to the teaching staff. The small, double-purpose, church-school building was soon overtaxed, and a building was erected to house the school in 1890. By 1891 there were 250 pupils enrolled, taught by a staff of 4.

After seventeen years of service in founding and building the school, the Reverend Johnston died in 1903, and the Reverend T. C. Ogburn was commissioned to fill the position. The Ogburns devoted seventeen packed years in an effort to alter the deplorable situation which they found in Pine Bluff. So much was to be done that a decade or more seemed too brief in which to achieve any transformation. In 1914 the Ogburns gave up the work, and the Reverend G. M. Elliott was commissioned to succeed them. Elliott was greatly concerned about the inadequacies of the boarding department which he explained to Dr. Gaston in a letter dated April 15, 1916:

We have not attempted for the past two years to keep any boarders, except in an incidental way. As yet the building is not suitably furnished for the purpose. In the past year, we had a young man for part of the time as a boarder. The amount paid by him was reckoned in the "Day Pupil's Account" because he was not in regularly. The boarding department consisted of the following persons: Mr. and Mrs. Zackery and their girl, Miss R. V. Torrence, myself and boy, Miss M. G. Purcell, seven in all, the young man referred to made eight. Because of the small salary received, the teachers were not charged board but all assisted with the general house work so there was no hiring. The department has been run from the current income of the school.[10]

Mr. T. S. Byers was also assisting with the instruction of the pupils that year. The fact that Elliott did not list him among the staff members might indicate that he was not commissioned by the Board. The Reverend G. M. Elliott remained at the school until 1919 when he resigned and was succeeded by the Reverend S. J. Elliott.

In 1921, the school was reported as a coeducational boarding school which offered junior and senior high school courses and ran thirty-two weeks annually. By 1932, however, the Richard Allen Institute had become the Richard Allen Community Station, in keeping with the Board's policy. This change of program, therefore, discontinued the school as a formal center for academic training.

Cotton Plant Academy
Cotton Plant, Arkansas

Cotton Plant, Arkansas, is one of those hard-to-find places on the map. Located on a country road out of the small town of Brinkley, it is about seventy miles from Little Rock, the capital of the state. The Board describes it in these words:

> Cotton Plant, Arkansas, . . . is well named. For miles around the village stretch wide cotton fields dotted with farm houses and cabins. Cotton and corn are the major crops, though many families have flourishing vegetable gardens for their own use.[11]

Cotton Plant Academy had a humble beginning. Back in the 1880s, educational opportunities for Negro children in this impoverished region were completely wanting. A small mission church for Negroes had been organized about 1883 in Cotton Plant and was called the Westminster Presbyterian Church. Reverend Davies, pastor of the Presbyterian church

[10] Letter from Rev. G. M. Elliott to Dr. Gaston, April 15, 1916.
[11] "Arkadelphia Cotton Plant Academy," *Brevities* (N.Y.: PCUSA, BNM, 1936), p. 1.

for whites, served as pastor of the Westminster Church at his conven-
ience until the Board of Missions for Freedmen sent two Negro ministers, the Reverends Alexander and MacMahan, into that part of the
mission field. Which of the two served as pastor of the church first has
not been officially established, as records vary.

The great need for a center for Christian education in the community
was first presented to the congregation of the Westminster Church by
Samuel R. Cowan, Scott Woods, and others who also sent their plea to
the Board of Missions for Freedmen.[12]

The local people were the first to respond. The concerned mothers
planted a cotton patch, cultivated it, picked the cotton, and sold it for
$375. With the money raised, the fathers and their sons purchased build-
ing materials and constructed a small frame, box-like, two-room school
house in 1886. The same year, the Board of Missions for Freedmen
commissioned the Reverend Francis C. Potter and his wife, Mrs. Cecelia
Potter, to take charge of the church and school program at Cotton
Plant. The first sessions of the school were held in the little box-like
structure and in the Potter home.[13]

The Potters were well educated, energetic, and sympathetically understanding of the community's needs. Mrs. Potter was adept at finding boys
and girls for the school. One day she had driven about ten miles from
town and saw some small boys playing in a red clay-dirt gulley. She
stopped and began the following conversation, "What are you little fellows doing?" "Jest playing," came the reply. "When do you go to
school?" she asked. "We don't go to school much out here," the boy by
the name of Albert replied. This answer set the tone for Mrs. Potter's
stock question: "Then, would you fellows like to go to town and attend
school there?" They all replied that they would. She asked, "Why do you
want to go to school?" All the boys answered, except one, "So we kin
go to school ever day cept one." Noticing that the one named Albert did
not join in the answer, she directed her next question to him, "And why
do you want to go to school?" He answered, "So when I get grown I can
preach." With the permission and assistance of their parents, she took
several of the boys to town and enrolled them in the school.[14]

Albert McCoy completed the course of study at Cotton Plant Indus-

[12] Mrs. L. D. Stinson, "History of the Westminster Presbyterian Church
and Cotton Plant Industrial Academy, 1910–1933." Copy in author's possession.
[13] Stinson, "History."
[14] Stinson, "History."

trial Academy and went to Lincoln University in Pennsylvania, where he completed both the college and seminary courses there. Albert McCoy was now the preacher he envisioned in his early youth. His rise was continuous—from the red clay-dirt gulley to the classroom and from the classroom to an executive position in the Presbyterian Church's Sunday School Missionary Division. Finally, he became the secretary of the Unit of Work With Colored People, the first Negro to attain this high recognition by the Presbyterian Church, U.S.A. After these and many other achievements, he returned to his hometown and the red clay-dirt gulley where it all began, but now it was different. He was Dr. Albert B. McCoy, a high official in the top rank of Presbyterian ministers. He was, however, still close to the people, and the townspeople greeted him with great joy as a hometown boy who had made good.[15]

Under the Potter administration, the school was strengthened and expanded. The little box-like structure was still standing in 1940. To this original building was added an industrial building with $2,000 sent by the Board of Missions for Freedmen. Following this addition, the school became known as The Cotton Plant Industrial Academy. Nicholas Hall, a dormitory for girls, was erected through the generosity of a Mr. Williams of Illinois. The building was named for Mr. Nicholas who gave more than thirty years to the training of Negro youths of Arkansas. It was dedicated in 1890. In this year also, a frame science building was constructed, an additional faculty member was commissioned, and more than 200 students were enrolled. By 1891, the coeducational institution enrolled 214 pupils, 37 of whom were boarders. The faculty consisted of Reverend and Mrs. Potter, Miss E. L. Jarvis, and Miss Sallie Means. The next year Miss Gertrude Butler and Miss Mattie Lewis were added to the faculty.

The institution suffered a great loss in 1893 when the boys' dormitory was destroyed by fire. This was also the year when the Board's financial crisis was at its peak. An appeal was made to the women's societies for $10,000 to replace the building.

Following Potter's death on November 6, 1900, Mrs. Potter became principal. She continued her husband's work with outstanding proficiency and dedication. Her faithful administration was terminated in 1902, which brought to a close sixteen years of highly successful administration by the Potters.

In the fall of 1902, the Reverend W. A. Byrd became the new execu-

15 Stinson, "History."

tive and might be safely called the "great builder." He immediately established himself in the community and won the interest and support of the people. He was considered an eloquent orator and, in addition, he was a shrewd and frugal administrator. Under his administration the curriculum was restructured and the plan significantly expanded. Turner Hall, a dormitory for boys, was built through the benefaction of Dr. Turner of Illinois; in 1905, a dormitory for girls was erected and completely equipped with modern facilities at a cost of $17,000; a frame building for laundry purposes was constructed in 1907. After seven years of work here, Byrd accepted a call from a church in New Jersey.

The Reverend H. M. Stinson became the new executive in 1910, and a new and lively spirit was stimulated throughout the school's program. He was twice a graduate of Biddle University, receiving the Bachelor of Arts degree in 1892 and the S.T.B. degree in 1895. He was an inspired and energetic leader with expertise in many areas of business management. The complete destruction of Turner Hall by fire in 1917 was a serious setback, but the zealous executive redoubled his efforts. In 1918 a double-duty building was erected at a cost of $4,200 and provided space for the chapel, for classrooms, and dormitory rooms for boys.

The next step which was taken by the scholarly executive was to enrich the academic program. In 1922, home economics was added to the curriculum, and in 1929 a concert choir was organized and began tours to win friends for the institution. The twelfth grade was added to the high school program, and its school term ran thirty-two weeks annually.

In 1933, the decision was reached by the Board to merge Cotton Plant Academy with the Arkadelphia Presbyterian Academy.[16] The identity of the two schools was preserved in its new name, Arkadelphia-Cotton Plant Academy, and the Reverend L. W. Davis, principal of the Arkadelphia School, continued as principal of the consolidated school.

Continuing efforts to strengthen the academic program, the school began dropping the primary grades in 1934. By virtue of the urgent pleas of concerned parents, however, a plan was effected whereby the grades were continued without the financial aid of the Board. The plant was further expanded by the construction of a frame building with salvaged building materials brought from the Arkadelphia plant. The equipment for this building was also brought from the Arkadelphia plant.

A gift of $2,000 from Mrs. George Russell, through the Women's Missionary Society of Lewistown, Pennsylvania, with an equal amount

[16] BNM, *Annual Report*, 1934, p. 63.

from the National Missions Building and Repair Fund, made possible the construction of another building in 1940. The building was named the "Russell Memorial Workshop and Science Building." Shop work was added to the curriculum and a special teacher was employed. The expansion trend was continued in 1941 when a teachers' cottage was erected. In 1943, a small dispensary and clinic building was added to the small house which had been donated by Dr. Albert B. McCoy. Funds for moving and installing this building on the campus were made up of proceeds from the sale of the Mt. Pleasant Arkansas Health Center and from sales of other Board property. Following these steps a trained nurse was added to the staff to develop a school and community health program.

This campaign of renovation and expansion created a hope for greater days for the academy, but this hope was blighted. On April 21, 1949, the Board of National Missions voted to close the school. The Board stated its reason for the closure as "the great outlay required to bring its plant up to minimum standards; the location not being central enough to the area being served." The Board also voted on that date to rent certain buildings to the public school authorities to care for the day students then enrolled at the academy, to continue to operate the clinic in cooperation with local doctors and to plan with parents and the church for a community playground and recreation program. In 1950, the principal's cottage was sold to the Reverend L. W. Davis, the school's last principal.

The Board voted in 1951 that since nurses to carry out the clinic program as planned were not obtainable and because the municipality had begun to provide clinical facilities for Negroes, the remaining property should be sold. In keeping with this latest action, the main building was sold to the local school board and the remaining property sold to various individuals. The total proceeds from these sales amounted to approximately $20,000.

The student records were transferred to Boggs Academy in Keysville, Georgia. With this disposition of plant and records, the Board's program of education for Negroes west of the Mississippi came to an end.

THE OKLAHOMA SCHOOLS   9

After the Board's program of education expanded westward across the Mississippi River into Arkansas and Texas, it experienced a stalemate before getting solidly established in the Indian Territory. On the plains of this vast open country, little influence of modern civilization was evident in the primitive folkways of the inhabitants. Inspired individuals, however, had been in the area over an extended period, attempting to awaken both the freedmen and the Choctaw Indians to a better way of life.

The Board of Missions for Freedmen reported to the General Assembly in 1892 that "Parson" Charles W. Stewart, the pioneer circuit rider of the Choctaw Freedmen, who had organized several preaching and teaching stations in the territory, was among the earliest Christian pioneers in that western frontier. Over a period of approximately eighteen years, the Board made frequent reports on the dedicated services of this slightly tutored Christian zealot. The Reverend Robert Elliott Flickinger, author of *The Choctaw Freedmen*, includes this excerpt in the narrative of the life of Parson Stewart, born in 1823.

Charles W. Stewart was a native of Alabama, and, at the age of ten in 1833, was transported with the Choctaws, to whom as a slave he belonged, to the southeastern part of the Indian Territory. John Homer was then his master, and he located about three miles northeast of the present town of Grant . . . .

Charles Stewart, a white man, keeping store at Doaksville, soon after became his owner and his previous name, "Homer" was then changed to "Stewart," after the name of his new master. About the year 1860, Samson Folsom, a Choctaw who lived eight miles southeast of old Goodland, became his new and last owner.[1]

Parson Stewart was ordained by a presbytery of the Presbyterian Church, U.S., in the Indian Territory, in the fall of 1870. He was officially assigned to the pastoral care of the congregations which he had previously developed. He had been furnished books and taught to read by Mrs. Stewart, the wife of his master, and began holding religious meetings as early as 1856 while he still belonged to the Stewarts. Sometimes these meetings were in the Reverend Cyrus Kingsbury's church for the Choctaws and sometimes under a brush arbor. According to Flickinger, the Oak Hill station was organized about 1865, soon after Stewart's freedom was obtained.

During the year 1883, the evangelical work of Parson Stewart was voluntarily transferred by the Southern to the Northern Presbyterian church. At the time of this transfer, the circuit rider was covering an area of about 118 or more miles to serve eleven or more stations. His services at Grant, Doaksville, Frogville, Sandy Branch, and two stations at Oak Hill were most effective and long lasting. When the Synod of Indian Territory was formed by the union of three presbyteries in 1886, his circuit included eight of the forty-three churches enrolled. Prior to 1890, Parson Stewart was the first and only Presbyterian minister who preached to the "colored" people of the Indian Territory.[2] He continued his pastorate of all these churches until 1893, when he was honorably retired. Parson Stewart then moved to a home near the Forest church and died there at the age of seventy-three, April 8, 1896.

The Reverend E. G. Haymaker, superintendent of the Oak Hill school, succeeded him as pastor of the Oak Hill church. Richard D. Colbert, with other elders, was appointed to direct the missions at Frogville and Sandy Branch and to keep the other stations operating.

The Board made the following report of progress in the territory in 1889:

In the Indian Territory, steady progress has been made by our schools. The Pittsburgh Mission at Atoka, under the care of Miss

[1] Robert Elliott Flickinger, *The Choctaw Freedmen* (Pittsburgh: Presbyterian Church in the U.S.A., Board of Missions for Freedmen, 1914), p. 352.
[2] Flickinger, *The Choctaw*, pp. 354–55.

Osborn and Miss McCoy, Miss Ahrens' school at Lukfata, and Miss Hunter's at Wheelock, have all been quietly at work banishing ignorance and superstition.[3]

Obviously by this time the Board's operation in the Indian Territory had achieved a degree of stability. Several stations sponsored by individuals had been taken under the care of the Board, and one of Parson Stewart's stations had been merged with the St. Paul Mission at Eagletown. The Wheelock Mission had been transferred; the Oak Grove church and school and the Bethany station were discontinued when the Kiamechi Presbytery was established.

During these formative years the work was difficult and living conditions were substandard in this impoverished region. These conditions and other negative factors limited the number of workers to the strong-hearted and dedicated few, who, when they accepted the challenge, also accepted the necessity for multiple services. In 1884, the Board's report to the General Assembly listed the Reverend Alexander Reed as superintendent of six mission schools. Several other missionaries are reported as working in two or more mission centers during the same time span. Miss Bertha Louise Ahrens, born in Berlin, Prussia, February 26, 1857, is an example of this multiple service record. After arriving in the United States, she settled in Iowa. She began her work in the Indian Territory by founding the Mt. Gilead Mission at Lukfata in 1885. While serving at Mt. Gilead at Lukfata, Forest at Doaksville, Hebran at Goodland, Beaver Dam at Grant, Oak Hill at Valliant, and Bethesda at Wynnwood. She is also listed as rendering invaluable services at other nearby stations.[4]

Miss Ahrens' mission at Lukfata continued to thrive throughout the lean years of the 1890s when many stations, of necessity, were merged, transferred, or discontinued. The Reverend Samuel Gladman directed the work there from 1897 to 1903 when he was succeeded by the Reverend K. Bridges who remained until 1914.

At Wynnwood, on November 1, 1899, two sisters, Clara and Carrie Boles, with the aid of concerned citizens, established the Bethesda Mission. The stated purpose of this mission was to provide a home and Christian education for orphans and homeless youths of the black population. Their conviction of the necessity was deeply anchored in the belief that "Go teach" was as much a Biblical imperative as was "Go preach." The gradual progress of the Boles sisters' mission was not un-

[3] BMF, *Annual Report*, 1898, p. 17.
[4] Flickinger, *The Choctaw*, pp. 311–313.

common in that section of the mission field, especially in the economic crisis of the 1890s. There was, however, noticeable revival of concern and benevolence at the turn of the century. This revival engendered a corresponding advancement in the creative innovations of the program in the territory. Fewer stations were attempted, and greater efforts were made to improve those which survived the difficult time.

In addition to greater concern and increased giving, there were major structural changes of national scope which affected the character and progress of the work in Indian Territory. The Oak Hill community became incorporated and was called Valliant in 1902, and the "Sooners' " land rights, which had prevailed since 1834, underwent a change when the Land Allotment Law of 1904–1905 went into effect. The Pittsburgh Mission was discontinued in 1904; token steps were taken to provide for a public school system in the territory in 1906. Finally, the Indian Territory acquired statehood in 1907 and became Oklahoma. The demand for more and better teachers became greater than the local communities could supply, and the movement of teachers into Oklahoma from Arkansas and Texas became common. The Board's appeal for preachers who could also teach was intensified. As the public school system began to become effective in the section, the Board felt the necessity for altering its policy of operation. Cooperative operation with the public school system was arranged in some schools and some mission schools were dropped. Missions at Caddo, Altoka, and Muskogee were among those dropped. In Oklahoma, one school stands out from all the others as central. The Oklahoma story is contained within it.

The Oak Hill-Alice Lee Elliott Academy
Valliant, Oklahoma

The Alice Lee Elliott Academy was the point at which the Board's program reached its peak in the Indian Territory. The story of its founding and development is used here as a typical example of the trials, successes, and failures of the Board's operation on this western front.

The school began as a parochial venture by inspired individuals soon after the close of the Civil War. Records of several church agencies, charged with the responsibility of executing the Board's work in this section, reveal the following narrative of how the school originated and grew. Two ministers, the Reverends Alexander Reed and John Edwards, who were missionaries to the Choctaw Indians, saw and sympathized with the grave needs of the freedmen in the area. Early in their experiences, they made an urgent appeal in the freedmen's interest to the Board of Missions for Freedmen. During these formative years Parson Stewart's influence was strong among the blacks of the area, and he urged intensification of the ministers' appeal. This was done and the Board was favorably impressed.

The fulfillment of the idea of a school for freedmen in the territory is credited to Parson Stewart and Elder Henry Crittenden. Elder Crittenden was ordained in 1869, about four years after he was accorded his freedom. He enjoyed the reputation of being a master mechanic, and, in addition, he had been trained during slavery as a blacksmith, tinsmith, and carpenter. Later he acquired the art of repairing jewelry. His intelligence, skills, industry, and religious fervor attracted customers from long distances after he opened his shop.[5]

The original planning session for opening the school was held at the Crittenden home in 1868, and the school was started the same year. It was called the "School for Freedmen." During the same year, the Oak Hill Presbyterian Church was organized, and Parson Stewart became its first pastor, with Wilson Homer as catechist. The establishment of the church made the school more secure. In 1876, the school also took on the name The Oak Hill School and, in 1878, the following teachers were reported at work there: George M. Dallas, Mary Roards, Henry Williams, and Lee V. Bibbs. About 1884, one of these teachers, Henry Williams, moved the school to an old log house. The reason for the removal was that there was no supply of good water at the old site, while at the new location a good well and a large vacant building were available. Parson Charles W. Stewart favored the change and under the guidance of Henry Crittenden, the "local trustee of the neighborhood, under the Choctaw law," it was decided that the "old log house" was the best place to establish the school.

The old log house was the pioneer home of a Choctaw chief Bazeel LeFlore, during the period prior to 1860. For more than a half century it had been the best building occupied by the Choctaws in the southeastern part of their large reservation. When occupied by the chief of the Choctaw Nation, its halls and spacious porches were the favorite meeting places for the administration of social and tribal affairs. About the year 1860, Chief LeFlore moved to Goodland, where he spent the remainder of his days. He left the log house to his nephew John Wilson, who occupied it for about twenty years and then left it to his son-in-law Frank Locke, its last Choctaw occupant. Frank Locke, after a few

[5] Flickinger, *The Choctaw*, pp. 108–109.

years, moved to a house in the Red River bottom and left the old log house to Robin Clark, the Choctaw freedman from whom it was obtained in 1884 for the use of the school. Robin Clark was an active member of the Oak Hill Church, and when he decided to move nearer the Red River, he generously tendered the free use of the building to the Oak Hill School. In 1885, Henry Friarson, another local teacher, was reported working at the school.

The school became more secure in 1886 when it was taken under the care of the Board of Missions for Freedmen. This was, in all reality, the beginning of a new chapter in the history of the school.

In January of 1886, Miss Eliza Hartford of Steubenville, Ohio, who had previously offered her services for missionary work, was commissioned by the Board, "and was sent in response to the appeal of the colored people of the Choctaw Nation."[6] She arrived at the mission on February 6, 1886. This is how Miss Hartford described the old log house upon her arrival:

> The windows are without sash or glass and the roof full of holes. The chimneys are of hewn stone, strong and massive. The house is of huge logs, two stories in height and stands high in the midst of a fine locust grove. The well of water near it seems as famous as Jacob's well.[7]

On Sunday, February 14, 1886, one week after her arrival, she organized a Sunday school and on Tuesday, February 16, 1886, she opened school with seven pupils in attendance. She became the first white teacher in the old log house. The building consisted of four rooms—two below and two above. After a survey of the community by the Reverend John Edwards, Miss Hartford and Miss Elder, a local friend, it was decided that the best place for Miss Hartford to stay was at the home of Elder Crittenden, three miles east. She was expected to make her daily journeys on horseback—the easiest mode of travel in the area at the time—and, in connection with the work of the school, to visit the people at their homes, furnish medicines for the sick, and give instruction in regard to their care.[8]

The opening session began by the reading of a chapter from the Bible, the singing of a hymn, and prayer by Elder Crittenden. Miss Hartford

---

[6] Flickinger, *The Choctaw*, pp. 296–297.
[7] Flickinger, *The Choctaw*, p. 107.
[8] Flickinger, *The Choctaw*, p. 108.

stated that she had never heard such a prayer of gratitude and thanks-giving at any school she had attended. He prayed for his people, the new teacher, the students and their parents, and for the prosperity of the school which was the fulfillment of the cries of his people to be delivered out of their ignorance and the darkness. On the following Monday, February 22, the enrollment had increased to fourteen. From this point on, the school's pace began to move more rapidly.

The Board of Missions increased its emphasis on industrial training at the school, in accordance with its policy in the late nineteenth century. With the addition of this phase of training at the Oak Hill School, its name was changed to "The Oak Hill Industrial Academy" on April 15, 1886. It was September of the same year that Oak Hill Industrial Academy became a boarding school with limited housing facilities. Following the establishment of the boarding facilities, students began to arrive from greater distances, and the old log house was soon overrun. Miss Hartford moved into the building with the boarding students and made a request to the Board for an additional teacher. In response, the Board commissioned Miss Priscilla G. Haymaker of Newlonsburg, Pennsylvania. She arrived at the school in April of 1887 and joined Miss Hartford in the old log house. Together, with the help of a skilled male student, they constructed the rustic furniture for the boarding department. When school opened in September of that year, eighty students enrolled, but housing could be provided for only thirty-six. The other forty-four were placed in homes of friendly neighbors.

Miss Haymaker's arrival was cause for community rejoicing, and during a community meeting that year an agreement was reached to erect a building to house both the school and the chapel. For this purpose, it was also agreed that all usable materials from the school house which was built in 1878 were to be salvaged. The Board allotted fifty dollars toward the project, and one of the school's original friends, the Reverend John Edwards, contributed twenty-five dollars. These donations were used to purchase additional lumber, and the men donated the necessary labor to construct the building. Miss Hartford and Elder Henry Critten-den assumed the responsibility for the rather large balance of the funds still needed. The project was a success, and the school and church moved into the new building the same year.

Miss Haymaker's first tenure at the school was cut short by failing health. Unaccustomed to the rough frontier life, she was unable to make the necessary adjustment and in November of 1887 was forced to give up the work and return to her home. Miss Anna E. Campbell of Midway, Pennsylvania, arrived two days after Miss Haymaker's departure and became Miss Hartford's assistant. Miss Campbell brought with her a large bell, which she had solicited from her father's farm. It was installed and summoned the parishioners to worship on the following Sunday after her arrival. She remained until the end of the school term, June 15, 1888. This left Miss Hartford without a staff and she felt constrained to return to her home in Ohio. There was no one left to direct the work and the school was closed.

Mr. and Mrs. James F. McBride of Kansas were commissioned to re-open the school, and they arrived on the campus on October 1, 1888 as superintendent and matron, respectively. The Board's explanation of these incidents at the school was made in its 1889 report:

> There has been a complete change of teachers at Oak Hill Indian Territory. Last year Miss Haymaker lost her health and was obliged to return home. Miss Campbell took her place, but by the end of the year she too was obliged to return home for the same reason. In the summer, Miss Hartford, who had been connected with the school from its organization, broke completely down and went home. We were fortunate, however, in securing Mr. and Mrs. J. F. McBride of Kansas and Miss C. L. Peck of Michigan, to take charge of the work. Miss Celestine Hodges of Scotia Seminary opened the school according to the requirements of the Choctaw law, in September and taught until the arrival of the other teachers in October, since which time she has acted as assistant.[9]

With the McBride administration, it is apparent that a new era in management at the school was inaugurated. Before 1888, the Board's ownership at the school consisted of farm buildings, the new school-church building, Robin Clark's gift of the old log house, and a barn purchased from him. In 1889, however, the Women's Department resolved to begin a building fund to erect a plain house for teachers, for it was their feeling that the failure in health of staff members and students resulted from exposure. A substantial dormitory, completed in 1889, was the result of their efforts. It was used to house the superintendent's family, teachers, and boarding female students. The old log house was renovated to house male students. The instructional staff was increased to five that year, including two Negroes.

[9] BMF, *Annual Report*, 1889, p. 17.

Not unlike their predecessors, the McBrides' enthusiasm and drive were pushed beyond the point of endurance by the post. After approximately four years, Mr. McBride died in 1892. His plans for a boys' dormitory and other progressive steps were arrested. Mrs. McBride and four teachers, Mary Coffland, Anna McBride, Bettie Stewart, a black teacher, and Rilla Fields completed the school year.

On October 1, 1892, the Reverend Edward Graham Haymaker of Newlonsburg, Pennsylvania, became superintendent of the Oak Hill School, with Miss Anna T. Hunter as principal. Miss Priscilla G. Haymaker, whose health had improved, had returned in 1890, and in the years that followed, several notable achievements were witnessed by the school. Plans for a boys' dormitory were completed, and a laundry and smokehouse had been completed by 1895. Despite this expansion of the physical plant, however, the undesirable location of the school continued to pose a problem. When Valliant was incorporated in 1902, the school was moved from beside the track in the Oak Grove section to a beautiful permanent site in Valliant. Prior to 1902, the nearest post office had been at Wheelock, ten miles to the east, and the nearest trading posts had been at Paris, Clarksville, and Goodland, Texas, twenty-eight miles to the west. Lumber and other materials for building purposes and food supplies had to be hauled from these distant posts. Many advantages, therefore, were gained by the move. Although the school remained co-educational, most of the students were girls, and the majority of all students were boarders.

During the early years of Haymaker's administration, a circular announcement was sent out in script form to acquaint interested patrons of the school with some of the changes and requirements at the school:

School opens Oct. 2nd and will continue for a term of six months. It is important that all who attend be on hand at the opening. The sum of $10.00 for citizens and $12.00 for non-citizens will be charged which must be paid in advance, or assurance given for its payment. The price of tuition has been raised by the Board as the Choctaw fund seems to be cut off. It only amounts of 1 cent a meal or 3 cents a day for board and 1½ cents for lodging. Cheap enough. The Board pays the large part of the bill.

Shoes must in all cases be provided by parents and guardians. Girls will be provided with other articles of clothing as far as possible, but no such provision can be made for boys. Books for all will be provided free, and all will be required to work certain hours each day. Boys will not be allowed to use tobacco.

A course of study has been arranged and pupils completing the course will be given a diploma. which will admit to any of the higher schools under the Board.[10]

These specifications were in no wise unique. With few exceptions, during the early years of the program the children of freedmen went to school "out of missionary barrels." Some students paid the entire cost of board and lodging through personal labor, while some others were "adopted" by various missionary groups who underwrote their entire bill.

Reverend Haymaker retired in the spring of 1904, and the school was again closed for a year since there was no available staff. A student was entrusted with the care of the buildings, stock, and crops until late in August of the same year, when Miss Bertha L. Ahrens, then at Grant, was commissioned as custodian of buildings and other Board property. Before Haymaker left the premises, however, he finalized several business contracts. The year of his retirement was also the year when land in the Indian Territory was allotted to the Indians and their former slaves, individually. Haymaker secured the allotment of two tracts of forty acres each (on which the buildings of the academy were located)—one to a graduate and the other to a full-blooded Choctaw woman. This was done with the understanding that, when ownership restrictions should be removed, the allottees or owners would sell them to the Board of Missions for Freedmen, to be held and used as a permanent site for the institution.[11]

The Reverend and Mrs. R. E. Flickinger of Fonda, Iowa, spent two weeks of voluntary service in the vicinity of the academy, visiting towns, churches, and schools in 1905. They traveled on horseback and made speeches in as many as eight different places the month before they opened the school again, for a three-month term, in February of 1905. The staff included Mrs. Flickinger, Miss Ahrens, and the Reverend and Mrs. W. H. Carroll.

When Flickinger assumed the executive role at the school in 1905, there were evidences of ill-repair which had developed the previous year while it was closed. Only a few students enrolled that year and the outlook was gloomy. With a creative and innovative approach, the new administration soon established a degree of order and some beauty. The piles of rubbish in every corner and the profuse growth of underbrush

[10] Flickinger, *The Choctaw*, pp. 134–135.
[11] Flickinger, *The Choctaw*, p. 154.

were cleaned out, and some of the buildings were neatly painted by the boys. Above all, the lagging spirit of the people concerning the continuation of the school was lifted and hope was revitalized. In fact, "enlargement and permanent improvement" became a driving force at the academy.

The Board's operation on this frontier received a tremendous boost in 1907 when the Indian Territory acquired statehood and became Oklahoma. Several actions regarding land ownership were taken. The Board had not secured clear titles to the allotments which the Reverend Haymaker had secured. The preventive restrictions were lifted with the acquisition of statehood, and the title to one small tract was promptly secured. A dozen other small tracts were added later at minimal prices, and the boundaries of the school property finally surrounded a 270-acre plot of beautiful and tillable land.

It was during this year also that Mrs. V. P. Boggs, secretary of the Women's Department of the Board of Missions for Freedmen, visited the school. Her observations and general impressions were later summarized as follows:

> Since the re-opening of Oak Hill Academy in February 1905 it has had an era of prosperity that promises permanency. Many improvements have been made, new buildings for farm purposes have been erected, much of the land has been refenced and is gradually being brought under a higher state of cultivation, and there is a general improvement in the appearance of the entire premises which reflects credit on the management as well as the boys who do the work. The literary work progresses under well trained teachers and a normal department has been added.[12]

Flickinger was patient and persevering, but his great staying powers were tapped when the "Fire Bug," to which the Board had referred frequently as "constantly ravaging the schools," severely attacked the Oak Hill School in 1908. In quick succession, the two largest buildings on the campus were destroyed by fire. One of these buildings was the boys' dormitory which had been erected in 1895. This disaster, as on many other Board school campuses, merely served as a motivation for redoubling efforts. A temporary dormitory was built and dedicated February 28, 1909. On Sunday, March 13, 1910, the girls' dormitory, which was built in 1889, the laundry, and the old log house were quickly con-

[12] Flickinger, *The Choctaw*, p. 158.

sumed in flames. This last burning left only the chapel and the boys' temporary dormitory intact. This was indeed a staggering loss, but rescue came.

In June, 1910, Mr. David Elliott of Lafayette, Indiana, gave $5,000 for a building in memory of his wife. With Flickinger serving as both architect and builder, the structure was built for $6,500, plus a gift of student and faculty labor. The concrete walls of Elliott Hall were the first of their kind in that vicinity, and five years later they were said to be the most substantial concrete walls in that part of the country. In addition to the new Elliott Hall, the name of the school was changed from the Oak Hill Industrial Academy to the Alice Lee Elliott Memorial School in 1910. Flickinger's concentrated goal, over the following two years, was the complete restoration of the school. At the end of the school year in 1912, Flickinger resigned. He remained until late October, directing the improvement of the plant and farm, publishing the last issue of "The Oak Hill Freedman's Friend," a newsletter intended to promote the interest of the Academy, and preparing and publishing a bulletin entitled *Approved Fruits for Southern Oklahoma*. The author's purpose for publishing this bulletin was to furnish a short and reliable textbook on horticulture for use in the academy and to supply the patrons of the institution with the information which they needed to secure early and profitable returns from their fruitbearing trees. Near the end of October he joined Mrs. Flickinger, who had returned to their "Airy View Farm" in Iowa following a serious injury in 1909.

The Reverend W. H. Carroll, principal, succeeded Flickinger as superintendent and presided over the testimonial service for Flickinger at his departure. Carroll was a product of both the college and seminary of Biddle University and was well acquainted with Flickinger's plans for expansion and improvement. Mrs. Carroll and Miss S. B. Neil joined the staff to assist with the instruction of the ninety-seven students enrolled.

In 1916, after four years of dedicated service under the Carroll administration, Miss Bertha Louise Ahrens resigned, donated a plot of twenty-one acres of land adjoining the Oak Hill farm, and returned to her home in Iowa. Carroll remained three years longer and then accepted the Board's commission to work at the Monticello Academy in Monticello, Arkansas. He was succeeded at Alice Lee Elliott by the Reverend J. D. Stanback the same year.

With the Reverend J. D. Stanback as superintendent, the Reverend Allen S. Meacham was commissioned as principal of the Alice Lee Elliott Memorial School in 1919. Two years later the Board made the following report to the General Assembly:

> Alice Lee Elliott, Valliant, Okla. must have a recitation building which would cost about $15,000.00. The good women of California are sending in contributions toward this object; meanwhile the principal and his workers are constantly besieging us to erect the building this summer.[13]

Alice Lee Elliott Memorial School was one of the thirty or more schools under the care of the Board that was affected by the retrenchment policy. Its doors were again closed, this time permanently, in 1940. The closure ended the Reverend Stanback's twenty-one years of service to the institution. He joined the host who faced the realities of the closure with deep regrets, and who, likewise, realized that the public school system could not fill the void created by the closure.

[13] *Minutes,* 1921, p. 344.

THE ALABAMA SCHOOLS   *10*

Although the impact of Presbyterianism was limited in the state of Alabama—at least in comparison to the work in several other states—both the Presbyterian Church, U.S.A., and the United Presbyterian Church had missions in the area before the merger of these two churches in 1958. In many ways, Alabama presents a miniature of the policies of these two churches before their coming together.

The United Presbyterian Church had established several parochial schools, but the strongest were five day schools in Wilcox County: Miller's Ferry, Prairie Mission, Camden Academy, Arlington Institute, and Canton Bend Academy. During the formative period of the program, the Women's General Missionary Society of the United Presbyterian Church took over the support and administration of Miller's Ferry, Prairie Institute, and Camden Academy, while the Board of American Missions supported and administered Arlington Institute and Canton Bend School. When these two missionary groups were merged to form the Board of American Missions on July 1, 1956, the consolidated society took over the administration of all five schools.

The United Presbyterian Church also established schools at Muscle Shoals, Summerfield, and Midway, but these were operated only a few years and then turned over to the public school system to operate. The five schools in Wilcox County were still operating in 1950, long after all such day schools had been closed by the sister denomination.

On the other hand, the Presbyterian Church, U.S.A., had one major school in Alabama, a boarding school for girls that eventually grew into a college, although there were a few parochial schools.

Shortly before the merger in 1958, the United Presbyterian Church had worked out an informal agreement with county public school officials whereby the county furnished the money for teachers' salaries and the full direction of the schools remained the responsibility of the church's agencies. Bible teachers were employed by the Board and the buildings were owned and maintained by it.[1] Perhaps it was this arrangement that permitted these day schools to continue, although no longer totally under church auspices.

Alabama presented a somewhat different environment than the churches encountered in other states. Incendiary bombs and the consequent destruction and danger of fire were strongly evidenced here. At the same time, wealthy white planters were often very strong supporters of the schools, donating land and money for their founding and continuation.

Barber Memorial College
Anniston, Alabama

Barber Memorial College, related to the Presbyterian Church, U.S.A., was founded in Anniston, Alabama, in 1896 by Mrs. Margaret Marr Barber of Philadelphia, Pennsylvania. It was a memorial to her late husband, Mr. Phineas N. Barber, whose expressed purpose it had been to provide an institution of this kind. The gift of Barber Memorial College was announced by the Board in the following words:

> At Anniston, Alabama, a commodious building is being erected for a girls' boarding school by Mrs. Phineas N. Barber of Philadelphia, who proposes to turn over to the Board a completed plant for the maintenance of a first class boarding school, capable of holding 150 girls. The Board accepts the responsibility of the management of the school on the condition that it is to have entire control, just as with its other large schools. The gift to the cause is a munificent one, and worthy of the generous founder of the "Barber Fund" now held in trust by the Trustees of the General Assembly for the benefit of the colored race.[2]

The physical plant was erected high on a hillside overlooking Anniston and the surrounding valley. The main building was a beautiful brick and natural stone structure, consisting of four stories and a basement. It was

---

[1] "Alabama Day Schools," *Briefly* (N.Y.: PCUSA, BNM, 1960).
[2] BMF, *Annual Report*, 1896, p. 10.

an enormous building, compared to the usual schoolhouses, and accommodated two hundred students and teachers. The main offices, teachers' living room, president's suite, classrooms, sewing room, and a chapel were on the first floor. The library, dean's office, additional classrooms, hospital, and college dormitory were on the third floor. On the fourth, dormitory space was provided for high school boarders. The basement housed the kitchen, dining room, domestic science room, printing shop, chemistry laboratory, and storage rooms. In addition to this all-purpose building there was a parsonage, a training house, and various other buildings. All of these were constructed at Mrs. Barber's expense. Chiseled in the marble cornerstone of the main building was the slogan, "For the Heart, the Head, the Hand."[3]

The school was formally opened on November 17, 1896, with the Reverend and Mrs. George B. Crawford of the Synod of New Jersey in charge of the school. Because of the natural beauty of its setting, the worthy principles for which it was founded, and the inspiration which it brought to the community, the school soon acquired the name, locally, "Barber the Beautiful."[4]

Immediately following the Board's 1897 report to the General Assembly concerning Mrs. Barber's generous gift, a message was flashed over the wires that the main building, which had been in use only six months, had been totally destroyed by fire. No lives were lost and, since it occurred near the end of the school term, the seriousness of the interruption was lessened. The Reverend George A. Marr, Mrs. Barber's brother, who had superintended the construction of the burned building, began reconstruction immediately without cost to the Board. The completed structure, which was considered better than the first, was presented to the Board of Missions on January 1, 1898.

The history of the Barber Memorial College is filled with several misfortunes and many great blessings. The main building was burned twice, but each time it was rebuilt on the same beautiful spot without cost to the Board. The last main building was large and imposing, with a huge veranda extending completely across the front, its length broken by attractive stone arches. The charm of the entire sixty-acre plot was heightened in the spring when the magnolia trees were in full bloom.

Like Mary Holmes Seminary, but unlike many other Board schools, Barber's beginning was on a large scale. Its first faculty consisted of

[3] *Barber Memorial College Catalog*, 1910, p. 3.
[4] "Barber Memorial College," *Brevities* (N.Y.: PCUSA, BNM, 1936).

seven members. About sixty pupils were comfortably housed and taught in what was then considered exceptionally fortunate surroundings.

The Reverend Crawford resigned in 1899 because of failing health and was succeeded by the Reverend S. M. Davis. By 1900, there were 117 pupils enrolled under the instruction of 10 teachers, and a greatly enriched curriculum had been structured. From 1896 to 1900 the basic curriculum had consisted of English, arithmetic, algebra, reading, spelling, penmanship, psychology, theory and practice of teaching, ancient history, and the Bible. Davis added to this curriculum many courses leading toward advanced study.

Mrs. Davis died in 1902 and Davis rededicated himself to their unfinished task. The enrollment for 1908 was 168 and the teaching staff had increased to 12. After fifteen years of a very successful administration, Davis retired in August of 1913 and, by Board action, was given the title of president emeritus. He continued his services at the institution as professor of the English Bible and Biblical Literature.

The Reverend Robert L. Alter of North Washington, Pennsylvania, was commissioned to fill the vacancy at Barber, and Mrs. Alter was elected principal. The outlook for the school was one of continued prosperity. The Alters began with 12 teachers and 153 students. After five years of creative leadership, Alter resigned and was succeeded by the Reverend J. F. Sherer in 1918.

The ten years during which Sherer charted the course for Barber were characterized by reorganization and expansion, primarily in the area of teacher-training, in view of the needs of the public school system for Negroes. In 1924 a college department was added and the first six grades were discontinued. The program of the junior and senior high school was restructured and enriched in order to prepare students for the college department. Sherer's administration came to a close in July of 1929, when the Reverend H. M. Hosack was commissioned to direct the program at the school.

Reverend Hosack arrived at Barber when its program was changing. In 1929 the Barber High School was accredited by the state Department of Education. The following year, however, the college department of Barber was merged with that of Scotia Seminary in Concord, North Carolina. Despite the reasonableness undergirding the action, it was met with deep regret in the Anniston community. In a speech made by President Hosack at the Workers' Conference in 1935, at Johnson C. Smith University in Charlotte, the reader may sense the deep emotional reaction to the transfer:

In 1930 there was the removal of the College Department to Scotia. We were happy at Barber to have had the privilege of starting our Presbyterian College for Colored Women on life's way; the college has left a blessing; our school is the better for having it in our midst for a while. We believe the college, too, will be forever better for having been born at Barber Seminary. Barber has always had a wonderful spirit that is characteristic, transmissible and persistent. Our prayer for our College for women, Barber-Scotia, is that baptized with the spirit of Barber, confirmed in the tradition of Scotia, and married with the manhood of Johnson C. Smith University, she will go on and on into the fullness of life and service to which Christ calls his own.[5]

Undaunted by the merger, however, Hosack placed increased stress on the junior-senior high school program and restoring the grades which had been dropped previously. In December of 1931, the Barber High School was approved by the Southern Association of Colleges and Secondary Schools. Two years later, 1933, Barber became coeducational after operating thirty-seven years as a seminary for girls. This change was occasioned by the consolidation of the South Highland High School with the Barber High School. South Highland High School, located not far from Barber, had been operated by the Board of Missions for Freedmen and for nineteen years had been under the leadership of the Reverend A. W. Rice. The Board had set a deadline, 1933, beyond which the day school program would not operate, unless valid reasons merited consideration. Therefore, the consolidation of South Highland with Barber was a fortunate action on the part of the Board for both schools. The Reverend Rice was appointed assistant principal of the consolidated school. In this position he recruited high school students from the area which South Highland served and brought most of the high school students to Barber. After seven years of operation, however, the consolidated Barber High School was discontinued in 1940.

Miller Memorial
Birmingham, Alabama

Barber was, by far, the most dynamic mission in Alabama sponsored by the Presbyterian Church, U.S.A., followed by the Highland High School in the same city of Anniston. Yet, there were some small parochial schools which rendered invaluable services to their respective communi-

[5] H. M. Hosack, Speech before the Workers Conference, Johnson C. Smith University, Charlotte, North Carolina, 1935.

ties for limited periods before they were discontinued. One such parochial school was the Miller Memorial in Birmingham, Alabama.

In 1894, the Reverend E. M. Clark, pastor of the Presbyterian church for Negroes in Birmingham, had 75 pupils enrolled. In 1895, the enrollment reached 115 and Miss Willie J. Clark was assisting with the instruction of the pupils. Miss Clark, industrious and creative, remained with it through the administration of the Reverend H. P. Therman in 1900. The Reverend L. B. Bascomb and Mr. E. J. Ravenah were conducting the work in 1901, and they were followed by the Reverend and Mrs. L. B. Ellerson at the end of that year. The Ellersons were assisted by the Misses Grier and Clark. The Reverend and Mrs. C. J. Barber were commissioned to take charge of the school in 1917, and they had five teachers assisting with the enrollment of 364. After four years of concentrated endeavor at the school, Barber resigned and was succeeded by the Reverend A. W. Sherard. Nine years later Miller Memorial was converted into the Miller Memorial Community Station and did not appear in the Board's report of schools after 1930.

In 1909 at Myrtlewood, the Cornerstone School, under the Reverend Vanhorn, was reported by the Board as active with sixty pupils enrolled. This mission never developed into a prosperous station and was shortlived. The Reverend E. B. Walthall was directing the school in 1921. There was also a parochial school at Greensboro under the direction of the Reverend D. L. Donnell in 1921, which had the same sort of history as the school at Myrtlewood.

The United Presbyterian Church at Work in Alabama

Miller's Ferry School
Wilcox County, Alabama

Miller's Ferry School was founded in 1884 in Wilcox County, Alabama, by the Freedmen's Board of Missions of the United Presbyterian Church of North America. The school began in an old log church on property donated by Judge William Henderson, a United Presbyterian planter of the North. He appealed to the Freedmen's Board of Missions to establish its program of education in Wilcox County and offered a site for the campus on his plantation. The proposal was accepted, and the program was started in Wilcox County, where no schools for Negroes existed, about one hundred miles from the Gulf of Mexico. In a 300-square-mile area in this section of Alabama, the Negro population was slightly less than the white. The Negroes eked out a meager existence

on large, fertile plantations or as sharecroppers. The educational, religious, and community-center program was intended for this rural population of freedmen at Miller's Ferry and the Board's other four parochial
schools in this county.

Miss Henrietta Mason was in charge of the Miller's Ferry School until
1887, when Professor P. C. Cloud was chosen principal of the school.
In 1889 the first school building was erected, and in 1895 this building
was destroyed by an incendiary bomb. The Reverend C. H. Johnson
became pastor and principal in 1893. At that time the plant consisted
of the school house, parsonage, two dormitories, a teachers' home, and
a printing and carpenter's shop.

In the late 1950s B. T. Ridgeway was principal of the Miller's Ferry
School with a staff that included one Bible teacher, three maintenance
workers—all under national missions—and several county teachers. The
school attendance was more than four hundred. In 1960 the school was
offering both elementary and high school work.

Prairie Mission School
Wilcox County, Alabama

The Prairie Mission School, founded in 1885 by the United Presbyterian Church, was five miles northwest of the Miller's Ferry School.
Professor H. J. Oliver was in the double role of superintendent of the
more than six-hundred-acre farm and principal of the school. He manned
these two positions until 1900, when N. B. Cotton, a Knoxville College
graduate, was appointed director of the farm, and the Reverend J. E.
James was commissioned as pastor and principal. At that time, the plant
consisted of the large farm, a school building which was also used for
church services, teachers' home, and a dormitory which was reconstructed from an old church that had stood on the grounds. The school
began as an elementary school and sent those who completed its course
of study to Miller's Ferry School for high school training.

In the late 1950s, Palmer E. Williams was the principal of the school
and working with him were one Bible teacher, one maintenance worker,
and county teachers.

Camden Academy
Wilcox County, Alabama

The next mission to be established by the Board in Wilcox County was
Camden Academy. It was founded in 1886 just outside the city limits of
Camden, the county seat, with Mr. Henry M. Green as principal. Mr.

Green remained only one year and was succeeded by the Reverend E. K. Smith in 1887. The plant was located on a hill known as "Hangman's Hill" because of the numerous hangings which had been conducted there. The plant consisted of four buildings: a combination school and church house, a teachers' home, and two dormitories. One of the dormitories was given by William Carson of the Sixth Church, Pittsburgh, Pennsylvania, in memory of his daughter, Miss Mary Carson, and the building was named "Mary Carson Memorial." The other dormitory resulted from the efforts of local patrons. The original plant, however, consisted of two small one-room churches.

In the late 1950s, A. A. Peoples, a Knoxville College graduate, was principal. With him were two Bible teachers, one dietician, three maintenance workers, county teachers, and more than eight hundred students.

Arlington Institute
Wilcox County, Alabama

Arlington Literary and Industrial Institute was the youngest of the Wilcox County Missions. It was founded in 1902 at Annemanie, a section unique in that at that time it was the only area in the county where Negroes could own property. Miss Janie Upton was in charge at the opening but remained only one year. The Reverend J. T. Arter was commissioned as pastor and principal in 1903.

K. P. Thomas, a graduate of Tuskegee Institute, was superintendent in the late 1950s, and assisting him were one Bible teacher, five maintenance workers, and county teachers. During this time the average enrollment was 400.

Canton Bend Mission
Wilcox County, Alabama

Canton Bend Mission was founded in 1896. A Mr. Bryant provided the land and his family remained substantial friends as long as the school lasted. The school was destroyed by fire in 1952 and the Board's operation there was discontinued. Canton Bend had begun under the guidance of Mr. and Mrs. J. N. Cotton at the request of surrounding planters, after seeing the benefits of such a school at Miller's Ferry.

Midway Mission
Wilcox County, Alabama

Midway Mission is said to have begun in 1901 four miles from Prairie with Mr. George Johnson as principal. Two planters in the vicinity donated ten acres each for the school. Mr. Johnson taught one year in a one-room cabin and was relieved in 1902 by Mr. T. R. Robinson. Further records of the work and closing date of this mission were unattainable.

THE TEXAS SCHOOL

The Texas story is the history of one school, Mary Allen Junior College in Crockett. A marker at the city limits of this small Texas town has the inscription, "Welcome to Crockett, Texas,—Twelve thousand pecan trees and six thousand inhabitants." Buffalo once roamed without fear in this rustic area north of the Gulf of Mexico and east of the Panhandle; profuse cacti deterred all who would pursue them. Surrounding Crockett, the prairieland levels off in all directions.

High upon a hill overlooking this marker is Mary Allen Junior College, dedicated to the memory of a woman who fought for the spiritual and intellectual liberation of a people.

How the Mary Allen Junior College became a reality is partially told by the Reverend S. M. Tenny, Curator of the Historical Foundation of the Presbyterian and Reformed Churches in Montreat, North Carolina, and son of the Reverend S. F. Tenny, who laid the foundation upon which the school was established. In essence, his narrative of his father's pioneering efforts reveals another paradox of those trying years: the Reverend S. F. Tenny, a minister of the Presbyterian Church, U. S., was born in the South and enlisted in the Confederate army in the Civil War. Following the surrender, however, he dedicated himself to the task of working for the unification of the nation and the complete liberation of the emancipated slaves.[1]

[1] S. M. Tenny, "Notes on the Work Among the Colored People of Crock-

He arrived in Crockett, Texas, during the Christmas week of 1870. In 1871, he accepted the pastorate of a local Presbyterian church, organized a Sabbath school and invited the freedmen to attend. They came in large numbers and were taught in a designated section of the church by volunteers from the congregation. The arrangement for conducting this Sabbath school prospered only for a short while, because unrest arose over the presence of the freedmen in the church edifice.[2]

Reverend Tenny realized that other arrangements had to be made for the continuance of the freedmen's phase of the Sabbath school. He, therefore, traveled throughout the North and into Canada soliciting funds for his Texas project. He brought back $538.49 in cash and $222.75 in supplies. The Texas Land Company deeded to the trustees of the local church land on which to construct a church building for the freedmen, May 26, 1875. Tenny writes of his father:

> He raised funds and erected a splendid, large church building with a tower and a bell, and painted it. He carried his people with him. Well do I recall that his best elder, a prominent merchant, superintended the colored Sunday School, and how the most popular music teacher in town, teacher of the primary class in her own church, a cultured devout soul, rode her little pony across town, and taught every Sunday in the colored Sunday School.[3]

This achievement apparently inspired the pioneer to expand his program. He again went on a travel campaign to St. Louis, Philadelphia, Pittsburgh, New York, Buffalo, and provinces in Canada, where he spoke and raised money with which he built an annex to the freedmen's church for a school room. He employed one of his best members, Mrs. C. O. Webb, to conduct a day school.[4] The son's narrative continues:

> His heart was set on establishing what his notebook calls "Moffatt Academy." Funds ran low. He had prepared for such a day and made our home the center for helping to educate five teachers: Alexander Turner, Maria Turner, Marian Clayborn, Viney Lane and Marie Green. . . . It was interesting how these would . . . often report at our door and ride out to the country to teach, then report

---

ett, Texas, Leading up to the Establishment of Mary Allen Seminary in 1886" (unpublished manuscript, 1939).

[2] Tenny, "Notes," pp. 1–2.

[3] S. M. Tenny, "Mary Allen Junior College" (unpublished manuscript, n.d.), p. 1.

[4] Tenny, "Notes," pp. 5–6.

back in the evening, and we children would help them to work arithmetic examples. This continued for two or possibly four years.[5]

Although the parochial school was apparently progressing, Tenny was not satisfied with its slow development and his finances were low. So he made an appeal to the Board of Missions for Freedmen. There was also a vital concern at the national level regarding entering the mission field of Texas. In 1885, the Board of Missions for Freedmen decided to found a boarding school for the daughters of freedmen in the state of Texas and consulted the superintendent of public instruction in the state regarding a suitable location. The Board's letter, which brought forth a number of favorable comments, was published in Texas papers. Through the letter and church periodicals, Tenny learned of the Board's intentions. He wrote the Reverend Richard H. Allen, at that time secretary of the Board of Missions for Freedmen, and invited him to visit Crockett. Allen accepted the invitation and was received cordially by Tenny and prominent businessmen, who assisted him in exploring the possibilities for maintaining the proposed school in that town.

Favorable events began to happen rapidly: some businessmen in Crockett offered a ten-acre, hilltop plot as a desirable location; Allen delivered a sermon at Tenny's church, and a definite agreement regarding the school was reached by the two ministers. Allen returned to Pittsburgh and recommended that the Board accept Crockett for the location of the proposed boarding school. The recommendation was approved. By this act, the Board took under its care in 1886 the parochial school and its funds which the Reverend S. F. Tenny had begun in 1880. The school began its new career on the beautiful, ten-acre plot.

Additionally, in 1884, the General Assembly had authorized the establishment of the Women's Executive Committee of the Board of Missions for Freedmen. Mary Esther Allen (Mrs. Richard H. Allen) chaired that new organization when it first met in December of 1884. Tenny had met Mrs. Allen during one of his trips to Pittsburgh and had won her interest in his Texas project.[6]

Mrs. Allen, convinced that the most permanent progress of a race depended, to a large degree, upon the elevation of its women, began immediately to activate the women of the church in the interest of the new school in Texas. She spoke at presbyterials and synodicals; she wrote

[5] Tenny, "Mary Allen," p. 1.
[6] *A Sketch of the Life and Work of Mrs. Mary E. Allen* (Philadelphia: Press of Henry B. Ashmead, 1886), p. 17.

numerous letters and published article after article with such titles as:
"Our New Work," "Earnest Words to Christian Women," "The Pittsburgh Mission," "The Children of the Freedmen," and "Our Texas
Boarding School for Colored Girls."[7] Her warm and sincere plea was
captivating, and she soon won the interest of the church women. Her
most captivating appeal, however, came through her final request delivered from her bed, shortly before she died:

> The school for colored girls in Texas stays on my mind and in my
> prayers. We must take steps at once to raise money for that build-
> ing. What has been done once, twice or thrice for these deserving
> children should be done a hundred times.
> The Christian education for Negro girls by means of such schools
> goes to the very heart of the Negro problem. What Scotia is doing in
> the east should be done in every section of the Southland. Don't let
> the work for colored girls in Texas lag.[8]

The organized women had already embraced Mrs. Allen's project but,
with these stirring words, it became their obsession. Mrs. J. P. E. Kumler
stressed this in remarks to the women: "Let us arise and build for her
memorial that house for the Texas Boarding-school for colored girls."[9]
Three days following the untimely death of Mrs. Allen, on March 3,
1886, the Board agreed that the official name of the school was to be
"Mary Allen Seminary."
The Reverend J. B. Smith had been commissioned to take charge of
the new seminary. S. M. Tenny writes:

> Late in 1885, Dr. J. B. Smith, his wife and Miss C. E. Logan ar-
> rived in Crockett and came to our home. Residence was secured for
> them near by where the Bromberg residence is now. Dr. Smith
> bought a good horse and buggy and went right to work.
> The Board reported that school opened at Crockett, Houston
> County, Texas, January 15, 1886, in an old two-story hotel, fur-
> nished by women of the church. The large frame structure was
> rented for the purpose.[10]

The Presbyterians were at this time considering a new building
and location. Dr. Smith bought the old church building, just as it
stood, placed it on rollers and moved it from its old site to the ten-

[7] *A Sketch of . . . Mary E. Allen*, p. 14.
[8] *A Sketch of . . . Mary E. Allen*, p. 17.
[9] *A Sketch of . . . Mary E. Allen*, p. 18.
[10] Tenny, "Notes," p. 9.

acre plot. This was something new in Crockett and attracted much
attention and many sightseers. The building served all purposes for
the institution until 1888. The citizens of Crockett donated another
twelve acres of land to the Board.

Dr. Smith was a very extraordinarily gifted man of good practical
judgment and sense and was an extra good business manager. He
threw his gifts into the new undertaking, and was shortly operating
a brick yard and erected the large building now standing. He established a good poultry yard, and secured some half dozen deer for
pets. He thoroughly identified himself with the town and its every
interest and supervised the erection of not less than six or eight of
the present business houses in Crockett. He, Mrs. Smith and the
teachers were all highly cultured and devout Christians.[11]

Mary Allen Hall was completed October 1, 1887 at a cost of $20,000
including furnishings. During the summer months of that year a normal
school for young men teachers in Houston County and a kindergarten
class were conducted. The school began as a day and boarding school,
offering courses at the primary, elementary, high school, and teacher-
training levels for girls only. Home economics and the choir were included in the initial program.

The seminary published its first catalog in 1887. In it, Mary Allen
Hall is described as a four-story brick structure with a basement, topped
by a mansard roof. It was an all-purpose building providing space for
boarding teachers and students, chapel, dining room, and kitchen. The
second term opened with forty boarders and increased to seventy-four
within three weeks.

Proud of their achievement at the Seminary, the women wrote in the
Home Mission Monthly that Mary Allen Seminary, like Scotia Seminary,
was designed on the pattern of the New England finishing schools and
was frequently referred to as "The Mt. Holyoke of the southwest for
Negro girls."

The institution's growth was rapid, as Mrs. Allen had hoped it would
be. In 1888–1889, the Grace McMillan Hall was erected with a gift of
$16,000 from James McMillan of Detroit, Michigan, in memory of his
daughter. Also in this year, 300 acres of land adjacent to the campus
were donated by James Snyder of Morrison, Illinois. Continuing the expansion of the physical plant in 1890, an addition to McMillan Hall and
a gift of books from the Reverend R. H. Allen made possible the beginning the school's library.

[11] Tenny, "Mary Allen," p. 2.

The Board did not give a detailed report of Mary Allen Seminary's progress along with the other schools for 1890, but Trinity Presbytery listed 8 teachers, in addition to the Reverend and Mrs. Smith, and 211 students. The Board's reports are almost silent regarding the progress of its schools during the difficult years of the 1890s and for the first eight years of the new century.

After twenty years of dedicated service to the school and town, President Smith resigned in 1910 but he remained at the school during the summer following his resignation, planning for the fall opening. He died in 1910 just when the future was beginning to look brighter for the school.[12]

The school term 1910–1911 was conducted by one of the senior teachers, Miss Ella Ferguson, acting president. *The Home Mission Monthly*, the freedmen number for 1913, paid a special tribute to Miss Ferguson:

> Miss Ella Ferguson of Union City, Indiana, . . . came to Mary Allen Seminary in the fall of 1889, almost at the beginning of this school, as assistant teacher in the literary department. She was sweet and kindly with a delightful vein of humor, which was a good medicine for depressed spirits and a dignity which prevented any undue familiarity.
>
> In 1891, she was made principal of the Seminary and in this position manifested her ability and clear mind in the management and discipline of over 200 girls who were untaught and untrained— the "raw material." She taught in the Seminary for 22 years.[13]

The 1910–1911 school year was not a pleasant experience at the seminary. Still striving to readjust following the death of Dr. Smith, the 213 boarders returned from the Christmas holidays to an epidemic of smallpox. When Miss Ferguson made the report to the Board, she was advised to close the school for the year. She insisted, however, that all persons had been quarantined in the school; all students, not infected, had been vaccinated; the teachers were willing to continue, and a large number of students who were candidates for graduation would suffer a great loss if sent home at that time. The Board of Missions directed the acting president to continue with her work.

In the fall of 1911, Dr. H. P. V. Bogue of Avon, New York, became the new president. Before the end of Dr. Bogue's first term, McMillan

---

[12] "Mary Allen Seminary," *Snapshots* (N.Y.: PCUSA, BNM).

[13] "Loving Tribute to Two Unusual Women," *Home Mission Monthly*, vol. 27, no. 6 (April, 1913), pp. 141–142.

Hall was completely destroyed by fire on January 13, 1912, but without loss of life. Miss Ferguson, however, who was seriously ill, had to be taken from the burning building on a stretcher. The building was insured for $16,000 but immediate replacement was impossible. The school was closed for the remainder of the school term, and Miss Ferguson died before the spring of the next year. Death and fire, added to the smallpox epidemic, struck the students and patrons with fear, and the enrollment was cut drastically.

A two-story McMillan Hall was erected over a basement by the fall of 1913; a third story was soon added. Mrs. Bogue died in 1917 and President Bogue resigned. The Reverend A. E. Hubbard of California was elected president of the seminary that year. The entire country was in a state of unrest at the time the Reverend Hubbard began his administration. Europe was at war and the United States was becoming seriously involved; benevolence was beginning to decline, and the prevailing uncertainty affected each phase of the institution's activities. Yet some gestures were made toward expanding and keeping the program alive. The enrollment dropped to thirty-five in 1923, and the Board considered seriously whether it would be wiser to attempt revitalizing the seminary or to discontinue it. Hubbard resigned in 1924.

The Board's indecision was resolved when, in 1924, it commissioned the Reverend Byrd Randall Smith to revitalize the program at the institution. This appointment terminated thirty-eight years of the school's career under white administrators, and time proved the wisdom of the Board's decision. Smith was a graduate of both the college department and the seminary of Biddle University, and he had thirteen years of experience as pastor and teacher within the Board's program. He possessed many attributes which enabled him to meet challenges with courage and optimism. He was intellectual, dynamic, a shrewd administrator, and also possessed a flare for the dramatic. He inspired his all-black faculty to top performance and stimulated the Board's original enthusiasm for the work at the institution. The Women's Department rallied vigorously to this ambitious program.

There were a number of problems. The library and science laboratory needed upgrading; the plant had to be repaired and reequipped to meet accreditation requirements; the curriculum had to be enriched and expanded; the home economics and music departments required serious attention, and the dining room was cramped and dismal. Only firm faith and a keen sense of humor, plus careful planning and wise administration, gave hope and optimism to the situation. To accomplish the desired goals, changes, additions, and deletions began immediately.

During the 1925–1926 school term, the high school department was accredited by the state Department of Education. In 1927, the first junior college class graduated. The policy of eliminating the lower grades continued, in order to make possible greater concentration on the higher levels.

A significant achievement was accomplished in 1932 when the Southern Association of Colleges and Secondary Schools gave its stamp of approval to the work at the seminary and awarded it the "A" rating. This action by the association made the seminary the first college with a Negro president to be so recognized in the state of Texas. It was a great day in Crockett and throughout the National Missions field. The Board of National Missions, through its Women's Department, flashed the good news across the field.

Continuing the policy of adapting its program to the conditions and needs of the community, Mary Allen opened its doors to men and became coeducational on September 18, 1933, by approval of the Board of National Missions. A cottage was built to house the male students and it was immediately filled. Following this change in policy the school's name was changed to "Mary Allen Junior College." [14]

The year 1935 marked the fiftieth anniversary of the institution, and during its celebration $10,000 was raised. In this same year, Mrs. Lucile Smith, wife of the president and the first Negro principal of the school, died leaving three children to be reared.

Commencement at Mary Allen, in June 1936, was an eventful occasion when the last high school graduating class marched down the chapel aisle, followed by the graduating college class. The processional symbolized the institution's progress.

During the ensuing decade the institution was justly dubbed the Board's "Prairie Queen." A library annex was constructed in 1936, and relatives and friends of Miss Martha Bray, former English teacher from Chicago, began a library in her memory. A major change which greatly enhanced the religious life of the campus was the moving of the Presbyterian church from across town to a spot in a beautiful pine grove on the campus in 1937. The sum of money raised during the fiftieth anniversary celebration was used to construct the Byrd Randall Smith Gymnasium, which was dedicated on November 11, 1938. Continuing the

[14] *Mary Allen Junior College Catalog*, 1934, back of front cover.

expansion of the plant in 1939, a farm shop was built and an agriculture department was added to the curriculum.

The graduating class of 1940 was the last to receive honors at the hand of President B. R. Smith. On June 20, 1940, his brilliant twenty-year administrative career was ended by a heart attack. The 210 students and a devoted and dedicated faculty had helped to make the year one of the most rewarding in the history of the school.

Professor Thomas Bayne Jones of the Agriculture and Technical University at Greensboro, North Carolina, was President Smith's choice for his successor. The Board honored his choice and in September, 1940, Professor Jones assumed the executive role at the institution. Professor Jones was also a product of Biddle University and held the master's degree from Northwestern University. President Jones, intellectual and energetic, set out to complete his friend's unfinished task.

On April 23-24, 1942, however, the Board in annual session considered suggestions from the Chamber of Commerce of Crockett, Texas, proposing that the property of the Mary Allen Junior College be donated toward a project calling for the initiation of a four-year college for Negroes under state control. The Board approved the proposal with the understanding that certain mineral rights would be reserved and authorized the Unit of Education and Medical Work to enter into negotiation with the Texas Department of Education. In 1943, again in annual session, the Board heard a report stating that the new situation created by World War II had prevented the Texas legislature from acting on the proposal for operating a four-year college for Negroes as proposed the year before, and it would be unable to do so until the next legislature convened in 1945.

In view of these developments and the fact that the Board did not feel that its finances would permit the expansion of Mary Allen Junior College into the four-year level, which the state education authorities considered essential at the time, the Board rescinded its action of 1942 and voted to close the college at the end of the 1942–1943 school term and to sell the property at the best price attainable. It also voted that the sale price of the institution's property would be used to erect a memorial building at one of the other Board schools for Negroes.

The Mary Allen property was sold during the summer of 1943 to Dr. C. W. Butler, Jr. for $13,000. Everything was sold: physical plant, equipment, and grounds. President Jones was transferred to the executive position at the Harbison Institute in Irmo, South Carolina. The Byrd R. Smith Fund for a library, $496.06, was transferred to Harbison to be used to strengthen the library there. Student records were transferred first to Harbison and in 1958, when Harbison was discontinued, to Barber-Scotia College in Concord, North Carolina.

What was once a thriving and dynamic educational center under the auspices of the Presbyterian Church, U.S.A., stood in 1970 as a four-year Baptist college, the Mary Allen Baptist College.

THE MISSISSIPPI SCHOOL 12

Mary Holmes Junior College
West Point, Mississippi

By the late 1880s the Board's program of education had established a number of schools, stretching from the Old Dominion to the highly regarded Mary Allen Junior College in Texas. Between these points, however, was a dense, untouched area.

The Board wanted to establish its program along this middle passage, and in 1891, this note rang in its annual report:

> We have the prospects of entering the state of Mississippi this coming year, a region, heretofore untouched by the Board. The ladies of Illinois propose to raise $6,000 toward the founding of a Boarding School for colored girls in that state to be known as the Mary Holmes Seminary.[1]

The next year the Board founded the school in Jackson, Mississippi, on twenty acres of land donated by Negro citizens of the vicinity. A large brick building was erected at a cost of $16,000. The building was completed in June, 1892 and the school opened on September 28 of the same year, filled to capacity. The school was named for Mrs. Mary Holmes, wife of the Reverend Mead Holmes of Rockford, Illinois, who for so many years worked for the Board of Missions for Freedmen, and

[1] BMF, *Annual Report*, 1891, pp. 7–8.

for Dr. Mary E. Holmes, who was a dedicated and tireless worker for the Monticello school in Arkansas and others in that southwestern sector of the Board's program.

This initial footing by the Board in the state of Mississippi began with a program of primary, elementary, and high school work for girls only and with Dr. Edgar F. Johnston as the school's first executive. Unlike many of the larger schools that evolved out of the small beginning of a parochial school, Mary Holmes was large from the very beginning, with 152 pupils enrolled for the year and 11 instructors, including the Johnstons. That year the Reverend H. N. Payne, field secretary for the Board of Missions for Freedmen, supervising the work out of Atlanta, Georgia, reported that the school was filled to capacity and that the women's societies of Illinois had undertaken to build an addition at Mary Holmes Seminary at a cost of $5,000. By 1894, the enrollment had increased to 169 and the faculty to 12 with the addition of Miss Ruth Johnston.

The joy of getting established in Mississippi was short-lived. After three years of progress, on January 30, 1895, the plant, its addition and improvements, valued at $27,000, were totally destroyed by fire. Only $15,000 insurance covered it.[2] School work was discontinued for one year and plans were begun immediately to replace all losses. In this case, as in many others among the Board's schools, the setback only motivated a solid commitment to continuance. The Board decided to change the school's location, moreover, and West Point was chosen as being the most desirable. The Board's reason for relocating the school was made in the following announcement:

> West Point was selected for a number of reasons: the white people were willing to donate a beautiful site of 20 acres of land on the outskirts of town, bored a good artesian well, yielding the best of water, on the premises, without expense to the Board; West Point was in the center of a large Negro population; the town itself was enterprising and interested in the project.[3]

The Board was greatly impressed by the West Point proposal and attitude. It let contracts for a building to cost $28,500 and the subsequent cost of heating, furnishings, and general equipment raised the total cost to $39,000. Sometime before the building was burned in Jacksonville, $5,000 had been contributed and sent to the Board for a con-

[2] *Minutes*, 1895, p. 289.
[3] BMF, *Annual Report*, 1897, p. 7.

templated enlargement. This, plus the insurance refund, went toward the reconstruction of a bigger and better Mary Holmes.[4]

When Johnston's health, never vigorous, began to fail, he resigned. Financial stress had forced the Board to discontinue the services of a field secretary, a position which had been held by the Reverend H. N. Payne, so the Board invited him to become the new executive of the Mary Holmes Seminary. After a lapse of almost two years, Mary Holmes began its new career on January 1, 1897. Mrs. Payne became the principal of the school. Dr. Mary E. Holmes tells the specifics of how the school began anew:

> Mary Holmes Seminary, "No. 2" was reopened January 1, 1897, Reverend H. N. Payne, D. D., as president. By his personal preference, not a member of the old faculty was asked to return and only two or three of the old students "entered" for the higher classes, with several of the lower classes, and the others were new pupils, the entire enrollment for the year was 91. Before the year closed the little church was reorganized with 21 members.[5]

The relocation and change of personnel and students, however, did not remove Mary Holmes from misfortune. First an epidemic of yellow fever attacked the school. Then, two years later, on March 6, 1899, the building and contents were destroyed by fire. Although no lives were lost, Dr. Payne, attempting to save office papers, was severely burned. The plant was insured for $29,000 and the Board, despite its drastic retrenchment policy, lost no time in planning for rebuilding.[6]

The new building for Mary Holmes Seminary "No. 3" was constructed on the same plan and foundation and was completed in December of the same year. In addition, a brick laundry and frame utility house were built. The buildings were dedicated and the school reopened January 1, 1900. This last construction amounted to $40,000. There were 118 pupils enrolled under the instruction of a staff of 11.

With the opening of the school term 1902–1903, Dr. and Mrs. Payne were temporarily detained in New York when Dr. Payne was hospitalized. The Board, the Paynes, and the teachers urged the Reverend Holmes and Dr. Mary E. Holmes to begin the session and carry on the

[4] *Minutes*, 1897, p. 268.
[5] Mary E. Holmes, "History of Mary Holmes Seminary" (a scrapbook). Copy in possession of present writer.
[6] Holmes, "History."

activities until the Paynes arrived. They consented and when the Paynes arrived the President's health was greatly impaired. Dr. Holmes tells the story in detail:

> They both with the teachers and the Board, urged us to come down and open the school for them and remain until they were able to return. On September 15, 1902, we came. Along with us were two very faithful teachers: Miss Susan Johnson and Miss Webb. School opened October 1, 1902, with auspiciously-full attendance and everything most promising. . . . After three weeks of this happy school life smallpox was discovered and 19 cases had developed and many others had very serious cases. . . . During our long quarantine of ten weeks not one single person died nor did a teacher become smitten. . . . Dr. Payne was so ill he could do little beyond conduct a half hour's service each day. . . . In March, Birmingham Presbytery held some of its sessions here in the chapel, including some evangelistic meetings. . . . The Baccalaureate sermon was preached that year by father at his 84th year.[7]

The Holmeses not only put their means and services into the founding and building of the school but also their hearts, thereby more than meriting the honor of the school bearing the Holmeses' name. Dr. Mary E. Holmes, "activating Founder," builder, and interim president, was ever a guiding and sustaining force, which prevented the seminary from falling apart during its most trying crises.

With the opening of the school year 1903–1904, Dr. and Mrs. Joseph A. Stevenson succeeded Dr. and Mrs. Payne. Dr. Payne died in 1904, and the Stevensons remained at the school two years longer.

Following the Stevensons' administration, administrative turnover at the school was rapid. The Reverend and Mrs. Austin H. Jolly assumed the executive position at the school in 1906. At that time 192 students were enrolled and fourteen teachers composed the instructional staff. A nurses' training department was added in 1907. The next year Dr. Jolly resigned and the Reverend E. F. Johnston, who had returned to the seminary a few years before, was again appointed president.

The domestic science building was completed at a cost of $35,000 in 1913. The Board was enthusiastic about this new facility:

> The Domestic Science Building of the Mary Holmes Seminary stands on the campus northwest of the Seminary Building. It was

[7] Holmes, "History."

originally put up as a hospital where the many patients of the school were cared for when the school had the terrible smallpox scourge several years ago. Later it was moved and used as a hospital to care for patients from the county and country round, and it was the hope of our Board that they might have a training school for nurses in connection with it; but the expense involved was so great, and so little interest was manifested in it by the people of the city, that it had to be given up, much to our sorrow.

Within the last year the little old building has been transformed into a pretty little home for the domestic sciences and sewing classes and a most delightful place they find it.[8]

In 1913 an additional strip of land adjacent to the school property was purchased. The music hall that was started in 1920 was completed in 1922.

Johnston again gave up the executive position at the school and was succeeded by the Reverend Graham P. Campbell. In 1932, the junior college department was added with a specific objective of training teachers for the state's elementary schools. Eight students enrolled in the department that year, seven girls and one male student, and in 1934 extension work was added to the curriculum. The extension work was conducted after regular school hours for five days and on Saturdays to provide Clay County in-service teachers an opportunity to continue their training. A practice elementary school, held in the old domestic science building and vacant classrooms in the main building, provided a laboratory for the in-service teachers and trainees.

In 1935, Mary Holmes officially admitted male students as day students only. The institution continued this emphasis toward meeting local needs by adding a spring quarter for in-service rural teachers. In the same interest, vocational agriculture and vocational home economics were added to the curriculum in 1938. This year also male students were admitted as boarding students.

On February 7, 1939, the main building and contents were destroyed by fire, but a new main building was immediately built on the same foundation at an approximate cost of $75,000. In 1940, a Jeans Fund supervisor was housed on the campus and, from her headquarters there, she supervised fifty-two one- and two-room elementary public schools.

[8] Florence A. Hall, "Domestic Science at Mary Holmes Seminary," *Home Mission Monthly*, vol. 27, no. 6 (April, 1913), p. 137.

In 1940, Mary Holmes' High School Department was one of the four high schools in the state of Mississippi available to Negroes, accredited by the Southern Association of Colleges and Secondary Schools.

In 1941 the school's name was changed to Mary Holmes Junior College. Many other changes and additions were made during the war years. A 163-acre farm was purchased in 1943 for $6,000. The call to military service decreased the male enrollment but the female students' enrollment increased during this period.

Following World War II, many of the Board's schools negotiated with the federal government for financial aids to veterans and temporary additions to plants. At Mary Holmes, President Campbell was authorized to execute contracts with the Veterans Administration for the purpose of securing tuition fees and other financial advantages for the veterans enrolled there. Two hundred fifty veterans were enrolled in the trades school, which had been established to offer courses in auto mechanics, radio services, and carpentry, all of which were approved by the Veteran's Administration. The Board entered into an agreement with the War Assets Administration for the purchase of certain supplies and buildings from the government for use in the new trades school.

President Campbell notified the Board on January 13, 1949 that the high school department had been given class "A" rating by the Southern Association of Colleges and Secondary Schools. This year also students being trained in the trades school built a two-story dwelling. On June 30, 1949, however, the trades school was discontinued, and the equipment was sold to J. D. Fatheree, a former teacher in the school, who continued to operate it, leasing the property from the Board.

President Campbell resigned on July 1, 1952 and Harry A. Brandt succeeded him. This year was also eventful in other ways. Mississippi standards for teacher certification were raised by requiring teachers to have at least two years of college training by 1954 and at least four by 1956. Mary Holmes restructured its curriculum to provide for these state changes and offered classes on Saturdays and a summer school session, designed especially for in-service teachers.

The academic progress of the institution was further evidenced in March of 1957 when the Junior College was accredited by the Commission on College Accreditation of the Board of Trustees of Institutions of Higher Learning of the State of Mississippi. During April of that year the library was dedicated, and general remodeling and expansion were made campus wide. The high school department at Mary Holmes was discontinued on August 31, 1959, following a study of Mississippi's public high schools for Negroes made by Dr. Milton and his committee, which had been appointed by the Board of National Missions. When President Harry A. Brandt was transferred to the Mevaul School, Mr. Horn was appointed vice-president and later president. In 1970, Mary Holmes was one of four educational centers under the direct sponsorship of the United Presbyterian Church, U.S.A.

SCHOOLS IN OTHER STATES   *13*

In areas bordering the heart of the Confederacy, the schools established by the agencies of the church within the black communities were few and short-lived. On a very small scale, Kentucky followed the pattern of Georgia and Tennessee. Florida had only a few day schools. In Kansas there was an attempt to follow the pattern of Texas and Mississippi, establishing a single, strong, higher level school. The attempt was not successful, however. Maryland was even less touched by Board activity. These schools, therefore, reflect the periphery of the work of the Board of Missions for Freedmen.

The Kentucky Schools

Fee Memorial Institute
Nicholasville, Kentucky

Several of the Board's schools in Kentucky were taken over by the Board after the schools had been started and operated for a while by individuals or groups outside of the church's organized program. The Board did not usually do this and gave strong reasons for making an exception in 1904 in Kentucky:

> The second case in which we have taken over an outside enterprise is that of the Camp Nelson School in Kentucky. It consists of school buildings and farm land estimated to be worth altogether

about $10,000. The property was made over to the Board without conditions. The effort to establish it as an undenominational boarding school managed by a Board of Trustees did not succeed. The main consideration which moved our Board to accept this trust was the fact that we have no other school in the whole state of Kentucky where there are something more than 280,000 colored people. Friends of our work in Kentucky were anxious for us to establish a school in that state, and the hope of the Board is that the Kentucky churches, favorable to our work, will make this school the special object of their benevolence, and that interest in the work in that region will increase their gifts to the cause more than enough to reimburse the Board for all it may expend in setting this enterprise in motion.[1]

In an early *Snapshots*, the Board traces the founding and development of the school before it was taken under its care. According to the Board's narrative in this publication, in 1864 at Camp Nelson, Kentucky, when the place was occupied as a military camp, a small Presbyterian church was organized for the freedmen. About 1868, Mr. and Mrs. John G. Fee donated nine and one-half acres of land, seven acres of which were designated as a plot for a school for the freedmen. A building was constructed on the plot in which a school began under the title "Ariel Academy." The name was later changed to honor its benefactors. The academy flourished for a while under the personal care and support of Mr. and Mrs. Fee.[2]

When the Board took the school under its care in 1904, the Reverend J. A. Boydon was commissioned as pastor of the church and as principal of the school. The next year, the Reverend W. C. Hargrave, pastor of two nearby churches in the vicinity of Burdick, Kentucky, Praigg and Calvary churches, assisted Boydon with the instruction of seventy-four pupils. In 1906, there were eighty-three pupils under the instruction of Boydon, and two teachers: Miss O. B. Feimster and Miss M. D. Spellman. The Reverend D. S. Colier had replaced Hargrave as pastor of the two nearby churches and had established in connection with them a parochial of forty pupils in 1908.[3] The next year, the Reverend and Mrs. Boydon were joined by Miss Francis Alexander and Miss A. Spellman. Together the four instructed the eighty pupils at the school.

[1] BMF, *Annual Report*, 1904, p. 8.
[2] "Fee Memorial Institute," *Snapshots* (N.Y.: PCUSA, BNM, 1936).
[3] *Fee Memorial Catalog*, 1907–1908, p. 8.

In 1910 the enrollment dropped to fifty and the Boydons lost the services of Miss Spellman. In its annual report for that year the Board described, in detail, the development of the academy:

Mention was made in our last report of the generous offer of $5,000 toward work among the colored people of Kentucky, if the churches of that state would carry out the resolution passed, in their Synod that year, to contribute $1,500 toward our work within the bounds of their state. Circulars were sent out to the Kentucky churches stating the case, and before the next meeting of the Synod the whole amount and a little more, was sent into the Board, for the improvement and enlargement of our school at Camp Nelson, Ky., known as the John G. Fee Memorial Institute. On the announcement that the $1,500 had been received, Mr. John A. Simpson, of Covington, Kentucky, promptly sent us his check for $5,000, to be invested permanently, the interest of which is to go to the promotion of the work at Camp Nelson; or should that fail, to any other similar work within the bounds of Kentucky, to which the Board might in the future wish to appropriate it.

The agricultural feature of the Camp Nelson School is being developed this year. The farm is being stocked with necessary implements, and portions of land are being assigned to the different boys, who are put in communication with the right authorities, at Washington, D. C., who are offering prizes to boys and young men who succeed best in their efforts at practical farming. A healthy impatience grew up in the minds of the boys during the winter, in their eagerness for the time to come when they could begin their competitive efforts at cultivating the soil.[4]

Although strenuous efforts were put forth, progress was slow at Camp Nelson. In 1911, Miss Irene Boydon had joined her parents and also Miss Kate Ross had been added to the teaching staff. After eleven years of striving at the pioneer level, Boydon resigned and the Reverend H. W. McNair was commissioned to fill the vacancy. The enrollment had dropped to fifty-five and conditions had begun to look dismal at the school.

McNair had received the S.T.B. degree from Biddle University Theological Seminary in 1912. He began an extended career at Fee Memorial Institute in 1915, which was to be characterized by the removal, remodeling, and redevelopment of the school. In 1920–1921, Fee Me-

[4] BMF, *Annual Report*, 1911, p. 11.

morial Institute was moved to Nicholasville, Kentucky, in the central part of the state about eighty miles southeast of Louisville. With the sale price of the property at Camp Nelson, the Board of Missions purchased an estate of thirteen acres with a large house and several smaller houses on it at the outskirts of the town of Nicholasville.[5]

When the school moved in from the country, the white population of Nicholasville felt that they were being swamped by the "colored folks." This attitude was gradually changed to one of sincere acceptance as the school created a pleasing atmosphere in a suburban section of the town. A prominent white citizen whose property joined that of the school apologized for his criticism and placed his farming tools at the disposal of the school without cost.[6]

The campus became one of the most beautiful spots in the community. Fee Memorial Institute gradually earned the warmest regards of the population of Nicholasville and the highest respect of the Board. The plant was expanded and the school's curriculum enriched. Training in elementary and high school work, offered thirty-six weeks annually, was of the highest quality for both day and boarding students. Unfortunately, however, the institute's enrollment dropped to thirty-six boarding students and eighteen day students in 1929 when the Board's cutback policy was gaining momentum. It survived the drastic cutback in the Board's operation of schools in 1933, but in 1935 it was merged with Ingleside Institute at Burksville, Virginia. The consolidated school was given the name Ingleside-Fee. The program at Nicholasville was continued as a community center for a period of time.

Bowling Green Academy
Bowling Green, Kentucky

Another educational project which the Board adopted in the state of Kentucky was the Bowling Green Academy that had been under the care of the black Presbyterian church in Bowling Green. Its management had been under the control of trustees of the Cumberland Church; however, financial difficulties prompted the trustees to appeal to the Board of Missions for Freedmen for aid.[7]

The academy began in 1902 with one student. As the enrollment increased, a Bible department was established headed by a graduate of

[5] "Fee," *Snapshots.*
[6] "Fee," *Snapshots.*
[7] "Bowling Green Academy," *Snapshots* (N.Y.: PCUSA, BNM).

Lincoln University.[8] Even before 1910, the Board had supported a teacher in the academy and explained its relationship to the school in the following statement:

> We still continue to sustain a teacher at the Bowling Green School, at Bowling Green, Ky. which belongs to the Colored Cumberland Church, and is in no way under the care and control of our Board. His work is to teach the Bible, and train, as far as he can, the young men of that Church, who are seeking to enter the Christian Ministry, many of whom are so poorly prepared to exercise the functions of so high and so sacred an office.[9]

The General Assembly had previously charged the Board with the responsibility of lending assistance to the Bowling Green mission whenever possible. In 1910, the following persons were in charge of the work at the school: the Reverend and Mrs. R. L. Hyde, the Reverend C. P. McLurkin, the Misses H. O. Brown and B. L. Tate and the Mesdames H. A. James, Lizzie Gordon, and A. Austin. The enrollment for 1910 was not reported but in all likelihood it was rather large, judged by the size of the staff.

The course of study at the Bowling Green Academy consisted of primary, grammar, and high school grades. Manual training and home economics courses were added to the curriculum as the school developed. During the summer months, a course in theology was offered for young men who planned to become ministers.[10]

In 1911, there were 154 students enrolled under the instruction of seven teachers, and the Reverend Hyde was still principal, assisted by the Reverend William Wolf.

The Bowling Green Academy came under the care of the Board in 1919 and was listed among its coeducational boarding schools for that year:

> The Board has taken over the school at Bowling Green, Ky. formerly managed by trustees for the Colored Cumberland Church, and hereafter will operate it along the same lines as our own schools, with the clear understanding that members and adherents of the Colored Cumberland Church will always be welcome at this school to all the benefits of a Christian education.[11]

[8] "Bowling Green Academy," *Snapshots.*
[9] BMF, *Annual Report*, 1911, pp. 11–12.
[10] "Bowling," *Snapshots.*
[11] *Minutes*, 1919, p. 433.

During the twelve-year span between 1919 and 1932, the academy made commendable progress under the Board's care. By 1931, it owned several lots on both sides of the street in a desirable location. The plant included two buildings and the home of the principal. The assembly building contained recitation rooms and a chapel on the first floor and dormitory quarters for boys on the second floor. The structure, which was once the home of a wealthy Southern artistocrat, was converted and became the quarters for the teaching of domestic science, the dining room for the entire school, and the dormitory for girls.

The Reverend William Wolf, who was supported in 1911 as the assistant principal to the Reverend R. L. Hyde, was reported in 1932 as principal with no explanation of when the change of administration occurred. He and his wife had four teachers working with them at the time. In 1932, there were 107 pupils enrolled, 19 of whom were boarders and 88 day students. This enrollment placed the school in the Board's classification of "day schools to be dropped." Despite this fact, however, the academy was placed on a list for further study and under the management of the Unit of Schools and Hospitals.[12]

This new arrangement for the academy did not last beyond a year. In 1933, the work in Bowling Green was redirected, and the Board reported the change in the following announcement:

With the closing of the academic work formerly offered at Bowling Green Academy, Bowling Green, Kentucky, the plant was turned into a home for students coming from rural and neighboring small towns to attend the Bowling Green public high school. Those in charge of the home are responsible for the extra curricular activities of the members of the family and guide each individual in the development of his religious life. Special classes in religious education are offered and the atmosphere of a Christian home is maintained. Student activities are largely worked out through a student council. Among other things this year they evolved a code of behavior which each resident pledged himself to observe. . . .

While the economic situation forced the Board to close the doors of the secular classrooms at Bowling Green, the executives have been able to continue their emphasis on the Christian program of the Church as a whole.[13]

By this action the Board's direct educational activities at the Bowling

[12] BNM, *Annual Report*, 1933, p. 82.
[13] BNM, *Annual Report*, 1934, pp. 62–63.

Green Academy ended. Information relative to the official date of the Board's complete withdrawal from the redirected program was not available.

Logan High School
Danville, Kentucky

The Logan High School of Danville was another mission under the care of the Board that flourished for a limited period in the Kentucky hills but was soon discontinued. When Logan High School was first reported as being under the Board's care in 1901, it was being directed by the Reverend and Mrs. J. A. Boydon who had 105 pupils under instruction. The high school, at that time, was offering twelve grades, and Miss Maggie Shelby was assisting with their instruction.

Boydon apparently gave up the work at Logan High School after the close of the 1903 school term. At that time, he assumed the responsibility of operating the Fee Memorial Institute when the Board took it over in 1904. The turnovers at Logan High were rapid thereafter, and enrollment dropped. The Reverend W. W. Todd became principal of the school in 1913 with thirty-four pupils enrolled.

Apparently, the persistent low enrollment at Logan High School influenced the Board's plans for the future of the school. Between 1901 and 1913, the enrollment dropped from 105 to 34—a loss of 71 pupils. At the end of the 1913 school year, Logan High School was dropped from the Board's list of day schools under its care. Despite this, however, people of Danville contend that the school operated until 1921 and that the students were taught by Mrs. J. A. Boydon and Mrs. Mary K. James.

A few other short-lived attempts were made by the Board to operate schools in the Kentucky hills. At Campbellsville, a school under the care of the Reverend J. W. Mallard was reported in 1911 with 21 pupils under instruction. This school thrived under the Board's care for a short period; however, it was discontinued as a Board-operated school. Likewise at Louisville, Kentucky, a school connected with the Knox Presbyterian Church met the same fate. Mrs. H. Parker was the instructor of the 150 pupils, yet the school was either discontinued or operated outside of the Board's care. Also, in Concord there was a parochial school of 155 pupils under the pastorate and principalship of the Reverend D. Murry in 1881. He was assisted with their instruction by Miss Fannie Miller. In 1884, there were 96 pupils under instruction, and Mrs. E. Shurley joined Murry and Miss Miller. The school was no longer reported by the Board after this year.

The Florida Schools

Down the Florida peninsula into the Everglades, life for the freedmen, following their emancipation, was primitive and mean. Although by 1900 the Board has been successful in establishing three churches in that region—the Mount Vernon Church at Palatka, with the Reverend C. H. Uggams, pastor; the Mather-Peritt Church at St. Augustine, with the Reverend G. E. Elliott, pastor; and the Laura Street Presbyterian Church at Jacksonville, with the Reverend J. C. Scarborough, pastor—it made little mention of school work at these three places.

From 1895 to 1900, with the exception of one slight reference, the Board merely reported that the ministers were busy executing their church programs at the Florida stations. During these five years, the Board experienced its worst financial crisis and if parochial schools were operated, they were, in all likelihood, unassisted by the Board.

The Laura Street Parochial School
Jacksonville, Florida

There evidently had been some very early school efforts attempted in Jacksonville by a Reverend J. C. Gibbs, a black pastor, who is referred to in the General Assembly minutes in 1867.

In 1915, the Reverend S. A. Downer, who had been pastor of the Laura Street Presbyterian Church for several years, is reported as having 110 pupils under instruction at the Laura Street Parochial School. The enrollment dropped to 90 in 1916, and in 1917 only 80 pupils were enrolled. Mrs. S. A. Downer was assisting her husband with their instruction. The school was not listed among the parochial schools under the Board's care after 1918, and is presumed to have been closed after the enrollment dropped.

The Mellon Parochial School
Palatka, Florida

The Reverend C. H. Uggams, who had directed the Berean Parochial School at Gainesville for approximately seven years, opened a school in connection with his church program at the Mount Vernon Presbyterian Church at Palatka in 1901 and was assisted by Mrs. Mary McCloud Bethune with the instruction of 50 pupils. Inasmuch as Uggams's stay at this mission was brief, the Reverend W. F. Kennedy was commissioned to complete four months of his unfinished term in 1902. Mrs. Bethune, however, remained at the mission. The enrollment increased annually, from 85 pupils in 1902 to a peak number of 180 in 1906. In that year,

Mrs. Kennedy joined the teaching staff to assist with the instruction. Following this year, however, there was a gradual decrease in the enrollment, and in 1909, the Reverend Franklin G. Gregg became the pastor and principal of the Palatka Mission, which had only 60 pupils enrolled in the parochial school. There was, however, a brief increase in the enrollment. By 1912, the Reverend and Mrs. W. B. Coleman had 179 pupils. The turnover was rapid. The Reverend Gregg left Palatka in 1912 and was succeeded by the Reverend and Mrs. G. T. Ellison. With the assistance of Mrs. F. G. Browning, they instructed 74 pupils. The next year the enrollment dropped to 63 under the same teaching staff. In 1916, the Board announced:

> We were able during the year just closed to give the church at Palatka, Fla., a school building which the good people of that church had been asking for for some time and which they very much needed. We did this through the generosity of Mr. Thomas W. Mellon, Jr. of Pittsburgh, Pa. who gave us $1,000 for the purpose. After this gift and in the honor of the donor, the name of the school was changed to the Mellon School.[14]

In 1929, the Mellon School, with an enrollment of 120 pupils, was offering high school work twenty-four weeks annually. In 1932, however, it was classified as an elementary school, operating twenty-four weeks annually, and offering eight grades. Sixty-nine pupils were enrolled. The Mellon School probably closed at the end of this school year. It was not listed among the thirty-five day schools discontinued in 1933 and did not appear on subsequent lists.

The Mather-Peritt Parochial School
St. Augustine, Florida

The exact date of the founding of the Mather-Peritt Parochial School or when it came under the Board's care cannot be established by written records. Dates cited by local residents and descendants of patrons and workers in the school vary widely. The Reverend J. H. Cooper, who received the S.T.B. degree from Biddle University in 1897, was reportedly in charge of the school and church there in 1909, with 78 pupils enrolled in the Mather-Peritt Parochial School. The enrollment increased to 105 by 1910. The Board's report that year said:

> At St. Augustine, Florida, the Board has just completed a very attractive and well planned building, made possible by the great

[14] BMF, *Annual Report*, 1916, p. 14.

generosity of the late Mrs. Flora S. Mather of Cleveland, O. the building and lot being her gift. In addition to this amount, $4,000, she left a bequest of $1,000 for the general work.[15]

There was a gradual annual increase in the enrollment; in 1918 there were 133 pupils enrolled under instruction of a staff of four. By 1932, the school had grown to junior high school status, offering nine grades twenty-four weeks annually. There were, however, only 42 pupils enrolled that year. The school was closed June 1, 1933, along with thirty-eight other day schools.

The Berean Parochial School
Gainesville, Florida

One of the earliest reports made by the Board of Missions of an organized program of education in Gainesville was made in 1887, stating, "The Mission at Gainesville, Florida, under Mrs. Hallock and Misses Lytle and Ainsworth, is prospering and doing a good work. They hope to occupy their new school house and church during the coming year."[16] A report of the further development of the school under the direction of the three women was not made. In 1889, however, the Board announced that the Reverend and Mrs. William Eugene Partee had been commissioned to take over the work there.

The Reverend Partee received his earliest formal training in the parochial school at Concord, North Carolina, under the guidance and inspiration of Dr. Luke Dorland. Upon completing the work of the parochial school there, he entered the preparatory department at Biddle University and received the A.B. degree from the college department in 1881. He went on to receive the S.T.B. degree from the seminary in 1884. His pastorate in Concord, still under the guidance of Dr. Dorland, gave him four years of invaluable experience. The Board made the following report:

> Our school at Gainesville, Florida, under the care of Reverend W. E. Partee and wife, others under the care of the Freedmen's Board, suffers from want of a proper building. It is now taught and preaching services are held in an old cabin of two rooms. The number of scholars is only limited by the size of the house. Through the exertion of a young invalid girl in New Jersey, a lot has been paid for upon which both church and schoolhouse could be erected. Three hundred dollars would put up a school building which could

[15] BMF, *Annual Report*, 1910, p. 10.
[16] Woman's Committee, *Annual Report*, 1887, p. 19.

also be used for church purposes until the people recover from the effects of the yellow fever epidemic and are able to build.[17]

The plea in the Board's announcement was rewarding. In its next year's report it was able to report, "At Gainesville, Florida, a house for our school has been built and is now in use, the money having been furnished by a generous lady in New Jersey."[18] Whether "the generous lady in New Jersey" was the same invalid young lady of New Jersey to whom the Board referred in its previous report is not made clear, but the Partees were happy to be more comfortably housed for school and church.

Partee apparently remained at the Gainesville mission about four years. In 1893 he was reported directing the Laura Street Presbyterian Church and parochial school in Jacksonville. The Reverend C. H. Uggams, who had been pastor of the Mount Vernon Church and principal of its parochial school in Palatka since 1900, was reported in charge of the Gainesville church and school.[19] With him was Miss Mamie J. Hughes, assisting with the instruction of ninety pupils.

After 1900, only two Florida schools were listed among those under the Board's care but the Berean School was not one of them, nor did it appear in subsequent lists.

The Kansas School

Quindaro High School
Quindaro, Kansas

The church made several efforts to establish schools in states near the boundary lines of the fallen Confederacy. In 1868, the Committee on Freedmen of the Old School branch of the church had high hopes of establishing a school of great respectability in the state of Kansas. The following description of this school was made in its annual report to the General Assembly:

> The High School in Quindaro, Kansas:—This institution was established under the auspices of the Assembly's Western committee, and was adopted by the Synod of Kansas. Under the superintendence of the indefatigable Dr. Blanchly it had gone quietly forward in the face of great discouragements. During the last year, it had

[17] BMF, *Annual Report,* 1889, pp. 16–17.
[18] *Minutes,* 1890, p. 10.
[19] *Minutes,* 1893, p. 403.

150 pupils on its roll who have made encouraging advancements. The school has accumulated property, consisting of the seminary building and three dwelling houses for teachers, valued at $6,200. On this there is a debt of $500. Efforts are being made now to obtain an efficient principal, who shall be able to give instruction to a theological class. Also to secure land for farming and gardening purposes, that the students must be instructed in agriculture, and trained to habits of industry.[20]

Despite the fact that the school was slow in progressing toward the planned goal, the Committee was still optimistic in 1869 about the potential:

> In this statement of schools, 38, there are three included which are intended to be of a higher grade than that of the parochial order, viz., Biddle, Quindaro High School, and Wallingford Academy.
>
> The Quindaro High School in Quindaro, Kansas, which is under the joint care of the Synod of Kansas and the Committee on Freedmen. This school had 145 pupils enrolled at the close of the year.[21]

The next year's report indicated the Committee's increasing ambition for the school. The name had been changed: "Freedmen's University of Kansas, has on its roll 180 pupils and has grounds with four buildings."[22]

Following the reunion of the Old and New School assemblies in 1870, the consolidated Committee of Missions for Freedmen included a statement in its report for 1871 which in all likelihood implies the reason for the school not appearing on its roll of schools thereafter:

> In view of the heavy indebtedness upon its work, the Committee, in making out its schedule of school work for the year, reduced it with but three exceptions, to that which is strictly parochial dropping with their teachers, such schools as had no individual church connections.[23]

The Committee spent several years attempting to lift the heavy debt incurred with the union. Although the Committee did not list the schools retained above the parochial level, the Committee's records reveal that Biddle, Scotia, and Wallingford Academy were retained, but no further mention is made of the Quindaro High School in Kansas. The school in Kansas had never had an individual church affiliation.

[20] *Minutes* (Old School), 1868, p. 736.

[21] *Minutes* (Old School), 1869, p. 90.

[22] Presbyterian Church in the U.S.A. (Old School), General Assembly, Committee on Freedmen, *Annual Report*, 1870, pp. 12–13.

[23] CMF, *Annual Report*, 1871, p. 5.

The Maryland School

Mount Zion Parochial School
Lothian, Maryland

In Lothian, Maryland, the Reverend J. B. Swann conducted a parochial school over an extended period of time in connection with his program at the Mount Zion Presbyterian Church. His work in this small Maryland town consisted of three churches: Mount Zion, Mill Run, and Calvary.

In 1892, when the first available report was made, the Reverend Swann had seventy-three pupils under instruction, which remained the average enrollment for approximately twenty-three years. In 1915, however, the enrollment reached its peak of 128 pupils and after that year, there was a sharp decrease. The public school system was beginning to develop for black youth, and after 1918 the Mount Zion Parochial School was no longer listed among parochial schools under the Board's care. It is presumed that the Board discontinued the school work there, considering it to be no longer necessary.

RETROSPECT AND PROSPECT *14*

Coming to the end of this long series of histories of individual schools, one needs to regain some perspective on the significance of the entire effort. It is a simple matter to classify these schools, list them, show the dates of opening and closing. Yet what becomes clear when so many particular schools are studied is the impact that each had on the community around it, even if its life was brief and its existence unknown a hundred miles away. That the effects of these schools, taken together, were enormous was partially the result of many small and often seemingly insignificant local schools. Few institutions rose to great prominence. Many disappeared without trace, except for the transformation of a few human lives.

From the foregoing survey one can see a variety of motivations for establishing the schools. On the part of the Presbyterian Church, U.S.A., a Northern and largely white institution, the efforts were made partly out of a sense of mission which reached its peak in the nineteenth century. In addition, for those who were actually involved in the work, there was a clear sense of social responsibility, always a motivating factor in human relations. The institutions—such as the church, the school, the hospital—that have survived the changing times have been those most concerned with the well-being of humanity. This concern was of foremost interest to those workers in the church schools presented in this study. This was true of the pioneer teachers, the philanthropists who were responsible for the funds and foundations, the tithers, and others who accepted the challenge created by the liberation of four million slaves. It was this commitment to a social issue that moved them to embrace a cause that involved breaking the shackles in the ex-slaves that bound the mind, the spirit, and the power to hope or dream. The Emancipation Proclamation did not dispel the deplorable consequences of the system from which they had physically emerged. Without a sense of direction and relegation to an abyss at the lowest level of human existence, they would still dwell within the grip of a slave system. Their plight was greatly intensified by living in the hostile territory of a defeated and embittered people who had lost their "human property" as well as their husbands, fathers, sons, brothers, lovers, and friends.

This Presbyterian adventure, therefore, had its origin in the torrid passion of the Civil conflict and the anguish of the subsequent Reconstruction period. The resolute determination of those "other carpetbaggers," therefore, was buffeted on every hand by barriers and discouragements. Yet, along the way, amazing advances were made.

On the other side, there was also enormous motivation on the part of the former slaves. In many places, the church schools presented almost the only opportunity for change, for healing, for hope.

These different motivations came together in the educational program of the church—and both sides benefited:

> Both the Church and the Negro have ample occasion for gratitude at the fruitage of the years. Both have abundantly given and both have even more abundantly received. Constantly and steadily the Church has quickened and enriched the spiritual life of the Negro, and again and yet again, the Negro has enlarged and vitalized for the Church, concepts of justice and Brotherhood, Oneness and service.
>
> Because of the Presbyterian Church, the Negro in America today is infinitely the richer in body, mind, and spirit; because of the Negro, the Presbyterian Church is immeasurably more responsive to human needs, more brotherly and more Christian.
>
> By the Grace of God, each, strengthening the other, has itself been strengthened; each transforming, has become radiant. May the future years be as fraught with blessing.[1]

The mission schools became the hub of the black community. Their religious and educational endeavors were held there, as were their social

---

[1] L. S. Cozart, "The Negro and The Presbyterian Church," *The New Advance*, March 15, 1940, p. 2.

and recreational activities. As the principal centers of community interest and concern, they furnished unification and common goals in which the community took pride. There developed a sense of possession at a time when many possessed nothing else. Their loved ones were born, reared, educated, died, and often buried within the shadow of the mission school.

The influence of these schools extended far beyond the churches and even the local community. Even those who were most hostile were forced by the accomplishments of these schools to realize the potential for black education in the South. This acknowledgment was usually grudgingly given, and programs of actions were belatedly put into operation. But had there been no example, even that small step would not have been taken:

> In the past, mission schools paved the way and set the standards for the schools for the Colored people. In pioneer days they served as the example for the public schools. Indeed, it was largely through them that the states developed a healthy interest in Negro education. It was primarily through the results of the mission schools that the states were made aware of the fruitful possibilities of Negro education as well as made conscious of their responsibility to provide adequate universal education for Colored youth.[2]

The accomplishments of the schools can probably best be measured by the quality and quantity of black leadership that was produced. Such leadership was evident at the very beginning of the program, especially in the black churches of the South. In the long run, however, the schools themselves became vehicles for this leadership when school after school was staffed and administered by the black leadership the schools themselves had produced. Ultimately, this necessitated a reconditioning of the American mind. A fundamentally changed black community had to be reckoned with in churches, in legislative halls, in courtrooms, in classrooms, by realtors, and neighbors.

It is no wonder then, that the black community was confused and shocked when it realized that these schools were to be discontinued. The community had become a part of the school and yet was powerless to restrain the closing.

The restlessness of the decade between 1960 and 1970 indicated a grave need for an immediate change from the system which dealt with the stereotyped plantation Negro to one that would recognize the pride, self-respect, and dignity of the transformed black American.

[2] BNM, *Annual Report*, 1930, p. 151.

There is no longer a "Negro Problem." It is now America's problem. America, as history records, braved all perils to secure a labor force of strong black backs, nimble black hands and legs capable of resisting the menaces of a wilderness in laying a foundation for a new nation. What the perpetrators failed to reckon with, however, was the fact that within their human commodity were intellectual faculties, keen insights, creative imaginations, and strong emotions, which, though crushed to a state of dormancy, had also the power of revival. The designers of the nation were interested in physical capabilities, and their original purpose was achieved. Now, if the American dream is to be realized, the nation has the unfinished task of facing reality honestly and justly dealing with the accompanying attributes of those whom it brought to its shores.

The church has made a zealous and rewarding effort to deal with this national problem. The church recognized the black American's "inalienable right to life, liberty, and the pursuit of happiness," and through education and evangelization has made the Negro unfit for slavery, awakened the power to hope and to dream, to seek after the truth that would make him truly free.

BIBLIOGRAPHY

Regrettably, official records regarding the pioneer work in education for black Americans are scarce, scattered, and often completely lost. In 1865 when the organized program was launched, only a few American blacks could read or write, and the rash of fires destroyed many of the missionaries' efforts to keep records of their experiences on the mission field. Yet, promotional literature, human interest stories, and oral history are helpful in piecing together pertinent information on the subject.

A great deal of information regarding this missionary work is to be found in the annual reports of the General Assembly's committees and boards charged with the responsibility of executing the program, especially the annual reports of the Presbyterian Church in the U.S.A., including the Board of National Missions, Board of Missions for Freedmen, Committee of Missions for Freedmen, Women's Board of Home Missions, Freedmen's Department, Women's Executive Committee on Home Missions (Freedmen's Department), (OS) Committee on Freedmen, and (NS) Committee of Home Missions (Freedmen's Department). A list and outline of the most relevant material have been filed by the author with the Presbyterian Historical Society in Philadelphia. Gerald W. Gillette, Research Historian for the Presbyterian Historical Society, is attempting to relocate a valuable card file which contains brief sketches of the founding and development of many of these schools. These record cards were compiled by Miss Catherine E. Gladfelter, while she was Secretary of the Medical and Educational Work, and her staff of the Board of National Missions. They were formerly housed in the office of the Unit of Work with Colored People in the Witherspoon Building in Philadelphia.

Minutes of the four original black synods—Atlantic, Blue Ridge, Canadian, and Catawba—contain references to the founding and development of the black schools within their boundaries. Many of the parochial schools were founded and operated jointly with the black churches and in the minutes of the sessions of these churches can be found information of historical value regarding the small schools. Various church periodicals are also useful. Prior to 1886, information regarding the work was recorded in *Presbyterian Home Missions*. After that date, however, most valuable information can be found in the *Home Mission Monthly*, the official voice of the Home Mission program. Much of this material, however, is not indexed. The first seven volumes of the *Home Mission Monthly* carry a section labeled "Words From Our Workers." Under this label will be found facts and human interest stories directly from the workers on the mission field. Under the title "Freedmen" are pertinent facts regarding the work among black Americans. Periodically an article on the work among the freedmen is written as an editorial. These are indexed. Beginning with the seventh volume there is an annual program outlined with each monthly issue being devoted to a particular phase of the Home Mission program. Under this new arrangement, information concerning work among the Freedmen is published in the April issue. By 1924, when the *Home Mission Monthly* was merged with *Women and Missions*, this policy was partially abandoned. The April issue in the new magazine was devoted first to the work in Africa and then to the work among the freedmen. After 1924, articles regarding work among the freedmen are to be found in issues other than April. Some of these are indexed and some are not. As in the case of the reports to the General Assembly, the author has filed with the Presbyterian Historical Society a list of the most significant material in these periodicals.

I. Selected Books, Pamphlets, Bulletins, and Articles in Journals

Ashmore, Harry S. *The Negro and the Schools*. Chapel Hill: University of North Carolina Press, 1954.

Barber, Jesse Belmont. *Climbing Jacob's Ladder*. New York: Board of National Missions, Presbyterian Church, U.S.A., 1952.

Bond, Horace Mann. *The Education of the Negro in the American Social Order*. New York: Prentice Hall, 1934.

Brameld, Theodore. *Minority in the Public Schools*. New York: Harper and Brothers, 1949.

Brown, Hugh Victor. *E-qual-i-ty Education in North Carolina Among Negroes*. Raleigh: Irvin-Swain Press, 1964.

Cable, George Washington. *The Negro Question*. New York: American Missionary Association, 1888.

Caldwell, A. B. (ed.). *History of the American Negro*. Atlanta: Caldwell Publishing Co., 1921.

Cushman, Robert F. *Leading Constitutional Decisions*. New York: Appleton, Century, Crofts, 1971.

Daniel, Sadie Iola. *Women Builders*. Washington, D.C.: The Associate Publishers, 1931.

Davis, Owena Hunter. *A History of Mary Potter School*. Oxford, North Carolina: no publisher given, 1944.

Delano, W. "Grade School Segregation: The Latest Attack on Racial Discrimination." *Yale Law Journal* 61 (1952), 730–44.

Drury, Clifford. *Presbyterian Panorama*. New York: Board of Christian Education, Presbyterian Church, U.S.A., 1952.

Fisher, S. J. *The Negro: An American Asset*. Pittsburgh: Board of Missions for Freedmen, Presbyterian Church, U.S.A., 1890.

Flickinger, R. E. *The Choctaw Freedman*. Pittsburgh: Board of Missions for Freedmen, 1914.

Franklin, John Hope. *From Slavery to Freedom; a history of American Negroes*. New York: Alfred A. Knopf, 1956.

Frazier, E. Franklin. *The Negro Church in America*. New York: Schocken Books, 1963.

George, Arthur (ed.). *Down Through the Years*. Charlotte, North Carolina: Dowd Press, 1961.

Goodrich, Francis. *A Devoted Life and its Results*. Pittsburgh: Board of Missions for Freedmen, Women's Department, n.d.

Green, Ashbell. *Presbyterian Missions*. Philadelphia: Randolph Company, 1893.

Harris, Janet and Hobson, Julius. *Black Pride*. New York: McGraw-Hill Book Co., 1969.

Hartshorn, W. N. (ed.). *An Era of Progress and Promise*. Boston: The Priscilla Publishing Co., 1910.

Hawkins, Hugh. *Booker T. Washington and His Critics: Problems of Negro Leadership*. Boston: Heath Press, 1962.

Hummel, Margaret Gibson. *The Amazing Heritage*. Philadelphia: The Geneva Press, 1970.

Hughes, Langston and Milton Meltzer. *A Pictorial History of the Negro in America*. New York: Crown Publishers, Inc., 1968.

Hughes, Langston. *The Dream Keeper and Other Poems*. New York: Alfred A. Knopf, 1932.

Leavell, Ulin Whitner. *Philanthropy in Negro Education*. Nashville: Cullen and Chertner Company, 1930.

Logan, Rayford W. *The Negro in American Life and Thought: The Nadir, 1877–1901*. New York: The Dial Press, 1954.

Marsden, George M. *The Evangelical Mind and the New School Presbyterian Experience: A Case Study of Thought and Theology in Nineteenth-century America*. New Haven: Yale University Press, 1970.

McCulloch, W. E. *The United Presbyterian Church and its Work in America*. New York: Board of Home Missions, The United Presbyterian Church of America, 1925.

McGranahan, Ralph W. (ed.). *Historical Sketch of the Freedmen's Missions of the United Presbyterian Church, 1862–1904*. Knoxville: Knoxville College, 1904.

McNaugher, John. *Theological Education in the United Presbyterian Church and its Ancestries*. United Presbyterian Board of Publication, 1931.

Murray, Andrew E. *Presbyterians and the Negro: A History*. Philadelphia: The Presbyterian Historical Society, 1966.

Myrdal, Gunnar. *An American Dilemma; the Negro Problem and Modern Democracy*. New York: Harper and Brothers, 1944.
Nichols, William H. *Southern Tradition and Regional Progress*. Chapel Hill: University of North Carolina Press, 1960.
Pearson, Paul M. (ed.). *The Speaker*, vol. II. New York: Noble and Noble, 1925.
Randall, Virginia Ray. *Shadows and Light*. New York: Board of National Missions, Presbyterian Church, U.S.A., 1941.
Richings, G. F. *Evidences of Progress Among Colored People*. Philadelphia: George S. Ferguson Company, 1902.
Seville, Janet E. *Like a Spreading Tree*. New York: Board of National Missions, Presbyterian Church, U.S.A., 1936.
Sherrill, Lewis J. *Presbyterian Parochial Schools, 1846–1870*. New Haven: Yale University Press, 1932.
A Sketch of the Life and Work of Mrs. Mary E. Allen. Philadelphia: Press of Henry B. Ashmead, 1886.
Smith, Captain John. *Works*. Ed. Edward Arbor. New York: AMS Press Inc., 1967.
Stewart, Archibald K. *May We Introduce Negro Misisons*. Pittsburgh: The Board of American Missions of the United Presbyterian Church, n.d.
Woodson, Carter G. *The Negro in Our History*. Washington, D.C.: Associated Publishers, 1927.

II. Newspapers, Periodicals, and Catalogs

The Africo-American Presbyterian. Specifically those issues publishing the series, "Blazers and Chips" by the Reverend William Lee Metz. Publication began January, 1927. A complete file of this important publication has not been preserved. Copies are to be found in the Presbyterian Historical Society in Philadelphia. Mr. Gerald Gillette is making an effort to complete the file. Other copies are to be found at the Presbyterian Historical Foundation at Montreat, North Carolina, the Interdenominational Theological Center in Atlanta, and the author also has some copies in her possession. Published by Johnson C. Smith University, Charlotte, N.C.
The New Advance. Supersedes *The Africo-American Presbyterian*. *The New Advance* was published by the PCUSA, Board of National Missions, Unit of Work with Colored People.
The Charlotte Observer, Charlotte, North Carolina. Annual spring issues on schools in the vicinity.
Press and Banner, Abbeville, South Carolina; *The Arkansas Gazette*, Little Rock, Arkansas.
Quarterly Review of Higher Education Among Negroes, Johnson C. Smith University Press.
Journal of Negro Education, Washington, D.C.: Howard University. Catalogs

and other publications of various Board Schools, especially Johnson C. Smith University, Charlotte, N.C.

Briefly, Brevities, Snapshots, pamphlet series published by the Board of National Missions.

III. Unpublished Theses

Anderson, Leon R. "History of Mission Work Among Negroes in Charlotte, North Carolina Area of Mecklenburg Presbytery," S.T.B. thesis, Johnson C. Smith University Theological Seminary, 1950. Now located in the library of the Interdenominational Theological Center in Atlanta.

Adair, Joseph H. "The Goodwill Larger Parish of Sumter, Claredon, and Lee Counties," S.T.B. thesis, Johnson C. Smith University Theological Seminary, 1951. Now located in the library of the Interdenominational Theological Center, Atlanta.

Givens, Howard W. "An In Depth Study of Burke County, Ga." S.T.B. thesis, Johnson C. Smith Theological Seminary, 1935.

Jones, Joseph T. "The Life and Works of Allen A. and Mary M. Jones," S.T.B. thesis, Johnson C. Smith University Theological Seminary, 1953. Now located in the library of the Interdenominational Theological Center in Atlanta.

Nelson, Grover D. "The Life and Works of George Waldo Long," S.T.B. thesis, Johnson C. Smith University Theological Seminary, 1949. Now lolated in the library of the Interdenominational Theological Center in Atlanta.

Shirley, Frank C. "An Introduction to the History of the Catawba Synod," S.T.B. thesis, Johnson C. Smith University Theological Seminary, 1949. Now located in the library of the Interdenominational Center in Atlanta.

Smith, James W. "A History of the Seventh Street Presbyterian Church," S.T.B. thesis, Johnson C. Smith University Theological Seminary, 1948. Now located in the library of the Interdenominational Theological Center in Atlanta.

Thompkins, Robert E. "History of Religious Education Among Negroes in the Presbyterian Church, U.S.A., Ph.D. dissertation, University of Pittsburgh, 1950.

Washington, John H. "The Life and Work of William Lee Metz on Edisto Island from 1916–1947," S.T.B. thesis, Johnson C. Smith University Theological Seminary, 1948. Now located in the library of the Interdenominational Theological Seminary in Atlanta.

IV. Unpublished Manuscripts

Shaw, George Clayton. "Seed Germination" and "A Glance Backward, a Present Meditation, A Forward Look." Now in the possession of Mrs. G. L. Shaw, Oxford, North Carolina.

Cooper, Charlotte. "Story of Mary M. Jones Life." 1941.

Metz, William. Study for the Catawba Presbytery. 1927.

Tenny, S. M. "Notes on the Work Among the Colored People of Crockett, Texas, Leading up to the Establishment of Mary Allen Seminary in 1886." 1939.

Tenny, S. M. "Mary Allen Junior College." N.d.

INDEX

Note: Each individual school has not been indexed. See *Contents* for complete listing of all schools described in the book.

About the Author

For four decades plus, Inez Moore Parker has been involved, as a student and as a teacher, in the program of education for black Americans by the Presbyterian Church, U.S.A. Her early academic training began in the Arkadelphia Presbyterian Academy, Arkadelphia, Arkansas.

With a Bachelor of Arts degree from Virginia Union University, Richmond, Virginia, she began her teaching career with the Board's program as instructor of English at the Mary Potter School, Oxford, North Carolina, 1933–1935. She spent the following year at the University of Michigan, Ann Arbor, Michigan, where she received the Master of Arts degree in June, 1936. She was then commissioned as chairman of the English Department at the Mary Allen Junior College, Crockett, Texas. During her six-year tenure there, 1936–1942, she provided additional services to the Board of National Missions of the Presbyterian Church, U.S.A. as its speaker at the Presbyterials of Kansas and Nebraska and attendance at the annual Workers Conference which brought together workers from the black mission field to assess and share successes and failures of the previous year.

Mrs. Parker's next appointment was as chairman of the English Department at Knoxville College, Knoxville, Tennessee, 1942–1944 (auspices of the United Presbyterian Church). Her present tenure at Johnson C. Smith University began in 1944, during which time she chaired the English Department for more than twenty-five years, continued her research which led to this book, and also continued her advanced studies at the University of Iowa, the University of Michigan, and Columbia University.

She is the author of *The Biddle Johnson C. Smith University Story*, published in 1975, and is a member of the Board of Directors of the Presbyterian Historical Society, the Charlotte-Mechlenburg County Bicentennial Committee, the North Carolina Historical and Literary Society, Mayor John Belk's Blue Heaven Committee, and the Alpha Kappa Alpha Sorority.